The Fruits of Freedom in British Togoland

The end of the First World War saw the former German protectorate of Togoland split into British- and French-administered territories, and by the late 1940s, a political movement known as Ablɔɖe (meaning 'freedom' in the Ewe language) called for the reunification of British and French Togoland into an independent multi-ethnic state. Despite its efforts, the United Nations trust territory of British Togoland was ultimately merged with the Gold Coast to become part of independent Ghana; three years later French Togoland achieved a separate independence as Togo.

Based on interviews with former political activists and their families, access to private papers and a collection of oral and written propaganda, this book examines the history behind the failed project of Togoland reunification. Kate Skinner challenges the marginalisation of the Togoland question from popular and academic analyses of post-colonial politics and explores present-day ramifications of the contingencies of decolonisation.

Kate Skinner is a lecturer in the History of Africa and Its Diasporas at the University of Birmingham.

For Simon, Nina and Tommy

The African Studies series, founded in 1968, publishes research monographs by emerging and senior scholars that feature innovative analyses in the fields of history, political science, anthropology, economics and environmental studies. The series also produces mature, paradigm-shifting syntheses that seek to reinterpret and revitalize the scholarly literature in these fields.

A list of books in this series will be found at the end of this volume.

The Fruits of Freedom in British Togoland

Literacy, Politics and Nationalism, 1914–2014

KATE SKINNER
University of Birmingham

CAMBRIDGE
UNIVERSITY PRESS

CAMBRIDGE
UNIVERSITY PRESS

32 Avenue of the Americas, New York, NY 10013-2473, USA

Cambridge University Press is part of the University of Cambridge.

It furthers the University's mission by disseminating knowledge in the pursuit of education, learning and research at the highest international levels of excellence.

www.cambridge.org
Information on this title: www.cambridge.org/9781107074637

First published 2015

Printed in Great Britain by Clays Ltd, St Ives plc

A catalog record for this publication is available from the British Library.

Library of Congress Cataloging in Publication Data
Skinner, Kate (Katharine Alexandra Collier)
The fruits of freedom in British Togoland : literacy, politics and nationalism, 1914–2014 / Kate Skinner, University of Birmingham.
pages cm. – (African studies series)
Includes bibliographical references and index.
ISBN 978-1-107-07463-7 (Hardback : alk. paper)
1. Decolonization–Ghana–History. 2. Ghana–History–Autonomy and independence movements. 3. Ghana–Politics and government–20th century. 4. Togo–Politics and government–20th century. 5. Ghana–Relations–Great Britain. 6. Great Britain–Relations–Ghana. I. Title. II. Series: African studies series (Cambridge, England)
DT511.S54 2015
966.7–dc23 2014045676

ISBN 978-1-107-07463-7 Hardback

Contents

Maps

Figures

Acknowledgements

This book has been a long time in the making, and my debts of gratitude are therefore many. I have organised them chronologically and hope that no one has been forgotten.

First, I must thank my parents, for raising me to know that history matters, and for helping me in numerous practical ways over the long period of time in which this book was researched and written. Second, as a product of British state education, I want to thank all the school teachers who were underpaid and undervalued by their employers, and yet found it within themselves to give to a young person who wanted to learn new things. I will always be grateful to Megan Vaughan, who introduced me to the field of African History. As an undergraduate, I benefitted from the intensive investment of my Balliol history tutors, particularly John Prest, Simon Skinner and Martin Conway. As a Masters student, I found the Centre de Recherche Africaine (Rue Mahler) to be remarkably tolerant of my shaky French, and I was helped through the study-abroad experience by Frédéric Herrmann, Agnès Delahaye, Lorna Wilson, and Angela Duff. When I became a PhD student at the University of Birmingham, Tom McCaskie and Lynne Brydon took care of me in many more ways than I had the right to expect, and they have continued to do so for many more years than I wish to remember. They are unique – as individuals and as a team. Lynne has generously shared with me knowledge accumulated through almost forty years of research on and in the region, whilst Tom has consistently challenged me to think about issues of due recognition and intersubjectivity in the lives of the people with whom this book is concerned.

I have been based at the Department of African Studies and Anthropology, Birmingham (formerly the Centre of West African Studies) for the entire period in which this book was researched and written. I thank Stewart Brown, Reg Cline-Cole, Benedetta Rossi, Paulo Farias, Toby Green, Katrien Pype, and Max Bolt for being supportive and entertaining colleagues. Karin Barber introduced me to many new and stimulating ideas about texts, while Insa Nolte shared her own intriguing experiences of writing political history. Most of all, Keith Shear's exceptional understanding and kindness and careful reading of my drafts enabled me to finally muster the courage to submit the manuscript (*akpe kaka!*). I am grateful to David Anderson for encouraging me to submit to Cambridge University Press, William Hammell and his team for helping me to complete the final stages, Harry and Louise Buglass for their help with maps and illustrations, Anne Frausing for German-English translations, and Anna McCaskie for her help with the bibliography.

Financial support has come in the form of an initial doctoral research grant from the old Arts and Humanities Research Board, and subsequent grants from the Nuffield Foundation (New Career Development Scheme), the British Academy (Small Research Grants Scheme), and the University of Birmingham (College of Arts and Law Research and Knowledge Transfer Fund).

My efforts with the Ewe language are ongoing, but in the meantime I have relied on the help of many bilingual Ghanaians and Togolese, including Lydia Osei-Brantuo, Daniel Adadjo, Richard Salifu, Frank Dedume, Richard Banibensu, Wilson Yayoh, Cecilia Dusi, Edem Adotey, and others. I received wonderful hospitality from Honorine Gbadamassi and Richard Amega in Lomé, from Cecilia Dusi in Kpandu, from Daria Mathilde Dzegblor and Betty Adinyra in Amedzofe, and many others in the course of my travels around the Ghana-Togo border area. In Accra I have always been very well looked after by Auntie Emily Asiedu, and I am grateful for support and advice received from other visitors to the Asiedu institute, particularly Stephan Miescher, Anne Hugon, Esperanza Brizuela-Garcia, and Jean Allman. I am also grateful for the assistance of staff at the National Archives at Kew, Rhodes House library in Oxford, the Public Records and Administration Department in Ho and Accra, and the Archives Nationales in Lomé; and to Sandrine Mansour Merien for her help in the Centre des Archives diplomatiques de Nantes.

A shorter version of Chapter 4 was previously published in the *Journal of African History* 48 (2007). Small amounts of material that appear in Chapters 5, 6, and 7 were previously published in an article in *History in Africa: A Journal of Method* 37 (2010), whilst small amounts of material that appear in Chapter 3 were also previously published in an article in

History in Africa: A Journal of Method 34 (2007). I am grateful to Cambridge University Press for their permission to reproduce this material.

Finally, I must thank all the people in Ghana and Togo who agreed to be interviewed for this project and shared their memories and their personal archives with a stranger with big eyes. Without their help this book would never have been possible.

A Note on Orthography

Ewe (Eʋe) is a tonal language with many dialectical variations. In the later nineteenth century, it was transcribed by missionaries and underwent a process of standardisation. In this book, key Ewe terms have been rendered in standard Ewe, using characters from the International Phonetic Alphabet. Place names and personal names have been rendered in their present-day English and French forms, although I have added comments in the footnotes where I think that further details are particularly important to readers' understanding. The language itself should properly be written 'Eʋe' but in this book I have used 'Ewe' because this is now normal practice in Ghana.

1

Ablɔɖe

African Political History, from Below and from Within

In the year 2010, a former teacher and member of parliament, Kosi Kedem, published a petition to the Ghana Constitutional Review Commission.[1] This petition analysed the mechanisms by which the former United Nations trust territory of British Togoland had been integrated with the neighbouring British colony of the Gold Coast and deemed a part of Ghana at Independence in 1957. Kedem concluded that the process of integration was deeply flawed, and he demanded negotiations over the terms by which British Togoland could remain in a union with the republic of Ghana in the twenty-first century. He thereby took up the central issue of a political movement which, from the late 1940s, had insisted that British Togoland had a political status quite distinct from that of the Gold Coast, to its west, and was thereby entitled to a form of Independence which would allow for its unification with French Togoland, to its east, in a single African state.

In his associated publications Kedem argued that this movement, the Togoland Congress, had a legitimate cause, but had fallen foul of the British government, which was fully committed to the integration of its trust territory with the Gold Coast.[2] Commenting on the role that the British administration was allowed to play in organising the popular consultation recommended by the United Nations and in interpreting its results, Kedem likened the plebiscite of 1956 to a judicial case between a hawk and a chicken: 'how [can] the hawk [Britain] ... objectively and

[1] Kosi Kedem, *2010 Constitutional Review and the Rectification of the Ghana-British Togoland Union* (Accra, 2010).

[2] Kosi Kedem, *How Britain Subverted and Betrayed British Togoland* (Accra, 2007).

sincerely preside over a case involving the chicken [Togoland]. It cannot happen! What justice or fairness would the chicken expect?'[3] Kedem concluded that, in allowing the integration of British Togoland with the Gold Coast, the United Nations had failed in its duty to the peoples of the trust territory, who had been denied their right to self-government. In Kedem's eyes, this failure was compounded by the treatment of Togoland Congress activists at the hands of the Ghanaian state after 1957. His publications and petitions therefore aimed to salvage truth and dignity for the 'men, women and the freedom fighters who were exiled, lost their lives and property, [and were] detained, imprisoned and suffered serious violation of their human rights during the struggle' that became known as *Ablɔɖe* ('freedom' in the Ewe language).[4] After a decade of research and campaigning, Kedem had forced open a controversial issue that historians of modern Ghana had considered to be dead.

Kedem's writings reflect his concern for the memory of Ablɔɖe activists, and can be read as attempts 'to give back to men of the past the unpredictability of the future and the dignity of acting in the face of uncertainty'.[5] He was challenging the 'construction of ignorance' and practices of 'sanctioned forgetting', which have threatened to edit the Ablɔɖe movement out of Ghana's national history.[6] Such editing makes Ghana's national borders appear far more certain than they ever really were, and thereby obscures not only the agency of the individuals who sought to challenge them, but also the political and diplomatic work which had to be undertaken by former colonial powers and by new African national governments in order to achieve and maintain what now looks like the status quo.

This book is about the people who directed and participated in Ablɔɖe from the late 1940s through to the present day. It explains who these people were, why they opposed the integration of British Togoland with the Gold Coast, and why they sought to preserve the possibility of a joint Independence with French Togoland. It also considers why they failed, and details the consequences of this failure for their families, livelihoods, and future political activity. It is a study of political activism, starting in

[3] Kedem, *2010 Constitutional Review*, 12–13.

[4] Kosi Kedem, *British Togoland: An Orphan or the Death of a Nation* (Accra, 2005), iii.

[5] Reinhard Bendix, *Force, Fate and Freedom: On Historical Sociology* (Berkley CA, 1984), 48.

[6] These phrases are used by Jean Allman, who argues for an 'agnotological approach' in her quest to understand why the key female activist Hannah Kudjoe 'got forgotten' in Ghana's national history. 'The Disappearing of Hannah Kudjoe: Nationalism, Feminism and the Tyrannies of History', *Journal of Women's History* 21 (3) (2009), 13–35.

the small towns and villages of southern British Togoland, and following individuals and networks through space and time. It maps the movements and connections of activists across borders in West Africa and beyond, shedding light upon their reorientation towards surprising new political projects in the post-Independence period.

On the most optimistic reading, this is a book about possibilities – it recovers alternative imaginings of nationhood and the creative labour of political struggle.[7] On the most pessimistic reading, it is the tale of a nation that never was, a historical sideshow to the main event. In writing about Ablɔḍe, I have sought to tell readers, whether of optimistic or pessimistic dispositions, one part of a larger story about the contingencies of decolonisation in Africa. The achievement of Independence and the subsequent consolidation of national territories become more remarkable when the full plethora of competing visions of nationhood is really understood; the dynamics of citizenship and the control of dissent in post-colonial nations are more comprehensible when the persistence of alternative political projects is revealed.

LOCATING ABLƆƊE

The Ablɔḍe movement grew up in the southern section of British Togoland, where Ewe is spoken by the majority, as a first, second, or occasionally a third language. Ablɔḍe had small clusters of supporters in the savannahs of northern British Togoland, but it was always stronger in the southern section, through the cocoa-growing areas of Buem (where Akan is widely spoken), in a series of mountain communities (some with their own distinct languages), and in the larger commercial and administrative centres of Kpandu, Hohoe, and Ho (where Ewe is spoken as a first language). The strength of Ablɔḍe in Ewe-speaking areas, however, does not mean that the movement should be interpreted as a form of Ewe nationalism, for the Ewe-speaking peoples experienced diverse historical trajectories and developed a range of political projects in the era of decolonisation.

The basic linguistic similarities between the Ewe-speaking peoples can be attributed to a common origin in Ketu (now in the republic of Benin) and a shared experience of seventeenth-century migration from Notsé

[7] In this sense it is consistent with Frederick Cooper's concern to avoid determinism and examine paths not taken. See 'Possibility and Constraint: African Independence in Historical Perspective', *Journal of African History* 49 (2) (2008), 167–96.

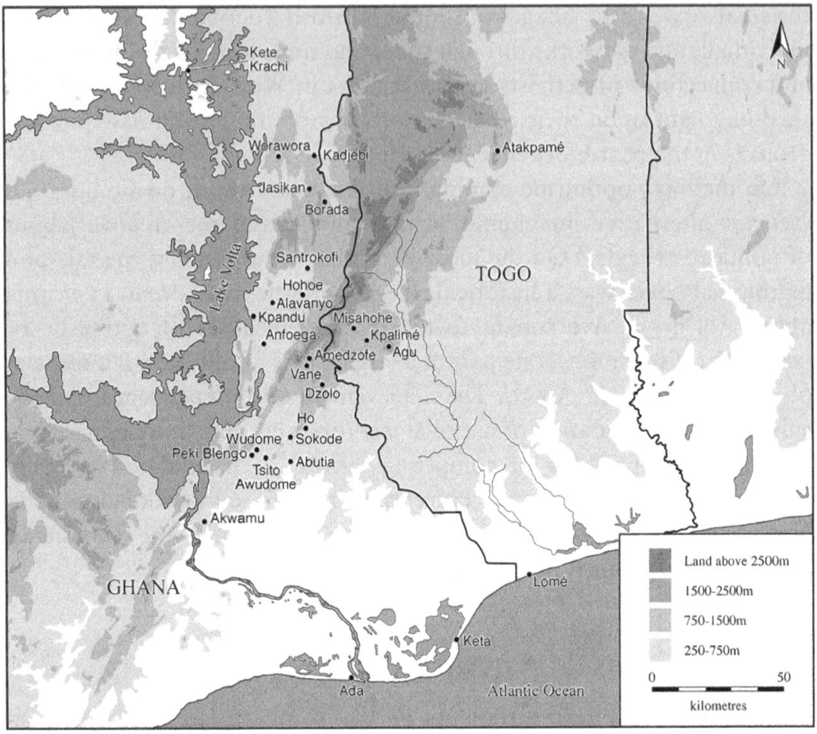

MAP 1: Physical Map of the Region

into the coastal and inland areas that now form the south-eastern quarter of Ghana and the southern quarter of Togo.[8] The inland areas include a forested mountain range, running NNE-SSW, from the settlements of Peki, in modern-day Ghana, into central Togo. (See Map 1.) These mountains accommodated many waves of migrants, and thus became home to a complex mosaic of small Ewe-speaking settlements interspersed with other distinct language groups.[9] Ewe-speaking settlements are also

[8] For a discussion of evidence drawn from oral history, archaeology, and historical linguistics, see Nicoué Gayibor (dir.), *Le Peuplement du Togo: état actuel des connaissances historiques* (Lomé, 1997).

[9] For an analysis of the linguistic diversity of the inland mountainous area, see Mary Kropp Dakubu and K. C. Ford, 'The Central Togo Languages', in *The Languages of Ghana*, ed. Mary Kropp Dakubu (London, 1988), 119–54. For historical context, see Paul Nugent, '"A Few Lesser Peoples": the Central Togo Minorities and their Ewe Neighbours', in *Ethnicity in Ghana: The Limits of Invention*, ed. Carola Lentz and Paul Nugent (London, 2000), 162–82; Paul Nugent, 'A Regional Melting Pot: The Ewe and their Neighbours in the Ghana-Togo Borderlands', in *The Ewe of Togo and Benin*, ed. Benjamin Lawrance

to be found on the flatter land to the sides of this mountain range, but as one moves south towards the coastal strip, the ecological characteristics are quite different. The southern and south-easterly areas of Ewe-speaking settlement lie in the Benin Gap – a savannah corridor which interrupts the belt of forest that otherwise stretches across West Africa. The Ewe-speaking migrants who settled on the coastal strip, 'between the sea and the lagoon', reoriented their livelihoods from farming towards lagoon fishing and then sea fishing.[10] Further inland, farming, along with hunting and river fishing, remained the dominant livelihoods.

To the Europeans who came to trade on the coast, the Ewe-speaking towns and villages were the 'upper Slave Coast'.[11] But whilst the settlements close to the coast coalesced into a state known as Anlo, Europeans remained unclear as to the nature of the Ewe-speaking interior, which they referred to as Krepe and regarded as a source of ivory and enslaved labour.[12] This perception of Krepe was also taken up by historians of the militarised expansionist states to the west, notably J. K. Fynn, who portrayed Krepe as a 'less sophisticated' region, which was plundered by its neighbours.[13] After 1730, the kingdom of Akwamu gradually established its suzerainty over Krepe with the aim of extracting ivory and enslaved labour and controlling the trade routes up the river Volta

(Accra, 2005), 29–43; and Wilson Yayoh, 'Krepi States in the 18th and 19th Centuries', *Transactions of the Historical Society of Ghana* 6 (2002), 67–81. Adangme-speaking clusters in the present-day Ghana-Togo border area resulted from an exodus of Adangme speakers from Accra in the aftermath of its invasion by Akwamu in 1680, as demonstrated by R. G. S. Sprigge, 'Eweland's Adangbe: An Inquiry into an Oral Tradition', *Transactions of the Historical Society of Ghana* X (1969) 87–128; and M. B. K. Darkoh, 'Note on the Peopling of the Forest Hills of the Volta Region of Ghana', *Ghana Notes and Queries* 11 (1970), 8–13.

10 On the distinctive ecology of the coastal strip, see Emmanuel Akyeampong, *Between the Sea and the Lagoon: An Eco-Social History of the Anlo of Southeastern Ghana, c.1850 to Recent Times* (Athens OH, 2001).

11 Hence the title of Sandra Greene's first book, *Gender, Ethnicity and Social Change on the Upper Slave Coast: A History of the Anlo-Ewe* (Portsmouth NH, 1996). There is a substantial literature on the Slave Coast, including Robin Law's authoritative *The Slave Coast of West Africa 1550–1750* (Oxford, 1991).

12 In 1764, the Governor of Cape Coast Castle on the Gold Coast tried to persuade the London Committee of Merchants that they should establish a fort close to the mouth of the river Volta in order to secure a regular supply of 'the very best slaves … called Crippes'. Cited in J. K. Fynn, *Asante and its Neighbours 1700–1807* (London, 1971), 127. The term 'Anlo' was often rendered as 'Awuna' by early European visitors, but was transcribed as *Aŋlɔ* in the 'standard' Ewe which emerged from missionary endeavours in the later nineteenth century. 'Krepe' was sometimes rendered as 'Crippe' or 'Krepi' by Europeans.

13 Ibid., 22–3.

to the market centres of the northern savannah zone.[14] As the value of these trade routes became apparent, coastal Anlo and inland Akwamu were drawn into alliances with each other and with the militarised expansionist Asante empire, making Krepe a kind of frontier between Asante (to its west) and Dahomey (to its east).[15] (See Map 2.)

The peoples of Krepe sought to shake off the suzerainty of Akwamu, and mounted a successful rebellion in 1833. However, as European traders on the central Fante-speaking Gold Coast gradually shifted away from the transportation of slaves into the Atlantic, and as conflicts between Asante and its southerly neighbours disrupted trade between the Asante interior and the Fante coastline, the river Volta and the Anlo coastline to its east became critical alternative routes for imports and exports, including firearms and slaves.[16] Thus in 1869, Asante invaded Krepe and temporarily reimposed control before European powers began exerting a greater presence in the region.[17]

When the Germans and British drew the border between their respective colonies of Togo and the Gold Coast at the end of the nineteenth century, their maps separated the speakers of Ewe in Anlo, and as far inland as Peki, from the speakers of Ewe further north-east, due east and south-east.[18] But this colonial border did not carve up a kingdom or an empire, because the linkages between the speakers of Ewe did not take the form of a large-scale centralised territorial kingship, and the inland Ewe-speakers lived in close proximity with numerous other small groups who were linguistically distinct and politically independent. The border

14 D. E. K. Amenumey, *The Ewe in Pre-Colonial Times: A Political History with Special Emphasis on the Anlo, Ge and Krepi* (Accra, 1986), 69. The river Volta connected the Atlantic coast to markets at Kete Krachi and Salaga.

15 On Anlo-Akwamu relations, see R. A. Kea, 'Akwamu – Anlo relations, c. 1750–1813', *Transactions of the Historical Society of Ghana* 10 (1969), 29–63. On the Asante empire, see T. C. McCaskie, *State and Society in Pre-Colonial Asante* (Cambridge, 1995); and Ivor Wilks, *Asante in the Nineteenth Century: The Structure and Evolution of a Political Order* (Cambridge, 1975).

16 On Anlo's post-abolition slave exporting boom and its social effects, see Sandra Greene, 'Modern "Trokosi" and the 1807 Abolition in Ghana: Connecting Past and Present', *William and Mary Quarterly* LXVI (4) (2009), 959–74. On Asante and other commercial interests in the region see Marion Johnson, 'M. Bonnat on the Volta', *Ghana Notes and Queries* X (1968) 4–17; and 'Asante East of the Volta', *Transactions of the Historical Society of Ghana* 8 (1965), 33–59.

17 Lynne Brydon, 'Constructing Avatime: Questions of History and Identity in a West African Polity, c. 1690s to the Twentieth Century', *Journal of African History* 49 (1) (2008), 23–42.

18 Peki was part of the 'Krepe interior', and led rebellions against Akwamu overlords in 1833. Peki was also involved in resistance to the Asante invasion of Krepi in 1869.

MAP 2: Pre-colonial States

between the British Gold Coast and German Togo cut across other types of ritual and material connections and exchanges, although, as Paul Nugent has argued, it was gradually transformed into a source of economic opportunity as well as constituting a barrier or an inconvenience.[19] In August 1914, at the outbreak of the First World War, the British advanced upon German Togo from their base in the Gold Coast colony to the west. Meanwhile the French advanced from their base in Dahomey to the east. When they converged, German Togo was divided into two spheres: British and French Togoland. (See Map 3.)

At the end of the war the border was redrawn, and as the two Togolands became mandated territories of the League of Nations, the British and the French were compelled to administer them under a measure of international supervision.[20] As Susan Pedersen has recently argued, 'one of the most innovative aspects of the mandates system ... was that it included the right of petition', and thereby created channels through which inhabitants of mandated territories could engage in 'claim-making, international lobbying and political mobilisation'.[21] Petitioning was a 'varied and complex practice', and the issues varied between the mandates.[22] One issue of lasting significance for the two Togolands was the extent to which mandated territories should be administered as separate entities, and the extent to which they could be incorporated into 'administrative unions' with the neighbouring British colony of the Gold Coast and French colony of Dahomey.

With the formation of the United Nations at the end of the Second World War, a new trusteeship system determined the framework within which the former mandated territories (now trust territories) could be administered. By article 76 of the United Nations Charter, the trusteeship

[19] Paul Nugent, *Smugglers, Secessionists and Loyal Citizens on the Ghana-Togo Frontier: The Lie of the Borderlands since 1914* (Athens OH, 2002). On the nature of spiritual and ritual relations between the Ewe-speaking peoples, and their metamorphosis under the influence of missionary Christianity and colonial rule, see Sandra Greene, *Sacred Sites and the Colonial Encounter: A History of Meaning and Memory in Ghana* (Bloomington IN, 2002).

[20] For a study of international supervision of mandated territories in Africa, see Michael Callahan, *Mandates and Empire: The League of Nations and Africa 1914–1931* (Brighton, 1999). Susan Pedersen's book on the mandates system was in preparation when my own book went into production.

[21] Susan Pedersen, 'Samoa on the World Stage: Petitions and Peoples before the Mandates Commission of the League of Nations', *Journal of Imperial and Commonwealth History* 40 (2) (2012), 231–61 at 231.

[22] Ibid., 239.

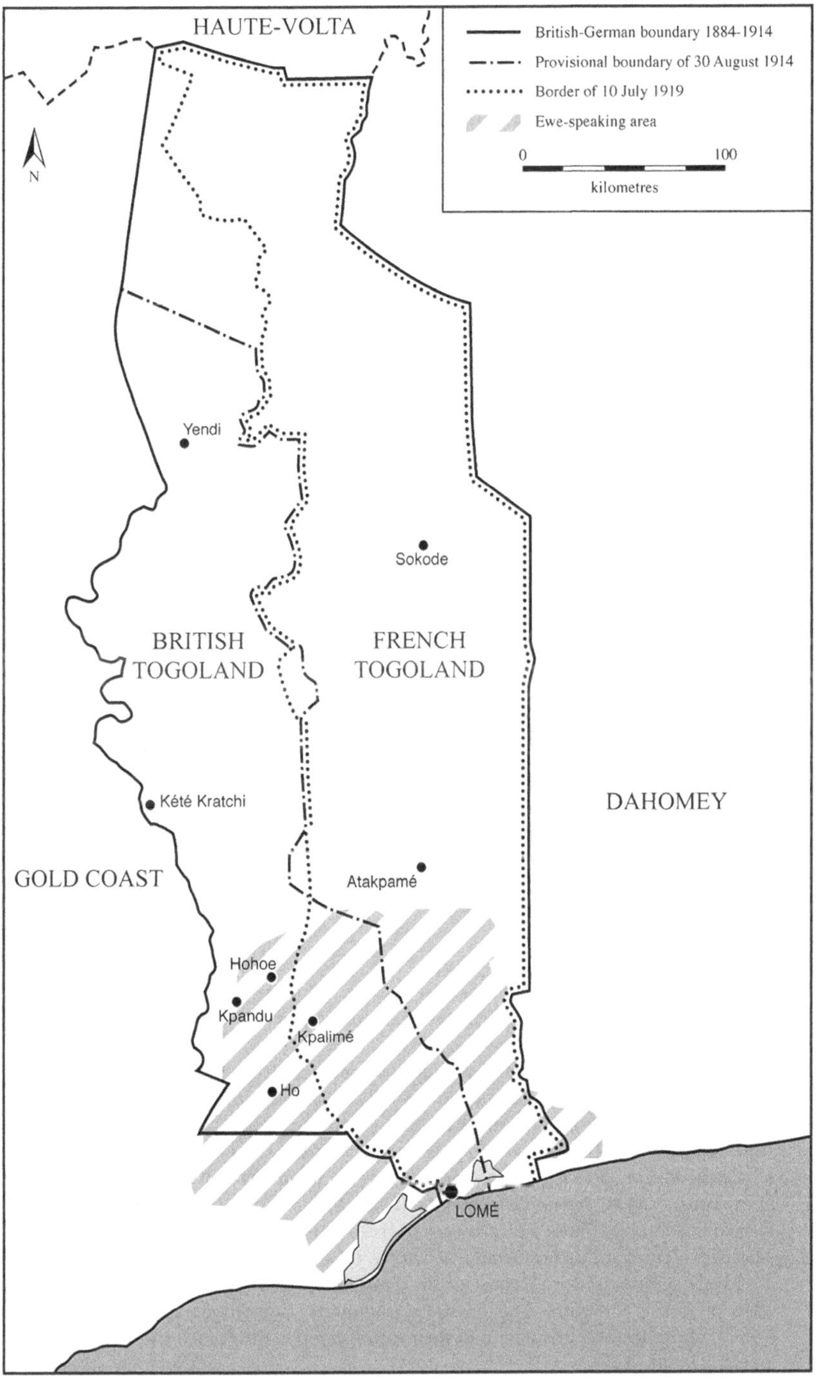

MAP 3: Changing Borders

system set out to 'promote the political, economic, social, and educational advancement of the inhabitants of the trust territories, and their progressive development towards self-government or independence as may be appropriate to the particular circumstances of each territory and its peoples and the freely expressed wishes of the peoples concerned, and as may be provided by the terms of each trusteeship agreement'.[23] In some respects, the degree of supervision over the administering authorities intensified, as international missions now visited the trust territories to make their own observations, and petitioners from the trust territories increasingly took up the opportunity to appear directly before United Nations bodies in New York.[24] This reduced the reliance of the United Nations on information provided by administering authorities, and increased the opportunities for Africans within the two Togolands (and indeed in Tanganyika and the Cameroons) to frame their claims within the broader principles of the trusteeship system and to present those claims to an international audience.[25]

The trusteeship agreements for individual territories, however, were drafted by the administering authorities, and whilst the General Assembly of the United Nations would only approve agreements that seemed consistent with article 76 of the charter, the administering authorities took the opportunity to set the terms of implementation. The agreement that was approved for British Togoland in 1946 was deliberately drafted so as to allow for an administrative union between the trust territory and the neighbouring British colony of the Gold Coast.[26] Initially, the British government justified administrative union on the grounds of necessity – the small size of the trust territory made an entirely separate structure of

[23] Charter of the United Nations, chapter XII, article 76, available at: www.un.org/en/documents/charter/chapter12.shtml [last accessed 2 July 2014].

[24] Petitioners targeted both the Trusteeship Council and the Fourth Committee of the General Assembly.

[25] The representations of Togolanders, and Ewe-speakers from the Gold Coast, are given detailed treatment in D. E. K. Amenumey, *The Ewe Unification Movement: A Political History* (Accra, 1989). For the Cameroon trust territories, see Meredith Terretta, *Petitioning for our Rights, Fighting for our Nation: The History of the Democratic Union of Cameroonian Women 1946–1960* (Oxford, 2013). For Tanganyika, see Ullrich Lohrmann, *Voices from Tanganyika: Great Britain, the United Nations and the Decolonization of a Trust Territory, 1946–1961* (Münster, 2007).

[26] This is explained in further detail in Chapter 3, but the key documents and clauses are effectively summarised in 'Report of the Trusteeship Council on administrative unions affecting Trust Territories and on the status of the Cameroons and Togoland under French administration arising out of their membership in the French Union', (New York, 1952), 4–6 and 23–6.

administration impractical.[27] However, once the British were faced with a wave of anti-colonial protest in the neighbouring colony of the Gold Coast, where they responded by moving towards self-government, they were also able to justify the relationship between the trust territory and the colony on the grounds that it was politically progressive.

This is the context in which the particular goals of the Ablɔɖe movement were shaped. The position of the British government appeared consistent with the principles of the United Nations Charter in the sense that the trust territory could advance towards self-government through its relationship with the Gold Coast. Inhabitants of the trust territory, however, debated long and hard over whether this form of self-government could really deliver the kind of 'freedom' they wanted. Ablɔɖe activists marshalled impressive evidence that the relationship between British Togoland and the Gold Coast effectively subordinated the interests of the former to the latter, and compromised the political, economic, social, and educational advancement of the trust territory *as a distinct entity* in ways which contravened a series of United Nations resolutions.[28] Activists mobilised considerable support, particularly in the southern section of the trust territory, where Ewe was the majority (but by no means the only) language. They set out to highlight and protect the special status of British Togoland, and held out for a separate constitutional arrangement that would keep open the possibility of reunification with French Togoland and a joint Togoland Independence. Had they succeeded, they would, in effect, have created an independent African state with the same borders as that of the former German colony of Togo. On the face of it, then, Ablɔɖe, or 'Togoland reunification', was a peculiar political project.

COLONIALISMS AND NATIONALISMS: THE PECULIAR PROBLEM OF TOGOLAND REUNIFICATION

The demand for the reunification of the two Togolands sits uneasily at the edge of a substantial literature on decolonisation in Africa because it has resisted categorisation as an ethno-nationalist project without gaining full acceptance as a form of anti-colonial territorial nationalism. By no stretch of invention, imagination, or cultural work could the peoples living

[27] Ibid., 4.

[28] These included General Assembly resolution 224 (III) of 18 Nov 1948 and Trusteeship Council resolution 81 (IV) of 27 Jan 1949.

within the borders of the two Togolands be conceived of as a single 'ethnic' group, and not even the strongest advocates of Togoland reunification made a sustained effort to argue this case. The northern sections contained but a tiny handful of Ewe-speaking migrants. The peoples of the northern savannahs of British Togoland have usually been categorised not as a single group of 'non Ewes', but rather as a series of mutually antagonistic groups, who divided according to their degree of adherence to, assimilation with, or resistance against, centralised territorial kingship.[29] The differences between the so-called decentralised peoples, the factions within and rivalries between the major centralised states, and the complex interactions of the former with the latter, all point to high levels of linguistic diversity and political contestation within the northern section.

Even in the southern section of British Togoland, those who spoke Ewe as a first language were interspersed with those who spoke it only as a second or third language, and in some cases, not at all. As Nugent's recent comparative study also suggests, there is little evidence that the people who spoke variants of the Ewe language actually thought of themselves as 'the Ewe' or identified themselves as such in juxtaposition to their neighbours during the seventeenth and eighteenth centuries.[30] The emergence of 'the Ewe', then, is a phenomenon of the later nineteenth century, associated with missionary Christianity. Certainly, there were some vocal advocates of Ewe political and cultural unity during the twentieth century, but we have no reason to assume that ethnic nationalism had an automatic appeal or a primary claim on the political allegiances of all the various speakers of Ewe who lived in the two Togolands.[31]

The demand for Togoland reunification had as its final objective an independent and multi-ethnic state. In this sense, it is best described as a form of territorial nationalism. The latter term, however, has usually

[29] For a critical commentary on the distinction between centralised (Dagomba/Nanumba) and non-centralised (Konkomba) peoples in northern British Togoland, and a re-evaluation of their relations, see Benjamin Talton, *Politics of Social Change in Ghana: The Konkomba Struggle for Political Equality* (New York, 2010).

[30] Paul Nugent, 'Putting the History Back into Ethnicity: Enslavement, Religion, and Cultural Brokerage in the Construction of Mandinka/Jola and Ewe/Agotime Identities in West Africa, c.1650–1930', *Comparative Studies in Society and History* 50 (4) (2008), 920–48.

[31] This is where Nugent parted company with D. E. K. Amenumey, who had suggested that Togoland reunification cut across a primordial Ewe identity and had thus undermined demands for Ewe political unity. Cf Nugent, *Smugglers, Secessionists and Loyal Citizens* and Amenumey, *The Ewe Unification Movement*.

been set in juxtaposition to ethnic nationalism in circumstances where a political movement which aimed to take over the *whole* territory encompassed within a colonial border found itself operating in opposition to political movements *inside* those borders which preferred to mobilise specific groups on the basis of shared ethnicity.[32] Togoland reunificationism was 'territorial' in the sense that it was not based on ethnic exclusivity, but even its advocates were sensitive to the accusation that they could not be considered fully 'anti-colonial' if they were aiming to separate off a portion of British-administered territory in order to re-establish the physical borders of a former German colony.[33]

The apparent peculiarity of the Togoland reunificationist project has attracted a series of scholars who have seen in it the possibility of an intriguing case study for a larger theory or research question. James Coleman assessed the role of international supervision in Independence settlements in the trust territories of Togoland and Cameroon; Claude Welch traced the challenges of ethnic and territorial nationalism to visions of pan-African unity; D. E. K. Amenumey examined how the possibilities for ethnic nationalism among the Ewe were squeezed by territorial nationalism on the Gold Coast and in the two Togolands; and David Brown analysed the struggle of the Ghanaian political 'centre' to control its Togoland 'periphery'.[34] More recently, Paul Nugent demonstrated that even those colonial borders which appeared to ignore linguistic and physical boundaries could provide opportunities to those who lived in their vicinities. He thus concluded that it is through people's agency that the Ghana-Togo border has cohered in the post-colonial era. This agency

[32] In Ghana, the classic example is the struggle between the National Liberation Movement and the Convention People's Party. The former was confined to Asante and sought some form of autonomy for Asante, whilst the latter claimed that it could mobilise people of every region and ethnic group within the borders of the Gold Coast/Ghana. See Jean Allman, *The Quills of the Porcupine: Asante Nationalism in an Emergent Ghana* (Madison WI, 1993).

[33] Frederick Cooper pinpoints the different possibilities of territorial, regional, and ethnic nationalisms during the period of decolonisation. See his 'Alternatives to Nationalism: the political imagination of elites in French West Africa, 1945–1960', in *Elites and Decolonization in the Twentieth Century*, ed. Jost Dülffer and Marc Frey (Basingstoke, 2011), 110–37.

[34] James Coleman, 'Togoland', *International Conciliation* 509 (1956), 2–91; Claude Welch, *Dream of Unity: Pan-Africanism and Political Unification in West Africa* (Ithaca NY, 1966); Amenumey, *The Ewe Unification Movement*; David Brown, 'Politics in the Kpandu Area of Ghana, 1925 to 1969: A Study of the Influence of Central Government and National Politics upon a Local Factional Competition' (PhD thesis, University of Birmingham, 1977).

consisted in the capacity of individuals and groups to connect national customs regimes, national political parties, and the opportunities of national citizenship to tangible localised interests in land, commerce, chieftaincy, and elected local government. For Nugent, it is these localised interests, and not primordialist ethnic identities, which explain why people in British Togoland gradually embraced, or at least reconciled themselves to, citizenship in an independent Ghana.[35]

Nugent's explanation of the outcome of the struggles over the future of British Togoland focussed attention on the numerous disputes which emerged in the face of economic change (particularly cocoa cash cropping) and colonial interventions in local power structures. The evidence for such disputes is particularly substantial for the inter-war period, when British administrators desperately sought to create order amongst the 'veritable hotch potch of tribes' whom they encountered in Togoland, and indeed elsewhere.[36] In their efforts to build structures of indirect rule, administrators set about navigating between forms of authority which appeared to be 'traditional' (in the sense of corresponding to particular understandings and representations of a pre-colonial past), whilst also creating opportunities for colonial subjects to practise techniques of 'modern' government. In a wider interpretative frame, these efforts appear familiar: they were, at least in part, attempts to categorise and thus to render governable subjects whom colonial administrators could neither fully understand nor subject to the more expensive and coercive regimes of direct rule and intensive infrastructural development. But of course across the empire such attempts were underscored by more specific agendas and they encountered particular local challenges.

In the northern section of British Togoland, attempts to govern via indirect rule entailed the resolution of disputes within the large centralised kingdoms, as well as the establishment of new means of control over the historically decentralised peoples who did not have 'chiefs'.[37] British

[35] Nugent, *Smugglers, Secessionists and Loyal Citizens*.

[36] This phrase is cited in Benjamin Lawrance, 'Bankoe v. Dome: Traditions and Petitions in the Ho-Asogli Amalgamation, British Mandated Togoland, 1919–39', *Journal of African History* 46 (2005), 243–67 at 261, fn 98. It is drawn from PRAAD, Accra, ADM 39/1/227 and 670, Notes of 17 March 1930.

[37] The British-German border, for example, had divided the eastern Dagomba capital of Yendi from western Dagomba and thus from the colonial administrative centre at Tamale. Much time was spent during the 1930s in trying to identify and render functional a constitution which would reunite the Dagomba. See Martin Staniland, *The Lions of Dagbon: Political Change in Northern Ghana* (Cambridge, 1975). For the treatment of decentralised groups such as the Konkomba, see Talton, *Politics of Social Change*.

attempts to introduce indirect rule in southern Togoland during the 1930s confronted a rather different obstacle: the various Ewe-speakers and the non-Ewe minorities were not, strictly speaking, acephalous and could not therefore simply be placed under a larger neighbouring kingdom or have their own chiefs invented for them. Chieftaincy had been practised in the southern section, but mostly on a very small territorial scale. Whilst British administrators may have believed that grouping numerous small independent units into larger 'amalgamated states' would ultimately lead to more effective local administration, it in fact provoked a proliferation of disputes over the relative seniority of previously independent chiefs, and it divided chiefs who were willing to amalgamate from subjects who were not, and vice versa.[38]

Each of these disputes was usually connected to a range of other issues relating to the value, availability, and allocation of land; the administration of justice in tribunals with all its problematic reference to 'native custom'; and the powers of chiefs to raise revenues in the form of fees and fines. Administrators deployed, in rough chronological order, strategies of persuasion, coercion, negotiation, and ultimately compromise, all of which generated an enormous volume of records. These are susceptible to analysis in the mode deployed by Ann Stoler for the Dutch East Indies – records fashioned 'grids of intelligibility' from 'uncertain knowledge' and were thus 'artifices of a colonial state declared to be in efficient operation'.[39] If the colonial state in British Africa was a 'thin white line' rather than a 'frame of steel', it is possible that in this context too, record keeping was a kind of psychological crutch, literally papering over small cracks and gaping holes in colonial understandings of their subjects, allowing administrators to create a feeling of order where there was none (or at least no order that they were able to discern and willing to endorse), and thereby permitting moments of confidence in the effectiveness and legitimacy of their own power.[40]

My interests here, however, lie less with the epistemic anxieties of colonial rule, and more with the implications of colonial record keeping for the study of African political history. In his efforts to track down and

[38] For a recent and detailed study of these disputes, see Wilson Yayoh, 'Local Government in Ewedome, British Trust Territory of Togoland (Ghana), 1920s–1970s' (PhD thesis, SOAS, London, 2010).

[39] Ann Stoler, *Along the Archival Grain: Epistemic Anxieties and Colonial Common Sense* (Princeton NJ, 2009), 1–2.

[40] Anthony Kirk-Greene, 'The Thin White Line: The Size of the British Colonial Service in Africa', *African Affairs* 79 (314) (1980), 25–44.

interpret the fragmentary evidence of an explosive and wide-ranging Christian revival movement, Derek Peterson concluded that 'East Africa's historians have been seduced by the logic of the archivist, the administrator, the census taker. The administrative grid structures the way we write history', and thereby renders some pasts more easily recoverable than others.[41] This is also a wider problem in African Studies. Historians can and do disagree over how consistent, considered, or coercive colonial administrators might have been; how far their projects were shaped by African intermediaries; and whether, through indirect rule, they established a powerful legacy of 'decentralised despotisms' (and thereby stunted the prospects for democracy in independent Africa), or simply built mutable political frameworks within which Africans were able to assert a range of social, economic, and cultural interests.[42] Wherever one comes down in these debates, the fact remains that in much of British colonial Africa, and in British Togoland in particular, an important consequence of indirect rule was an overwhelming administrative focus on disputes around the individual chiefs and the chieftaincy structures with which the colonial state sought to work. The resolution of such disputes was the day-by-day task of the district commissioner, and hence these disputes dominate his files, up until – and in some cases beyond – the shift towards elected local government during the 1950s. Africans appear in the record insofar as they respond to, or obstruct, the structures (or the last-resort and ad hoc compromises) that administrators tried to build.

Many useful histories have been written 'from below', by reading between the lines and against the grain of the detailed and voluminous records of district commissioners. In the case of Ghana, there are also impressive attempts to exploit alternative series of public records (particularly those of courts, boundary commissions, land registries, and customs services) in order to understand what was at stake in the numerous disputes with which district commissioners were endlessly concerned, and to identify how such disputes were connected to broader socio-economic changes. These records, particularly when set alongside those of missionary societies and African churches, have shed light on a range of

41 Derek Peterson, *Ethnic Patriotism and the East African Revival: A History of Dissent, c. 1935–1972* (Cambridge, 2012), 26.

42 Benjamin Lawrance, Emily Osborn and Richard Roberts, eds., *Intermediaries, Interpreters and Clerks: African Employees in the Making of Colonial Africa* (Madison WI, 2006); Mahmood Mamdani, *Citizen and Subject: Contemporary Africa and the Legacy of Late Colonialism* (Princeton NJ, 1996); and a review of the latter by John Lonsdale, *Journal of African History* 38 (3) (1997), 520–2.

struggles in rural areas, between genders and generations, indigènes and migrants, chiefs and commoners, local intelligentsias and their illiterate compatriots.[43] They also point to the key role of local political activists as points of articulation between such local struggles and the wider agendas of mass nationalist movements.

PARTY, PERSON, AND PLACE IN AFRICAN POLITICAL HISTORY

The seminal studies of mass nationalism in sub-Saharan Africa highlighted the role of intermediary figures who were capable of bridging a perceived gap between the particular localised concerns of the rural majority and the wider vision of independent nationhood which was articulated in the towns. The connection between rural-urban migration and the emergence of new political ideas and forms of mobilisation was spelled out by Thomas Hodgkin, who compared the African mass nationalist movements of the 1940s and 1950s, and particularly the rise of the Convention People's Party in the Gold Coast, to the Chartist movement in nineteenth-century Britain.[44] In his pioneering study of African political parties, which was based on his tours of the continent and his many encounters with anti-colonial nationalists, Hodgkin insisted on the town as the site of innovation. He directed students of African politics towards

> the new "proto-industrial" towns – products of the economic revolution which Europe has brought to Africa. For it is above all in these new urban societies that the characteristic institutions and ideas of African nationalism are born and grow to maturity; and from these centres that they spread to, and influence "the bush."[45]

The task of the anti-colonial nationalist movements, then, was to harness rural voters to agendas and ideas that were conceived in the urban environment. The centrality of towns was explained in terms of a series of connections between formal schooling, rural-urban migration, and new forms of political engagement. Hodgkin thus suggested that mass nationalism depended not only on urban activists harnessing rural voters,

43 For example, Sara Berry, *Chiefs Know Their Boundaries: Essays on Property, Power and the Past in Asante, 1896–1996* (Oxford, 2000); Jean Allman and Victoria Tashjian, *'I Will Not Eat Stone': A Women's History of Colonial Asante* (Portsmouth NH, 2000); Gareth Austin, *Labour, Land and Capital in Ghana: From Slavery to Free Labour in Asante, 1807–1956* (Rochester NY, 2005); Carola Lentz, *Ethnicity and the Making of History in Northern Ghana* (Edinburgh, 2006).

44 Thomas Hodgkin, *Freedom for the Gold Coast?* (London, 1951).

45 Thomas Hodgkin, *Nationalism in Colonial Africa* (London, 1956), 18.

but, in a series of prior steps, the extension of urban political activity from a tiny and highly educated elite at the start of the twentieth century, to the youth leagues and congresses of the 1930s, and finally to a considerably larger and rowdier contingent of disgruntled primary-school leavers at the end of the Second World War.

Studies of Ghana have been at the forefront of the scholarly literature on Africa's modern political history due to the country's early achievement of Independence in 1957, the dramatic rise and fall of its first president, Kwame Nkrumah, and its long experience of military and single-party rule up to 1992. Dennis Austin's pioneering *Politics in Ghana* (1964) followed Hodgkin's basic explanatory framework and applied it in a country-specific context.[46] In particular, Austin suggested that whilst African politics in the first half of the twentieth century could be read as a struggle between the chiefs and the intelligentsia for influence over colonial policy, the emergence of a critical mass of primary-school leavers in the urban centres was decisive in enabling the organisation of widespread anti-colonial sentiment after the Second World War.[47] In addition to the chiefs and intelligentsia, then, Austin added a third category of political actor, whom he considered most critical. This was the 'young man' who, by virtue of his status as a 'commoner', had been marginalised from the structures of indirect rule through which the British governed the Gold Coast and their other African colonies. Lacking a voice in a native authority system that was dominated by chiefs and their councils of elders, these commoners took their primary-school certificates to the towns. Here, however, they confronted intense competition for white collar jobs in European trading companies and in the civil service, and were often excluded from such employment by their lack of secondary-school certificates. This, according to Austin, was the socio-economic backbone of support for Kwame Nkrumah's Convention People's Party (CPP).

Despite his personal contact with many CPP activists, Austin did not set out to write a book about the CPP *per se*. He was equally concerned to trace connections between the dramatic events unfolding in Ghana's political centre (the capital city of Accra) and the kinds of issues that agitated the rural majority. It was these connections, he suggested, which explained how the CPP, unlike its predecessors, had become a 'mass'

46 Dennis Austin, *Politics in Ghana 1946–1960* (London, 1964).

47 Austin's work extended that of David Kimble, *A Political History of Ghana: The Rise of Gold Coast Nationalism 1850–1928* (Oxford, 1963).

rather than an 'elite' party, and thereby rewrote the rules by which its opponents had to play. One of the ways in which Austin explored these connections was by weaving through his Ghana-wide narrative a richly detailed case study of a single town, Bekwai, in the cocoa-producing region of Asante. The local case study quickly caught on, and became a standard method for researching twentieth-century African politics 'from below'. By imposing a tighter geographical frame, researchers hoped to 'drill down' to specific issues that agitated people in rural localities, and to identify the type of individual who was capable of channelling aggrieved rural voters towards a larger political party.[48]

The implication of such local case studies in British Togoland is that the commitment of most rural Africans to political parties was tenuous: encouraged by local activists, they looked beyond their hometown primarily to secure resources that would increase the likelihood of a favourable outcome in local problems or disputes. When local activists backed the right party, and could secure such outcomes in return for rural votes, they were deemed successful; when activists backed the wrong party, and failed to secure favourable outcomes in return for rural votes, the progress of their hometown was retarded, and they were castigated as failures. In both of the key local case studies of politics in British Togoland, the nature of the political party and its ideological position were deemed less important to rural voters than its capacity to deliver solutions to specific local problems and to resolve the many local disputes which had arisen from the misguided implementation of indirect rule.

If the rise of mass nationalist parties provided one framework for the study of local activists, the *Invention of Tradition* marked a starting point for alternative approaches.[49] The difficulties and disappointments of the first generation of African nationalist leaders prompted scholars to go beyond the accusations of 'tribalism' that had been levied at political opponents, and to explore how alternative imaginings of the past were mobilised in the struggles of the present and shaped ongoing debates

[48] Doctoral research in particular has often assumed the form of a local case study which can be related to wider trends or to analytical frameworks. This is the approach adopted in Brown, 'Politics in the Kpandu Area of Ghana' and in Paul Nugent, 'National Integration and the Vicissitudes of State Power in Ghana: The Political Incorporation of Likpe, a Border Community, 1945–1986' (PhD thesis, SOAS, London, 1991).

[49] Eric Hobsbawm and Terence Ranger, eds., *The Invention of Tradition* (Cambridge, 1983).

about identity and citizenship.[50] The analytical lens thus widened beyond the explicitly political work of harnessing rural voters to parties, and encompassed a wider range of processes by which ethnic identities were constructed within the framework of the colonial state and reworked according to the opportunities presented by its demise. In these analyses, formal schooling was important not simply because it gave rise to rural-urban migration and thus to new forms of political mobilisation, but because it enabled individuals to view themselves and their societies from diverse perspectives, to explore the means by which particular elements of the past could be used to confer legitimacy on competing versions of the present and future, and to deploy the tool of literacy in 'meaning making' activities.[51] The scope of studies of intermediary figures thus widened beyond the specific tasks associated with party-political mobilisation to include the processes of research, reflection, and persuasion in which diverse individuals invested much effort.[52]

For Derek Peterson, 'the architects of eastern Africa's ethnic patriotisms' were hardly politicians at all: 'they were not involved in the anti-colonial struggle for political self-government. Neither were they engaged in the effort to build nations. They were driven by the urgent need to find institutions that would protect civic virtues and define honourable conduct.'[53] In this analysis, urbanisation was not, as Hodgkin claimed, the *sine qua non* of mass anti-colonial nationalism. Rather, it produced cohorts of marginal men who sought social capital by disciplining women and resisting the shame that prostitution brought upon their group. In this context, histories were constructed in order to define what was normative and honourable for that group: 'in their textual work, patriots were creating a patrimony.'[54] For Peterson, then, ethnic nationalism was, fundamentally, a product of patriarchal struggle, not party politics.

The *dramatis personae* in this book sit uneasily between such scholarly frameworks. Firstly, Ablɔɖe leaders and activists spent much of their time

[50] Of particular importance were the two-volume study by Bruce Berman and John Lonsdale, *Unhappy Valley: Conflict in Kenya and Africa* (London, 1992) and Leroy Vail, ed., *The Creation of Tribalism in Southern Africa* (London, 1989).

[51] For a classic study, see Steven Feierman, *Peasant Intellectuals: Anthropology and History in Tanzania* (Madison WI, 1990). For a more recent intervention, see Derek Peterson and Giacomo Macola, eds., *Recasting the Past: History Writing and Political Work in Modern Africa* (Athens OH, 2009).

[52] For a recent example, see Carola Lentz, 'SWDK Gandah (1927–2001): Intellectual and Historian from Northern Ghana', *Africa* 82 (3) (2012), 343–55.

[53] Peterson, *Ethnic Patriotism and the East African Revival*, 16.

[54] Ibid., 24.

in rural settings, and this is where most of their political ideas and initiatives developed. Their interest in ending colonial rule and in competing visions of Independence was not necessarily dependent on, or sparked by, an urban experience which enabled or compelled them to set localised issues in a wider political framework. In contrast to the model set up by Hodgkin, the lives of pioneering political figures in southern British Togoland did not revolve around rural-urban labour migration. Nor, however, do these figures match up neatly with the 'ethnic patriots' described by Peterson for eastern Africa, or indeed with 'the first Yoruba' whom John Peel describes as 'Christian evangelists [who] were, unavoidably, ethnic missionaries too'.[55] Many Ablɔḍe leaders, activists, and supporters were trained in missionary or church schools. They took with them the tool of mother-tongue literacy and the capacity to select from historical experience in order to formulate narratives which directed their readers and interlocutors towards collective action in political and social projects. But what is interesting about the Togoland case is that those individuals who were the most intensively exposed to German Protestant ideals of the Ewe as a *volk* – and who might therefore appear particularly well-equipped for what Peel calls 'the cultural work' of 'ethnogenesis' – did *not* always put the tool of mother-tongue literacy to work in the construction of an ethnic Ewe identity.[56] They were not particularly interested in policing the boundaries of 'Ewe-ness', nor did they affiliate themselves *en masse* to demands for an Ewe homeland. In their hands, mother-tongue literacy was also deployed to construct transnational networks, to advocate for a multi-ethnic nation-state, and to debate varieties of citizenship that seemed plausible in the 'the possibilities of the post-war moment'.[57]

BEYOND IDENTITY: BIOGRAPHY, TIN TRUNKS, AND CREATIVE WORK

In 1999 and 2000, I began to seek out individuals who had been active in the Ablɔḍe movement from the later 1940s. I wanted to know who had joined and why, what their 'activism' had actually entailed, how they

[55] John Peel, 'The Cultural Work of Yoruba Ethnogenesis', in *History and Ethnicity*, ed. Elizabeth Tonkin, Maryon McDonald, and Malcolm Chapman (London, 1989), 198–215 at 201.

[56] Ibid. Peel's argument about missionary Christianity and ethnogenesis is developed in greater detail in *Religious Encounter and the Making of Yoruba* (Bloomington IN, 2000).

[57] Frederick Cooper, *Africa Since 1940: The Past of the Present* (Cambridge, 2002), 38.

sought to persuade others, why they were unable to achieve their objectives, and how they experienced and adapted to political failure through the second half of the twentieth century. In short, I wanted to write the history of a political movement 'from within'. This was not unprecedented, but whilst the anti-colonial nationalist struggle has been documented and analysed in almost every African country, there are relatively few book-length studies which attempt to 'get inside' African political movements, particularly those that found themselves on the losing side, for whom freedom was to produce bitter fruit. The most-studied movements tend to be those which fought liberation struggles against settler regimes in southern Africa and those which remained at the forefront of national politics for prolonged periods (such as the Tanzania African National Union).[58] For Kenya, Daniel Branch has demonstrated how much can be gained by studying the people who were 'loyal' in the face of the Mau Mau insurgency.[59] More recently, for Niger and Cameroon respectively, Klaas van Walraven and Meredith Terretta have sought to place the rise and fall of left-wing anti-colonial movements into a broader African context, highlighting the work undertaken by the French in order to ensure the success of more acceptable African politicians.[60] For Ghana, on the other hand, there has been no major study of any political movement since Jean Allman's *Quills of the Porcupine*.[61] It is also striking that two of the studies most explicitly concerned with grassroots activism in other parts of late colonial Africa make a determined effort to recover the experiences of women, and bring social and gender history approaches to bear on the study of politics.[62]

Given that many of the individuals whom I interviewed had spent periods in preventive detention or political exile, experienced punitive transfers or dismissals from formal employment, or witnessed 'destoolments'

[58] Susan Geiger, *TANU Women: Gender and Culture in the Making of Tanganyikan Nationalism, 1955–1965* (Portsmouth NH, 1997); Jocelyn Alexander and JoAnn McGregor, 'War Stories: Guerrilla Narratives of Zimbabwe's Liberation War', *History Workshop* 57 (1) (2004); Stephen Ellis, *External Mission: The ANC in Exile 1960–1990* (London, 2012).

[59] Daniel Branch, *Defeating Mau Mau, Creating Kenya: Counterinsurgency, Civil War, and Decolonization* (Cambridge, 2009).

[60] Klaas van Walraven, *The Yearning for Relief: A History of the Sawaba Movement in Niger* (Leiden, 2013); Meredith Terretta, *Nation of Outlaws, State of Violence: Nationalism, Grassfields Tradition, and State-Building in Cameroon* (Athens OH, 2013).

[61] Allman, *Quills of the Porcupine*.

[62] Elizabeth Schmidt, *Mobilizing the Masses: Gender, Ethnicity, and Class in the Nationalist Movement in Guinea, 1939–1958* (Portsmouth NH, 2005); Geiger, *TANU Women*.

of chiefs on the losing side of a political divide, it is unsurprising that some of them had developed a deep suspicion of 'politics' and recalled their periods of activism with bitter regret.[63] Some of the people from whom I had the most to learn had little reason to revisit difficult periods of their lives, or to provide detailed accounts of their political activities to a 'stranger with big eyes'.[64] Whilst it was always clear that I had come to them because of my interest in a particular political movement, my visits, correspondence, and conversations increasingly revolved around biography. Rather than devising closed questions that aimed to establish whether factor A or factor B was more important in determining an individual's party affiliation, I talked to people about the course of their lives – where they were born, what their parents did, whether and where they had been to school, how they earned a living, whom they had married, where they had travelled, and when and why. In generating these biographical accounts, individual activists plotted their movements through the border area, into other parts of what are now the republics of Ghana and Togo, and, in some cases, across continents. They pinpointed the times and places in which they formed relationships with other activists, and recalled some of the social and economic interactions around which a particular political project would ultimately coalesce. When individuals had already passed away, I was often able to talk with their relatives or colleagues, and the biographies contained within their funeral pamphlets helped me to reconstruct some of the major events and relationships in their lives.[65]

This biographical approach exposed the limitations of analyses which treat political activists either as ethnic nationalists or as points of articulation between highly localised rural grievances and the mass anti-colonial parties that grew up in the towns. My point is not that political activists never served these functions, for earlier studies demonstrate that they sometimes did. But a biographical starting point for research

[63] In southern Ghana, among the Ewe-, Ga-, and Akan-speaking peoples, chiefs sit on stools, and thus the process of a removing an individual from his chiefly office is described as 'destoolment'. In northern Ghana, chiefs sit on skins, and are therefore 'deskinned' rather than 'destooled'.

[64] This is an approximation of *Amɛdzro ŋku gã me nya xɔdome* o (usually translated as 'a stranger with big eyes can never see all the corners of the town').

[65] For an intriguing study of the origins and popularisation of obituaries in Ghana, and an example of ways in which such texts promoted particular political projects, see T. C. McCaskie, 'Writing, Reading and Printing Death: Obituaries and Commemoration in Asante', in *Africa's Hidden Histories: Everyday Literacy and Making the Self*, ed. Karin Barber (Bloomington IN, 2006), 341–84.

on political activism points to the need to widen the lens beyond local-national and ethnic-national dichotomies, and to heed the possibilities implied in Frederick Cooper's argument: 'Politics takes doing; it implies persuading people to think of linkages they may not have perceived before.'[66] The Ablɔɖe movement was something *more than* an agglomeration of parochial disputes. In order for activists to build a movement at all, they needed to develop and disseminate ideas that were capable of bringing different and potentially antagonistic individuals and groups together. If some of this work was directed at connecting a vision of territorial nationalism to tangible localised interests, other elements sought to widen, not narrow, the horizon. Ablɔɖe therefore led individuals across colonial borders and, in some cases, took them as far as New York, Berlin, Warsaw, and London, where they forged surprising new relationships in their articulation of a distinctive vision of freedom.

Interviews, then, were important in revealing the physical and intellectual range of political activists, and highlighting the need for further research that would connect 'the political cultures of particular locales to territorial and transregional political currents', and thereby consider the local, territorial, and global 'in the same analytical plane'.[67] Rather than plugging the gaps in, or layering new perspectives upon, narratives constructed largely on the back of the district commissioners' files in the national archives, interviews with elderly activists (or their surviving relatives) directed me to an alternative form of archive which contained the evidentiary fragments of their persuasive work. Although a few of the people I interviewed held very explicit opinions on contemporary politics, and therefore tended to recount their earlier activities as a prelude to or an explanation for their present positions, many others were unaccustomed to speaking to strangers about their political pasts and, unlike Peterson's East African revivalists, they had no practised genre of testimony to fall back upon. In the course of tentative or exploratory conversations, however, elderly activists (or their surviving relatives) recovered other texts. From a series of 'tin trunks' I was shown maps, newspaper cuttings, United Nations documentation, local histories, obituaries, poems, fiction, and, most importantly, political pamphlets.[68]

[66] Cooper, *Africa since 1940*, 48. [67] Terretta, *Nation of Outlaws*, 20–1.

[68] Karin Barber, 'Introduction: Africa's Hidden Innovators' in *Africa's Hidden Histories*, ed. Barber, 1–24, explains that the rapid spread of primary schooling in the first half of the twentieth century gave rise to new forms of self-representation and subjectivity, and argues that the texts stored by individuals in their tin trunks can shed new light on social and cultural history.

Recent explorations of writing in colonial contexts have emphasised how critical it was to the exercise of state power. For Sean Hawkins, 'more than steamboats, quinine, breechloading rifles, machine guns or any other material instruments commonly associated with conquest, writing made colonialism possible.'[69] It was a technology of control which categorised people, extracting them from a world of their own experience, locating them in 'the world on paper', and thereby enabling their appropriation as the subjects of bureaucratic regimes. Whilst Ann Stoler sees the colonial archive as both 'a corpus of writing' (created out of the particular conventions of record keeping) and as 'a force field that animates political energies and expertise', ultimately she too is concerned with how the archive 'inscribes the authority of the colonial state and the analytic energies mobilised to make its assertions'.[70]

Cooper's premise that 'politics takes doing' invites alternative perspectives which allow for the critical role of writing in the work of persuasion. This is particularly valid for regions where the rapid spread of primary schooling had given rise to substantial new African readerships by the middle of the twentieth century, creating further opportunities for activists to make use of writing in a range of political and social projects. The political pamphlets that I was handed are not simply pieces of evidence which recorded at first hand what their authors thought at a given point in time about particular issues of the day. They *can* be set in juxtaposition to texts produced by colonial administrators, in order to identify specific areas of contention, but this is hardly the limit of their use as evidence. These texts were also the outcomes of a traceable sequence of local and transnational relationships and encounters – between school pupil and teacher, author and printer, buyer and seller, political ally and opponent; they were material objects which circulated through space and time, and amongst networks of people who engaged in impromptu translation and debate; they became personal valuables, deemed worthy of preservation and inclusion within the larger documentary record of an individual author's or reader's life. Inside tin trunks, then, are individual cross sections of the kind of shifting literary landscape identified by Pier Larson in his work on Madagascar.[71] The same trunk

69 Sean Hawkins, *Writing and Colonialism in Northern Ghana: The Encounter Between the LoDagaa and 'The World on Paper', 1892–1991* (Toronto, 2002), 3.

70 Stoler, *Along the Archival Grain*, 22.

71 Pier Larson, *Ocean of Letters: Language and Creolization in an Indian Ocean Diaspora* (Cambridge, 2009).

might contain texts written in different languages and genres for different purposes, and such texts could also be read in different modes – publicly, for the purposes of dissemination, translation, or debate; or privately, for the purposes of increasing knowledge, stimulating reflection, or improving the individual self.

In viewing texts from tin trunks as evidence of persuasive work, and as elements in a varied literary landscape, it becomes apparent that Ablɔɖe activists did not simply address themselves to 'the' Ewe-speaking readership that was formed through missionary Christianity and formal schooling. The history of pre-colonial warfare in the region, the experience of a three-way (German, British, and French) colonisation, the peculiarities of local administration under international trusteeship, and the existence of numerous linguistic minorities through the areas in which Ewe was the majority or vehicular language, meant that political activists could not rely on potential voters to 'self identify' in obvious, neat, or mutually exclusive categories. Whilst the production of texts in Ewe, and the informal translation of English or French texts into Ewe, was a key feature of the persuasive work of political activists, it was also part of what Larson describes as a 'bundle of associated [literary] practices with varied social and political implications, involving fractured and often contending publics'.[72] This perspective allows us to understand how, in spite of their exposure to German missionary understandings of the Ewe as a *volk*, and even when they were writing in standard Ewe, Ablɔɖe authors could also display scepticism of 'Ewe-ness' as a basis of nationhood and work to summon a more diverse and multi-lingual constituency of 'Togolanders' into being.[73] History was pressed into service, and as Ablɔɖe authors articulated the protective and developmental benefits of a sovereign Togoland state, they also alluded to earlier experiences of invasion and raiding by neighbouring groups.

Ablɔɖe authors were aware that they were operating in a crowded field populated by writers of other English, French, and Ewe-language texts, who invoked different aspects of history, and thereby sought to persuade the same readers to adhere to alternative political projects, including some which prioritised unity amongst all the Ewe-speaking peoples of

[72] Pier Larson, 'Literacy and Power in Madagascar', 2 (emphasis original), paper presented at the Wits Institute for Social and Economic Research, 12 Aug 2013, available at: http://wiser.wits.ac.za/system/files/seminar/Larson2013.pdf [last accessed 13 Aug 2014].

[73] This point about the ways in which texts can summon new constituencies is well made in Derek Peterson and Giacomo Macola, 'Homespun Historiography and the Academic Profession', in *Recasting the Past*, ed. Peterson and Macola, 1–30.

the Gold Coast and the two Togoland trust territories.[74] Given this work of persuasion in a crowded field, authors of propaganda would often take on and criticise quotable excerpts from the work of a competitor, and refer readers back to 'arbiter' texts, such as the United Nations Charter or even the Bible, in a bid to set the parameters of debate.[75] English, French, and Ewe-language writings, in conjunction with the numerous political chants and songs which former activists allowed me to record, were the print and oral forms through which rural Africans built new constituencies, debated the role of the state, and mobilised support behind particular political projects.[76]

The dissemination, reception, and impact of competing political propaganda were shaped not only by the force of argumentative content, or by the choice of language, but also by relationships of trust and respect between leaders and their supporters. This may explain why texts were retained by activists in processes of self-archiving, and why some of the activists who spent most of the time with me expressed the hope that I would use what they told me to produce a kind of potted biography that they might later instruct their relatives to incorporate in their funeral pamphlets.[77] When propaganda texts (oral and written) are read in the light of biographical information about individual authors and activists, they offer intriguing opportunities to explore the practices of 'spokesmanship' in specific historical circumstances. The gendered implication of this term is not accidental, for as we shall see, women were 'foot soldiers' more frequently than they were 'spokespersons'.

Ablɔḍe leaders in southern British Togoland regarded themselves very explicitly as an indigenous intelligentsia, quite distinct from the graduate lawyers, doctors, newspaper owners, and wealthy merchants of the

[74] The most important texts which advocated a pan-Ewe approach were: *The Ewe Newsletter*, which envisaged an Ewe homeland, first under British rule and then as an independent state; and *Eve Kɔnuwo* (Ewe Customs) by S. J. Obianim, which advocated Ewe unity within the framework of an emergent Ghana. The latter was adopted as a reader in church schools in British Togoland during the 1950s.

[75] My reading of political propaganda as a specific genre within a 'textual economy' has been influenced by Karin Barber, *The Anthropology of Texts, Persons and Publics: Oral and Written Culture in Africa and Beyond* (Cambridge, 2007). Any errors, however, are my own responsibility.

[76] For some examples of these sources, and my preliminary analysis of their significance, see Kate Skinner, 'Reading, Writing and Rallies: The Politics of "Freedom" in Southern British Togoland 1953–1956', *Journal of African History* 48 (1) (2007), 123–47. A more detailed examination is provided in Chapter 5 of this book.

[77] I wrote an outline of such a text for M. K. Asase, of Ho-Dome, whom we shall encounter in Chapters 5 and 6.

coastal urban centres of the Gold Coast. This coastal/inland distinction is not entirely peculiar to British Togoland and the Gold Coast. For Nigeria, Philip Zachernuk has argued that while the terms 'elite' and 'intelligentsia' are often conflated in depictions of the early African nationalists and pan-Africanists of the nineteenth century, by the mid-twentieth century, 'the intelligentsia' was much larger, more geographically dispersed and internally differentiated, and even rather amorphous. Two further observations from his Nigerian case study seem applicable to British Togoland: the rapid expansion of schooling during the first half of the twentieth century created a 'thin but well-distributed' layer of literates through the southern hinterland, 'reaching beyond the larger cities and by no means disconnected from village life'; 'leading provincial figures were . . . more likely to be clerks, clergymen and teachers than doctors and lawyers, but this did not prevent them from entering national forums in their own right'.[78] Ablɔḍe leaders knew that they lacked the higher academic qualifications and more substantial financial resources of their urban coastal counterparts, but they nonetheless regarded themselves as more authentic and legitimate spokesmen for the people of the trust territory. What, then, was the basis of this claim?

The ability to work across local and colonial languages, and in written and oral forms, became a prerequisite to political spokesmanship – not least for the obvious reason that all the major national and international forums in which British Togolanders sought to present their case were dominated by English and (to a lesser degree) French. But if facility in English and a high level of literacy became a necessary condition of spokesmanship, it was by no means sufficient. Authors of texts always insisted that literacy and multi-lingualism were not purely technical skills: they also conferred responsibilities and, more specifically, the duty to challenge the esoteric bases of power and thereby enlighten a wider readership as to the means of its deception and oppression.[79] Whilst texts could and did travel between anonymous and potentially interchangeable readers, the authorial voice frequently asserted its own honesty, consistency, and prior record, drawing unfavourable comparisons with more

[78] Philip Zachernuk, *Colonial Subjects: An African Intelligentsia and Atlantic Ideas* (Charlottesville VA, 2000), 128 and 130–1.

[79] Peterson also argues that eastern Africa's ethnic patriots went about their writing with 'a sense of duty' and 'an obligation to create useable knowledge'. In his case, however, he indicates that these efforts were aimed at creating patrimony. *Ethnic Patriotism*, 22 and 23.

wilful and unpredictable opponents who were bringing comparable skills of literacy and translation to bear upon competing political projects.

Political pamphlets often circulated and were purchased at rallies, where this emphasis on personal trust and reliability was further reinforced in leaders' appearances before their supporters and their exposure to public scrutiny. In this sense, texts do not only record the ideas that spokesmen sought to disseminate. They also tell us about the self-understandings of Ablɔḍe leaders, the intermediary work of grassroots activists, and the basis on which they sought to forge new relationships with potential supporters who could be either familiar or unknown. The production of English, French, and local-language texts, and their impromptu translation and discussion in social spaces, was a key element in the creative labour undertaken by political activists, who carried out their work of persuasion along and across the oral and literate spheres, and were, above all else, skilled multi-lingual communicators.[80]

'THE FRUITS OF FREEDOM'

Despite these significant investments of creative labour, the Ablɔḍe movement failed to achieve its objectives. The mounting sense of internal division and external interference was depicted by a local author-activist, G. K. Tsekpo, in his political pamphlet, *Togo Nukae Hiawo?* (Togo, what do you need?) (See illustration on this book's front cover.) Tsekpo envisaged freedom as a tree that bore fruit. Rather than helping each other to climb that tree and harvest the fruit, however, people within the trust territory were struggling against one another, according to the designs of the colonial powers (represented as onlookers in suits). The rapid pace of political change on the Gold Coast forced a 'solution' to the Togoland problem. In British Togoland, a plebiscite was organised by the administering authority under United Nations supervision in May 1956. As we shall see, the problematic process of voter registration, and disagreements over the interpretation of the results, have remained sources of grievance for Ablɔḍe activists and their descendants into the twenty-first century. Nonetheless, the United Nations accepted the

80 My interest in 'creative labour' and the work of political persuasion is influenced by Derek Peterson, *Creative Writing: Translation, Bookkeeping, and the Work of Imagination in Colonial Kenya* (Portsmouth NH, 2004). The circumstances of the Kikuyu and the Togolanders, however, were rather different, and this is reflected in the different orientations of the primary texts considered in our respective studies.

plebiscite as a basis for termination of the trusteeship agreement over British Togoland, and the trust territory thereby achieved Independence as part of Ghana in March 1957. The southern section of British Togoland is still part of the Volta Region of Ghana, whilst the northern section became part of Ghana's Northern Region. French Togoland achieved a separate Independence from France in 1960, and the Ghana-Togo border today remains essentially the same as that agreed by the British and the French in 1922.

When Paul Nugent conducted field work at the end of the 1980s, he concluded that the border had, in spite of its colonial origins, cohered remarkably well.[81] The Independence settlement was not the kind of 'freedom' that Ablɔɖe activists had demanded, but nonetheless it had gradually yielded fruit. In the former British Togoland, the descendants of those who had struggled for Ablɔɖe now appeared to consider themselves 'model Ghanaians', and indeed even amongst the older generation, Nugent detected little interest in secession from Ghana or reunification with the francophone republic of Togo.[82] Some former activists expressed similar sentiments when I began my own field work ten years later. According to E. K. Datsa in Amezofe-Avatime in 1999, Togoland reunificationism was 'an old man's issue'. People did not concern themselves with it, because they would rather get on 'with the opportunities that were open to them', particularly through formal education and public sector employment in Ghana.[83] I, like Nugent, began to think that the issue was dead.

Then, in December 2000, presidential and legislative elections ushered in a new political era. President Jerry Rawlings' long tenure of power in Ghana was brought to an end as John Agyekum Kufuor led the New Patriotic Party into government. Elderly Ablɔɖe activists, often supported by children or younger siblings, voiced longstanding grievances at the National Reconciliation Commission in 2004. It is against this backdrop that the former teacher and member of parliament, Kosi Kedem, petitioned the Ghana Constitutional Review Commission on the manner in which the former British Togoland had been integrated into Ghana and demanded negotiations on the terms by which a union could be

[81] This is the main argument of his PhD thesis, 'National Integration and the Vicissitudes of State Power', and it is developed in *Smugglers, Secessionists and Loyal Citizens*, on the basis of a series of further local case studies and an investigation into the specific opportunities that were provided by the border in the form of contraband trade.

[82] Nugent, *Smugglers, Secessionists and Loyal Citizens*, 218.

[83] Interview with E. K. Datsa, Avatime-Amedzofe, 3 June 1999.

maintained. The resurrection of the Togoland question in post-Rawlings Ghana prompted me to return to the material I had gathered and to reconsider the apparent demise of the Togoland question during the long periods of single-party and military rule on both sides of the border, when 'freedom' had yielded bitter fruit.

The preventive detention and political exile experienced by Ablɔɖe activists in the 1960s reoriented their networks and their activities. Those who crossed from Ghana into the republic of Togo as political refugees became embroiled, first in that country's Independence settlement, and later in its domestic politics. Ewe-language print played a critical role in maintaining the 'loss' of British Togoland to Ghana as a key issue in the political life of the new francophone republic of Togo, whilst those who were taken into preventive detention within Ghana formed new relationships with individuals in the Ghana-wide opposition to Kwame Nkrumah. Following a spate of secessionist activity during the mid-1970s, Togoland reunification became a less explicit priority, and in Rawlings' Ghana, it receded from view. Since the year 2000, however, significant changes in the political environment in Ghana reveal that some of the organisational and ideological aspects of Ablɔɖe were never fully 'neutralised', but rather became embedded, and left their traces, in alternative political projects.

The format of this book is broadly chronological. This is, in some sense, an artificial and post-facto construction because, for the reasons outlined above, what I have learned about Ablɔɖe was shaped by the circumstances of the present, and by what former activists were willing to share with me. What I present here, then, is not *the* history of Ablɔɖe, but *one* history, written from the vantage point of the early twenty-first century. It is organised around three sets of questions. Chapters 2 and 3 ask why teachers played such a central role in the politics of southern British Togoland. How did teachers come to conceive of themselves as a cohort and why did they believe they had a right, or even a duty, to speak on behalf of others? How did their experiences of formal schooling shape their understandings of citizenship, and how did they achieve recognition from those around them? Chapter 4 investigates the arguments that were made by Ablɔɖe leaders and activists during the mid-1950s to persuade voters against the integration of British Togoland with the Gold Coast and in favour of the reunification of the two trust territories of British and French Togoland. How were these arguments articulated in speech and in print? What might oral and written texts tell us about the nature of political activism and the engagement of leaders with potential supporters? Chapters 5, 6, and 7 are concerned with the post-Independence period and 'the fruits of freedom'. They ask how the Togoland question continued to influence the politics of both Ghana and Togo after the defeat of the reunificationists in 1956 and 1957, and what the acknowledgement of political failure meant for individuals who had invested so much effort in establishing their right and duty to speak for others.

The people with whom this book is concerned were born after colonial conquest, struggled as adults for a particular version of Independence, and were forced in their later lives to accommodate themselves to political failure. When I began researching Ablɔɖe, it was still possible to talk to many grassroots political activists, to hear their chants and songs, read their pamphlets, and ask about their lives. This 'Independence generation' has since passed away, and the possibilities for understanding their experiences have narrowed. By telling their stories here, I am responding to the interest they expressed in documenting and memorialising their own lives. I did not presume that I could provide their descendants with a usable past, and whether I have done so is not for me to judge.[84] None of these individuals needed me to create a legacy for them. Traces of their experiences, and of the choices that they made, are already embedded in popular histories that circulate close to home and in far-flung places, influencing younger generations in unpredictable ways.[85]

[84] Stephen Ellis, 'Writing Histories of Contemporary Africa', *Journal of African History* 43 (1) (2002), 1–26.

[85] Some of these unpredictable influences are identified in Kate Skinner, 'Local Historians and Strangers with Big Eyes: The Politics of Ewe History in Ghana and its Global Diaspora', *History in Africa* 37 (2010), 125–58.

2

Godly Teachers and Clever Rascals

Southern British Togoland's Intelligentsia

Teacher-politicians were ubiquitous in the era of decolonisation, and in Africa more than any other continent.[1] A few, such as Julius Nyerere (*Mwalimu*, meaning 'teacher' in Swahili) became figures of international renown.[2] But teachers were also over-represented amongst grassroots party activists and in the first legislatures to be elected on the basis of universal adult suffrage. In the 1951 House of Assembly in the Eastern Region of Nigeria, 32 per cent of members were teachers; in the 1954 Gold Coast Legislative Assembly, 29 per cent of members were teachers; in the Kenya African elections of 1957, 32 per cent of nominees were employed as teachers.[3] The preponderance of teachers in the Ablɔɖe movement, then, is striking but not wholly exceptional. This chapter therefore poses two questions which can be answered with reference to the distinctive features of British Togoland, but have a wider resonance in African political history: why did teachers believe that they were well-equipped to articulate political projects; and why did people around them not only accept that this was the case, but expect and even demand that teachers assume leadership roles beyond their classrooms?

Ablɔɖe's teacher-politicians, like many others across colonial Africa, emerged from a system of formal schooling initiated by Christian missionaries and maintained by African successor churches, which accepted

[1] Linda Dove, 'Teachers in Politics in Ex-Colonial Countries', *Journal of Commonwealth and Comparative Politics* 17 (1979), 176–91 at 177.

[2] Andreas Eckert, 'Julius Nyerere, Tanzanian Elites, and the Project of African Socialism', in *Elites and Decolonization in the Twentieth Century*, ed. Jost Dülffer and Marc Frey (Basingstoke, 2011), 216–40.

[3] Dove, 'Teachers in Politics', 178–9.

colonial regulation and inspection in return for funding. The particularities of British Togoland can thus be interpreted in relation to other analyses of missionary encounter and its role in generating 'causes of complaint and a rhetoric of protest'.[4] In their influential study of the Tswana of South Africa, Jean and John Comaroff argued that, in their emphasis on bodily discipline, physical and mental industry, monogamous marriage, and refined consumption, missionaries sought to 're-form Southern Tswana personhood' and thereby stimulated in their converts a sense of themselves as rational, enlightened, autonomous, rights-bearing individuals.[5] Missionaries were therefore critical to the emergence of a 'register of radical individualism', but they were also implicated in a contradictory 'register of primal sovereignty', 'which defined people by virtue of their membership in "customary" political communities' and ascribed to them 'an ineffable, essential primitivism'.[6] This 'register of primal sovereignty' was given its initial impetus by missionary objectification of African cultures, and was subsequently solidified in structures of administration which allowed Africans access to governmental resources and a very limited political voice only within the context of their 'tribe'.

These contradictory registers existed within, and were critical to, racially coded colonialism and they bequeathed a legacy of 'double-consciousness to match the two-faced character of the discourse of rights itself'.[7] The 'register of radical individualism' stimulated one form of political protest, as like-minded individuals mobilised to challenge the gap between the rights that their encounter with missionary Christianity had seemed to promise, and their bitter experience of subordination. The 'register of primal sovereignty' stimulated an alternative form of protest, in the form of rebellions which appeared 'at once to embrace and parody the fierce communalism' that was attributed to 'the Bechuana'.[8] The Comaroffs believe that it is this same legacy of 'double consciousness' which manifested itself in the 1990s, in the bitter contest between the liberal-modernism of the African National Congress and the ethnonationalism of the (Zulu) Inkatha Freedom Party.[9]

In British Togoland, the connections between missionary education and African political protest are puzzling. Schools and colleges explicitly

[4] Jean Comaroff and John Comaroff, *Of Revelation and Revolution: Christianity, Colonialism and Consciousness in South Africa, vol. 1* (Chicago, 1991), 12.

[5] Jean Comaroff and John Comaroff, *Of Revelation and Revolution: The Dialectics of Modernity on the South African Frontier, vol. 2* (Chicago, 1997), 370.

[6] Ibid., 370. [7] Ibid., 400. [8] Ibid., 400. [9] Ibid., 401–2.

aimed to build 'Christian nations' out of pagan 'tribes' and were therefore implicated in the objectification of African cultures.[10] Yet connections between missionary endeavour, 'a register of primal sovereignty', and ethno-nationalist politics were neither inevitable nor straightforward. African school and college leavers in fact went on to lead a range of competing political projects, among them Ablɔɖe, which entailed a scepticism of ethnicity as a basis of nationhood and the envisioning of a different form of citizenship within a reunified Togoland. In this chapter and the one that follows, I propose an alternative to 'double consciousness', and seek other means of explaining how formal education connects the realm of 'culture, symbolism and ideology' to the realm of 'political economy'.[11] Whilst it is tempting to focus on the ethos of institutions and the values that they sought to inculcate in cohorts of students, here I suggest that ultimately it is the differentiating impact of education which matters most – that is, the ways in which formal schooling structures opportunities in specific socio-economic contexts and creates new avenues through which educated individuals can secure recognition from the people around them. By plotting some of the changes within educational systems between the 1890s and 1950s, it is possible to identify how the mundane functions of formal schooling cohered with the capacity of literate and multi-lingual individuals to navigate between different educational projects, to select from them, and to forge political movements which went beyond what any European educationist had intended or predicted.

'THE BRAINS BEHIND IT'

In a funeral pamphlet prepared for E. O. Kofi Dumoga in 1993, his brothers John W. Kodzo and Daniel K. Kwami made the following observation:

> Historians will tell you that the Togoland Teachers' Union later became the Togoland Union [also known as the Togo Union] and then the Togoland Congress. From fighting for the rights of teachers, it became necessary to fight for the political rights of the peoples of Mandated Togoland.[12]

[10] Reverend J. G. Christaller, cited in Cati Coe, *Dilemmas of Culture in African Schools: Youth, Nationalism, and the Transformation of Knowledge* (Chicago IL, 2005), 41.

[11] Comaroff and Comaroff, *Of Revelation and Revolution, vol. 1*, 8. The Comaroffs acknowledge the need for further research on the impact of formal education in stimulating novel and contradictory forms of consciousness. *Of Revelation and Revolution, vol.* 2, 412.

[12] Funeral pamphlet for E. O. Kofi Dumoga, buried at Anfoega-Akukome in 1993.

Dumoga came from Anfoega, near Kpandu, where his father Jonathan had been a chief. Just like G. O. Awuma, who was a pioneering political figure in the regional administrative capital of Ho, Dumoga had attended senior primary school in the mountain-top village of Amedzofe, undertaken a teacher training course in the Gold Coast, and returned to a series of postings in Presbyterian schools in southern British Togoland. As we shall see, both Awuma and Dumoga later fell out with the Togoland Union, which had its headquarters further north, in the commercial town of Hohoe. But when the Togoland reunificationist project took on a clearer shape and a new organisational form at the start of the 1950s, the leadership again comprised individuals who shared a similar educational background. Among the signatories to the early documents which established the Togoland Congress were V. O. Anku, E. K. Datsa, and A. K. Tse, all of whom were trained teachers and Presbyterians. S. G. Antor, who became leader of the Togoland Congress and represented this party in the Gold Coast parliament, was also a teacher. Like his fellow parliamentarian, F. R. Ametowobla, Antor had undertaken part of his primary schooling at Amedzofe, and both men attended the same Presbyterian teacher training college at Akropong in the Akuapem area of the Gold Coast.[13] Ametowobla also became a pastor in the Evangelical Presbyterian church.

Of course, Presbyterian teachers were not the only people involved in the Ablɔɖe movement. Within the ranks of the leadership was A. K. Senoo, a Roman Catholic from the Bla quarter of Hohoe, who worked first as a teacher and then as a mail runner, tribunal registrar, postal agent, and store keeper, before becoming president of the Togoland Union.[14] M. C. Batse had served in the Royal West African Frontier Force, whilst Kodzo Ayeke had worked in customs and excise before joining the staff of a private secondary school and then seeking election to the Gold Coast parliament. He eventually became a lawyer. Amongst those who mobilised support for the Togoland Congress at the grassroots were cocoa farmers, goldsmiths, transport owners, motor drivers, traders, and mass education assistants. The Ablɔɖe movement, then, was not a monolith of Presbyterian teachers, but the importance of teachers within it was acknowledged by friends and enemies alike.

British officials initially took comfort in the prominence of the 'teacher class' in the Togoland Union, believing that this would restrict its appeal

[13] I am grateful to Lynne Brydon for sharing her research notes on the Ametowobla family.
[14] Interview with Modestus Senoo, Hohoe, 15 April 2013.

to the wider population.[15] This assumption proved wrong, and Ablɔḍe became the dominant political force in southern British Togoland in the mid-1950s (albeit temporarily). Following the defeat of the Togoland reunificationists and the integration of British Togoland into Ghana at Independence, the government of the Convention People's Party remained suspicious of the political influence of teachers. Thus, members of the teaching staff at Mawuli secondary school in Ho were removed from their posts on the grounds that their presence in the former trust territory was not conducive 'to the security and the success of the work of the [Ghana] government'.[16] According to Michael Senoo (son of A. K. Senoo, and a teacher himself), these individuals were removed from Mawuli because of their position in the reunification movement: 'They were the brains behind it. The teachers were the elite, our intelligentsia.'[17]

The people who initiated the Ablɔḍe movement and became prominent spokespersons for Togoland reunification were trained in schools and colleges which, whilst formally controlled by African-led churches, remained under the influence of European missionaries through the Second World War. In this sense, the political activists of the mid-twentieth century were the products of a longer engagement between missionaries and the peoples of the areas that later became the Gold Coast and British Togoland. As we shall see, the objectives, failures, and triumphs of this particular set of missionaries in West Africa have long been the subjects of mission-centric research, whilst more recent studies have provided stimulating insights into the changes in materiality and subjectivity that emerged from the African encounter with, and appropriation of, Christianity. These studies, however, did not set out to explore the specific connections between formal education and the articulation of explicitly political projects by mission-trained teachers in southern British Togoland. Here, I suggest that former studies have usually focussed on the aims of missionaries in building Christian nations and have underestimated the significance of changes that took place within the educational systems of the two Togolands and the Gold Coast in the 1930s and 1940s.[18] This is important because it has inhibited our

[15] Public Records and Archives Administration Department (PRAAD), Ho, Ghana. DA/D113: Undated memorandum by district commissioner, cited in Nugent, *Smugglers, Secessionists and Loyal Citizens*, 171, fn 99.

[16] This incident is analysed in further detail in Chapter 6.

[17] Interview with Michael Senoo, Hohoe, 13 Sept 2000.

[18] Meera Venkatachalam has also questioned the degree to which missionary Christianity gave rise to Ewe identity, but her interests lie more in the integration of enslaved Krepe

understanding of the particular social status that attached to teachers in southern British Togoland and the ways in which the specific issues that agitated them as an occupational group could be translated into a broader political agenda.

MISSIONARY EDUCATION AND ETHNOGENESIS

German-speaking Pietists came into the Ewe-speaking areas in the mid-nineteenth century under the auspices of the Bremen-based Norddeutsche Missiongesellschaft (NMG). Their first station was established in coastal Keta in 1853. Further stations were opened at Waya in 1856 and Anyako in 1857, whilst the first real foothold in the inland area came a few years later, in 1859, when the mission established a station at Ho-Wegbe. This meant that the mission's first successes were amongst the coastal Anlo Ewe, and it was this dialect of Ewe which the missionaries first learned and transcribed.[19] Recognising that the dialects in and around Ho-Wegbe were mutually intelligible with Anlo, the missionaries were convinced that the speakers of this language shared a common origin, and they attributed observable differences to the degenerative effects of paganism, slave trading, and warfare. Imbued with romantic nationalism, missionaries sought to standardise and develop the Ewe language in a bid to render it a fit vehicle for revelation, and 'to express and give form to the *Volksgeist*' of an Ewe nation.[20] These efforts were later supplemented by the propagation of narratives of migration from Notsé, through which missionaries sought to unearth a monotheistic past and to revive 'a dormant common national Ewe consciousness'.[21]

women into Anlo society in the aftermath of 1869 and more recently. 'Between the Devil and the Cross: Religion, Slavery and the Making of the Anlo-Ewe', *Journal of African History* 53 (1) (2012), 45–64.

19 Birgit Meyer, 'Christianity and the Ewe Nation: German Pietist Missionaries, Ewe Converts and the Politics of Culture', *Journal of Religion in Africa* 32/2 (2002), 167–99, particularly 177–8. Missionary Lorenz Wolf had made an attempt at evangelisation in Peki in 1847 but this was unsuccessful.

20 Ibid., 173.

21 The quotation is drawn from Hans Debrunner, *The Church in Togo: A Church Between Two Powers* (London, 1965), 122. A more recent analysis of the missionary work of ethnogenesis can be found in Rainer Alsheimer, *Zwischen Sklaverei und christlicher Ethnogenese: die vorkoloniale Missionierung der Ewe in Westafrika (1848 – ca 1890)* (Münster, 2007). For an analysis of narratives of migration from Notsé, see Sandra Greene, 'Notsie Narratives: History, Memory and Meaning in West Africa', *South Atlantic Quarterly* 101 (4) (2002), 1015–41.

The fragility of the mission's progress, and the enormity of its self-appointed task in consolidating the Ewe as a *volk*, were manifested in the disaster that befell Krepe in 1869. The Bremen mission station at Ho-Wegbe was destroyed by the Asante armies who marched east across the river Volta. The Basel mission society, which had established stations along the river Volta and further north in Buem, was also affected, and missionaries Ramseyer and Kühn were famously taken captive and endured the ordeal of a march to, and imprisonment in, the Asante capital Kumasi.[22] Whilst Krepe was devastated by the invasion itself, and by the period of occupation and plunder which followed, coastal Anlo remained immune through its alliance with Asante.[23]

Missionaries were aware of the historic role of traders along the Anlo coast in supplying European African and African-Brazilian buyers with slaves from further inland, and in procuring imports of firearms, gunpowder, and manufactured goods. This long-standing coastal/inland, Anlo/Krepe cleavage, however, was complicated by the fact that Krepe itself was highly differentiated, consisting of numerous small independent *dukɔwo*.[24] Some of the *dukɔwo* had developed alliances with Anlo, Akwamu, or Asante at different points in time, arguably to the detriment of their Krepe neighbours.[25] The invasion of 1869 gave rise to new

[22] This ordeal was subsequently publicised in their famous narrative, F. Ramseyer and J. Kühne, *Four Years' Captivity in Ashanti, Related in Accordance with the Diaries of the Missionaries Ramseyer and Kühne, by P. Steiner* (London, 1901 [1875]).

[23] The cataclysmic nature of the invasion is depicted in Lynne Brydon, 'Constructing Avatime: Questions of History and Identity in a West African Polity c. 1650 to the Twentieth Century', *Journal of African History* 49 (2008), 23–42. The extraction of slaves from Krepe was a key objective of the invasion. See Donna Maier, 'Asante War Aims in the 1869 Invasion of Ewe' in *The Golden Stool: Studies of the Asante Center and Periphery*, ed. Enid Schildkrout (New York, 1987), 232–323.

[24] *Dukɔ* (s), *dukɔwo* (pl), is a difficult term to translate into English, because it is used to refer to political units on a variety of scales. In the context of eighteenth- and nineteenth-century Krepe, the term *dukɔ* is probably most accurately translated as 'microstate' – that is, a cluster of settlements whose people acknowledged their ties to each other in distinction to other settlements, and recognised the authority of a senior or 'paramount' chief or *fiaga*. This problem of definition is considered in Benjamin Lawrance, *Locality, Mobility and 'Nation': Periurban Colonialism in Togo's Eweland 1900–1960* (Rochester NY, 2007), particularly the introduction and chapter 1.

[25] Taviefe, for example, claimed an Anlo origin, whilst Peki played a sub-imperial role for much of Akwamu's century-long suzerainty over Krepe before turning the tables in an armed rebellion in 1833. Sandra Greene, *West African Narratives of Slavery: Texts from Late Nineteenth- and Early Twentieth-Century Ghana* (Bloomington IN, 2011), 86–7; D. E. K. Amenumey, *The Ewe in Pre-Colonial Times: A Political History with Special Emphasis on the Anlo, Ge and Krepi* (Accra, 1986), 66–85; C. W. Welman, *The Native States of the Gold Coast: History and Constitution, Part I, Peki* (London, 1969 [1924]).

hostilities between Krepe settlements, because those who resisted the Asante forces risked death in battle or mass enslavement in defeat, and therefore resented those who sought to mitigate these risks by submitting to and assisting the Asante forces.[26]

After the Asante withdrew in 1871, the Bremen missionaries gradually resumed their work in Krepe, rebuilding, consolidating, and then expanding their influence in a bid to uplift and unify the Ewe-speaking peoples. As evangelism met with greater success, and as more children were brought into mission schools, the use of standard (Anlo) Ewe provided a basis of shared communication, regardless of the colonial border which was drawn between the British Gold Coast and German Togo in 1884. Whilst the German administration pursued a policy of Germanisation in Togo, the impact was limited by two inconvenient realities: firstly, English retained its utility as a commercial lingua franca; secondly, missionaries and African converts continued to use and develop standard Ewe and extended its popularity amongst linguistic minorities in southern Togo.[27] Later studies, conducted under the auspices of the International Missionary Council in the 1960s, insisted that continued missionary emphasis on Ewe language and history reflected their long-standing aim to build an indigenous church.[28] This was achieved rather sooner than the missionaries had anticipated, for once the British and French had ousted the German colonial regime at the outbreak of the First World War, the German-speaking missionaries fell under suspicion. By 1916, all but Bürgi (who was a Swiss national) had been expelled, and African pastors established their control of the Ewe Church.[29]

For Hans Debrunner, the intentions of missionaries in recovering a common Ewe history and propagating the gospel in standard Ewe worked in tandem with the unanticipated consequence of the First World War to produce a cultural renaissance and a confidence in the capacity for African leadership: 'the *growth of the Church* led to the *growth of*

[26] The bitter legacy of these strategies was specifically mentioned by a British official, Gouldsbury, as cited in Brydon, 'Constructing Avatime', 34.

[27] Benjamin Lawrance, 'Most Obedient Servants: The Politics of Language in German colonial Togo', *Cahiers d'études africaines* 40 (159) (2000), 489–524.

[28] The research in Debrunner, *The Church in Togo* was conducted under the auspices of the IMC.

[29] E. E. Grau, 'The Evangelical Presbyterian Church (Ghana and Togo) 1914–1946: A Study in European Mission Relations Affecting the Beginning of an Indigenous Church' (PhD thesis, Hartford Seminary Foundation, 1964).

the Ewe nation.'[30] This sense of nationhood appeared to have withstood the redrawing of the colonial border between British and French Togoland at the end of the First World War, and was reflected in the name Ewe Church, which was adopted by the new African leadership. (Later, the Ewe Church was renamed the Evangelical Presbyterian Church in order to take account of the other language groups who formed part of its congregation.) Debrunner's assessment of the role of the Ewe Church was subsequently incorporated into the analyses of political historians, who saw cultural nationalism as a pre-condition of political nationalism.[31] For D. E. K. Amenumey, it was this cultural nationalism, combined with Africans' keen awareness of differences between the administrations of the French and the British in their respective portions of Togoland, which formed the background to the political demand for an Ewe homeland, as articulated by the All Ewe Conference (AEC) in the aftermath of the Second World War.

The AEC was initiated by highly educated Ewe-speakers from the Anlo and Peki areas that lay within the British Gold Coast Colony. The AEC sought to expand its support base into the southern section of British Togoland but, as Paul Nugent has pointed out, there is no reason to assume that its ethno-nationalist agenda had an automatic appeal to the peoples of the trust territory or a primary claim on their political allegiances.[32] Certainly, it is possible to identify individuals within British Togoland who were trained by mission and church schools, embraced the study of Ewe language and history, and were interested in the political unification of the Ewe-speaking peoples.[33] What concerns us here, however, is why so many other Ewe-speaking teachers in southern British Togoland were sceptical of the ethno-nationalist project of the AEC, and mobilised instead behind a peculiar form of multi-ethnic territorial

30 Debrunner, *The Church in Togo*, 123 (his emphasis).

31 Amenumey, *The Ewe Unification Movement*, 28–9. See also D. E. K. Amenumey, 'The Pre-1947 Background to the Ewe Unification Question: A Preliminary Sketch', *Transactions of the Historical Society of Ghana* X (1969), 65–85 at 78–9. Lawrance, 'Most Obedient Servants' argues that, whilst the German administration was concerned to establish the precedence of German over English, the use and spread of standard Ewe was to prove a 'powerful unifying tool for Africans' (491) and created a basis for 'proto-nationalism' (494).

32 Nugent, *Smugglers, Secessionists and Loyal Citizens*, 188–98.

33 S. J. Obianim, who came from the Siyase-speaking enclave of Gbadzeme-Avatime, wrote a book entitled *Eve Kɔnuwo* (Ewe Customs), which was adopted as a reader in church primary schools after 1952 and which advocated unity amongst the Ewe-speaking peoples.

nationalism, which sought the restoration of the borders of the former German colony. Put differently, why did the mission's view of 'nation' fail to translate into a single, coherent, ethno-nationalist project, even amongst the relatively small cohort of Ewe-speakers whom the mission had trained?

For Nugent, who is interested in the 'limits of invention', the missionaries' construction of 'the Ewe' as a *volk* had limited salience because it was insufficiently grounded in pre-colonial historical realities.[34] Other sub-ethnic and localised issues therefore proved more important than 'Ewe identity' in articulating the relationships between rural communities and the colonial state. Whilst the analyses of Nugent and Amenumey diverge over the extent to which ethnic nationalism appealed to the diverse groups of people who could communicate in Ewe, they espouse a similar explanation for the particular role played by mission-trained teachers in articulating an alternative political project. This explanation points to the rivalry between those in British Togoland and their counterparts in the Gold Coast, who enjoyed a wider range of scholarly and occupational opportunities. Amenumey thus points to the

> resentment felt by the Ewe of British Togoland particularly the educated class – the majority of whom were teachers – against the Anlo and Peki of the Gold Coast. The former were jealous of the positions of prominence attained by the Gold Coast Ewe both in the fields of education and in the administration of British Togoland. The prominence of the Anlo and Peki Ewe in the AEC was also resented.[35]

Amenumey thus located the origins of demands for Togoland (as opposed to Ewe) political unity in the teachers' associations of the British trust territory – a view echoed in the funeral pamphlet of E. O. Kofi Dumoga, albeit from a rather different point of view.

Like Nugent, I am wary of mission-centric narratives of Ewe cultural nationalism, for if we accept this as the basis of political consciousness, it is difficult (without resort to 'double consciousness') to explain why individuals who had been trained in exactly the same ethos and institutions ended up mobilising behind opposing political projects. Unlike Nugent and Amenumey, however, I see the Togoland teachers as something more than a small interest group chafing against their subordinate positions within church and school hierarchies. In order to understand

[34] Carola Lentz and Paul Nugent, eds., *Ethnicity in Ghana: The Limits of Invention* (Basingstoke, 1999).

[35] Amenumey, *The Ewe Unification Movement*, 118–9 and fn 2.

why teachers arrogated to themselves the work of articulating wider political projects, and why others were willing to confer leadership roles upon them, we need to explore two further areas: firstly, how individuals who passed through missionary and church institutions were able to reinterpret and select from the intentions of those Europeans who sought to educate them; and secondly, how they related what they learned within those institutions to the people who lived around them.

MATERIALITY, ENLIGHTENMENT, AND RELIGIOUS ENCOUNTER

Although four Bremen mission stations were constructed in the 1850s, Werner Ustorf has emphasised the painfully slow progress of the missionaries, who achieved just fourteen conversions in their first decade of evangelistic endeavour. The difficulties in converting free Africans contributed to missionary interest in the manumission of slave children, and approximately one hundred such children were purchased, 'liberated', and converted in the period between 1857 and 1868.[36] This strategy of conversion by manumission was subsequently criticised by key mission supporters, not least because the maintenance of the children proved more costly and problematic than anticipated. Manumission was also deemed less necessary once missionaries were able to attract free children into their schools, and this realisation encouraged a reconsideration of mission strategies.[37]

The significance of the Asante invasion of 1869 lies not simply in its exposure of the divisions between the different Ewe-speaking groups, but in the social and economic devastation wreaked upon the local

[36] Werner Ustorf, 'Norddeutsche Mission under Wirklichkeitsbewätigung: Bremen, Afrika under der Slavenfreikauf', in *Mission im Kontext: Beiträge zur Sozialgeschichte der Norddeutschen Missionsgesellschaft im 19. Jahrhundert*, ed. Werner Ustorf (Bremen, 1989), 121–215. From a variety of primary sources, Ustorf concludes that the total figure was 109. Biographies of manumitted slave girls at Keta are included in Alsheimer, *Zwischen Sklaverei und Christlicher Ethnogese.*

[37] In her more detailed study of Wegbe, however, Sonja Sawitzki stresses that conversion through schooling was by no means unproblematic or guaranteed, either before or after the Asante invasion: free Africans could be deterred from sending their children to classrooms that were associated with former slaves; free children were also deemed more difficult to control, in terms of their eating habits and their adherence to the timetable. See Sonja Sawitzki, *Ho/Wegbe: Die Etablierung einer Missionsstation in West-Afrika* (Bremen, 2002). I am grateful to Anne Frausing for bringing this book to my attention and for her assistance with German-English translation.

population: settlements were deserted as people fled the advancing armies or were taken captive; agricultural activities were abandoned; the markets that connected different settlements within Krepe, and served as links into trade routes to both north and south, ceased to function.[38] Lynne Brydon thus explains how the re-establishment of mission stations was part of a wider process of social and economic reconstruction in Krepe. The number of African Christians was initially boosted by the return of numerous individuals who had experienced conversion during periods of absence in the Gold Coast. Some of these people had fled the invasion of 1869, whilst others had been taken as slaves and were subsequently converted by Basel missionaries at their stations in Abokobi and Maiera (near Accra) in the aftermath of British anti-slavery proclamations in 1874.[39] Evangelisation in the Siyase-speaking enclave of Avatime gathered pace after 1889 because the construction of a mission station in the mountain-top village of Amedzofe generated an association between Christian settlements and the new knowledge and skills that were shown to facilitate the re-entry of dislocated individuals into the labour market and into new forms of cash-earning agricultural production.

A similar process to that identified by Brydon was also observed by Birgit Meyer in Ewe-speaking villages. Converts were required to separate themselves from the heathen life of the village, and move to the *kpodzi* (hill top), whose 'materiality' was 'impressive and entirely different from the usual standards'.[40] Missionaries usually lived in two-storey houses that were surrounded by a veranda and had wooden doors and windows. One of the first tasks of an African male convert was to construct a similar home for himself and his nuclear family (albeit on a more modest one-storey plan). Local people earned cash by carrying materials up to the *kpodzi* where they observed skilled labourers from the coast, and sometimes the missionaries themselves, engaging in the crafts of carpentry, bricklaying, and masonry.

[38] Brydon, 'Constructing Avatime', 32–6.

[39] Lynne Brydon, 'Extensions of Extended Families: a case study from Avatime, Ghana', Working Paper No. 1 of the Missione Etnologica in Bénin e Africa Occidentale (2007), available at: www.mebao.org/uploads/wps/mebao_wp01.pdf [last accessed 14 Feb 2013].

[40] Birgit Meyer, 'Christian Mind and Worldly Matters: Religion and Materiality in Nineteenth-Century Gold Coast', *Journal of Material Culture* 2 (3) (1997), 311–37 at 318. The Basel missionaries on the Gold Coast also promoted separate settlements for their Christian converts. See Noel Smith, *The Presbyterian Church of Ghana 1835–1960* (Accra, 1966), 49.

It was through learning a craft that many young men first started to associate with the mission, and this in turn forged a connection between Christianity and new forms of labour and consumption.[41] The connection was reinforced as the missionaries began to promote peasant cash cropping, thereby facilitating means of earning cash amongst those whose skills lay in agriculture.[42] Once these connections were established, mission schools began to expand more rapidly, for whilst the Bremen missionaries, like their Basel counterparts, 'conceived of schooling as a first step in a total conversion process', schools were also recognised by local populations as an entry point to new forms of knowledge, skill, employment, production, and consumption.[43]

In areas closer to the coastal trading centres, there was a wider range of avenues through which Africans could explore and select from novel forms of labour and consumption. However, in the inland farming areas, the mission itself became a (sometimes *the*) major broker between rural lifestyles and a new material culture, and missionaries' responses to these motivations for, and mechanisms of, conversion were conflicted.[44] They required converts to adopt a 'distinct material culture', which included new forms of clothing, furniture, and housing, but they conceived of this in terms of minimum standards of 'decency'.[45] They were thus disturbed by the propensity of Africans to value material goods, and they feared that converts were preoccupied with the exterior manifestations of their new status (and particularly clothing) to the detriment of their inner lives and the quality of their individual relationships with God. Herein lay a prolonged source of tension

[41] Brydon has noted a similar process in Amedzofe-Avatime, where the missionaries constructed a chapel and a school and trained Africans as carpenters and masons, as well as teachers and catechists. *Lives and Livings* (unpublished book manuscript).

[42] Meyer, 'Christian Mind and Worldly Matters', 321. See also Stephan Weissflog, 'Vietor und sein Konzept des Leistungsfähigen Afrikaners', in *Mission im Kontext*, ed. Ustorf, 293–304. Weissflog argues that, as head of a trading firm and a member of the mission board, J. K. Vietor was well-positioned to press his economic interests: he saw the stimulation of agricultural production in the tropics as a means of increasing import/export activity whilst promoting a Christian peasant lifestyle.

[43] Coe, *Dilemmas of Culture in African Schools*, 39. This emphasis on the association between Christianity and 'the good things in life' bears resemblance to the dynamic identified by J. D. Y. Peel, *Religious Encounter and the Making of Yoruba* (Bloomington IN, 2000), 243

[44] This point is made in Meyer, 'Christianity and the Ewe Nation', 183.

[45] Meyer, 'Christian Mind and Worldly Matters', 331.

between missionary emphasis on asceticism and African Christians' understanding of enlightenment.[46]

In his dictionary, Missionary Westermann defined the Ewe term *ŋkuvuvu* as 'having the eyes open, briskness, cleverness, knowledge, civilisation'.[47] Meyer's preferred translation is 'civilisation' – a term which is still widely used in Ghana – and her explication bears some similarity to that offered by John Peel for the Yoruba term *ọlaju*: 'To the Ewe, "civilization" meant the adoption of new things seen elsewhere and found worthwhile to supplement, or even to replace, the familiar'.[48] There are two elements of this definition which invite further exploration. The first is that, in Meyer's analysis, *ŋkuvuvu* refers primarily to individuals: through experiences such as travel, trade, formal schooling, or artisanship, individuals acquired new skills, knowledge, and attributes, and became 'enlightened'.[49] This enlightenment could be both manifested by the individual, and rendered visible and explicit to others, through material goods. Clothing, then, along with housing and furniture, was critical to the self-fashioning of individuals and their assertion of a new identity. In his discussion of the apparently similar concept among the Yoruba, however, Peel notes how *ọlaju* stood in relationship to other terms which were used to describe the progress (*ilọsiwaju/itẹsiwaju*) or growing up (*idagbasoke*) of a town. In other words, he sought to explain how individuals' self-identification as 'enlightened', and their recognition as such by others, was connected to a more collective sense of advancement.[50]

Peel suggests that, amongst the Yoruba, progress was understood as an aggregate of individual achievements. Towns advanced by virtue of being home to a multiplicity of individuals who had achieved enlightened

[46] Meyer's early research sought to historicise and explain the rise of schismatic charismatic churches and the 'prosperity gospel' in Ghana. See Birgit Meyer, *Translating the Devil: Religion and Modernity Among the Ewe in Ghana* (Edinburgh, 1999).

[47] Diedrich Westermann, *Evefiala or Ewe-English Dictionary* (Berlin, 1973 [1928]), 197 (Ewe-English section). This draws from Westermann's earlier Ewe-German work, *Wörterbuch die Ewe-Sprache* (Berlin, 1905 and 1906).

[48] Meyer, 'Christian Mind', 316; see also J. D. Y. Peel, '*Ọlaju*: A Yoruba Concept of Development', *Journal of Development Studies* 14 (1978), 139–165.

[49] The term 'civilised' is widely used in Ghana, while its French equivalent ('civilisé') is used in Togo, and in this respect Meyer's translation is authentic. I remain uncomfortable with its connotations. Here I prefer 'enlightened', which I think better captures the Ewe term *vuŋku* and its association with awakening from slumber or emerging from darkness into light. See also Westermann, *Evefiala*, 114 (English-Ewe section).

[50] Peel, '*Ọlaju*'.

status. The Yoruba, of course, have a distinctive urban history arising out of nineteenth-century warfare, whilst in the more rural areas of Krepe, settlements existed on a very small scale through to the second half of the twentieth century.[51] Nonetheless, Peel's depiction of progress as an aggregate of individual achievement points to the need to explore whether one enlightened individual was expected to open up opportunities for others to achieve that status, and if so, how exactly he or she might do this. This presupposes a significant shift between the status that derives from esoteric knowledge and the status that derives from displaying and disseminating the knowledge that one has in order that others can admire it, acquire it, and turn it to their own advantage and advancement.[52]

The progress of a town was similar to that of a person, in the sense that it could be manifested, and made visible and explicit to others, through a change in materiality. The construction of new physical infrastructure and amenities in the 1930s, 40s and 50s thus served a range of concrete purposes, but it also displayed a town's progress because it was indicative of the presence of enlightened individuals who were capable of generating consensus around the desirability of particular projects and initiating collective efforts. In this definition, the progressive town was not simply a town which was home to enlightened individuals who had their own resources; it was also a town in which people were able to perceive the wider benefits derived from the construction of a feeder road, a primary school, a community centre, or a post office, and organise themselves towards the realisation of such projects.[53]

Teachers became important in southern British Togoland because they were deemed capable in both respects. Within their schools, teachers were expected to transmit specific knowledge and skills, and thereby open up new opportunities for a multiplicity of individual children, who in turn were required to share their success with their families. Beyond their schools, teachers – in collaboration with other literate school leavers – also played a key role not only in deciphering the demands of the colonial state, but also in bringing people together (*ɖekawɔwɔ* – unity) to forge collective responses and to organise collective endeavours. Teachers were

[51] For a study of the town of Ibadan and a commentary on the distinctive urban history of the Yoruba, see Ruth Watson, *'Civil Disorder is the Disease of Ibadan': Chieftaincy and Civic Virtue in a Colonial City* (Oxford, 2001).

[52] Peel, '*Ọlaju*', 149.

[53] For a discussion of how Asante chiefs asserted their legitimacy in terms of bringing unity (*nkabɔmu*) and/or progress (*nkɔsɔɔ*), see Ivor Wilks, '"Unity and Progress": Asante Politics Revisited', *Ghana Studies* 1 (1998), 151–79.

thereby able to initiate *ŋgɔyiyi / yi ŋgɔ* (progress, noun/verb) and *dudzadzrado* (town improvement, lit. making the town nice). In these respects, *ŋkuvuvu* is an important concept for understanding the self-fashioning of individuals, but taken on its own, it is insufficient for understanding intersubjectivity and the changing terms on which teachers could secure due recognition from those around them.[54] For this reason, it is necessary to undertake a more mundane analysis of the development of schools and colleges, and the new form of training that was given to teachers after the First World War, and to locate these changes within their economic context. This will allow us in later chapters to grasp teachers' claims to leadership and the nature of their spokesmanship in the Togoland reunification movement. It will also provide a basis for understanding responses to political failure.

TRAINING TEACHERS AND PREACHERS: GERMAN APPROACHES

For the Bremen mission, the work of the teacher and evangelist was inseparable. This connection between the provision of formal schooling to children and the monitoring of the religious lives of members of a wider community was maintained beyond the Second World War, despite some resistance on the part of trainee and practising teachers. The struggles around the model of teacher-catechist have usually been interpreted as part of a conflict between the different missionaries who continued to exercise either an informal influence, or a direct supervision, over the Ewe Church after the First World War.[55] Here, I suggest that struggles over the teacher-catechist model between the 1880s and the 1940s provide an important entry point to the self-understandings of teachers and the peculiar status that was accorded to them. For this reason, it is worth retracing the origins of the model, before examining how it gradually became untenable in the light of teachers' responses to the formalisation of educational structures in British Togoland.

Recognising that schools were the most effective instruments of evangelisation, the long-serving Bremen mission inspector, D. F. M. Zahn, concluded that the training of teachers, and thus the education they would later provide for African students, should be aimed not at

[54] My interest in the terms of due recognition is derived from Axel Honneth, *The Struggle for Recognition: The Moral Grammar of Social Conflicts* (Cambridge, 2005 [1995]).

[55] This is a recurring theme in Grau, 'The Evangelical Presbyterian Church'.

Germanisation, but at the realisation of a distinctively Ewe Christianity. In this respect, the Bremen mission espoused a similar ethos to that of its Basel counterpart, which, in its work among the Akan-speaking peoples to the west, also aimed to make 'Christian nations out of the tribes of the Gold Coast'.[56] The Bremen mission, however, undertook a distinctive experiment when it brought twenty young Ewe-speaking men for training in Württemburg between 1884 and 1900. In the analysis of Birgit Meyer, Zahn's approach sought to confine Africans within the reified version of their culture endorsed by European missionaries. Under the guise of training, European educators denied autonomy to African students by limiting their opportunities for independent explorations of life in Germany and preventing their 'creative trespassing of boundaries' between cultures.[57] The African trainees were envisaged not as future leaders, but as 'humble, efficient and reliable workers, as assistants to the missionaries, as wise educators to the pupils, and shining examples of all that is good'.[58] Indeed, the training was not freely given, for the trainees were bonded to serve the mission on their return to Africa in order to ensure that the knowledge and skills acquired in Württemburg were deployed only for the purpose that the mission had intended.

Missionaries recognised that, through their familiarity with, and capacity to navigate between different cultures, the first-generation converts had the potential to exercise subtle but significant powers of brokerage. Thus, whilst missionaries recognised their own dependence on these cultural brokers for the further propagation of the gospel, they also devised a programme of training which sought to limit the autonomy of trainees and thereby rebalance the power relationship in favour of the mission. A recent prosopographical study by Kokou Azamede points to some patterns in the careers of the trainees which suggest that missionary control turned out to be rather more limited than the latter would have wished.[59] According to Azamede, then, Isaac Kwadzo attributed

[56] Reverend J. G. Christaller, cited in Cati Coe, *Dilemmas of Culture in African Schools: Youth, Nationalism, and the Transformation of Knowledge* (Chicago IL, 2005), 41.

[57] Meyer, 'Christianity and the Ewe Nation', 169.

[58] Johannes Binder, cited in Meyer, 'Christianity and the Ewe Nation', 184. This emphasis on the controlling attitude of missionaries, and their insistence on their superiority vis-à-vis the African mission personnel, is also evident in Werner Ustorf, *Bremen Missionaries in Togo and Ghana 1847 to 1900* (Legon, 2002 [trans. James Greig]).

[59] Kokou Azamede, *Transkulturationen? Ewe-Christen zwishcen Deutschland und Westafrika, 1884–1939* (Wiesbaden, 2010). I am grateful to Anne Frausing for her assistance with German-English translation.

great importance to his work as a teacher, but showed little concern for combating 'pagan' practices, and continued to participate in enstoolment ceremonies in Peki; Gebhard Christophe Komla Mensa excelled as a teacher, but was deemed to show little aptitude as a priest, possibly because he was ready to compromise on issues such as mixed marriages; Zacharias Deku was also deemed unsatisfactory in his preaching, but continued to work as a teacher; Elisa Kende, Nathaniel Kwami, and Ludwig Medenu all left the services of the mission, and were able to pay back the costs of their training by finding salaried employment within the German colonial administration or within commercial firms.[60]

Within the hierarchy of the Bremen mission, teachers served also as evangelists and only after lengthy and successful service might they aspire to become a pastor. What Azamede's biographies suggest, however, is that the 'Ewe-Württemburger' developed their own ambitions, and several of those who remained within the remit of the mission directed their energies towards teaching. In their more strictly religious functions, the returnees were obliged to survey the intimate affairs of converts and to implicate themselves in interventions that either disrupted converts' continued obligations to their extended families and their hometowns or resulted in their dismissal from the congregation.[61] The pursuit of this task was necessary to accede to the rank of pastor, yet it demanded the assumption of superiority over extended family, neighbours, and friends, which easily gave rise to resentment.[62] In the school room, on the other hand, the returnees may have exercised greater latitude in selecting from among the mission's values those that they believed to be most useful to people around them. As teachers, they were more easily tolerated as agents of progress and enlightenment, because they were opening up new opportunities to the children of the town.

The returnees thus sought to navigate between different sources of status. Within the structures determined by the mission, the most successful returnees were those who were promoted from school teaching through ordination as pastors. For some of the returnees, however, the

60 Azamede, *Transkulturationen?* Here, I use the term 'mixed marriages' to refer to marriages between Christians and non-Christians.

61 Greene, *West African Narratives of Slavery*, 27–31 also notes that the mission's evangelist Aaron Kuku found little popularity through his new religion.

62 This may explain why those who did accede to the rank of pastor were often drawn from successive generations of the same family, where individuals could safely assume that most of their relatives were already practising Christians – e.g. the Ametowoblas and the Kwamis.

position of teacher was preferable because it enabled them to enjoy better relationships with the people amongst whom they had to live. For others, their education allowed them to leave the employ of the mission – either when their bond expired, or sooner if they could afford it. After 1900, the NMG decided to train its African teachers and evangelists within Togo, but a similar pattern persisted. Indeed, a report produced by a Gold Coast education officer after the First World War suggested that 50 per cent of the teachers working in the Bremen mission schools were under bond – in other words, numerous individuals had preferred to take up alternative opportunities in the civil service and in commerce once they completed their five-year bonded service.[63] Thus, if first-generation converts were key cultural brokers between the mission and African societies, the embedding of the German colonial state and German commercial interests opened up a range of other intermediary occupations and alternative spheres of influence for those who had mastered the skill of reading and writing in a European language.

THE FATE OF THE 'GERMAN SCHOLAR'

A minority among the 'Ewe-Württemburger' did accede to the position of pastor, and, upon the departure of the German missionaries in the First World War, they constituted the new leadership of the Ewe Church.[64] However, for other Africans who had acquired competence in written and spoken German, the demise of the German regime threatened their usefulness as teachers, translators, interpreters, and clerks. The professional dislocation of the 'German scholars' and their petitioning activities have been attributed some significance in studies of Togoland. They represent an indigenous elite – albeit a very small one – which had a specific objection to the separate mandates given by the League of Nations for the British and French administration of the former German colony, and a vested interest in the promotion of a territorial Togoland identity. Between 1925 and 1936, there was scope for this small interest group to

63 PRAAD, Accra, ADM 39/5/461 'Mission Schools in British Mandatory, Togoland' by Aitken (n.d.) and letter from Major Jackson (Commander of British Forces in Togoland) to Colonial Secretary, Accra, 12 Nov 1920.

64 Azamede, *Transkulturationen?* thus explains how Timotheo Kofi Ametowobla was finally made a pastor by the Swiss missionary Bürgi in July 1916, at a time when all the German nationals had been forced to leave both the British and French zones of Togoland. The first synod of the Ewe Church was held under the leadership of a senior 'Ewe-Württemburger', Andreas Aku, in 1922.

forge connections with two other grievances which pertained to a wider range of people: in the British zone, there was enormous resentment against attempts to bring together into larger 'amalgamated states' the numerous small chieftaincies that had been recognised by the Germans; in the French zone, there were deeply felt objections to the coercive nature of the regime and to the direct taxation that it sought to impose.[65]

The activities of the Bund der Deutschen Togoländer in the inter-war period have been well analysed by Benjamin Lawrance, particularly in relation to grievances in the zone that came under French administration.[66] For the British zone, David Brown emphasises the presence of 'nostalgia' for German rule amongst those born at the turn of the twentieth century, but he also notes that the most vocal advocates of Togoland reunification from the late 1940s were not those who had suffered at first-hand from professional dislocation upon the demise of the German regime.[67] The activists of the late 1940s and 1950s belonged to the next generation, whose professional opportunities were much more directly shaped by the process of formalisation that the new British administration imposed upon mission/church schools in their sphere of Togoland. This process of formalisation served to widen the gap between the religious and educational functions of teachers, and created different opportunities for individuals to achieve and to serve. These changes were points of departure in a new set of dynamics whereby individual opportunities became enmeshed with emerging forms of local leadership and a growing sense that the people of southern British Togoland were severely disadvantaged in relation to their counterparts in the Gold Coast. It is these dynamics, and not a rose-tinted nostalgia for German rule, or a mission-derived sense of 'Ewe-ness', which increasingly oriented teachers in the trust territory

[65] On the exodus from French Togoland into the cocoa growing areas of British Togoland during the interwar period, see Benjamin Lawrance, '"En proie à la fièvre du cacao": Land and Resource Conflict on an Ewe Frontier, 1922–1939', *African Economic History* 31 (2005), 135–81. On the predicaments of the unamalgamated divisions, see Wilson Yayoh, 'Local Government in Ewedome, British Trust Territory of Togoland (Ghana), 1920s–1970s' (PhD thesis, School of Oriental and African Studies, 2010), and 'Protests Against Amalgamation in Colonial Ewedome, British Mandated Territory, 1920 to 1948', *Journal of History and Cultures* 2 (2013), 1–16, available at: http://historyandcultures.files.wordpress.com/2013/02/jhac-2-journal-of-history-and-cultures-issue-2-february-20132.pdf [last accessed July 2014].

[66] Lawrance, *Locality, Mobility and "Nation"*, chapter 5.

[67] David Brown, 'Politics in the Kpandu Area of Ghana, 1925 to 1969: A Study of the Influence of Central Government and National Politics upon a Local Factional Competition' (PhD thesis, University of Birmingham, 1977) 240.

towards political projects, and which provided one of the most important bases upon which a case for Togoland reunification could be made.

When the British occupied the western half of German Togo during the First World War, their attitude to the Bremen mission schools was in keeping with the voluntarist approach that was applied in their other African territories. There was no move to dismantle the Bremen mission schools and replace them with direct governmental provision. The problem was how the mission's schools were to be regulated and financed. The five African pastors who struggled, alongside the lone Swiss missionary, Bürgi, to maintain every mission station after the expulsions of 1916, had insufficient funds to pay the teachers' salaries. In a bid to arrest the precipitous decline in the regularity of teaching and in school attendance, an education officer was appointed to conduct a survey and identify whether a government grant could be made.[68]

The government, however, wanted the African pastors and teachers to be supervised by a British missionary organisation, and thus approached the Free Church of Scotland (FCS). At first, the FCS insisted that it had insufficient funds to maintain all the former Bremen stations, and could work only in the areas that fell within the Gold Coast, where it had already agreed to supervise schools established by the Basel mission. The government persisted, and finally, in October 1921, the FCS assumed supervisory responsibilities in British Togoland.[69] Similarly, in the French zone, the new administration wanted African pastors and teachers to be supervised by a French missionary organisation, and selected the Société des Missions Evangéliques de Paris for this purpose. The African pastors resisted new European interventions, and thus convened their own synod at Kpalimé, in French Togoland, in May 1922 and inaugurated the Ewe Church. Despite the concern of African pastors about the divisive potential of French and Scots supervisory arrangements, the lack of funding for schools forced their hand.

In January 1920, the Bremen mission schools in British Togoland were closed and teachers were paid their salaries during a period of retraining in English. Not all teachers accepted this retraining and some left the profession, which delayed the reopening of schools. But Eugene Adom

68 PRAAD, Accra, ADM 39/5/46: 'Mission Schools in British Mandatory, Togoland' by Aitken (n.d.) and letter from Major Jackson (Commander of British Forces in Togoland) to Colonial Secretary, Accra, 12 Nov 1920.

69 The main Bremen stations in the Gold Coast were those at Peki and Keta, whilst the main stations in British Togoland were those at Ho, Amedzofe, Akpafu, and Kpandu.

from Hohoe recalled that his father, a Bremen mission teacher, had attended the special classes at Amedzofe and in 1925 passed an examination which re-established his right to teach in British Togoland and enabled him to take up a post at Wusuta.[70] Mathias Agbodza, from Santrokofi-Benua, also recalled that his father had passed through a process of retraining in English.[71] When the Bremen missionaries began to return after November 1922, they were forced to accept the carving-up of their mission field, as ordained by the British and French administrations, and in British Togoland they had to submit to the supervision of the FCS in all matters pertaining to education. Their capacity to pursue a distinctive vision of Ewe Christianity through the school curriculum and through the training and management of school teachers was abruptly curtailed. Some of these returning Bremen missionaries directed their attention to educational work amongst people who were largely excluded from schools – notably adult women. Lynne Brydon has thus outlined how Luise Funke worked with local women to form the Women's Bible Class.[72] Later, we shall revisit examples of educational work among adult women, but first let us see how, in spite of efforts to maintain a shared religious ethos, church schools in the two Togolands gradually diverged from each other and became integrated into the respective systems of the British and the French.

According to Marie-France Lange, the French administration quickly began to open public (as opposed to mission/church) schools with the aim of eliminating German influence and building up a cadre of French-speaking African intermediaries in their portion of Togoland.[73] The administration also insisted on the use of French in all schools from 1922. However, initial efforts to expand state provision were subsequently scaled back in the face of the fiscal pressures of the global economic depression, and anxieties amongst local officials about the deracination of a growing number of school leavers from their communities. Direct governmental provision remained essential at the higher levels of schooling, but through

[70] Interview with Eugene Adom, Hohoe, 13 Sept 2000. Adom also showed me photographs of the classes that were organised at Amedzofe for the purpose of retraining teachers in English.

[71] Interview with M. K. Agbodza, Santrokofi-Benua, 19 Sept 2000.

[72] Lynne Brydon, 'Religious Encounter in Amedzofe: Women and Change through the Twentieth Century', in *Christianity and Social Change in Africa: Essays in honour of JDY Peel*, ed. Toyin Falola (Durham NC, 2005), 471–88.

[73] Marie-France Lange, *L'école au Togo: processus de scolarisation et institution de l'école en Afrique* (Paris, 1998), particularly chapter 3.

the inter-war period a substantial proportion of the school population was still concentrated in institutions established by the Bremen, Wesleyan, or Roman Catholic missions.[74] Whilst many missionaries contested the administration's French language policy, they were also constrained by it in their schools (less so in their churches). Mission schools in British Togoland, on the other hand, were increasingly drawn into the ambit of policy and regulation that was decided in the Gold Coast capital, Accra, with reference to an advisory committee of colonial educationists based in London.[75] As the administration in Accra relied heavily on the FCS to implement its policies and regulations, it was the FCS mission which became the most important in shaping the schools of southern British Togoland in line with the Gold Coast system, and in determining the nature of the training and the rewards that teachers received.

GODLY TEACHERS AND CLEVER RASCALS: BRITISH APPROACHES

The leadership of the FCS approved of the educational ethos promoted by Governor Guggisberg and of the government grants that could relieve financial pressure on the mission and enable it to work towards what it deemed to be a better quality of education. Reverend Wilkie therefore noted in his 1925 report that the Gold Coast Education Ordinance 'should not be a source of fear for good teachers'.[76] In order to achieve the status of 'assisted school' and thus to receive grants that met most of the cost of teachers' salaries, schools in British Togoland had to adjust their curriculum to include more English-language instruction, and submit themselves to the regime of inspection pertaining to schools in the Gold Coast.[77] Schools in British Togoland were gradually reorganised so as to conform to the Gold Coast–wide structure, whereby the first three years were classified as 'infant primary'; the second three years were

[74] In 1936–7, there were approximately 5000 pupils attending public schools and a similar number attending mission/church schools. Lange, *L'école au Togo*, 111–12.

[75] For a review of the literature on colonial education policy in Africa, see Clive Whitehead, 'The Historiography of British Imperial Education Policy, Part II: Africa and the Rest of the Colonial Empire', *History of Education* 34 (4) (2005), 441–54; for prosopographical study of key colonial education advisors, see Clive Whitehead, *Colonial Educators: The British Indian and Colonial Education Service 1858–1983* (London, 2003).

[76] The Scottish Mission, Gold Coast Colony Reports, 1925, 7–8. Copies available at the Akrofi-Christaller library, Akropong, Eastern Region, Ghana.

[77] Grau, 'The Evangelical Presbyterian Church', 44–8, 77, 113, 154–7, and 180–85.

classified as 'junior primary' and sub-divided into standards I–III; whilst the final four years were classified as 'senior primary' and sub-divided into standards IV–VII. Standard VII was envisaged as the terminal qualification for the majority.

In particular, the FCS was pleased that the old Basel mission seminary at Akropong was to be transformed into a 'modern' teacher training college by a special vote of government funds, for they hoped that this would generate a cohort of well-trained teachers for the Presbyterian schools in the Eastern Province of the Gold Coast. The old seminary at Amedzofe-Avatime in British Togoland became a senior primary school, which took pupils through to standard VII, and was not used again for teacher training until after the Second World War. In principle, pupils could proceed from Amedzofe directly to secondary school but, for reasons explained later, this was not a realistic prospect for the vast majority. Those who completed standard VII could either try their hands in the labour market or undertake a competitive entrance examination in order to secure one of the places at Akropong that was reserved for boys from the old Bremen mission field. There, boys could train either for four years, to be a 'certificate A teacher' (who was allowed to teach up to standard VII) or for a shorter period of time to become a 'certificate B teacher' (who could teach up to standard III). The boys who were trained at Akropong under the auspices of the Ewe Church were also required to undertake a seminary year, in which they received further training for their role as catechists.

In his report on the official opening of the upgraded College in 1928, Reverend Wilkie set out his vision and emphasised the extent to which it cohered with that of Guggisberg. Referring to the 'amazing rapidity' of social change on the Gold Coast, Wilkie expressed his concern that amongst the Africans living there,

> thought will be directed mainly towards material prosperity and that progress will be measured by material rather than spiritual change ... It is a cause of great thankfulness that so many in the highest places of Government are equally alive to the danger. Sir Gordon Guggisberg referred to it in a personal message to the General Assembly of the Scottish Church in 1926. "It is my sincere belief," he said, "that education without character training is a serious evil in any country ... and that character training that is not based upon the real life and teaching of Jesus Christ is not character training at all."[78]

[78] The Presbyterian Church of the Gold Coast, Reports and Accounts for 1928, 9.

Achimota College has been more intensively studied than Akropong, but there are some similarities in the ethos of the two institutions and their approaches to teacher training.[79] Despite the disgruntlement of the old Bremen missionaries about the inclusion of more English-language instruction, both of the 'modern' teacher training colleges at Achimota and Akropong shared the government's concern that primary education should be 'adapted' for rural Africans. Teachers were trained mainly in English and were exhorted to use modern methods to engage their pupils, but they were expected to deliver a curriculum in which English was envisaged as the language of instruction only at the senior primary level, and in which emphasis was placed on building the moral character of pupils through discipline, an ethic of service, and a readiness to engage in manual labour.

The colonial education advisors who promoted 'adapted education' believed that it was necessary to stem the tide of rural-urban migration and to reintegrate primary-school leavers more effectively into the social and economic life of the rural communities from which they came. Arguably, the rhetoric of 'adapted education' revolved around a similar understanding of African culture to that which had been endorsed in Württemburg fifty years earlier: African culture was, on the one hand, separated from its living context (where it risked contamination by paganism) and reified as an object of study; on the other hand, it was assigned to a position of ongoing inferiority by educators who insisted on their own right to determine what progress meant in an African context and how it could be achieved.

The staff at Akropong therefore encountered some familiar challenges from African students. In their struggles over clothing, students asserted their autonomy and claimed the right to creative trespassing and self-fashioning. But there were other struggles too in which students demonstrated an awareness of the ways in which educational structures determined their own access to the labour market, to cash incomes, and to the opening of further opportunities for their siblings, children, and future pupils. It is in the context of these struggles that students from southern British Togoland developed a sense of being a cohort with particular responsibilities, and a basis from which to mobilise a much wider constituency.

[79] See Coe *Dilemmas of Culture in African Schools*; and Cati Coe, 'Educating an African Leadership: Achimota and the Teaching of African Culture in the Gold Coast', *Africa Today* 49 (3) (2002), 23–44.

Clothing was a persistent source of disagreement. Best known is the case of the Peki teacher Ephraim Amu who was dismissed from his post at Akropong in 1933 for teaching students how to drum and for preaching in 'native attire'. The back story to this case is revealing for, as Cati Coe observes, it was the African and West Indian members of the Presbyterian Synod Committee who were most concerned to eliminate from the college anything that they associated with paganism.[80] Some of the Europeans on the staff were much more concerned by the propensity of trainees to value imported clothing and to invest in expensive European suits. Reverend Ferguson (who was then principal of the college) wrote in 1929 about the need for a more 'refined' consumption:

> An effort is being made, by introducing a College uniform, to train the students in simplicity and neatness of dress, but the efforts of the staff in this direction are being thwarted to some extent by public opinion, which holds that the educated man must be distinguished by his dress. For this reason parents and guardians buy expensive European clothes for their children. Books would be a better investment.[81]

College regulations might have had some effect whilst trainees were in attendance, but once they had taken up their posts they exercised their freedom to spend their salaries on items of their own choosing. E. K. Datsa attended the seminary year at Akropong in 1940. By 1949, he was secretary general of the Togoland Youth Association and in 1950 he was a signatory to the founding documents of the Togoland Congress. He described in his memoirs how one of his teacher colleagues at Ho-Kpodzi was also acting as an agent for a clothing company based in Britain. Mr Datsa recounted how, in 1942, 'I too joined the craze for foreign clothes … and placed an order for one three-piece black suit, one blue herringbone double-breasted coat and a pair of cream flannel trousers.'[82] Unfortunately, when the package arrived at the local post office, the agent could not produce the import licence that was required under wartime shipping regulations, and Mr Datsa was prevented from taking possession of his parcel. The strength of feeling around clothing is indicated in his description of his colleagues' reactions: some of them sympathised

[80] Coe, *Dilemmas of Culture*, 50.

[81] The Presbyterian Church of the Gold Coast, Reports and Accounts for 1928, 10. Stephan Miescher, *Making Men in Ghana* (Bloomington IN, 2005), 77 also notes the concerns of missionaries about clothing and their desire for a uniform.

[82] E. K. Datsa, *Doing My Duty: Memoirs of a Ghanaian Educationist* (Accra, 2006), 57.

'in sincerity, others with crocodile tears'.[83] In this insistence on the rights of teachers to choose their own style of clothing, and in their belief that a teacher ought to be well-dressed, the Ewe-speaking trainees and practising teachers were very similar to those from the Akan-speaking areas, with whom they mixed freely in the classrooms and the house systems at the training colleges.[84]

For the leadership of the Presbyterian Church of the Gold Coast and for the Europeans on the teacher-training staff, clothing was not necessarily the most insidious manifestation of the 'worldliness' that they detected in trainee teachers and their families. As early as 1925, in the context of plans to upgrade the college buildings, Reverend Murray explained the need to increase the bond from £30 to £100 for the new crop of trainees. As trainees usually had to raise the bond through pledges from family members, neighbours, and friends, this was felt to be a useful means of encouraging the interest of a wider circle of adults in an individual's successful completion of the training course, thus providing some informal monitoring of the trainees during the long summer vacations away from the college.[85] Through the inter-war period, the Presbyterian Church of the Gold Coast (which was the successor to the Basel mission and worked mainly in the Akan- and Ga-speaking areas) consistently expressed its concern that Christian families were not sending their best sons into teacher training, and that those boys who took up their places at Akropong as a second-best option were too easily tempted away by the promise of more lucrative employment in the towns of the Gold Coast.[86]

Four years later, the Presbyterian Church held a discussion on 'How to Hold Ex-Senior School Boys'. This was a pressing concern because boys who had benefitted from church expenditure on primary schooling were failing in adolescence and adulthood to become regular contributing members to their congregations. Reverend Watt suggested that the Twi (Akan) and Ga districts of the church should open a separate school so that boys ear-marked for teaching training would be taught separately from other boys for standards VI and VII. In this segregated environment,

[83] Datsa, *Doing My Duty*, 57.

[84] Miescher, *Making Men*, 109 also indicates that in his interviews with the Akropong-trained teacher E. F. Opusuo in Kwahu the latter recalled how proud he felt when ordering for the first time a shirt from London at the cost of 27 shillings.

[85] Reverend W. M. Murray in The Scottish Mission, Gold Coast Colony, Reports, 1925, 9.

[86] One hundred and forty boys took the entrance exam in 1926, competing for fifty places, but many of those with the best marks did not take up their places. Report for 1926, 10.

they 'would not be disturbed by the talk of other boys about fine jobs and big salaries'. He emphasised that the boys' 'characters could be carefully watched' because 'the Church needs a Godly teacher more than a clever rascal'.[87] This difficulty in attracting the highest achieving students into teacher training was combined with a fear that those who did train would either drop out or prove inadequate to the work. Trainees who did not go on to teach well were a poor investment and this was particularly pertinent in the context of the financial crisis that confronted the Presbyterian Church by the end of the 1920s and persisted through most of the 1930s. The first black Synod Clerk, Reverend N. T. Clerk, therefore emphasised that whilst government grants in the 1920s had enabled the upgrading of teacher training facilities, the government's emphasis on the modernisation and professionalisation of teaching had brought some undesirable consequences.

In particular, territory-wide salary scales reached far beyond what the church could afford to pay teachers in the non-assisted schools (i.e. the church schools that had not yet passed inspections and were not in receipt of government grants).[88] In Clerk's view, this compromised the use of church schools as instruments of evangelisation as well as encouraging a worldly and materialistic attitude amongst the certificated teachers:

> We were deeply concerned when Government caused the salaries of teachers to be raised considerably, for we knew what temptations were connected therewith for the teachers of the Church, who are expected to lead a modest and moral life as examples. Instead of that, it taught them to be careless. The Church too, which had the welfare of children in the non-assisted schools at heart, was brought under the obligation of giving too high salaries.

Reverend Clerk's solution was a moral one: 'let us be prepared to deny ourselves.'[89] But it did not work.

In the face of cuts in government spending on education, and difficulties in meeting shortfalls through increased contributions from church members (who were negatively affected by falling world prices for cocoa), the numbers of teacher-training places had to be reduced. In 1935, the teacher training college at Akropong did not admit a single first-year

[87] The Presbyterian Church of the Gold Coast, Reports, Accounts and Statistics for 1930, Synod Minutes, 44.

[88] Miescher, *Making Men*, 105, fn 83, indicates that Akropong-trained teachers were earning £6 per month in 1938.

[89] Reverend N. T. Clerk in The Presbyterian Church of the Gold Coast, Reports, Accounts and Statistics for 1930, Synod Minutes, 5.

student; in 1936, it admitted only twenty-five. In order to train any teachers at all in this period, the Ewe Presbyterian Church had to send its students to Achimota instead. When the number of places at Akropong was once more able to expand at the end of the 1930s, the church continued to rail against the failure of its members to put their 'best' young people into the college:

> We know of examples of good Christian parents who have thought that the ablest of their sons should not enter the Church's service, but should seek training for medicine or law or a government appointment ... Do you offer our College the "second best" of your sons? Is the "second best" a fit offering for Christ's service?[90]

The professionalisation of teaching, which had taken place as a matter of government policy and under the supervision of the FCS mission, was problematic for the church hierarchy. This was because it entailed greater expense in the provision of a more 'modern' training, whilst at the same time loosening the control of the church over its teachers. Those in possession of certificate A or B were, in principle, employable in any part of the Gold Coast or in a government school once they had completed their service to the church which had sponsored them. The possession of such a certificate also meant that individuals who remained within the service of a church education unit had particular entitlements – particularly in terms of their pay – which did not pertain to the untrained teacher.[91]

Teachers trained by missionaries had long been confronted by different orders of status: within the hierarchy of the mission and later the church, the most successful teachers were those who achieved promotion to the rank of pastor through ordination. Amongst those who eschewed this path, there were two options: to remain in the lower ranks of the mission/church hierarchy and fulfil the role of teacher-catechist, or to leave the remit of the mission/church and pursue more 'worldly' opportunities elsewhere – for example, as commercial clerks, as secretaries to the 'native authorities' (councils of chiefs and elders), or in the junior ranks of the civil service. In the inter-war period, however, the provision of a 'modern'

[90] The Presbyterian Church of the Gold Coast, Reports, Accounts and Statistics for 1938, 5.

[91] The stark distinction in status between the trained and the untrained teacher is also observed in Miescher, *Making Men* and in Penelope Roberts, 'The Village Schoolteacher in Ghana', in *Changing Social Structure in Ghana: Essays in the Comparative Sociology of a New State and an Old Tradition*, ed. Jack Goody (London, 1975), 245–60.

training, the issuing of transferable certificates, and the introduction of territory-wide salary scales enhanced the status that pertained to teaching itself.

Church leaders grasped the significance of territory-wide salary scales in 1928, when they realised that the more experienced certificated teachers were being paid more than some ministers of the church. Given the historic emphasis on *promotion* from the ranks of the teacher-catechist through ordination, the new pay differential was highly problematic, and Reverend Clerk's exhortations to self-denial did not erase the sense that the trained teachers were becoming too proud. The synod debated the issue of salaries at its meeting in Akropong in October 1928, but it was difficult to find a solution 'as the income of the church does not make it possible to raise the salary of the ministers to the same scale'.[92] The synod then discussed how to grade teachers on the new scale, and expressed the views that 'character and not merely certificate qualification must be an element in all grading' and that increments should be 'dependent upon satisfactory work and conduct'.[93] They also moved to strengthen their control by preventing teachers under threat of dismissal from voluntarily resigning their posts and seeking employment elsewhere.

Those who graduated from Akropong (and indeed from Achimota) saw themselves as qualified professionals, and as noted by Stephan Miescher, by the late 1930s they were forming associations to protect their terms of service and rates of pay during periods of cuts in government education grants.[94] The aspirations of this new cohort of trained teachers might still include ordination (as in the case of F. R. Ametowobla who remained within the Evangelical Presbyterian Church, or G. O. Awuma who became an Anglican), but increasingly, trained teachers were interested in a new avenue of advancement. They wanted to upgrade their professional qualifications by obtaining university education to join the new elite of graduate teachers. In order to have any prospect of achieving this, they needed to acquire the certificates that were prerequisite to university entrance – that is, the equivalent of secondary education. As we shall see in Chapter 3, church hierarchies struggled first to contain and then to accommodate this new ambition.

[92] Presbyterian Church of the Gold Coast, Gold Coast Colony and Ashanti: reports and accounts for 1928, Synod Minutes, October 1928, 60.

[93] Ibid., 63.

[94] Miescher, *Making Men in Ghana*, 107–8.

'BEST SONS': ECONOMIC CHANGE AND EDUCATIONAL OPPORTUNITY

Within the walls of the training colleges, both at Achimota and Akropong, there was no segregation of students by origin or language. According to Mathias Agbodza, who entered Akropong in 1942, and later became a Togoland reunificationist, the only distinction came in the teaching of African languages: as the Ewe-speaking students were expected to be posted in Ewe-speaking areas, they had their own language classes, separate from those of the Akan-speaking majority, so that they could learn how to produce teaching aids (including plays and short stories) in Ewe.[95] But despite the overall similarity in trainees' experiences of the curriculum and the disciplinary environment, the students from southern British Togoland had different perceptions of opportunity and status than those who came from the Gold Coast. Whilst the Presbyterian Church of the Gold Coast was concerned that it could not attract 'best sons' into teacher training, primary-school leavers from British Togoland regarded teacher training as the very best option that was open to them. This gap in perceptions of opportunity needs to be located firstly within a broader economic comparison between the trust territory and the Gold Coast, and secondly within an analysis of the changing education system.

In the census of 1931, the total population of British Togoland was 293,714 of which 125,566 resided in the southern section. Population increase during the 1920s has been attributed to an influx of migrant labour from French Togoland to the cocoa-growing areas of British Togoland (particularly to the north of Hohoe).[96] Despite this, southern British Togoland remained overwhelmingly rural. It had only two towns (Ho and Hohoe) with populations of 3,000 to 5,000, with Kpandu a close third and Jasikan in fourth place at 2,150. The southern, Colony area of the Gold Coast, on the other hand, had five towns with populations of over 10,000 and fifty towns with populations of 2,000 to 3,000.[97] Even within the towns of British Togoland, the numbers of individuals whom census enumerators deemed to have had 'education' was tiny: Hohoe, for example, had 120 such individuals, whilst the rural division

[95] Interview with M. K. Agbodza, Santrokofi-Benua, 19 Sept 2000. See also Grau, *The Evangelical Presbyterian Church*, 186.

[96] Lawrance, '"En proie à la fièvre du cacao"'.

[97] Gold Coast, *Appendices Containing Comparative Returns and General Statistics of the 1931 Census* (Accra, 1932), 17.

of Logba (home to the future Togoland Congress leader S. G. Antor) had only 29.[98] The data on occupations are given as raw numbers, rather than being converted into a more comparable measure (e.g. per thousand of population) and their accuracy is questionable. Nonetheless some of the figures are striking. In the whole of the trust territory, only 30 individuals were identified as commercial clerks, as compared with approximately 4,000 such individuals in the Colony; for motor drivers, the numbers were 59 in Togoland versus over 3,000 in the Colony.[99]

Mr Datsa, who started as a boarder at the senior primary school in Amedzofe in 1931, later recalled it as an excellent school that catered to children from a backwater. Far from the talk of 'fine jobs and big salaries' that the Presbyterian Church hierarchy attributed to boys at senior primary schools in the Gold Coast Colony, Mr Datsa recalled the utter lack of worldliness on the part of the students at Amedzofe in southern British Togoland. For their Saturday night entertainment, the students put on their own plays, including one entitled 'The Prodigal Shopkeeper', which told the story of a young man who, upon completing his standard VII, 'succeeded in securing the enviable job of shopkeeper in the big commercial firm ... The sudden affluence turned his head. He became extravagant, ostentatious ... Before long, his wealth began to dwindle ... he started pilfering the goods ... was taken to court ... and sentenced to imprisonment.'[100] According to Mr Datsa, with the frequent and repeated dramatisation of this play, 'the idea struck deep root in our minds that commerce or trading was the type of work so inevitably fraught with insurmountable temptations that anyone who chose it was sure to end in disaster.'[101]

Like commerce, the law was also held in great disrepute: 'A classmate who had attended school earlier in Accra told me that because of the heinous lies that were told by lawyers, whenever any of them died, his corpse was put into the coffin face down, for he dared not look God in the face.' Such stories, suggested Mr Datsa, limited the aspirations of the students at Amedzofe:

> The only professions considered respectable and "holy" were farming, fishing, artisanship and at the top of the ladder, teaching and the ministry of the Gospel ... The civil service was not regarded as bad, for though it too was fraught with temptations, these were not as irresistible as in shopkeeping ... As for professions like nursing, medicine and engineering, they were considered as too high ranking for us the children of the working class. They were the professions of wealthy

[98] Ibid., 243–4. [99] Ibid., 19. [100] Datsa, *Doing My Duty*, 10. [101] Ibid., 11.

people . . . It was no wonder then, that we not only looked up to our teachers as people in a very noble profession, but we also aspired to follow their example.[102]

On the back of cocoa cash cropping, the mandated territory gradually became less of an economic backwater. Nugent notes that cocoa production increased from 6,172 tons in 1930/1 to 16,539 tons in 1939/40.[103] By the time of the 1948 census, the total population of the Ho district (which for the purposes of the census was roughly equivalent to the southern section of British Togoland) was 172,530.[104] The populations of both Ho and Hohoe had now passed 5,000, whilst Kpandu's population had grown to 4,000, and fifteen other towns now supported populations of over 1,500.[105] The percentage of the population to have completed an education up to standards III to VI was 4.8 for the Ho district, as compared to 2.4 for the whole of the Gold Coast and Togoland together, whilst the percentage to have completed standard VII and above was 1.8 for the Ho district, as compared to 1.6 for the whole of the Gold Coast and Togoland together. In Cape Coast, however, the percentages were 10.7 and 14.2.

Given the high proportion of the population that was under the age of 15, these percentages do not provide a very good insight into the rapid increase in primary schooling in southern British Togoland. The 1949 United Nations visiting mission noted that there were 359 primary schools in the southern section, and that 72.5 per cent of the school-aged population (34,500 children) were attending school. In the northern section, the equivalent percentage was 1.8. The visiting mission noted that the total enrolment for British Togoland had grown by 4,000 pupils in just two years, and it had increased threefold since 1936.[106] The substantial increases were all in the southern section, and the gulf between opportunities here and those in the northern section was enormous. The occupational data for British Togoland in the 1948 census is based on a sample of only 4,928 individuals whose data was collected via form B, and, like the data for 1931, its accuracy is questionable. It suggests an increase in the number of 'white collar' workers (110 individuals

[102] Ibid., 11.

[103] Nugent, *Smugglers, Secessionists and Loyal Citizens*, 54. These statistics are based on the Colonial Office's *Togoland Annual Reports*.

[104] Gold Coast, *Census of Population 1948, Report and Tables* (London, 1950), 43.

[105] Ibid., 28.

[106] United Nations Trusteeship Council, *Report of the First Visiting Mission to the Trust Territory of Togoland Under British Administration* (New York, 1950), 46.

self-identified as teachers) and an increase in wood, textile, and metal working, manufacturing industries, and road transport.[107] Nonetheless, the gap between the trust territory and the more prosperous areas of the Gold Coast was still considerable.

Opportunities within the exchange sector in Togoland were expanding on the back of cocoa cash cropping, and perhaps those who schooled at Amedzofe a decade after Mr Datsa were more worldly than the barefoot pupils he remembered from the early 1930s. But, in a story that is familiar from other parts of the forest belt of West Africa, the sons of cocoa farmers did not aspire to become cocoa farmers – they wanted their parents to put them through school.[108] This meant that whilst the exchange sector expanded, so did the education sector, particularly at the primary level, and this raised the question of what primary-school leavers could do next. The trust territory had no secondary school of its own until 1950. Parents who wished to send their children to secondary schools had to meet not only the cost of the fees, but all the expenses associated with travelling to and boarding at institutions in the Gold Coast. In effect, secondary education was beyond the reach of all but a tiny number of families.

One should not exaggerate the ease with which secondary education was available elsewhere. It was only in the major towns along the coast that secondary education was available in the first three decades of the twentieth century, and even there it remained very expensive.[109] For people in the Eastern Province, the breakthrough came in 1938 when the Presbyterian Church opened a secondary school at Krobo-Odumase – which may of course have compounded their problems in attracting 'best sons' to Akropong. For the Ewe-speakers of southern British Togoland, the Anlo-Ewe area of the Gold Coast was an important point of comparison. Here, three secondary and business schools were opened in the towns of Anloga and Keta during the 1930s.[110] As Philip Foster demonstrated back in the 1960s, the popular perception of a shortage of secondary provision and a widespread desire for expansion was evidenced in the proliferation of private non-assisted secondary schools

[107] Gold Coast, *Census of Population 1948*, 371.

[108] See Sara Berry, *Fathers Work for Their Sons: Accumulation, Mobility and Class Formation in an Extended Yoruba Community* (Berkley CA, 1985).

[109] Miescher, *Making Men*, 119, fn 77 indicates that Mfantsipim school (Cape Coast) charged £18 per year whilst the secondary school at Achimota (near Accra) charged £50.

[110] Emmanuel Akyeampong, *Between the Sea and the Lagoon: An Eco-Social History of the Anlo of Southeastern Ghana, c.1850 to Recent Times* (Oxford, 2001), 128.

across the southern half of the Gold Coast in the 1930s and 1940s.[111] In this sense, the lack felt within the trust territory was comparable to the lack that was felt elsewhere. Nonetheless, outside of the Northern Territories, southern British Togoland was the last administrative zone to have an assisted secondary school of its own. Some Togoland reunificationists were involved in a handful of attempts to establish private secondary schools, but these institutions were short-lived.[112] From the perspective of the twenty-first century – and indeed from the perspective of the first independent government – one of the most divisive legacies of the colonial era was the educational gap between the north of Ghana and the south. It may then seem surprising that the peoples of southern British Togoland considered themselves so disadvantaged, but for the generation that was coming of age in the 1930s and 1940s, the lack of a secondary school was felt to be a very critical issue.

Adolescents who completed standard VII could go no further in their education unless they were able to secure entry to teacher training college. Those who succeeded in the competitive entrance examinations for Akropong or Achimota were the very highest achieving students. In this respect, the Presbyterian and the Roman Catholic students in Togoland were in the same position. Michael Senoo (son of A. K. Senoo, former president of the Togoland Union) put it in the following terms: 'In my day, even before you could get to St Augustine's [the Roman Catholic training college near Cape Coast], you had to be a brilliant boy, liked by the church, with your father's influence, everything, just to get to training college.'[113] Those who succeeded were the crème de la crème. This situation gave rise to two phenomena which are important to the formation of the Togoland reunificationist project. The first is that the Togoland teachers developed specific grievances which mobilised them as a cohort against the Ewe-speakers from Anlo and Peki (in the Gold Coast) who formed the hierarchy within the Evangelical Presbyterian Church. The second is that, within rural postings, the teacher was typically the most highly educated individual in the village. He was thus the obvious

[111] Philip Foster, *Education and Social Change in Ghana* (London, 1965).

[112] Asante was just a few years ahead, with the opening of Prempeh College in 1947. In 1951, Kodzo Ayeke took up a teaching post at the newly opened private secondary school at Ve-Koloenu. In 1955, two activists, E. O. Kofi Dumoga and B. K. Kodzi, worked to open another private institution – The Togoland National College – at Akome. Neither institution lasted very long.

[113] Interview with Michael Senoo, Dansoman, Greater Accra, 14 July 2000.

(and sometimes the only) candidate for the intermediary work of deciphering the demands of the colonial state.

In writing about the intermediary role of teachers in West Africa, Jean-Hervé Jézéquel makes an important distinction between the French and British territories. Drawing on examples from the inter-war French Soudan, Jézéquel indicates that teachers operated in a closer and more direct relationship to the colonial state: the highest ranking teachers were trained in the *écoles normales*, became employees of the colonial state, and, when posted to relatively remote areas where people resisted formal schooling, they could enhance their own influence by writing reports on 'native custom' for use by French officials.[114] In the case of southern British Togoland, the relationship between teachers and the colonial state was less direct and more ambiguous: teachers usually trained at, and then worked in, institutions that were managed by the church, and inspected and subsidised by the state, and they were posted in areas where there was growing enthusiasm for formal schooling. Thus, whilst Jézéquel identifies individuals who carried out intermediary functions at the behest of the colonial state and in order to counter their isolation from local people, the evidence for British Togoland rather suggests that teachers were seen as resources by the communities in which they were posted. Teachers were thus prevailed upon to act as advisors, interpreters, and leaders of voluntary unpaid activities in the sphere of mass education and community development. Indeed, by the 1940s, district commissioners had reasons to worry that the teachers could influence and mobilise people more easily than the chiefs.

'WE WERE CAPABLE OF HOLDING POSTS'

Although it was the Presbyterian Church of the Gold Coast and the FCS missionaries who ran the teacher training college at Akropong, once teachers were posted to schools within the southern section of British Togoland, they came under the remit of the Ewe Church (later renamed Evangelical Presbyterian Church). Within this church, however, they began to note discrepancies in two areas. The first was the allocation of scholarships, and the second was the prominence of Anlo- and Peki-Ewes

[114] Jean-Hervé Jézéquel, '"Collecting Customary Law": Educated Africans, Ethnographical Writings, and Colonial Justice in French West Africa', in *Intermediaries, Interpreters and Clerks*, ed. Lawrance, Osborn and Roberts, 139–58. Jézéquel concedes, however, that literate Africans had diverse motivations for writing ethnography.

within the church hierarchy. These issues became connected in 1948, when the Togoland teachers within the Evangelical Presbyterian education unit came together in a campaign to oust Reverend C. G. Baeta (an Anlo) as synod clerk and replace him with a Togolander. This campaign was grounded in suspicions over the allocation of scholarships, which Togolanders considered to work disproportionately in favour of Anlos and Pekis from the Gold Coast. In the eyes of the teachers, this contributed to a circular situation: the Anlos and Pekis held historic advantages in education because they had always been within the English-speaking Gold Coast Colony and, unlike the Togolanders, they had not been disrupted by a shift between colonial languages; due to these advantages the Anlos and Pekis were able to monopolise the leadership of the Evangelical Presbyterian Church; if they were not prepared to allocate scholarships to people from the trust territory in order that they could upgrade their qualifications and assume leadership positions, the historic advantages would only become more entrenched.

Mathias Agbodza explained the need for a change in terms of a generation gap. His father was a 'German scholar' who had retrained in English after the First World War:

> My father learned English, but he never spoke it really well. He used to say the funniest things. Once I asked him, "Father, where have you been?" and he answered me, "I wenting to Hohoe to license my gun." ... At that time there was a very sharp division here between Eweland here [i.e. in the inland areas of the trust territory] and the Anlos and the Pekis. And that brought a division in our church. Like I was saying, my father's English was "I wenting" so someone with English like that could not hold any important post. But we, the younger generation, we had learned English from our youth. We were capable of holding posts. So we were uniting so that when any elections came for posts in the church, we could vote together and win.[115]

Teachers who had passed the competitive entrance examination for Akropong or Achimota and were in possession of a nationally recognised teaching qualification were disinclined to remain permanently in the lower ranks. They felt that they deserved scholarships as much as anyone else. Reverend Baeta was in fact replaced as synod clerk in 1948 by G. K. Ampofo, but in 1950 F. R. Ametowobla – a Togolander from the mountainous Siyase-speaking enclave of Avatime – was elected. He remained in the post until 1954 when he entered the Gold Coast parliament.[116]

[115] Interview with M. K. Agbodza, Santrokofi-Benua, 19 Sept 2000.

[116] Technically, Ametowobla was an independent member of parliament, but his close association with the Togoland Congress was widely known, and following the passage

On the face of it, these were very specific issues of interest only to the educated minority, and they provided an unlikely basis for wider political mobilisation. But whilst E. O. Kofi Dumoga was busy mobilising the teachers as an occupational group in the Togoland Teachers' Union, in Ho another connection was forged. Here, the Awuma family of the Ahliha quarter were amongst the earliest adherents to the Bremen mission. Elia Awuma was one of the 'Ewe-Württemburger' traced by Kokou Azamede. After serving for a period as a teacher, he became a member of the tiny elite who acceded to the rank of pastor within the Ewe Church. From there, he became moderator of the church, a position which he held from 1927 to 1939. Gerald Otto (G. O.) Awuma was his son. When G. O. was born in 1902 his father was serving in Bremen mission schools and stations which fell within German Togo – in Kpalimé, Atakpamé, and Tové. G. O.'s primary-school years were thus spent speaking Ewe and German, but after the partition of German Togo during the First World War, he moved first to Lomé (where he learned French) and then to Anum in the Gold Coast (where he learned English). Awuma completed his training at Akropong in 1927 before taking up postings in primary schools in Akpafu, Keta, and Ho.[117]

During the 1930s, the Evangelical Presbyterian school at Ho provided education only up to standard III, and those who wished to go further had to become boarders at Amedzofe. For those who were unable to secure a place, or whose parents could not afford the costs associated with boarding and the loss of their children's labour, standard III represented the limits of their educational opportunities. Local demand for senior primary education was much in evidence, however, firstly in the form of financial contributions and then through contributions of unpaid labour.[118] It is difficult to prove that G. O. Awuma was at the forefront of these efforts – a contemporary observer referred only to 'a very intelligent and active man' – but his interest in the expansion of educational opportunities appears to have been endorsed when he was appointed to the district education committee.[119]

If Awuma exercised some influence in Ho through the pupils he taught at the primary school and through his status as a qualified teacher, this

of the Preventive Detention Act in 1958, he went into political exile, first in French Togoland and then in Liberia.

117 Interview with F. Y. Awuma, Ho, 21 July 2000.

118 Reinold Schober, 'Native Co-operation in Togoland', *Africa: Journal of the International Africa Institute* 9 (4) (1936), 485–94 at 491.

119 Ibid., 491.

influence soon found an outlet in local politics. The enormous resentment that surrounded British attempts to amalgamate the numerous small chieftaincies in southern Togoland into larger 'native states' for the purposes of indirect rule have been studied in considerable detail elsewhere, and shall be summarised only briefly here to highlight the role played by teachers.[120] In and around Ho, disputes lasted for almost three decades and centred on three related issues. The first was a disagreement between the three chiefly lineages of Ho-Dome as to whose turn it was to present a candidate for the Dome chieftaincy; the second was a disagreement between Ho-Dome and Ho-Bankoe as to whose chief was subservient to whom; the third disagreement stemmed from the second, because once the decision was taken by long-serving district commissioner Captain Lilley to amalgamate the formerly independent divisions in and around Ho into the Asogli State, whoever was successful in the Dome-Bankoe dispute would also secure the paramountcy of the amalgamated state for himself and his own division. In Asogli, Mote Kofi II of Ho-Dome secured this position.

In some newly amalgamated states – and particularly in Buem where the terrain was suitable for cocoa cash cropping – prolonged disputes between chiefly candidates and between different stools tended to reflect tensions over the allocation of land, the rights of stools to charge migrant or 'stranger' farmers for usufruct, and the rights and responsibilities of these 'strangers' vis-à-vis their 'hosts'.[121] In other areas, the disputes between formerly independent divisions were more concerned with control over tribunals (and the revenues that accrued from fees and fines), the rights of native authorities to raise levies, and the allocation of revenues such as market tolls – which, as Wilson Yayoh has remarked, were raised at least partly on the backs of female traders but were controlled by the male chiefs in the amalgamated states.[122] In Asogli, the chiefs of formerly independent divisions were particularly aggrieved by the use of the state council as an appellate court, and these grievances came to a head in December 1945. The secretary to the state council, F. Y. Medie, refused to record a verdict of the state council in a land case between Agbade

120 For the inter-war period, the Asogli disputes are analysed in Benjamin Lawrance, 'Bankoe v. Dome: Traditions and Petitions in the Ho-Asogli Amalgamation, British Mandated Togoland, 1919–39', *Journal of African History* 46 (2005), 243–67.

121 These issues are well captured in Nugent's discussion of Buem. See *Smugglers, Secessionists and Loyal Citizens*, 132–8.

122 Yayoh, 'British policy of direct taxation among the Northern Ewe of Ghana' (article in preparation).

Kwasi of Sokode and Elia Awuma of Ho-Ahliha. The paramount chief accused Medie of refusing to record the verdict because it overturned an earlier decision made by 'his bossom [sic] friend' the divisional chief of Sokode, Tenkoloe Kwaku II, which had been in favour of Agbade Kwasi.[123]

What matters for our purposes here is that although the British had clearly hoped to establish strong paramount chieftaincies, based on the Akan model of the Gold Coast, what they found in Asogli was that Mote Kofi's authority was consistently challenged by a significant number of the divisional chiefs who supposedly served under him on the Asogli state council. Mote Kofi was also at loggerheads with his own state secretary for much of the 1940s, but was blocked by successive district commissioners in his attempts to dismiss Medie from his position. The district commissioners' approval of Medie may have been based on the good service he had rendered in persuading formerly independent divisions to amalgamate to the Asogli state, or more specifically because he had mediated a peace settlement between Dome and Bankoe in 1943 and his continued presence as state secretary was deemed important to retaining Bankoe within the amalgamation.[124] In any case, lacking both chiefly and secretarial support, Mote Kofi increasingly looked for support from the 'youth' (commoners) who, under the influence of G. O. Awuma, formed themselves into the Asogli Youth League and the Asogli Taxpayers' Association.

Awuma was increasingly regarded by the district commissioners as a trouble maker, and in 1947 he was dismissed from his position on the district education committee. Awuma made his feelings abundantly clear, relating his situation to the marginalisation of the peoples of the trust territory by 'adventurers' from 'Gold Coast Eweland'.[125] He thus challenged the Colonial Secretary, Accra, with the following question:

> Should the inborn Togolander thus be judged unreasonable when he rightly concludes that the Gold Coast Government, the Missionary Societies and the

[123] PRAAD, Accra, ADM 39/1/67: Mote Kofi II to District Commissioner, Ho, 8 Dec 1945; and Mote Kofi II to Commissioner of Eastern Province, Koforidua, 17 Dec 1945.

[124] The former point is made in Nugent, *Smugglers, Secessionists and Loyal Citizens*, 70, based on Nugent's reading of PRAAD, Ho, DA/D78: Handing over notes from C. M. Weatherburn to A. V. Cameron, 1950. Looking a little further back into the dispute between Bankoe and Dome, it appears that the notes on the 'Customs Tending to Peace Settlement in the Ho Division' in PRAAD, Accra, ADM 39/1/54, were actually written by F. Y. Medie in March 1943. According to these notes, both the Howusu (chief of Ho) and Fia Apede of Bankoe thanked Medie for his mediation, with Fia Apede describing Medie as 'a stranger who laboured for production of this peace'.

[125] This was quite possibly a reference to F. Y. Medie, who is frequently referred as 'a stranger' – although it is not completely clear that he was an Anlo.

Merchant Houses seem to have conspired to support the Gold Coast Ewes in their intrigues and trickery to set up a Totalitarian Tyranny in Togoland and dominate, supplant and oppress the Togolander in his own home?[126]

The divisional chiefs were outraged by Awuma's attempts to initiate political organisations within their divisions without their express permission, and they resented Awuma's influence over Mote Kofi. By 1949, the divisional chiefs openly blamed Mote Kofi for the 'rawdism [sic] in Ho town young men and women to hoot at and throw abuses at Chiefs of this Asogli State', whilst district commissioners were concerned by the influence of Awuma over Mote Kofi, whom one official described as a 'puppet' poised to 'dance to the tune' of the young men who supported the Togoland Union.[127] Whilst Medie was a 'staunch supporter of the AEC' and thus of ethnic unity between the Ewe-speakers of the two Togolands and the Gold Coast, Awuma was deemed critical in influencing the young men of Ho – and indeed some of the outlying divisions of Asogli – in favour of Togoland reunification.[128] Amongst these young men were Moses Kofi Asase and Christian Baxter Attah, who had been students of Awuma in the primary school at Ho-Kpodzi and became active Togoland reunificationists. Attah became a councillor after the introduction of elected local government in the early 1950s, and both men were taken into preventive detention in 1960 on suspicion of planning a civil disturbance aimed at reversing the integration of the trust territory with Ghana.[129] We shall return to their stories in Chapter 6.

Whilst the dynamics of disputes within the amalgamated states differed from case to case, they clearly contained a capacity – unremarked in some previous studies – to mobilise individuals who were concerned by the limited educational opportunities within the trust territory. In Hohoe and in Kpandu, teachers were also protagonists in disputes over amalgamation and in the mobilisation of opinion in favour of Togoland reunification. Teachers were viewed with some trepidation by district commissioners and chiefs alike, because of their ability to mobilise former and aspiring students. The role of teachers in these localised disputes was

126 PRAAD, Ho, DA/D113. G. O. Awuma to Colonial Secretary, Accra, undated. Cited in Nugent, *Smugglers, Secessionists and Loyal Citizens*, 124.

127 PRAAD, Ho, VRG 2/110 Asogli Native Affairs: 'Memorandum on the Political Situation in the Asogli State', 6 Dec 1949.

128 PRAAD, Accra, ADM 39/1/456: Handing over notes from C. M. Weatherburn to A. V. Cameron, 1950.

129 Interviews with M. K. Asase, Ho, 24 March 1999, 18 May 1999, 20 July 2000, 11 Aug 2000; and interview with C. B. Attah, Ho, 20 Sept 2000.

given a further, albeit inadvertent, fillip in the government's introduction of mass education campaigns in the trust territory in 1948.

MASS EDUCATION AND THE MORAL GRAMMAR OF SOCIAL CONFLICTS

Under pressure from the Colonial Office, which wished to see a more pro-active implementation of its advisory committee's memoranda on *Mass Education in African Society* (1943) and *Education for Citizenship* (1948), the administration in Accra appointed A. G. Dickson as Social Development Officer. The level of enthusiasm for mass education was rather lower amongst officials in Accra than it was amongst advisors based in London, particularly in the context of anti-colonial riots in the towns of the Gold Coast in the spring of 1948. Once Dickson was appointed, there was a question mark over what exactly he ought to do, and where he should be sent. It is not completely clear why the two trust territories were selected, but colonial administrators were certainly aware of the need to muster up evidence for the United Nations visiting mission of their efforts in preparing the peoples of the trust territory for self-government.[130] Dickson was therefore tasked with organising experimental courses in mass education in British and French Togoland in 1948 and 1949. The main purpose of these courses was to recruit volunteers who could then be trained in the organisation of improving activities – such as physical training, boxing, singing choirs, brass bands, and handicrafts – and stimulate such activities within their home communities.

Dickson rapidly proved a controversial figure. He was explicit in questioning the policy direction advocated by one of the Colonial Office's most prominent educational advisors (Dr Margaret Read) and expressed in print his doubts that illiteracy actually was 'the single biggest obstacle to progress in peasant societies'.[131] Having worked in an army education unit during the Second World War, he was optimistic about the possibilities of teaching directly in English to Africans who were illiterate: 'If it is what people want, and want for reasons that are readily understandable, and if it will help to release reserves of goodwill and voluntary endeavour,

[130] PRAAD, Accra, ADM 39/1/472, Mass Education: John Dixon, senior district commissioner, 'Report on Social Development in the Ho/Kpandu/Keta districts' (n.d. but probably summer 1949): 'It would not, perhaps, be without interest to the Trusteeship Council Commission to see the [mass education] team actually at work in the field'.

[131] A. G. Dickson, 'Mass Education in Togoland', African Affairs 49 (194) (1950), 139.

should we not at any rate investigate ways and means?'[132] Despite these heretical views on the primacy of mother-tongue literacy, however, he was firmly on board with the agenda of *Education for Citizenship*: he considered it his mission to 'challenge the awakening sense of nationalism' among the Gold Coast's young men and to make real citizens of them by teaching them how to organise voluntary and improving activities in their home communities.

The finer distinctions between the AEC and the Togoland Union, and the cleavage between the Ewe-speakers of Anlo and Peki in the Gold Coast on the one hand, and the peoples of the trust territory on the other, may have escaped Dickson's grasp. But he was clearly aware of the political mobilisation that was going on all around him, and hoped that he could capitalise on it: 'The Ewe are increasingly conscious of their own nationhood, and this is a positive factor in any campaign for Mass Education ... With their demand for unification of their people on both sides of the Togoland frontier, they are coming to have news-value (or is it nuisance-value?).'[133] Perhaps unsurprisingly, Dickson's relationship with the district commissioners in British Togoland was problematic, and in fact he was removed from his post after a bare eighteen months. In the meantime, confronted by what he saw as inadequate levels of support from the administration, he was forced to turn to the Evangelical Presbyterian Church for assistance.

Dickson was not particularly interested in attracting teachers as future leaders of mass education activity. He wanted to avoid mass education becoming an extension of the school system, believing that its main purpose was not so much 'utilitarian instruction' of illiterate adult students, but the harnessing of energy among the young, mobile, literate population towards beneficial activities in their communities. He envisaged such people as 'lorry-drivers, artisans, the poorer clerks, petty traders, subordinate Government staff and a host of others'.[134] He hoped that, after such individuals were trained in the arts of mass education in exciting residential courses, they would return to their home communities as a 'creative minority' or 'the yeast that leaven the lump'.[135] What Dickson discovered, however, was that 'whether it be Boy Scouts, Red Cross, Literacy or any other worthwhile cause, it is always left to the teachers'.[136]

[132] Ibid., 140. [133] Ibid., 137. [134] Ibid., 136. [135] Ibid., 138–9.
[136] PRAAD, Accra, ADM 39/1/472 Mass Education: A. G. Dickson to senior district commissioner, Ho, 20 Jan 1949.

Reverend Baeta had already begun work on an Ewe primer, which volunteers could use in classes with illiterate adults. But it was Mathias Agbodza, a teacher from Santrokofi-Benua, who produced the Laubach picture syllable chart from which all such classes began.[137] In order to organise the choirs, Dickson relied on help from William Tsistsiwu, who had trained with E. K. Datsa, and taught at Amedzofe and at Akropong.[138] Within southern British Togoland, V. O. Anku was a skilful teacher of carpentry, and taught in Hohoe and Amezofe, before moving to Mawuli school in Ho. At the joint Anglo-French mass education course held in Kpalimé in July 1949, H. K. Asamany – a teacher at the Presbyterian school in Hohoe and son of the famous ivory carver from Kpandu – taught a range of arts and crafts.[139] Dickson also imported help from other regions – and he was particularly grateful to Mr Asante (an Achimota-trained teacher at the Swedru Industrial School) for directing the participants away from the frivolity of paper flower making towards the more serious and improving activity of carpentry.[140]

Dickson attributed the dominance of teachers in the mass education courses to a lack of effort on the part of the district commissioners in recruiting from the native authority clerks, and he even accused government departments of failing to allow his circulars to penetrate down to the target group of junior civil servants.[141] He expressed his belief that mass education was 'something quite new' and gave vent to his frustration about the difficulty of recruiting mass education leaders from beyond the ranks of teachers: 'I believe that Africans can be "jollied" into doing things that they might otherwise not have done for themselves, especially by their senior officers: that is, isn't it, the reason why we are still in Africa?'[142]

Dickson's frustrations, however, stemmed partly from his difficulty in appreciating that, in many respects, the kinds of activities that he was

[137] Interview with M. K. Agbodza, Santrokofi-Benua, 19 Sept 2000. Mr Agbodza was also able to show me a copy of the picture chart he had designed.

[138] Ibid., 146. Soon after this mass education campaign, Tsitsiwu went to Scotland to pursue higher education. He served briefly as Ghana's ambassador to Togo during the Acheampong era, and we shall encounter him again in Chapter 6.

[139] PRAAD, Accra, ADM 39/1/138: Mass Education in Togoland, press release dated 23 July 1949. The Asamany family were prominent reunificationists in Kpandu, whilst V. O. Anku and E. K. Datsa were among the signatories to the earliest Togoland Congress documents.

[140] Dickson, 'Mass Education in Togoland', 148.

[141] PRAAD Accra, ADM 39/1/472 Mass Education. A. G. Dickson to senior district commissioner, Ho, 20 Jan 1949.

[142] Ibid.

promoting were *not* something entirely new. The annual reports of both the Scottish Mission and the Presbyterian Church of the Gold Coast consistently commented through the 1920s and 1930s on the willingness of students at Akropong to engage in voluntary work, which included boy scouting activities with local youths and the teaching of vernacular literacy to local women. Given Dickson's heretical views on the primacy of mother-tongue literacy, he was unprepared for the extent of the demand that was exhibited for it, particularly among adult women. He thus recounted his surprise when a voluntary leaders' residential course attracted a large crowd of women who expected and demanded to be taught how to read in Ewe. Dickson was apparently unaware of the efforts of women since the 1930s to organise themselves for the purpose of learning to read the bible in Ewe.[143] Nor did he consider that although women formed the majority amongst the contributing adult membership of the Evangelical Presbyterian Church, they had received relatively scant educational resources in comparison to the younger males who were the primary beneficiaries of the system of formal schooling. Older women and younger men could be considered, respectively, as net contributors to and net beneficiaries of the church, and it therefore conceivable that women saw voluntary unpaid teaching by younger males as part of their duty to give something back.

As a pragmatist, Dickson was willing to integrate the unanticipated demands of women into his residential course, and he saw mother-tongue literacy as something akin to a mobile cinema van – if people wanted it and it drew them in to his broader project, then why resist? But fundamentally, Dickson was uninterested in women: 'Despite the fact that women formed the large majority of those touched by our mass literacy work,' he wrote in his account of his experiments, 'the writer remains convinced that the key to this problem of social development lies not with the illiterate young women of the villages, but with the quasi-educated young men.'[144] It might have surprised Dickson to learn that Regina Asamany – daughter of the ivory carver from Kpandu and the only woman to make it into the first rank of the Togoland Congress leadership in the 1950s – began her career in the Department for Social Welfare, which took over responsibility for mass education after Dickson's departure.[145]

[143] See Brydon, 'Religious Encounter in Amedzofe'.
[144] Dickson, 'Mass Education in Togoland', 149.
[145] Interview with anonymous member of the Asamany family, Kpandu, 7 June 2010.

A great deal more could be said about the career of A. G. Dickson (who later went on to establish Voluntary Service Overseas), and indeed about mass education in British Togoland.[146] For our purposes here, however, two points are worth emphasising. The first is that mass education was retained and expanded through the first half of the 1950s, and was supported by both the main parties that emerged in southern British Togoland – the Convention People's Party as well as the Togoland Congress. In Dickson's first experiment in 1948 some 4,000 adults participated in literacy classes, whilst by 1952 some 28,000 adult learners were registered in southern British Togoland and in the Ewe-speaking areas of the Gold Coast colony. Amongst the learners who sat the literacy exam, women outnumbered men by nine to one.[147] The extension of mass education activities therefore created a much wider pool of literate individuals, who later became the readers of a range of Ewe-language histories, novels, plays, and indeed political propaganda, as we shall see in Chapter 4. Literacy in and of itself did not necessarily orient people towards either of the main political parties that emerged in southern British Togoland, but it did establish the possibility of new forums and mediums of debate about the future of the trust territory.

Secondly, there was a clear overlap between the people who assumed leadership of mass education activities and those who engaged actively in political debates around the status and future of the trust territory. In his study of Kpandu, Brown thus explains that a mass education course held in Anfoega in 1948 was a direct stimulus to the formation of the Akpini Youth Society, which was 'composed mainly of Kpandu men who were teacher training college graduates'.[148] The society petitioned for a new post office, organised the construction of a community centre, and established a branch of the People's Education Association. It was also in close contact with G. O. Awuma, Harry Anku Morny, and S. G. Antor, who, as we shall see in the next chapter, were all busy pressing the Togoland reunification agenda in Geneva, London, and New York. Trained teachers in and around Kpandu were therefore gradually drawn into the remit of the wider reunification movement whilst simultaneously asserting their contribution to, and leadership of, mass education and community development.

[146] Ben Page has been pursuing further research into the legacies of early experiments in mass education and community development, particularly in Cameroon, where A. G. Dickson went after his departure from the Gold Coast/Togoland.

[147] Department of Social Welfare and Community Development, *Literacy Campaign 1952* (Accra, 1952), 13 and 15.

[148] Brown, 'Politics in the Kpandu Area of Ghana', 248.

My point here is not that Togoland reunificationists were the only people to participate in, or assume leadership of, such efforts. It is clear that a wide range of youth and hometown improvement associations were engaged in similar efforts to establish literacy classes, build amenities, and organise leisure in the small towns and villages of southern British Togoland, and doubtless some of the members of these associations affiliated themselves with political parties or projects which were opposed to Togoland reunification. My point is rather that those who became active advocates of Togoland reunification almost invariably based their claims to articulate and represent the interests of a wider public on the basis of their contributions to communities. Whilst teachers were not the only people to organise mass education or community development activities, they considered themselves particularly well-equipped, and indeed duty-bound, to do so. By 1951, teachers from the Evangelical Presbyterian education unit were working in co-operation with Roman Catholics to elaborate a 'professional code' which explicitly tied the occupational interests of teachers, and their desire to upgrade their qualifications and appointments, to the interests of the wider population of the trust territory. Better educational provision, they suggested, was necessary for the progress of Togoland, and this could be best achieved by Togoland 'nationals' who had the requisite training and whose interests were sincere.

The code thus imposed the following obligations upon its members:

> It should be the duty of each and every Togoland Teacher to regard Togoland as his most precious possession and as such should endeavour to seek her progress and welfare in all things.
>
> It should be a ruling passion in every Togoland teacher to make himself qualified for appointment to any of the higher posts within the educational set-up namely Headmaster, Supervisor of Schools, Minister of Religion, and any other future posts herein not named.
>
> Every Teacher should make a keen interest in Mass Education and the upliftment of Togoland from its present state of ignorance and illiteracy.[149]

By making themselves responsible for the 'upliftment' of Togoland, teachers were also claiming a specific insight into its needs and a track record of service to its people, thereby highlighting their own potential for effective leadership. In effect, the teachers' code articulated the

[149] 'Togoland Teachers' Union, Professional Code, adopted at Jasikan Buem, this twenty-second day of August, in the year of our Lord nineteen hundred and fifty one'. From the private archive of M. K. Agbodza of Santrokofi-Benua.

'moral grammar' of their social struggle, and pinpointed the basis on which they expected to secure recognition from a wider population.[150] The teachers who formed the backbone of the Togoland reunificationist movement thereby positioned themselves as agents of enlightenment and progress, who could open up opportunities for a multiplicity of individual students and organise collective endeavour.

[150] Honneth, *The Struggle for Recognition.*

3

Education, Citizenship and the 'Sacred Trust'

Chapters 1 and 2 outlined the peculiarities of the colonial encounter in southern British Togoland and explained why mission- and church-trained teachers in particular gained popular recognition as spokespersons for the peoples of the trust territory. This chapter extends my analysis of the influence of educational experiments and systems on the formulation and leadership of distinctive political projects, but it approaches the subject from a different angle. Here, I begin by outlining the key external factors which were brought to bear upon local debates about the future of the trust territory. Initially, these external factors appeared to open up opportunities for people to explore new forms of citizenship and they gave rise to a flourish of educational and developmental activity in the small towns and villages of southern British Togoland. Ultimately, however, external factors worked to close down political possibilities. Teachers were particularly active in challenging the terms of colonial educational interventions and devising their own initiatives for education in citizenship, but as experimentation and debate were curtailed under external pressures, teachers' energies were increasingly channelled into the formation of antagonistic party organisations which directed voters to choose between two mutually incompatible versions of self-government.

External pressures emanated from three arenas: London, New York, and Accra. Firstly, in Britain, the general election of July 1945 brought the Labour Party to power. During the inter-war period, party members had evinced scruples about the exercise of empire, and had suggested that the administration of all non-self-governing territories should be subjected to more rigorous international oversight.[1] The inability of the League of Nations to prevent a further world war, and the contribution of the empire to the Allied victory over a genocidal racist Nazi regime, stimulated the party to re-evaluate Britain's relationship to colonised peoples and to the new institutions of global governance that were established by the United Nations Charter of 1945. The post-war Labour leadership accepted that the United Nations could serve as a 'peripatetic inspectorate' and thereby check potential abuses of non-self-governing peoples.[2] But the party leadership also became more assertive about its own interpretation of 'the sacred trust' of administering non-self-governing territories and its own capacity to formulate policies which served the interests of the inhabitants and assisted them in their progressive development towards self-government.[3]

In London, this new-found assertiveness translated into a better informed and more pro-active post-war colonial policy. Since its establishment in 1940, the Fabian Colonial Bureau (FCB) had amassed considerable knowledge of colonial affairs, and this knowledge was mobilised within the wartime Labour Party and the post-war Labour government, as leading members of the FCB were appointed to Colonial Office Committees. As a former chair of both the FCB and the party's Advisory Committee on Imperial Questions, Arthur Creech Jones brought insight and energy to his new portfolio as Secretary of State for the Colonies from 1946 to 1950.[4] In collaboration with his assistant under-secretary for African affairs, Andrew Cohen, Creech Jones stimulated more active consideration within

[1] R. M. Douglas, 'An Offer They Couldn't Refuse: The British Left, Colonies and International Trusteeship, 1940–1951', in *Imperialism on Trial: International Oversight of Colonial Rule in Historical Perspective*, ed. R. M. Douglas, Michael Callahan and Elizabeth Roberts (Lanham MD, 2006), 139–66. 'Non-self-governing territories' was a broad category which encompassed crown colonies and protectorates. The mandated territories of the League of Nations, which later became trust territories of the United Nations, were a specific category of non-self-governing territory administered under international oversight.

[2] Ibid., 149.

[3] Article 73 of the United Nations Charter established the core obligations of administering authorities vis-à-vis all non-self-governing territories, including crown colonies and protectorates; article 76 dealt specifically with those territories which had been placed under the new system of international trusteeship.

[4] Patricia Pugh, 'Jones, Arthur Creech (1891–1964)', in *Oxford Dictionary of National Biography* ed. H. C. G. Matthew and Brian Harrison (Oxford, 2004), online edition edited by Lawrence Goldman (2011) available at www.oxforddnb.com/view/article/34224 [last accessed 27 Nov 2013].

the Colonial Office of the practical means of preparing colonial subjects for citizenship. The famous circular despatch of February 1947 announced a shift away from indirect rule and a new emphasis on strengthening the foundations for future self-government by building representative institutions from the localities and districts up to centre.[5] But Creech Jones also considered the expansion of formal schooling, adult education, and new communication technologies in the African colonies.[6]

These developments in London shaped the attitudes that British representatives took to New York. As former mandated territories of the League of Nations were transformed into trust territories of the United Nations, the administering powers drafted their own trusteeship agreements and thereby sought to create latitude for their own interpretations of the core principles outlined in the United Nations Charter. By article 76 of the charter, the British government was obliged to 'promote the progressive development [of its trust territories] towards self-government or independence'. But it resisted the elision of this obligation with the right of small nations to self-determination. According to R. M. Douglas,

> In the light of the ruthless expansionism of the Axis powers, small ethnically homogenous states were now perceived at best as easy prey for aggressive neighbors, and at worst as unviable political and economic entities whose inherent inability to meet the needs of their citizens carried the seeds of future wars. Large multinational polities, on the other hand, with their combination of economic efficiency, cultural diversity, and military self-sufficiency, were best qualified to maintain the peace.[7]

When the post-war Labour leadership envisaged future self-governing states, it envisaged them as larger units with multi-ethnic populations and economies that could support the expenses of modern government, infrastructural development, and social services. The post-war vision therefore bore some of the marks of an older strand of socialist paternalism, which posited that 'the non-adult races' would need to undergo a process of modernisation before they could be trusted to use self-

[5] John Cell, 'On the Eve of Decolonization: The Colonial Office's Plans for the Transfer of Power in Africa, 1947', *Journal of Imperial and Commonwealth History* 8 (3) (1980), 235–57.

[6] Advisory Committee on Education in the Colonies, 'Education for Citizenship in Africa' (London, 1948).

[7] Douglas, 'An Offer They Couldn't Refuse', 146.

government towards the greater aims of economic development and social equality.[8]

The trusteeship agreement proposed for British Togoland pursued this vision insofar as article 5(a) sought to establish the right of the British government to administer the trust territory 'in accordance with the Authority's own laws as an integral part of its territory'.[9] The phrase 'as an integral part of its own territory' did not mean that British Togoland would be administered as an integral part of the United Kingdom in a manner consistent with the French vision of their colonies as parts of *la plus grande France*. In this particular case, what the British government was trying to establish was its right to administer its Togoland trust territory within the framework of a union with the neighbouring colony of the Gold Coast. This was highly controversial. The USSR boycotted the Trusteeship Council in 1947, partly on the grounds that the trusteeship agreements provided inadequate safeguards against the annexation of trust territories to neighbouring colonies.[10] The General Assembly also recognised the possibility that arrangements for administrative union might have 'practical consequences' that would tend towards 'a *de facto* establishment of a political union' and thereby threaten the distinctive status and integrity of the trust territory. By resolution 224 (III), the General Assembly insisted that unions should 'remain strictly administrative in nature' and should not obstruct the 'separate development of the Trust Territory in the fields of political, economic, social and educational advancement, as a distinct entity'.[11] In January 1949, the Trusteeship Council decided that it was necessary to establish the Standing Committee on Administrative Unions to monitor the thin line between administrative convenience and political integration,

[8] The term 'non-adult races' was used by Sidney and Beatrice Webb in 1918. Ibid., 143 and 152. See also Ronald Hyam, 'Africa and the Labour government, 1945–1951', *Journal of Imperial and Commonwealth History* 16 (3) (1988), 148–72 for a discussion of the ways in which proposals for political advancement were bound up with concerns about economic development.

[9] United Nations, 'Trusteeship Agreement for the Territory of Togoland under British administration: as approved by the General Assembly on 13 December 1946', (New York, 1947).

[10] Gordon Morrell, 'A Higher Stage of Imperialism: The Big Three, the United Nations Trusteeship Council and the Early Cold War', in *Imperialism on Trial*, ed. Douglas, Callahan and Bishop, 111–38 at 118.

[11] United Nations, 'Report of the Trusteeship Council on administrative unions affecting Trust Territories and on the status of the Cameroons and Togoland under French administration arising out of their membership in the French Union', (New York, 1952), 4–6.

but by this point debates in New York had already been overtaken by events in Accra.

The wave of protest that rocked the towns of the Gold Coast in February and March 1948 catalysed a process of rapid constitutional reform, and thereby added urgency to debates about the future of British Togoland. As the Coussey Commission deliberated on constitutional reform for the Gold Coast, it provoked a series of discussions about whether the administrative union of the trust territory with its neighbouring colony could actually 'remain strictly administrative in nature' if the colony itself was marching quickly through agreed stages on a road to self-government. The commission's proposals ultimately resulted in greater 'democracy', in the form of the enhanced powers held by the Gold Coast Legislative Assembly that was elected in February 1951, and in the introduction of elected local government in 1952–3. But the process of constitutional reform in and for the Gold Coast also defined the structures through which political opinion in British Togoland could be articulated, and raised concerns about the erosion of the distinctive status of the trust territory.

These pressures from London, New York, and Accra did not take place above the heads or beyond the view of people living in the small towns and villages of southern British Togoland. The implications of each new development were carefully scrutinised and vigorously debated in new forums and public spaces. Connections were made between alternative proposals for national self-government, and the specific opportunity gaps and local grievances identified in Chapter 2, and these connections were in turn cast on a wider canvas of post-war international citizenship. Here, then, I begin with an experiment in education for citizenship which arose from Labour's evolving colonial policy. This experiment was not originally intended for the 'thin but well-distributed layer' of literate, English-speaking school leavers who could be found throughout the southern section of the trust territory, and there were moments when Togolanders challenged the terms on which such education had been offered to them.[12] Yet, there was also considerable enthusiasm for the extension of educational opportunities beyond the system of formal schooling, not least because the latter had its own constraints. Thus, a metropolitan initiative in adult education was reshaped and made locally acceptable, producing new forums in which people made their own connections between local,

[12] The phrase is borrowed from Philip Zachernuk, *Colonial Subjects: An African Intelligentsia and Atlantic Ideas* (Charlottesville VA, 2000), 128.

territorial, and global issues, and engaged each other in debate over the nature of self-government and the rights and responsibilities of citizenship.

EDUCATION FOR CITIZENSHIP

In 1948, David Kimble arrived at the newly established University College of the Gold Coast on a two-year secondment from the Oxford Delegacy for Extra-Mural Studies. He was tasked with introducing to the Gold Coast a model of adult education which explicitly intended to prepare colonial subjects to become citizens of self-governing nations. There are numerous studies of the emergence of the 'Oxford model' of adult education in late nineteenth- and early twentieth-century Britain, as well as several studies which question whether it was ever suitable for the African colonies.[13] In this chapter, then, I shall confine myself to a brief examination of the assumptions underlying the Colonial Office's post-war interest in voluntary educational activity and associations in Africa, and then concentrate on exploring how such activity and associations became embedded in southern British Togoland.

Kimble's peculiar mission was worked out between the Oxford Delegacy and the Colonial Office from 1946 to 1948 in a series of negotiations which called upon the close and longstanding relationship between adult education and the labour movement in Britain. These negotiations ran alongside the work of a sub-committee of the Advisory Committee on Education in the Colonies (ACEC), which was appointed at the behest of Arthur Creech Jones. In investigating the possibility of 'Education for Citizenship' in the colonies, individual members of the sub-committee drew on their personal experiences and knowledge of British adult education and of the British labour movement, and asserted a direct analogy between the situation of colonised Africans in the mid-twentieth century and that of the nineteenth-century British working class.

[13] Kwa Hagan, *Oxford University and an Adult Education Experiment in Ghana, 1947–1950* (Legon, 1974); Abelwahid Aballa Yousif, *The Origins and Development of University Adult Education in Ghana and Nigeria, 1946–1966* (Bon-Bad Godesberg, 1974); Roger Fieldhouse, *Adult Education and the Cold War: Liberal Values under Siege, 1946–51* (Leeds, 1985); Colin Titmus and Tom Steele, *Adult Education for Independence: The Introduction of University Extra-Mural Work into British Tropical Africa* (Leeds, 1995); Albert Amedzro, 'University-Based Adult Education in Ghana 1948–2000' in Kobina Asiedu, Kate Adoo-Adeku, and Albert Amedzro eds., *The Practice of Adult Education in Ghana* (Accra, 2004), 48–68.

The suitability of a British adult educational model for the African colonies hinged on the shared experience of urbanisation, whose effects were assumed to be universal.[14] The sub-committee thus anticipated that as new forms of associational life developed in towns, Africans, like their British working-class counterparts, would increasingly organise themselves on a voluntary basis to acquire the new knowledge that would enable them to articulate their collective interests and press their claims to political representation. The ACEC already favoured the creation of departments of extra-mural studies in order to ensure that new institutions of higher education in West Africa would reach out beyond their own walls and shoulder responsibility for educating public opinion and preparing colonial subjects for a gradual extension of the franchise. It was envisaged that these departments would meet Africans' self-expressed needs for education, in a manner akin to the provision made by Oxford University's Delegacy for Extra-Mural Studies to the working-class Britons who organised themselves through the Workers' Educational Association.

Whilst colonial education advisors saw the extra-mural class as a vehicle for educating public opinion, they also remained convinced that citizenship was as strongly equated with 'character' as it was with knowledge. Citizens, they argued, could not be trained through a straightforward transfer of knowledge and skills from the universities to the broader population: '[t]he democratic habit of mind resembles religion – with which it has much in common – in that it cannot be taught merely from text-books.'[15] Indeed, in Britain, they claimed, the very

> demand for adult education was closely linked to the desire for social progress, and the initiative has come largely from the people themselves, particularly those who were most concerned to secure political and social reform, from the early trade unionists, co-operators and radicals of the nineteenth century onwards.[16]

The Colonial Office might facilitate the provision of adult education in the colonies, by financing experimental courses, but it could not create the demand. When the secretary of the Oxford Delegacy, Thomas Hodgkin, first approached the Colonial Office in 1946, his proposals concerned the provision of experimental courses in the urban centres of Nigeria and the

[14] Kate Skinner, 'Agency and Analogy in African History: The Contribution of Extra-Mural Studies in Ghana', *History in Africa* 34 (2007), 273–96.

[15] ACEC, 'Education for Citizenship', Ibid., 9. [16] Ibid., 34–35.

Gold Coast, where he believed that such demand was concentrated.[17] And when J. A. McLean arrived in the Gold Coast in May 1947, his twelve-week experimental lecture series in 'Economic History and Problems' ran in Cape Coast, Sekondi, Kumasi, and Accra.[18] The small towns and villages of southern British Togoland lay well beyond the extra-mural horizon during this experimental phase.

Then, between 28 February and 16 March 1948, a series of riots in the urban centres of the Gold Coast gave rise first to the Watson Commission on the causes of popular discontent and then to the Coussey Commission on constitutional reform. When David Kimble arrived in April 1948, he threw himself wholeheartedly into the political drama. From his base at the new University College of the Gold Coast, where he went on to create the Department of Extra-Mural Studies (now the Institute of Adult Education), Kimble travelled out to offer 'sessional courses', lasting twenty-four weeks, on 'Problems of Modern Government' at Accra, Cape Coast, Kumasi, and Sekondi; and 'terminal courses', lasting ten weeks, on 'The Machinery of Government' at Ho, Koforidua, Swedru, and Tarkwa. He also invited leading Gold Coast nationalists to speak at a series of one-day schools in the larger towns, on the themes of 'The Press and Public Opinion', 'Problems of Municipal Government', 'Mass Education', and 'The Place of Chiefs'.[19] Perhaps most importantly, Kimble convened a residential conference at Aburi in February 1949, which drew together those who had participated in, or lectured at, these early adult education events. The conference culminated in the inauguration of a new nation-wide voluntary association, the People's Education Association (PEA).

Kimble's focus on urban centres may have derived from an underlying belief that urbanisation was the fundamental socio-economic dynamic that would steer the political life of African colonies along a trajectory comparable with that of nineteenth-century Britain. But as Kimble started out in the Gold Coast as a one-man-band, the urban focus of his activities was also practical: it enabled him to reach larger audiences in a shorter period of time. By November 1949, a new resident tutor, Lalage Bown, had been allocated to the area east of the river Volta, and by June 1950,

[17] The National Archives (TNA), Kew, UK. CO 554/135/2 Higher Education in West Africa, Study Courses Arranged by the Oxford Extra-Mural Delegacy, 1946. Hodgkin was also able to quote back to the Colonial Office sections of the Asquith and Elliot commission reports, which emphasised the benefits of including extra-mural departments in the new university institutions of West Africa.

[18] University of Oxford Delegacy for Extra-Mural Studies, *Adult Education in the Gold Coast: A Report for the Year 1948–49 by the Resident Tutor* (Achimota, 1949), 3.

[19] Ibid., 12–13.

she had completed ten-week courses on 'Modern Political Systems' at Hohoe, Kpandu, Ho, Amedzofe, Anfoega, and Nkonya, in the trust territory of British Togoland, as well as in several towns in the Ewe-speaking areas of the Gold Coast. In June 1952, Bown reported that the demand for extra-mural classes in her 'Trans-Volta Togoland' area had expanded so much that a second resident tutor was required, and she added that, beyond her own classes, members of the PEA were also volunteering themselves in mass literacy campaigns, community development projects, women's work, and vernacular discussion groups.[20]

Trans-Volta Togoland was regarded by tutors as a model region because whilst the extra-mural classes enabled students from different localities to come together to inform themselves about national and international issues and events, the class members were deemed to be unusually pro-active in tapping into older forms of solidarity within small towns and villages, and mobilising communities behind self-help projects. Lalage Bown was convinced of the importance of adult education in forging productive linkages between the new 'horizontal' identities and interests of the young, mobile, literate, class members, and the older 'vertical' solidarities of the rural communities from which they came. Bown thus identified herself with a dynamic movement which would empower citizens and hasten the achievement of democratic self-government in Britain's African colonies.[21] As a young, single woman, embarking determinedly on a mission that ultimately took her all across the continent in the period of anti-colonial nationalism and Independence, Bown's life story is worthy of research in its own right. Her exceptional levels of energy and commitment, however, are not a sufficient explanation for the rapid expansion of PEA membership and activities through the southern section of the trust territory. In order to understand this, we must look to the members themselves.

'ANOTHER CAMOUFLAGE OF COLONIAL PLATITUDE FROM OLD OFFICIALDOM'

In the year 2000, I met two brothers, Michael and Constant Senoo.[22] They came from the Bla quarter of Hohoe, where their late father,

[20] Annual Report, 1951–2, 11.

[21] Interview with Lalage Bown, Cheltenham, 30 March 2000.

[22] Interview with Constant Senoo and Richard Banibensu, Madina, Greater Accra, 11 July 2000; interview with Michael Senoo and Richard Banibensu, Dansom, Greater Accra, 14 July 2000.

A. K. Senoo, had been president of the Togoland Union. Whereas most of the Presbyterian teachers whom I met had trained at Akropong in the Akuapem area of the Gold Coast, Michael and Constant's father was a Roman Catholic, and so the boys went to train at St Augustine's in Cape Coast. Michael was there during the riots of 1948 and described his political initiation in the following terms:

When Nkrumah and the Big Six were arrested, he [Kofi Baako, the future government minister] came round the schools and colleges to organise the students to go on strike. He went to Adisadel, Mfantsipim, and St Augustine's, and the strike started on 15 March 1948. At that time there were a lot of lectures by prominent people – I remember hearing Kobina Sekyi . . . My father did not understand why we should have joined this strike. He told us that we were Togolanders, that we should be supporting our own people, not involving ourselves with Gold Coast affairs, that we were a different people from the colonial Gold Coast. Of course that was in 1948, we were students, we wouldn't listen to anything that our parents told us! Two years later, I moved back to the trust territory, and especially when I was stationed in Hohoe in 1954, well that was the centre of the Togoland movement, and I became involved with that. It was clear, now that we have left Cape Coast, now that we are at Hohoe, the centre of the region, there was no sense in supporting the political aspirations of the Gold Coast, so we joined the Togoland Congress. We also formed the Togoland Students' Union.[23]

When Senoo finished his training, he took up his first posting as a middle-school teacher at Nkonya-Ahinkro in the trust territory. His brother Constant had just been posted back to Hohoe, and they both joined Lalage Bown's extra-mural classes and decided to become members of the PEA.

Despite the enthusiasm of these young school teachers, the leadership of the Togoland Union eyed the expatriate tutors with some suspicion. At some point in 1948–9, Kimble received a letter from the Union's secretary, which informed him, 'We have been reading of your activities in the Gold Coast Press from time to time, we viewed them as another camouflage of colonial platitude from old officialdom.' But the members of the Togoland Union also wanted Kimble to know that they were prepared to give him the benefit of the doubt. They had resolved to form an adult study group, and they asked Kimble to support their efforts.[24] In his annual report for 1948–9, Kimble described this letter in terms of a more

[23] Interview with Michael Senoo and Richard Banibensu, Dansoman, Greater Accra, 14 July 2000.

[24] University of Oxford Delegacy for Extra-Mural Studies, *Adult Education in the Gold Coast* (Achimota, 1949), 3.

general suspicion across the Gold Coast that extra-mural classes were a metropolitan initiative intended to teach acceptance of colonialism, and he listed his many efforts to demonstrate that this was not the case. The objection of the Togoland Union, however, was much more specific.

The expatriate extra-mural tutors saw the 1948 riots as a turning point in the political history of the Gold Coast, and indeed this is how they went on to write about them later in their academic careers. The seminal account remains that of Dennis Austin, who argued that the post–Second World War period witnessed a shift from elite politics to mass politics, in which competition between the chiefs and the intelligentsia for influence over colonial policy was overtaken by the demands of a growing group of primary-school leavers.[25] By virtue of their commoner status, these people had found themselves marginalised in rural areas by the structures of indirect rule which privileged the chiefs. But they also lacked sufficient education to enter the professional elite in the urban areas. In Austin's view, they went on to form the backbone of Kwame Nkrumah's Convention People's Party (CPP) when it formally separated from the United Gold Coast Convention in June 1949. It was this same group of marginalised, and as yet largely disenfranchised, school leavers whom Kimble sought to reach through adult education. In southern British Togoland however, the riots had more specific consequences, because the likelihood of constitutional reform in the Gold Coast added urgency to debates over the future of the trust territory.

It is against this background, then, that the Togoland Union's suspicion of extra-mural tutors should be interpreted. The Aburi residential conference which first established the PEA in February 1949 envisaged four main organisational districts, and, as Ho was the only place in British Togoland where Kimble had held a class at this point, it appears to have been assumed that the areas east of the Volta would simply be tacked on to the eastern district of the Gold Coast PEA. In the six months that followed Lalage Bown's arrival in November 1949, however, eleven new extra-mural classes had been established east of the Volta, whilst PEA branches at Peki, Tsito, Keta, and Kpandu were particularly active. Thus at the first PEA annual conference in 1950, a new organisational structure was adopted, identifying five regions, including 'Trans-Volta and Southern Togoland'. In other words, the PEA adopted an organisational structure which mirrored the proposal

[25] Dennis Austin, *Politics in Ghana 1946–1960* (London, 1964).

of the Coussey Commission (whose report was published in October 1949) to include the southern, largely Ewe-speaking, portion of southern British Togoland in a single administrative unit with the Anlo and Peki Ewe-speaking areas of the Gold Coast.

The expatriate tutors were pleased to report upon the expansion of extra-mural classes and other forms of PEA activity east of the river Volta, and they regarded the formation of a Trans-Volta and Southern Togoland region as a practical solution to the problem of allocating scarce teaching resources. It is clear, however, that this measure was opposed by some of the PEA members in the trust territory, 'who most strongly advocate political dichotomy', and tutors had to work hard to persuade them to 'see Trans-Volta Gold Coast and Southern Togoland combined as one P.E.A. Region'.[26] Kimble's annual report for 1949–50 indicates that members had accepted that 'intolerance can balk the pursuit of truth', and he appears to have considered the matter to be closed. He was wrong. In May 1951, the Togoland Union sent a petition to the General Secretary of the United Nations in which they complained about the PEA and the Department of Extra-Mural Studies. In particular, they referred to

> a week-end conference at Kpandu in British Togoland in April, 1951, where University Lecturers in a most subtle manner condemned the United Nations, the Trusteeship Council and the Trusteeship System and explained to attendants that the best thing for Togoland was to demand abolition of the Trust System and ask for annexation to the Gold Coast.[27]

As we saw in Chapter 2, David Brown's study of Kpandu identified an overlap between the Akpini Youth Society, membership of the PEA, and support for Togoland reunification in Kpandu, and this may explain why feelings ran high at this particular event in April 1951.[28] Those who participated directly in other extra-mural classes did not recall deliberate bias on the part of expatriate tutors. According to Michael Senoo, '[Tutors] did not tell us how to play our politics. They were just teaching us. They were not biased.'[29] Togbe Akoto II of Liati, writing to me in October 2000, also insisted that adult education classes were not party

[26] University College of the Gold Coast, Department of Extra-Mural Studies, 'Progress in Adult Education', 20.

[27] Public Records and Archives Administration Department,, Ho, Ghana. DAO (D) 113 Togo Union: M. Batse, Togo Union, to The Secretary General, United Nations, 11 May 1951.

[28] Brown, 'Politics in the Kpandu Area of Ghana', 248.

[29] Interview with Michael Senoo and Richard Banibensu, Dansoman, Greater Accra, 14 July 2000.

political.[30] The Togoland Union's perception of bias, then, seems to have been related to the organisational structure of the PEA and to the nature of the classes and other events which the department promoted.

Kimble was quite clear about the value of the PEA at this particular stage of the Gold Coast's political development:

> The role of voluntary independent associations *can* play in creating a practical democracy is probably not sufficiently realised in the Gold Coast [sic]. They can become agencies for the expression of specialised public opinion; and men and women are able to feel that through their particular association, they have influenced governmental action. They can act as nurseries of democratic life ... members are able to acquire at first hand the technique of managing or mismanaging their own affairs. They can develop certain social qualities. For as active members of such an association, doing something together, people are able to grow in social stature, because they find an outlook for capacities denied to them in their work-a-day life.[31]

Like A. G. Dickson, who organised the early mass education campaigns described in Chapter 2, extra-mural tutors envisaged that, through membership of voluntary associations, and through their leadership of self-help projects, PEA members would develop an ethic of service to others, and thus meet the responsibilities that were the flip side of the rights that literate school leavers were increasingly demanding. The difference was that whilst Dickson's mass education campaigns had focussed on British Togoland before expanding through the Gold Coast, and had actively promoted cross-border co-operation with French Togoland, the PEA had developed first in the Gold Coast and was now extending into British Togoland. Thus, whilst the Togoland Teachers' Union had committed itself to mass education and the spread of mother-tongue literacy, the Togoland Union appeared to worry about the potential of extra-mural studies and the PEA to draw the younger generation of literate English-speaking school leavers into a Gold Coast–centred network that would divert their attention towards the political drama unfolding in Accra, and away from the distinctive status of the trust territory and its potential reunification with French Togoland.

It was difficult for the Togoland Union to accept the organisational structure of the PEA because it mirrored that proposed by the Coussey Commission, to which they were bitterly opposed; it was also difficult for them to accept the mission of the extra-mural classes in preparing colonial

30 Letter from Togbe Akoto II of Liati to the author, 9 Oct 2000.

31 University of Oxford Delegacy for Extra-Mural Studies, *Adult Education in the Gold Coast*, 22 (emphasis original).

subjects for self-government because the unit of citizenship envisaged by expatriate tutors was that of an independent Gold Coast and not a reunified Togoland. In October 1949, the Togoland Union wrote to the chiefs in the trust territory, warning them of the 'great noise' that was taking place in the Gold Coast around the release of the Coussey report, and insisting that they should not allow the trust territory to be drawn in:

> We hasten to make it crystal clear here that should any of the disturbances or the philosophy of Positive Action filter through to our Togoland under United Kingdom Trusteeship by way of advices, inducements or adverse programmes, you should stand firm to point out to any busy-body that we of the Trust Territory are not in any way concerned and therefore shall have absolutely no hand in anything.[32]

The Union watched from a distance as Nkrumah launched his Positive Action campaign in January 1950, but A. K. Senoo stuck to his position. Thus in November 1950, he informed the United Nations that British Togoland 'has not accepted the Coussey Recommendations in practice and will accordingly not register and elect or vote for people to the New House of Legislative Assembly for the Gold Coast and will not participate in the various organs of the Gold Coast Government'.[33]

The Department of Extra-Mural Studies, on the other hand, prided itself on having its fingers on the pulse of political reform and in making direct contact with those who were becoming active participants in the new elected institutions of the Gold Coast. The report of the Coussey Commission was discussed in classes up and down the country in the 1949–50 session. Following the elections of February 1951, which brought a CPP majority into the new Legislative Assembly in Accra, the department turned its attention to the development of elected local government. In the 1951–2 session, the Department organised three weekend conferences for newly elected members of the Legislative Assembly on the themes of 'Local Government', 'Public Administration', and 'The Cost of Living'.[34] Bown noted in her report on Trans-Volta Togoland in the 1951–2 session,

[32] PRAAD, Ho, DAO (D) 113, Togo Union: Togoland Union, Hohoe, to Togbi/Nana, 14 Oct 1949, signed by A. K. Senoo.

[33] Public Records And Archives Administration Department, Accra, Ghana. 39/1/691: Resolutions of the Natural Rulers, States, Native Authorities, Principal Political Bodies and Organisations and People of Togoland Under United Kingdom Trusteeship, 13 Nov 1950, signed by A. K. Senoo, President of the Togo Union, and sent to the Secretary-General of the United Nations, New York.

[34] Annual Report, 1951–2, 35.

Regular class members in Southern Togoland include two chiefs, four state secretaries, and a member of the District Education Committee . . . Class members have been energetic in explaining the new local government proposals to the public, and several are standing for election to the new local councils.[35]

The following year, she noted that the subject of Local Government had again 'pre-occupied students, both in classes and at conferences' through the TVT region and that 'Councillors have been members of most of the regular classes'.[36] She concluded, 'Throughout the Region, such sober discussion and thought has helped the smooth establishment of the new local government system.'

In Chapter 4, we shall see that the establishment of the new local government system was far from smooth, and that amongst the councillors were political activists who raised numerous objections to the ways in which the new local, district, and regional council boundaries blurred Ewe-speaking areas of the Gold Coast with those of the trust territory, and thus compromised the distinctive constitutional status of the latter.[37] For now, however, the most important point is not that extra-mural tutors were deliberately biased. The point is that when the Department of Extra-Mural Studies thought about training citizens for self-government, their frame of reference was the Gold Coast and the process of constitutional reform that was set in motion by the urban riots of 1948. Embedded in the organisational structure of the PEA was an assumption that southern British Togoland could be grouped along with the Ewe-speaking areas of the Gold Coast, leaving northern British Togoland to be absorbed within the Northern Territories. This was precisely what the Togoland reunificationists feared would happen to the trust territory as Gold Coast Independence came closer into view. There were, however, mechanisms that enabled adult students in southern British Togoland to take ownership of the classes and assert some of their own agendas. It is these mechanisms which explain why the objections of the Togoland Union between 1949 and 1951 did not ultimately prevent the expansion of adult education in the trust territory, or indeed its popularity amongst

35 Annual Report, 1951–2, 15. The two chiefs were probably Togbe Akoto of Liati and Togbe Tepre Hodo of Anfoega, both well-known PEA activists.

36 Annual Report, 1952–3, 9.

37 This point is also made by Wilson Yayoh in his careful and valuable study of local government in the inland Ewe-speaking areas. 'Local government in Ewedome, British Trust Territory of Togoland (Ghana) 1920s-1970s' (PhD thesis, School of Oriental and African Studies, London, 2010).

individuals who opposed the integration of the trust territory with the Gold Coast/Ghana.

From the outset, Kimble was attached to 'the principle of freedom of enquiry'. He believed that adult students should not simply accept whichever courses the extra-mural tutors had to offer, but should also organise themselves into PEA branches that would articulate potential academic interests to which the tutors ought to respond. Michael Senoo thus recalled, 'The students themselves picked the subjects, and in British Togoland they asked to be taught about the UN [United Nations].'[38] The resident tutor also noticed that in the 1952–3 session 'International Affairs' was the 'deliberate choice' of several groups, and she attributed this to the students' desire 'to set knowledge gained in previous sessions against a wider background'.[39] At Nkonya (where Michael Senoo was teaching middle school), this was the subject chosen by a group of thirty-seven adult students. In 1953–4, 'International affairs once more had a particular appeal', but this time, requests for the subject coincided with a measure that Lalage Bown was forced to introduce in order to meet the expanding demand for extra mural tuition. Thus, class members from Likpe, Lolobi, Fodome, and Hohoe all combined for fortnightly sessions in which the students formed two groups of fifty. Whilst Bown lectured on 'West Africa and the World' to one group, the other group learned about psychology from a part-time tutor, Mr Coleman. Halfway through the evening, the two groups switched over.[40]

Bown's teaching notes focus on the significance of the Gold Coast, which was 'likely to be the first colonial territory in Tropical Africa to have self-government handed over to the indigenous inhabitants', and contain no detailed lectures on the Togoland question. But the notes are fairly skeletal because discussion was a significant component of all extra-mural classes. One of the discussion questions was, 'What international machinery is there through which the voices of small nations may be heard?' Others asked about 'the significance of the UN's specialised agencies' and the difficulties of operating an international body.[41] These

[38] Interview with Michael Senoo and Richard Banibensu, Dansoman, Greater Accra, 14 July 2000.

[39] Annual report, 1952–3, 9.

[40] Annual report, 1953–4, 7.

[41] My copy of the syllabus for this and other courses was given to me by Lalage Bown. A significant volume of materials, including Annual Reports of both the PEA and the Department of Extra-mural Studies, numerous discussion pamphlets, and records of one-day and weekend events are available in Rhodes House, Oxford, Lalage Bown papers, MSS.Afr.1877.

discussion topics, and Senoo's recollections of the sessions, raise the possibility that whilst the PEA was formed largely in anticipation of the achievement of Gold Coast Independence, and whilst extra-mural tutors sought to develop a sense of territorial or national citizenship, the Togoland members were interested in the emergence of new organs of global governance and their peculiar status as persons administered under international trusteeship.[42] What students were taking away from extra-mural classes, then, was very likely shaped by the political concerns which Togolanders were already beginning to debate among themselves before David Kimble or Lalage Bown arrived.

AWUMA, MORNY, AND THE INTERNATIONALISATION OF THE TOGOLAND QUESTION

G. O. Awuma appears in the district records, and in subsequent studies that draw upon them, as a leader of the young men in and around the administrative capital of Ho, and as a protagonist in the disputes between chiefs in the amalgamated state of Asogli. As we saw in Chapter 2, Awuma was influential in persuading the paramount chief of Asogli – Mote Kofi II – to transfer support from the All Ewe Conference (AEC) to the Togoland Union, and as such he incurred the displeasure of successive district commissioners. As a trained teacher, Awuma was able to develop a following amongst his students, but he was also an articulate and ambitious international traveller.

Writing from London in the summer of 1949, Awuma explained that 'the small and insignificant territory of Western Togoland [i.e. British Togoland] ... has formed an Association in support of the United Nations, and has done quite a good job already by bringing the United Nations and its specialised Agencies to the notice of her people'. According to Awuma, this association had also sent a delegation of three (including Awuma himself and Harry Anku Morny of Hohoe) to the assembly of the World Federation of United Nations Associations in Geneva in September 1948.[43] The federation had been formed in 1946, when a group of twenty-two national associations met in Luxemburg to co-ordinate existing efforts to promote the aims of the United Nations

[42] A one-day school on United Nations Trusteeship was also held at Leklebi-Liati-Ve – see Annual Report, 1953/4, 28.

[43] PRAAD, Ho, DAO (D) 113, Togo Union: G. O. Awuma's address for radio broadcast, dated 21 July 1949.

Charter and to raise public awareness of United Nations institutions and programmes. The Togoland United Nations Association (TUNA) had been founded for similar purposes and therefore sought membership within the federation. In August 1948, V. O. Anku, who was then teaching at Amedzofe, wrote to inform the Colonial Secretary in Accra that the Togoland Union was incorporating the TUNA, and by 1949 they were sharing the same headquarters at Hohoe, where Harry Anku Morny acted as general secretary.[44] According to the Togoland Union's 1949 statement on 'What it is and how it functions', the TUNA was a 'non-sectarian' group within the Union, whose task was to receive and distribute United Nations publications to study groups, who would discuss the publications and 'compile small local libraries'.[45]

The TUNA, then, became the educational wing of the Togoland Union, whose broader aims were: 'to fight exclusively for equal development in Togoland under United Kingdom Trusteeship with the Gold Coast Colony', 'to educate the indigenous people for the full enjoyment of the RIGHTS of the Trusteeship System', to 'obtain independence for Togoland under United Kingdom Trusteeship in the shortest possible time', and 'to contact Togoland under French Government Trusteeship for UNIFICATION of the two trust territories as early as possible incorporating various tribal groupings'. Whilst the Togoland Union noted that its publication programme was 'at present infant' in 1949, the Hope Press at Hohoe, owned by G. K. Tsekpo, would deal with the printing of 'enrollment forms, admissions cards and notices'. Those who paid the enrolment fee of two shillings and joined the TUNA committed themselves to 'obey the rules and regulations of the Association and at all times and in all circumstances to advance the cause of the United Nations and Togoland without flinching'.[46]

Metropolitan initiatives in adult education were intended to prepare Africans for citizenship within the framework of a self-governing Gold Coast, but in British Togoland these initiatives coincided with local efforts to disseminate information about the United Nations and to highlight the new system of international trusteeship. Arguably, at this point, the

[44] PRAAD, Accra, ADM 39/1/651 Togoland Union and Togoland Association for the United Nations Organisation: Letter from V. O. Anku, Amedzofe, to Colonial Secretary, Accra, 9 Aug 1948.

[45] PRAAD, Ho, DAO (D) 113, Togo Union: 'The Togoland Union, incorporated with the United Nations (What it is and how it functions)'.

[46] A copy of a TUNA membership card is available in PRAAD, Ho, DAO (D) 113, Togo Union.

Togoland Union's framework of citizenship was a narrow one: it did not invoke the Universal Declaration of Human Rights (which was formally adopted by the United Nations in December 1948), but rather emphasised the distinctive status of the trust territory, and the particular obligations that the British government had incurred towards its peoples.[47] Whilst David Kimble's classes on 'the machinery of government' spread through the Gold Coast, in small towns and villages of British Togoland, literate English-speakers – and particularly teachers – looked to test the strength of Britain's own parliamentary system, finding ways to bring to the attention of Britons' own elected representatives the nature of its administration in its trust territories.

During his visit to London, en route to the World Federation of United Nations Associations conference in Geneva, Harry Anku Morny met with Dr Rita Hinden, secretary to the FCB.[48] Hinden was a very useful contact, who worked in close association with Arthur Creech Jones and might have been expected to wield some influence. On his return to Hohoe, Anku Morny maintained a steady stream of correspondence with Hinden, providing her with a report on the condition of Togoland in February 1949, in which he claimed that the trust territory's progress was impeded by its lack of a secondary school. Anku Morny listed the numerous professions in which Togolanders were grossly under-represented, or from which they were entirely excluded, and sought to persuade her that 'Togoland has apparently had to play second fiddle to the Gold Coast in educational facilities'.[49] Hinden in turn channelled Anku Morny's information to the British parliamentarian, Reginald Sorensen, who in May, June, and October 1949 confronted the secretary of state with a series of challenging parliamentary questions.

[47] I agree with Merredith Terretta's broader argument about the international outlook of African nationalists, and understand why the suppression of radical political parties in Cameroon stimulated local appeals to universal human rights. I am not convinced that, at this stage, the Togoland reunificationists in the British zone exhibited the same degree of interest, but I return to this point in Chapter 7. See Meredith Terretta, '"We Had Been Fooled into Thinking that the UN Watches over the Entire World": Human rights, UN Trust Territories and Africa's Decolonization', *Human Rights Quarterly* 34 (2) (2012), 329–60.

[48] Patricia Pugh, 'Hinden, Rita (1909–1971)' in H. C. G. Matthew and Brian Harrison eds., *Oxford Dictionary of National Biography* (Oxford, 2004), online edition edited by Lawrence Goldman (2011), available at: www.oxforddnb.com/view/article/59962 [last accessed 27 July 2014].

[49] Fabian Colonial Bureau papers, Rhodes House, Oxford. MSS Brit.Emp.s.365, box 89, file 1, 'Togoland – a British Trust Territory' by H. Anku Morny (n.d., but judging from the other correspondence, Feb 1949).

Sorensen began by referring to the complaints of the Togoland Farmers Association about the marketing of their cocoa through the Gold Coast Cocoa Marketing Board, and the continued lack of provision for roads, schools, and health facilities in the trust territory. This was followed up by a request for the secretary of state to provide parliament with concrete details as to progress in the building of hospitals and schools in the trust territory and the numbers of Togolanders in receipt of government scholarships. Sorensen also argued that it was primarily through local efforts that any new roads had been constructed, and suggested that 'in view of the amount of revenue derived from these people', the secretary of state should find out whether any attempt was being made by the government of the Gold Coast to improve their roads.[50] Anku Morny, then, was attempting to shame the secretary of state into greater vigour in the development of the trust territory by ensuring that he faced questions from his own party's benches in the House of Commons. Ironically, it was the same secretary of state – Arthur Creech Jones – who had founded the FCB with Hinden in 1940, and who had approved the Oxford Delegacy's original proposals for experiments in extra-mural studies in West Africa.

Thus, if extra-mural tutors may initially have thought of education for citizenship in terms of informing class members about the constitutional developments within the Gold Coast, and encouraging a wide debate about their implications, the kinds of people most likely to become class members within southern British Togoland were more than capable of asserting that citizenship had an international as well as territorial dimension and that the British government still had much to learn about trusteeship. The TUNA believed that an 'educated public opinion' in Togoland necessarily entailed reference to the new organs of global governance and a means of ensuring that the British government was held accountable for meetings its obligations.

IDEAL SPEECH ACTS IN A RURAL PUBLIC SPHERE

The willingness of tutors to accommodate the requests of students for particular subjects goes some way to explaining why Togolanders signed up to the PEA and attended extra-mural classes in spite of the early suspicions expressed by the Togoland Union. The resident tutor often pondered the particular enthusiasm with which students participated in

[50] Letters from Rita Hinden to Anku Morny, 14 June 1949 and 8 Nov 1949, including excerpts from Hansard.

her classes, and she attributed this to the 'sense of mental isolation' that the region's literate population experienced 'because of the barrier of the [river] Volta, the particularly poor roads, and the absence of radio and newspapers in many areas'.[51] At this level, classes were social occasions, which were likely to attract interest in the absence of alternatives. But extra-mural classes and PEA activities continued to be popular for over a decade, which suggests that students may also have enjoyed the sessions.

Tutors were deeply attached to adult teaching methods and emphasised that extra-mural classes should be very different from the notoriously authoritarian and hierarchical environment experienced by students in church schools and teacher training colleges. Constant Senoo therefore emphasised his surprise at the sense of equality between tutor and adult student: 'You know, we liked it so much. When we went on residential courses, there was no distinction, we had common dining and common dormitories ... It was through the PEA that we realised that we could be equal to a white man.'[52] Former tutors also commented in interviews on the extent to which their own understanding of history and politics had been shaped by discussion with students whom they encountered up and down the country in their extra-mural work.[53] In principle at least, there was a strong commitment that tutors should learn from students, and that students should learn from each other as well as from the tutor.

In these respects, both tutors and students described extra-mural classes and residential courses as a rural African version of the public sphere which, according to Jürgen Habermas, emerged in the salons and coffee houses of eighteenth-century enlightened Europe: adults participated as equals in discussions based on reason, and thereby developed a conception not only of their own interests, but also of the common good.[54] Kimble wrote at length in his first annual report about his desire to raise the quality of class discussions by training students to adduce evidence for their opinions and reasons for their claims. Tolerance was treated by tutors as a measure of the quality of discussion, because tolerance rested on class members' confidence that each of their number was capable of justifying his or her views and was sincere in seeking the common good. Classes aimed to provide a mechanism through which

[51] Annual report, 1951–2, 12.

[52] Interview with Constant Senoo and Richard Banibensu, Madina, Greater Accra, 11 July 2000.

[53] Interviews with Lalage Bown, Shrewsbury, 30 April 2000 and 12 July 2004.

[54] Jürgen Habermas, *The Structural Transformation of the Public Sphere: An Inquiry into a Category of Bourgeois Society* (Cambridge, 1989 [trans. Thomas Burger]).

disagreement could be channelled into debates governed by mutual respect between individuals.

Tutors were quite explicit in their intention that the discourse ethics learned in the extra-mural class should be internalised by students and applied in a range of other political and institutional contexts. Thus in 1954, Lalage Bown argued that adult education had 'encouraged a more balanced public opinion and a more tolerant outlook in the Region', which was evidenced in an increased willingness of individuals 'to listen to political views with which they are out of sympathy'. She was optimistic that this 'spirit of tolerance will be carried to the new Assembly [the Gold Coast Legislative Assembly elected in 1954], for rather more than one-half of the election candidates in the Region have attended either regular extra-mural classes or residential courses organised by the Department'.[55]

STATUS, RECOGNITION, AND ACCESS

There is little evidence to suggest that adult students rejected the ideal of the PEA as part of a widening public sphere, but the rules of discourse operating within the four walls of an extra-mural class or a PEA weekend conference were not necessarily the same rules that governed other forms of speech or structured access to state institutions or even the voluntary organisations themselves. Ironically, whilst much of the content of extra-mural classes developed Togolanders' awareness of new opportunities for participation in the processes of constitutional change in the Gold Coast, the organisational aspects of the PEA, and the experience of meeting other members from around the Gold Coast, often served to heighten a sense of marginality and disadvantage. If within the four walls of each weekly class, every adult enjoyed being treated as an equal interlocutor, the placing of individuals within the structure of the organisation tended to reflect their differences, and particularly the level of formal schooling and qualification that the individual had achieved.

In the context of small towns and villages, membership of the PEA and attendance at an extra-mural class was in itself a marker of achievement, for active participation was open only to those who were already literate and confident in spoken English.[56] The 1952–3 report for the Department

[55] Annual report, 1953–4, 7–8.

[56] Although former tutors indicated in interviews that their classes were sometimes attended by people who could not speak English well but nonetheless wanted to get a sense of what was going on.

of Extra-Mural Studies made a rough attempt to record and analyse the occupations of 'effective' class members. The numbers appear rather small because only those who had followed an entire course under a tutor appointed by the department in the 1952–3 session were categorised as 'effective' class members, whilst a much larger number of people were members of the PEA or ad hoc participants in its other activities. Nonetheless, the more anecdotal observations in all the other annual reports indicate that this snapshot provided a reasonably accurate picture of the larger PEA membership. The largest single category was 'unclassified' (620). Of those who were classified, the largest category by far was middle-school teachers (380), followed by commercial and business clerks (276), primary-school teachers (205), head teachers (115), and civil service clerks (110). The rest of the class members were drawn from what might loosely be termed 'white collar' occupations, including letter writers, stenographers, dispensers, cashiers, and sanitary inspectors; along with a handful of artisans, such as masons, carpenters, tailors, and 'fitters' (car mechanics); and self-employed traders, transport operators, and store keepers.[57] The membership was also overwhelmingly male.

In the more specific context of southern British Togoland, these patterns were replicated, but the dominance of school teachers in the class membership was even more pronounced. The 1955 report of the Department of Extra-Mural Studies provided a breakdown of occupations of class members in five sample classes. One of these was Leklebi-Liati-Ve in the trust territory, where the class members comprised sixteen teachers (almost certainly middle- and primary-school level), three headmasters, three farmers, two produce checkers, one produce examiner, one postal agent, one carpenter, and one chief (Togbe Akoto of Liati).[58] Adult students, then, did not belong to a 'bourgeoisie' in the Marxist sense of the term. Nor did they resemble the urban working class for whom the extra-mural class in England was originally intended.[59] But in the context

[57] Annual report, 1952–3, 39. [58] Annual Report, 1955, 39.

[59] Goldman suggests that despite the emphasis that the Oxford Delegacy placed on the industrial working class, participants in English adult education classes were mainly drawn from 'the respectable, upper reaches of the working class … an assortment of clerks, teachers, trade unionists and co-operators'. 'Intellectuals and the English working class 1870–1945: The Case of Adult Education', *History of Education* 29 (2000), 281–300 at 283. The ethos and social appeal of adult education in Scotland was slightly different.

of rural southern Togoland, participation in classes was a meaningful and visible marker of social status. Tutors were well aware of the difficulties that class members experienced in travelling along bad roads in the evenings, and those tutors who owned cars would sometimes drive around the villages to pick up their adult students in order to make sure their class could convene on time. This meant that attendance at a class was witnessed by an individual's relatives and neighbours, and physically demonstrated a commitment to the widely endorsed strategy of self-improvement through education. Thus in their own interviews with the long-serving adult educationist, Richard Banibensu, Titmus and Steele were told, just as I was, that in village settings, everyone who was anyone wanted to join, 'postmasters, catechists, and chiefs'.[60]

The class members constituted the intelligentsia in their own villages. But there was an important distinction between tutors and their adult students: tutors had to hold a university degree, and they were paid to teach, whereas much of the organisational work amongst class members was done on a voluntary unpaid basis. In principle, race was irrelevant in the internal hierarchy of adult education. The Department of Extra-Mural Studies could employ any graduate to give classes on a part-time basis, and in the towns of the Gold Coast, the African graduate teachers of prestigious secondary schools were employed on this basis, whilst those whom we might describe as 'public intellectuals' were invited as key note speakers to numerous day schools, weekend conferences, and other events. The sociologist Kofi Busia and the lawyer J. B. Danquah were also invited to write for the department's series of discussion group pamphlets, published by the Bureau of Current Affairs.[61] The availability of part-time graduate tutors facilitated the spread of adult education in Gold Coast towns, whilst the very lack of such individuals inhibited it in the more sparsely populated areas of southern British Togoland, and posed a very significant barrier in the North.[62] All of the department's annual reports emphasised the struggle of a single resident tutor to meet the growing demand for classes in the TVT region where travel along poor roads took much of her time, and where few graduates

[60] Titmus and Steele, *Adult Education for Independence*, 65.

[61] See, for example, K. A. Busia, *Education for Citizenship* (London, n.d.) and J. B. Danquah, *Obligation in Akan Society* (London, n.d.).

[62] Interview with Bill Tordoff, Chapel-en-le-Frith, 13 April 2004. Tordoff indicated that, amongst the tutors, the North was recognised as a very tough posting, mainly because the tutor had to teach almost every class him/herself and drive considerable distances on a weekly basis.

(local or expatriate) were available to act as part-time tutors. As the PEA itself was structured along the lines envisaged in the Coussey Commission, and represented a kind of training ground for a self-governing Gold Coast, there was little to reassure Togolanders that their area would not end up playing the role of disadvantaged periphery.

Expatriate tutors may have seen membership of the PEA and participation in extra-mural classes as a means of stimulating a sense of Gold Coast citizenship and a better-informed participation in the new organs of elected government. But the effect was by no means automatic because the PEA also provided a frame of reference through which Togolanders became acutely aware of their lack of a graduate intelligentsia and the ways in which this would inhibit the full and equal participation of the area in Gold Coast–wide organisations and institutions. Until 1950, the trust territory did not have a school which could prepare students for any qualification above standard VII. Only pupils from the very wealthiest families could afford to travel to the Gold Coast for secondary education, and thus for the great majority, the new University College remained beyond the realm of the possible. The problem was circular, for without graduate teachers, it was difficult to open new secondary schools; without a regular cohort of secondary-school leavers, the trust territory would be under-represented in the University College; without a stream of university graduates, it would be difficult to build up a cohort of graduate teachers who were willing to be posted in the trust territory.

As Michael Senoo pointed out, whether one looked west, to the Akan-English-speaking areas of the Gold Coast, or east, to the Ewe/Mina elite of coastal French Togoland, the sense of relative disadvantage was the same for the inland Ewe-speakers of southern British Togoland:

> On the French side, there were lots of real academicians, lawyers, university teachers, people like the Olympios, who exerted more influence on us than our own people ... In those days we did not have highly educated people from our own area – lawyers and so on – we didn't have them. Most of us needed a quick job and we became teachers. If the Germans had stayed, we would have been the second or third generation of graduates.[63]

Richard Banibensu concurred with Senoo's emphasis on the disadvantages under which British Togoland had laboured, explaining how

[63] Interview with Michael Senoo and Richard Banibensu, Dansoman, Greater Accra, 14 July 2000.

measures of achievement had changed between the generations which came of age in the first half of the twentieth century. 'Our fathers [first or second generation converts] who had become teachers were content with themselves. They had reached the elite of society.' For his own generation, coming out of the training colleges in the 1930s and 1940s, this was no longer enough. '[Our fathers] had seen being a primary-school teacher as their achievement, but we who saw a future for ourselves, we thought of being a middle-school teacher as just a beginning. We wanted to go further, to keep learning. We who saw a future for ourselves started to follow the PEA.'[64]

Retrospective accounts of adult education in African countries often emphasise a split between expatriate tutors and local students over the question of certification. The tutors who came to the Gold Coast via the Oxford Delegacy in the late 1940s and early 1950s espoused an idealised view of education that would prepare individuals to lead ethical lives in which they served others by bringing enhanced powers of reason to bear upon the complex questions facing local communities and new nations. Tutors believed that the primary aim of education was citizenship, and that the collective ethos of adult learning would be undermined by competitive examination and the issuing of certificates to individual students.

Dennis Austin, who returned to Ghana at various points through the 1960s and 1970s, noted how quickly this opposition to certification had evaporated, and began to question whether the type of education that the first generation of extra-mural tutors provided had ever really corresponded to the true nature of local demand. In this analysis, extra-mural classes were only popular *faute de mieux*, and once expatriate tutors began to move on to academic posts elsewhere, students no longer bothered to disguise their individualist aspirations and their instrumentalist approach to education. Austin, who had served as resident tutor first in the Northern Territories, and then in the Ashanti Region, was well aware of the educational bottleneck through which many students were attempting to squeeze: 'Only about 13 per cent of the very large middle school population actually got to a secondary school, and . . . only about a quarter to a fifth of these succeeded in reaching the fifth or sixth forms, [so] most of our adult students were from the middle schools.'[65]

[64] Ibid.

[65] Dennis Austin, 'Et in Arcadia Ego: Politics and Learning in Ghana', *Minerva* 13 (2) (1975), 236–69 at 254.

As soon as it was elected in February 1951, the new Legislative Assembly in the Gold Coast sought to address the 'problem' of the standard-VII school leaver. The 1951 Accelerated Plan for Education therefore reorganised the senior years of primary school (standards IV to VII) into middle school (forms I to IV). Those students who passed the competitive entrance examinations, and whose families could afford for them to take up the place, would leave halfway through middle school and proceed to secondary schools which prepared them for the GCE examinations.[66] Those who failed the examination, or whose families could not afford for them to take up a place, completed two further years in middle school, leaving at form IV. The Middle School Leaving Certificate required students to pass a combination of academic and vocational subjects, and was thus intended to widen their employment aspirations to include skilled manual work, and improved farming, as more 'realistic' alternatives to scarce white collar jobs. The government's priority, in 1951, was to make a full primary education available to all school-aged children, and particularly those in the Northern Territories, where provision was still very limited.[67] In much of the southern part of the country, however, the plan was unpopular, because it treated the Middle School Leaving Certificate as a 'terminal' qualification for the majority, and did not commit to meeting rapidly the ever-growing demand for secondary education.[68]

Austin believed that British observers of adult education in the Gold Coast had failed to grasp its underlying dynamics.

> Fresh from Oxford or London, they were eager to translate what they saw into their own experience. They lectured to, and even talked with, a number of students, but found it hard to grasp that although the chairman, secretary treasurer and librarian [of PEA branches] were commoners – the office of president usually being bestowed on the chief – they were certainly not 'levellers', except in the sense that they wished to level themselves up.[69]

[66] GCE (General Certificate of Education) was introduced in Britain in 1951. It was divided into O'level and A'level, the latter being the requirement for university entrance. Before 1951, the main secondary qualifications in the United Kingdom were the School Certificate and the Higher School Certificate, the latter being required for university entrance. The term 'matriculation' was often used to refer to qualifications that allowed students to enter universities.

[67] See R. B. Bening, *A History of Education in Northern Ghana* (Accra, 1990).

[68] This is well explained in Philip Foster, *Education and Social Change in Ghana* (London, 1965), 179–201.

[69] Austin, 'Et in Arcadia Ego', 253.

More specifically, adult students wanted to obtain the GCE qualifications that would open the doors to university, the professions, the higher ranks of the civil service, and a range of other possibilities. They were prepared to attend extra-mural classes because they thought they might learn something that would help them in their private study for fee-paying correspondence courses. But their ideal was that the extra-mural class should teach them directly for the exam, at a much reduced fee. According to Austin, then,

> Over the years, [those who were] home-grown in extra-mural studies tended, paradoxically, to place greater emphasis on certificate education, based on external standards of examination . . . To the early – largely expatriate – tutors . . . such a programme would have seemed heresy, a perversion of intentions: Caliban has cast out Ariel. I do not doubt but that the change reflects the wishes of students now and in the past.[70]

Austin was not condemning the adult students, whom he believed laboured under heavy burdens of obligation to extended families, and could not afford the luxury of time spent on forms of education that would not enable them to present specific qualifications to potential employers. His criticism, albeit implicit, was directed at the naivety of the tutors who expected that the Oxford model of education for citizenship could be transplanted to societies which lacked either a substantial industrial working class or a productive indigenous bourgeoisie. The changes within the PEA and the Institute of Adult Education after Independence, he thought, were dictated by much the same dynamic that he identified throughout the new organs of elected government and the civil service: adult students were primarily interested in forms of learning that would have a tangible and positive impact on their earning power, giving them a head start in the desperate scrabble for scarce white-collar employment opportunities, many of which were underwritten by state expenditure.

Austin's interpretation of the increasing shift towards certification in the later 1950s casts the earlier period of PEA activity in terms of a binary that is familiar in debates on the nature and purpose of education around the globe: an idealistic vision of education – which was most strongly advocated by those who were already university graduates and could afford to espouse it – was inevitably eroded by the more pragmatic and material concerns of individuals seeking to better their economic

[70] Ibid., 253 and fn 83.

positions. Given what we know about the peculiar status of teachers in southern British Togoland, however, I think that this binary fails to capture the more complicated mixture of beliefs and motivations on the part of those who participated in the PEA. As we saw in Chapter 2, there were numerous and explicit discussions within Togoland about the social and political responsibilities that education conferred on individuals, particularly teachers. Adult students were keenly aware of the ways in which educational attainment could be used to structure access to the civil service, the professions, the church, and even voluntary associations themselves. Clearly this gave rise to a desire on the part of individuals to move further up the ladders on which they found themselves. But it also gave rise to frequent reflections on why those ladders took the form that they did, whether they served the common good, and whether they could be changed. In order to interrogate this further, and outline why unequal access to education was a core issue for the Togoland reunificationists, we will examine in greater detail the academic and political career of Mr E. K. Datsa from the Siyase-speaking enclave of Amedzofe-Avatime.

BENZIES, BOOK BOXES, AND 'A SACRIFICIAL WORK'

During the second half of the nineteenth century, Africans who were trained by the Bremen mission were expected to assume the responsibilities of moral guardianship in idealised Christian peasant communities. In the course of the twentieth century, the responsibilities of teachers continued to extend beyond the classroom and into rural communities, but they assumed new forms, particularly in mobilising collective responses to the opportunities and constraints posed by the colonial state, and in helping illiterate individuals to respond to its demands. New responsibilities were often embraced willingly and enthusiastically, particularly in mass literacy and community development campaigns. In their own accounts of their careers, then, teachers often instanced acts of service to the community as key components of their ethical lives, and were prone to advise the younger generation on the need to embrace the opportunity to serve and to desist from impossible demands for more comfortable living and teaching accommodation in the rural stations. Even today, teaching is often referred to, approvingly, as 'a sacrificial work' and this is a dominant theme in Mr Datsa's memoir, which he entitled 'Doing My Duty'.

A closer look at Mr Datsa's life, however, reveals some of the ways in which individuals chafed against the limitations of the training they received and how this oriented them towards the Togoland reunificationist project. Some of them objected to the requirement that teachers who had trained to Certificate A under the auspices of the Evangelical Presbyterian Church also had to spend a further year at a seminary in order to train as a catechist.[71] This opposition was more likely to reflect family responsibilities than incipient secularisation: many of the newly qualified teachers needed to work in order to meet the cost of schooling for their younger siblings. Equally significant was the resentment against the restrictions that church institutions placed on trainee teachers in order to curtail the amount of time they could spend studying privately by correspondence. Practising and trainee teachers thus lived with the tension between a shared expectation of sacrifice and service on the one hand, and on the other, a desire to understand and make their own way within changing socio-economic circumstances. This tension is captured in an incident recounted by Mr Datsa in his memoir.

Having trained for Certificate A at Achimota, and having worked as a teacher back in his home village of Amedzofe in 1939, Mr Datsa was then sent to Akropong in the Akuapem area of the Gold Coast for his seminary year. In June 1940, the seminary students engaged in a protest against an inspection of the boxes and trunks that they kept in their dormitories:

> The aim was for the college authorities to discover and seize any books other than those prescribed and approved by the college for use by the students. (No student was allowed to be studying any subject privately, besides those on the curriculum.) Textbooks in Latin, Greek, Advanced Mathematics, Geography or History for study for any examinations were strictly forbidden.[72]

Those who had already completed Certificate A and were at Akropong for the seminary year were exempt from this rule, which applied only to the trainee teachers. The seminary students therefore looked after the banned books for their juniors who wished to study privately in addition to training for their Certificate A. In a bid to stop this practice, inspections were extended to the seminary students, who refused to open their boxes.

[71] This is described in E. E. Grau, 'The Evangelical Presbyterian Church (Ghana and Togo) 1914–1946: A Study in European Mission Relations Affecting the Beginning of an Indigenous Church' (PhD thesis, Hartford Seminary Foundation, 1964). Grau was sent to Togoland in 1946 for the purpose of training catechists and future pastors. He therefore wrote at length on the model of the teacher-catechist and the objections that were raised to this model during his time in Togoland.

[72] E. K. Datsa, *Doing My Duty: Memoirs of a Ghanaian Educationalist* (Accra, 2006), 50.

The college threatened to close the seminary altogether and to physically withhold certificates even from those who had already completed their teacher training, thus effectively rendering them unemployable.

Mr Datsa and the other seminary students formed a delegation and appealed for the intervention of the Synod Clerk. Whilst they were awaiting the resolution of this dispute, they received gifts of food from some of the African tutors at the college, as well as from the district pastor (an African) and his wife, and some of the local townspeople in Akropong, who apparently sympathised with the seminary students' case against the college principal, Benzies, a Scots missionary. When the Synod Clerk arrived, he was met by a delegation of church elders demonstrating in favour of the seminary students and shouting, 'Benzies must go!' The support of the church elders for the seminary students, and the perception that opposition to private study was stronger among the expatriates than the African tutors, points to an interesting development in attitudes towards the nature and purpose of education.

Church and missionary training through the 1920s, 30s and 40s continued to revolve around a dominant ideal of the teacher-catechist living an exemplary life of service in his rural station. There was constant concern about the propensity of young trainees to succumb to the temptation to drop out of teaching in order to join the ranks of waged workers in the towns and enjoy exposure to all the material luxuries, sensual pleasures, and immoral temptations that urban life could offer.[73] As primary provision expanded through the inter-war period, there was a growing number of literate school leavers and standard VII was often not enough to secure entry to positions in the large import-export companies or the lower ranks of the civil service. In the absence of direct governmental provision in the trust territory, the churches remained the dominant providers of post-standard VII opportunities, which came in the form of teacher training courses. In the case of the Presbyterians at the teacher training college in Akropong, the desire of trainees to acquire further qualifications via private correspondence courses was regarded as evidence of a lack of commitment to the work of a rural teacher-catechist and an intention to pursue more worldly opportunities elsewhere. Trained teachers who did not go on to teach were a poor investment:

[73] The excitement and danger of the city in this period is well captured in the film *The Boy Kumasenu*. See Peter Bloom and Kate Skinner, 'Modernity and Danger: The Boy Kumasenu and the Work of the Gold Coast Film Unit', *Ghana Studies* 12/13 (2009/10), 121–53.

the churches subsidised the cost of training teachers in the expectation of future service, and indeed teachers could be bonded to ensure that the churches could recoup their expenditure. By the 1940s, however, attitudes to further study seemed to be changing.

In his memoirs, then Mr Datsa explained how he had navigated between the expectation of service to the church, to pupils, and to communities, and his own desire to acquire a higher level of formal education. Having finished his seminary year, Mr Datsa returned to teaching, first at Ho-Kpodzi and then back at Amedzofe, but he also studied privately by correspondence with Wolsey Hall, alongside with his friend Stephen Ohene from Abutia. In 1945 both men sat the London Matriculation Examination, and in 1946 Mr Datsa was recommended by the Evangelical Presbyterian Education Unit for a scholarship that enabled him to go back to Achimota for his intermediate degree. In the short term, he indicated that his own students, and even some of his fellow teachers, felt that his departure to Achimota had come at the expense of the pupils at Amedzofe who were about to sit their standard VII exams and needed his help. Within the church education unit, however, there appears to have been a gradual recognition that in order to retain teachers and to provide staff for even a small number of church secondary schools, there had to be some opportunities for higher education. After completing two years at Achimota, and teaching in the Presbyterian secondary school at Krobo-Odumase in the Gold Coast, Mr Datsa was recommended for another scholarship, this time to complete his university education in the United Kingdom. Thus in August 1949, he and William Tsitsiwu (the choir master) proceeded to Glasgow. Under the same scheme, Mr A. K. Tse went to St Andrew's, and Mr Datsa's friend, Stephen Ohene, also gained his degree.

After the opening of Mawuli secondary school in the trust territory's administrative capital, Ho, Mr Datsa and Mr Tse both had suitable jobs to go to when they returned to British Togoland in 1953, and they became integral parts of an institution which opened up opportunities hitherto denied to the vast majority of primary/middle-school leavers. As there was only a tiny handful of university graduates in the trust territory, their services were also in high demand for adult education work. Mr Datsa taught a class on 'Elementary Economics' at Vane in 1953–4 and a similar class at Ho in 1955, as well as judging the PEA's regional essay competition. Mr Tse also taught 'Introductory Economics' at Awudome (just beyond the border of the trust territory) in 1953–4, and wrote up for the Department of Extra-Mural Studies a 'Syllabus for a Course of Study on Some Economic Principles'.[74] The classes they taught did not provide GCE certificates for students, but Mr Datsa recalled his extra-mural work as a form of service nonetheless, and indicated that at least some students were sufficiently stimulated to go back to formal education and improve themselves in life.[75]

In a pattern recognisable in other memoirs written by individuals in this generation, Mr Datsa used his own life story to advise a younger generation: his readiness to sacrifice and to serve, and his endurance in the face of adversity, was not only virtuous; it had ultimately yielded greater personal rewards.[76] There is something very Presbyterian about this aspect of Mr Datsa's memoir, and when he started writing it at around the age of 80, he was absolutely sincere in his desire to stimulate an ethic of service in younger men and women teaching in rural areas.[77] Mr Datsa would probably not have recognised the competition that Austin posited between individual achievement (education for certification) and an ethic of service to others (education for citizenship). The relationship that Mr Datsa posited in his memoirs was one of mutual reinforcement: education conferred a responsibility to serve; the proper discharge of this responsibility would enhance the individual's own prospects of reward in the form of opportunities for higher education; higher education would in turn incur a heightened responsibility to serve.

But there are other, more contemporaneous written expressions of Mr Datsa's feelings about the nature of the opportunities that were open to Togolanders in the late colonial period, and of the connections he made between lack of access to education and the undesirability of the integration of the trust territory with the Gold Coast. Whilst he was in the United Kingdom, Mr Datsa did not forget about the Togoland question. Rather, he seems to have picked up on the connection with the FCB that was forged in August 1948 by G. O. Awuma and Harry Anku Morny, and

74 Annual Report, 1951–2, 11; Annual Report, 1953–4, 36; Annual Report, 1955, 9.

75 Draft version of Mr Datsa's memoir in author's possession – details on extra-mural were cut from the final version due to constraints of space.

76 See, for example, Stephan Miescher, '"My Own Life": A. K. Boakye Yiadom's Autobiography – the Writing and Subjectivity of a Ghanaian Teacher-catechist', in *Africa's Hidden Histories: Everyday Literacy and Making the Self*, ed. Karin Barber (Bloomington IN, 2006), 27–51.

77 I am very grateful to Lynne Brydon for introducing me to Mr Datsa, who taught me a great deal about Togoland. I am also very grateful to Mr Datsa for corresponding with me and allowing me to see his extended draft memoir before the slightly shorter version was completed and published.

joined in the effort to challenge the rather rosy picture that the British government presented to the United Nations in its annual reports on the trust territory. In September 1949, someone called Datsa began writing to the FCB and sent them a copy of the founding document of the Togoland Youth Movement.[78] Initially, the Youth Movement appeared to favour the reunification of the two Togolands, followed by their achievement of self-government with the Gold Coast, and indeed this position had been agreed in 1948 at a joint meeting of the AEC, the Comité de l'Unité Togolaise (CUT), and the Togoland Union – a copy of which was also sent to the FCB.

By February 1950, in the aftermath of the publication of the Coussey report, the position required clarification. Mr Datsa again contacted the FCB with a letter, parts of which he wanted them to publish in their *Venture* magazine. This letter explained that whilst the longer-term goal of the youth was a West African Socialist Republic, in which the two Togolands and the Gold Coast could be joined, their immediate goal was 'National Independence for Togoland as an entity'. Mr Datsa supported the earlier effort of Harry Anku Morny to challenge the image that the British had sought to present to the United Nations. He argued that when the latter announced that it would send a visiting mission to British Togoland in 1949, the administering authority had sought to cover up its neglect of the trust territory: it 'hurriedly sank a few wells', 'a Mass Education team was rushed into the territory', and 'scanty sums of money were granted to certain towns to build community centres'. Mr Datsa emphasised that educational provision in the trust territory was inadequate, and that political freedom was not all that it appeared. In particular, he questioned whether the emergency powers that were used to deal with Nkrumah's Positive Action campaign in the Gold Coast could be legitimately applied to the trust territory.[79]

[78] Rhodes House, MSS.Brit.Emp.s.365, Box 89, file 1: Letter from E. Datsa, secretary-general of the Togoland Youth Movement, 30 Sept 1949.

[79] MSS.Brit.Emp.s.365, Box 89, file 1: Letter from Datsa to FCB 2 Feb 1950. In comparing the signature of Mr Datsa in the FCB correspondence with his signature on other documents, including letters to me, I feel sure that this is the same E. Datsa. Certainly, the name is uncommon, although there is a possibility that some of the letters, particularly those dating from 1950 (i.e. after E. K. Datsa was in the United Kingdom for university), were signed by another E. Datsa – perhaps E. K. Datsa's younger brother, Eliezer. It should be noted that the Togoland Youth Movement also used the name Togoland Youth Association.

After 1950, the letters from the Togoland Youth to the FCB petered out – possibly because of Mr Datsa's extended absence from Togoland, but possibly because the FCB itself began to express doubts as to the feasibility of the reunificationist cause. In fact, in October 1949, in the immediate aftermath of the release of the Coussey report, Reverend Forrester-Paton of the Free Church of Scotland mission wrote to Hinden from his post at Amedzofe with his own views of the Togoland question, which were rather different from those expressed by Mr Datsa. The FCB replied to the Forrester-Paton and then to Mr Datsa, in both cases expressing doubts about the viability of small nations.[80] The following year, faced with continued correspondence from Togolanders, the FCB produced a detailed internal report on the Togoland question. The author (probably Hilda Selwyn-Clarke) accepted that British Togolanders 'had not been consulted on the present set-up', and that, in view of this, their grievances might perhaps be addressed by holding a national constituent assembly. Her own conclusion, however, was that 'fighting for unification is a waste of time', not least because the French were so unlikely to cede their portion of Togoland.[81]

Mr Datsa clearly maintained an awareness of, and concern for, the impact of the Coussey Commission on the status of the trust territory, and, as we shall see in Chapter 6, he was later accused of masterminding the reunificationist project and transferred out of his post at Mawuli school. But in the time that Mr Datsa was away, the organisation of reunificationist sentiment was undergoing a transformation. In the summer of 1949, there was still scope for an agreement between the Togoland Union, the AEC, and the CUT that British and French Togoland could be reunified, with a view to subsequent unification with Ewe-speakers in the Gold Coast. At this stage, there was no necessary conflict with Nkrumah's CPP, and indeed there was some potential for convergence with his longer-term pan-African vision. By the time Mr Datsa returned, the CPP had captured the new organs of elected government which emerged from the Coussey Commission, and had committed themselves explicitly to the integration of British Togoland in a self-governing Gold Coast. Those who believed that the distinct status of the trust territory must be preserved, and that its reunification with

[80] MSS. Brit-Emp.s.365, Box 89, file 1: Letter from FCB to Forrester-Paton, 24 March 1950; letter from Rita Hinden to E. Datsa, 5 April 1950.

[81] MSS. Brit-Emp.s.365, Box 89, file 2: 'Togoland' (n.d. but file labelled 1951–2, author not given, but judging by other correspondence, probably Hilda Selwyn-Clarke).

French Togoland must be prioritised, had reorganised themselves into the Togoland Congress, under the leadership of Senyo Gatro (S. G.) Antor.

'FOUL THREATS AND MURDEROUS CONSPIRACIES'

Finally, then, let us examine this process of reorganisation in response to the Coussey Commission, and suggest why the discourse ethics that were so widely endorsed in PEA and in extra-mural classes did not ultimately govern the ways in which the Togoland question was actually resolved. The reorganisation of reunificationist sentiment under the leadership of S. G. Antor was accompanied not only by rancorous debate in the press, but also by deep personal bitterness, and by accusations that were levied against individuals' characters as much as at the political positions they assumed. Given the pressures imposed by the Coussey Commission and the pace of constitutional reform in the Gold Coast, it is perhaps unsurprising that the ideals of debate espoused within the adult education movement were eroded in a series of urgent and unpalatable choices that were thrust upon Togoland's intelligentsia. And given the tendency of individuals to base their claim to articulate the wider interest of the people on their prior record of service, it is perhaps also unsurprising that politics became very personal. As we shall see in Chapter 4, the divisions that emerged between 1949 and 1951 introduced a particular dynamic into the relationships between reunificationist leaders and their supporters, and they also account – at least in part – for some of the difficulties in mobilising secessionist sentiment after Independence.

Extra-mural classes and PEA events were protected spaces in which matters of interest could be raised and debated. Although these protected spaces, with their explicit rules of engagement, were often conceived as training grounds for self-government, they differed fundamentally from real institutions of government, which were formed with specific geographical and policy remits, and exercised the power to raise and distribute revenue. Between 1949 and 1951, debates over the future of British Togoland became increasingly bitter because individuals had very limited control over the organs that would determine their political future, and they became distrustful of the motivations of those who sought to co-operate with the new institutions that they had had little hand in creating.

Two related disputes were critical in shifting Togoland politics away from debates about what was possible and desirable, towards concrete and unpalatable decisions about how to respond to the nature and pace of change set in Accra and in London. The first dispute concerned the

Enlarged Anglo-French Consultative Commission. This commission was proposed in 1950 as an elected body that could debate specific issues pertaining to the two Togolands but would not have legislative powers. The CUT in the French zone objected strongly to the process by which representatives were selected for the commission, because an indirect election of representatives by chiefs was used instead of direct election of representatives by the people. Both the AEC and the CUT argued that as the chiefs were themselves largely appointed or removed according to the whim of the French administration, the process was intended to exclude anyone who was critical of the French administration, including the CUT itself.[82]

In British Togoland, there were other concerns in the run-up to the elections to the commission. The Togoland Youth Association was anxious about the potential for Gold Coast Ewes to dominate the commission, and about the unsuitability of some of the traditional rulers. It thus resolved that only candidates whose paternal ancestry lay within British Togoland could stand for election, and that all candidates must be literate.[83] The Togoland Union appears to have had similar concerns, because it objected to the provision of a seat to the AEC, which, it claimed, was based in the Gold Coast and could not therefore be represented on a commission that was strictly concerned with the two trust territories. The union also endorsed a literacy qualification for candidates.[84] The leadership of the Togoland Union therefore met with chiefs from the amalgamated states and the non-amalgamated divisions, along with representatives of the Togoland Farmers' Union and the Togoland Youth Association, at a 'congress' in Buem-Borada in early November 1950. The congress decided to petition for a deferment of the first session of the Consultative Commission until the objections from both sides of the border could be 'fairly considered'. Harry Anku Morny gathered the signatures of the representatives and despatched the petition.[85]

82 PRAAD, Accra, 39/1/691: E. Amu, All Ewe Conference, Achimota, to Co-Presidents of the Anglo-French Consultative Commission, 27 Oct 1951.

83 PRAAD Accra, 39/1/691: Resolution re Joint Enlarged Ango-French Consultative Assembly, presented by Togoland Youth Association, 12 Aug 1950.

84 PRAAD Accra, 39/1/691: A Petition from the Togoland Union on the Enlarged Joint / Anglo-French Standing Consultative Commission for Togoland (n.d.) and Representations from the Togoland Union on the Standing Consultative Commission for Togoland, election of representative of Togoland under U.K. Trusteeship (n.d.).

85 PRAAD, Accra, 39/1/691: Resolution by the Supreme Council of the six states of Togo including the three non-amalgamated divisions, the Togo Union, Togo Farmers' Union, Togo Youth Assocation, at Borada-Buem on 3 Nov 1950.

However, the general secretary of the Togoland Union, E. O. Kofi Dumoga, favoured participation and indeed he went further in attempting to forge an agreement between the Togoland Union and the Parti Togolais du Progrès in the French zone.[86] Dumoga appears to have thought that it would be beneficial for the Togoland Union to make a marriage of convenience with le Parti Togolais du Progrès, partly because the latter was opposed to the project of ethnic Ewe unification, and partly because it enjoyed much better relations with the French than did the CUT. Dumoga's effort to conclude such an agreement on behalf of the Togoland Union was quickly and angrily revoked by the rest of the union's leadership and Dumoga was removed from his position as general secretary in mid-November.[87]

Dumoga felt sufficiently strongly about his break with the Togoland Union to respond to a request from the senior district commissioner for information about the organisation of the Togoland Union, in which he named the branch officers and the members of the executive.[88] It is possible that the skeletal outline provided by Dumoga did not increase significantly the district commissioners' understanding of the union membership or agenda, which had been elaborated in other correspondence between the union and the administration. It did, however, connect his own dispute with the union over the Enlarged Anglo-French Consultative Commission to a second dispute, over whether Togolanders should register as voters or organise a boycott of the Gold Coast elections that were scheduled for February 1951.

As we have seen, under the leadership of A. K. Senoo in Hohoe, the Togoland Union wanted to hold the line against any structures that would draw the trust territory into a closer relationship with the Gold Coast. The Togoland Union thus participated in another meeting of the congress of chiefs and political bodies at Buem-Borada on 13 November 1950, at which Senoo claimed there was a clear majority in favour of a boycott of the Gold Coast elections. He therefore pressed the congress' demand for the Southern Togoland Council (of chiefs) to be transformed into an

[86] The correspondence between Dumoga and le Progrès, including a handwritten copy of the convention dated 25 May 1950, is available in PRAAD Ho, DAO (D) 113, Togo Union. Accounts of the dispute are offered in Amenumey, *The Ewe Unification Movement*, 118–33; and Nugent, *Smugglers, Secessionists and Loyal Citizens*, 178–9.

[87] PRAAD Accra, ADM 39/1/691: A. K. Senoo, President of the Togo Union to Governors of British and French Togoland and district commissioners, 6 Dec 1950.

[88] PRAAD, Ho, DAO (D) 113, Togo Union: E. O. Kofi Dumoga, E. P. Senior School, Anfoega Akukome to Senior District Commissioner, Ho, 23 Jan 1951.

elected legislative body, enabling budgetary and administrative autonomy for British Togoland.[89] Presumably, the resolution reflected an acceptance of the unlikeliness that the French would agree to cede their portion of Togoland and a hope that, if British Togoland's separation from the Gold Coast could be maintained in the immediate term, reunification with French Togoland could be effected later on, when the obstacles posed by the French had been overcome. The stance outlined at Borada continued to guide the reunificationists until 1956.

The reunificationist leadership, then, was split between those who wished to participate in the new elected organs – including Dumoga on the Consultative Commission, and G. O. Awuma and F. Y. Asare (from Buem-Borada) in the new Legislative Assembly – and those who wished to hold the line against participation. The latter group, which included those who had been members of the Togoland Union, Togoland Youth Association and Togoland Farmers' Association, were probably surprised by their difficulty in preventing a quarter of the eligible voters in British Togoland from registering for the 1951 Gold Coast elections. They were also infuriated by the victories of Awuma and Asare, both of whom had started their careers within the Togoland Union as reunificationists but, by February 1951, were sat in the Gold Coast Legislative Assembly on the basis of the support of the minority of voters who had registered.

Dumoga appears to have been shocked by the extent of the hostility that was expressed towards him by those reunificationists who favoured the boycott. In correspondence with his friend and mentor, Awuma, he complained that 'Anku Morny, Batse and other Hohoe gentlemen' [i.e. the leadership of the Togoland Union] were making 'defamatory pronouncements against me'.[90] Dumoga felt that he was the victim of a character assassination attempt in which he was reported to have accepted £2000 plus a government scholarship in exchange for his attempts to persuade people in British Togoland to participate in the Consultative Commission. He also believed that his enemies in Hohoe and in Anfoega had turned Reverend Motte against him, which led to discrimination against him within the Evangelical Presbyterian education unit:

[89] PRAAD, Accra, 39/1/691: Letter from Togo Union to Secretary-General of the United Nations, 13 Nov 1950, signed by A. K. Senoo, and containing Resolutions of the Natural Rulers, States, Native Authorities, Principal Political Bodies and Organisations and People of Togo Under United Kingdom Trusteeship.

[90] PRAAD Accra, 39/1/691: Letter from Dumoga to Awuma, 1 June 1951.

> Apart from the salary one receives, prestige also counts and to some us the latter even matters more. Since my coming here [to the Evangelical Presbyterian School at Anfoega] I have been made to work on the staff of my juniors and less efficient teachers as headmasters and even now under my own old school boys as head-teachers. Is this not very insulting?[91]

Dumoga was discovering to his cost that if a claim to articulate the interests of Togoland could be made on the basis of a track record of service and evidence of good character, so this process could also work in reverse: his political stance was undermined, partly by the arguments that the other reunificationists continued to make about the appropriate forums for resolving the Togoland question, but partly also by intense scrutiny of his personal motivations.

If Dumoga was upset by this, Awuma was angry, particularly with Antor, whom he blamed for the closing of ranks by those who had endorsed a boycott strategy at the Buem-Borada congresses of November 1950. After receiving several letters from Dumoga about his treatment at the hands of the Togoland Unionists, Awuma wrote directly to Antor – who was then in New York, representing the reunificationists at the United Nations – and accused him of leading a 'fanatic Boycott Party' and mobilising the population 'through every unscrupulous form of malicious false propaganda' including 'foul threats and murderous conspiracies'.[92] Awuma also believed that he was himself the victim of a character assassination attempt at the hands of Kodzo Ayeke, who was writing about the Togoland question in the Gold Coast press under the pseudonym 'Adjisam's Special Political Observer'. As the son of a pastor, and as a trained teacher who had travelled through Europe, spoke three European languages, and was now representing the Togolanders of Asogli in the new Legislative Assembly, Awuma objected to being criticised by Ayeke, whom he described as 'an embittered junior Customs employee, dismissed for insubordination, who now wanders about without a job'.[93] Awuma also accused Antor of abusing his influence over 'the masses whose imagination ... is darkened by illiteracy and ignorance' by fabricating a letter which threw into question the commitment of Mote Kofi II of Asogli to the reunificationist cause and implied that the chief was nothing but a puppet of Awuma himself.

The rapid turn of events between 1949 and 1951 moved the Togoland question out of the realm of debate and into the realm of reality. The

[91] PRAAD Accra, 39/1/691: Letter from Dumoga to Awuma, 25 May 1951.
[92] PRAAD Accra, 39/1/691: Letter from Awuma to Antor, 5 June 1951. [93] Ibid.

extra-mural classes and the PEA weekend conferences continued, and they were enjoyed by numerous articulate and assertive individuals who were keen to dissect the arguments about the future of the trust territory. But the rules of discourse that governed the extra-mural class discussion and the PEA weekend conference debate clearly did not govern the exchanges between individuals as they realigned themselves behind new political organisations and agendas. Those who favoured a boycott were bitterly opposed to those who favoured participation, and both sides comprised individuals who had staked their claims in similar ways: a track record of service that gave them a privileged insight into the needs of the people, and a level of educational attainment that would enable them articulate those needs to others. Individuals interrogated each other's characteristics and motivations, and often found each other wanting: the political was personal. But having been caught on the back foot in the legislative elections of 1951, the reunificationists now recognised the need to wrest control of the new elected institutions away from those who argued that the inclusion of the trust territory in the Gold Coast would serve its people's interests. Under the leadership of S. G. Antor, then, those who had participated in the congresses at Buem-Borada formed a new political party, the Togoland Congress, which continued to press the reunificationist case at the United Nations, whilst fielding its own candidates in local, district, and legislative elections until 1958. It is to this new movement and its work of political persuasion that we must now turn.

4

Revealing Stepfather's Secrets

Making and Losing the Case for Togoland Reunification

In the previous chapter we saw how pressures from London, New York, and Accra influenced the nature and timing of debates on the future of British Togoland, and how people integrated local, territorial, and international developments into their deliberations on the different possibilities of citizenship. In focussing on the new forums that were opened up through adult education, I demonstrated that 'political cosmopolitanism' was not restricted to a tiny elite, but permeated the growing population of literate English-speaking schools leavers in the small towns and villages of the trust territory.[1] This chapter considers how such debates were 'vernacularised' amongst a larger and more diverse electorate: through processes of translation into written and spoken Ewe, through linkages between ideas about *Ablɔɖe* (freedom) and a range of local grievances, and through scrutiny of the motivations and reliability of the individuals who acted as spokespersons.[2] Having considered how the case for Togoland reunification was made, I will then explain how it was lost.

Bitter disagreements amongst the reunificationists between 1949 and 1951 provide de facto evidence of the divisive potential of tactical dilemmas, localised disputes, and personal vendettas. But after the Gold Coast elections of 1951, and particularly after the local government reforms of 1952, the reunificationists confronted a British-CPP diarchy

[1] Meredith Terretta, *Nation of Outlaws, State of Violence: Nationalism, Grassfields Tradition and State-Building in Cameroon* (Athens OH, 2014), 5.

[2] Ibid., 6. Terretta uses the term 'vernacularization' but emphasises the ways in which international political discourses – and particularly 'human rights talk' – became integrated with Cameroonian nationalism.

which had consolidated its control over the electoral, administrative, and diplomatic structures within which the Togoland question had to be resolved. It therefore became imperative for those who opposed the integration of the trust territory with the Gold Coast, and favoured reunification with French Togoland, to gain demonstrable popular support in subsequent electoral contests. It was against this background that S. G. Antor, a trained teacher from Logba, set out to reorganise reunificantionist sentiment, to establish the Togoland Congress as the dominant reunificationist organisation, and to marshal popular support behind its chosen vision of self-government and strategies for achieving it.

Antor would no doubt have related to Frederick Cooper's reflection that 'politics takes doing: it implies persuading people to think of linkages they may not have perceived before'.[3] This chapter, then, explores the work of persuasion through an examination of some of the print propaganda and oral texts that were produced in Ewe and in English and circulated in the small towns and villages of southern British Togoland. At the most obvious level, print propaganda provided a means by which leaders might win over the undecided by constructing and circulating arguments against integration and in favour of reunification. Here, I identify those arguments and demonstrate how they intersected with the popular chant and song that was invented and enacted in the trust territory.

Print, however, was more than just a vehicle for rhetoric or an opportunity to mobilise locally embedded ideas behind the reunificationist cause. It also offered some more distinctive means by which writers sought to enhance their credibility. The defections or expulsions of G. O. Awuma, F. Y. Asare and E. O. Kofi Dumoga in 1950–1 were significant for the evolution of the relationship between leading spokespersons of the Togoland Congress and their grassroots supporters. Formal education was accepted as a prerequisite for the representation of Togoland interests in Gold Coast and international forums, but it could no longer be regarded as a guarantee of constancy or efficacy. Spokespersons could use printed materials to appeal to shared reasoning and solidarity of objective, but authors were also aware of the potential for distrust and suspicion on the part of their readership and worked hard to overcome this.

By obtaining printed matter from political opponents, and quoting from it in their own work, reunificationist spokesmen exposed the secret

[3] Frederick Cooper, *Africa Since 1940: The Past of the Present* (Cambridge, 2002), 48.

intentions of those who sought to subvert the Togoland cause. By warning their readerships of these plans to deceive them, authors of both Ewe and English texts demonstrated that literacy enabled them to undermine the esoteric basis of their opponents' illegitimate power. Authors thereby cast the Togoland question in terms of a binary division between their opponents and themselves, suggesting that whilst the former relied on secrecy and deception to wield power over others, the latter were engaged in the work of enlightening people as to their true interests, and could therefore claim both the technical skills to articulate those interests and the moral authority to represent them.[4] When those texts were published abroad, their very physical presence back in the trust territory provided concrete evidence of spokespersons' efforts to articulate Togolanders' interests and mobilise external support for their cause, particularly at the United Nations.

PRINT POLITICS AND A 'DEMOCRACY OF CONTENT'

The texts considered here do not come from a series that is catalogued in any national archive. They were acquired piecemeal, from people who attended rallies as observers, or from people whose work as grassroots activists required them to transport, sell, and interpret texts. Whilst there is an undeniable element of chance in the selection presented here, there is also coherence, in the sense that the authors of these texts were known to one another, and engaged in exchange and dialogue beyond the printed page. The first text, *Togo Nukae Hiawo?* (Togo, What do you Need?), was written in Ewe by G. K. Tsekpo, whom we encountered in Chapter 3 as the owner of a printing press in Hohoe. As the chair of the Ewe Presbyterian Literature Committee, Tsekpo had both authored and edited texts which, while of varying genres (novels, short stories, plays, hymn books, farmers' almanacs), shared an objective in stimulating moral scrutiny and self-improvement among an Ewe-language readership. He established the Hope Press (which produced membership cards for the Togoland Union) in Hohoe in the late 1940s, and later appears to have moved to Accra where he opened the Mawuli Press. By 1955, Tsekpo was publishing his own Ewe-language newspaper, *Mia Denyigba* (Our Homeland), whilst by 1961 he had moved his press to Lomé, where

[4] For a comparative perspective on 'the division of textual labour and the ownership of knowledge', and the possession of secrets, see Karin Barber, *The Anthropology of Texts, Persons, and Publics: Oral and Written Culture in Africa and Beyond* (Cambridge, 2007), 86–101.

he was living in exile.[5] In 1953, the publication of *Togo Nukae Hiawo?* represented a major contribution to the debate on the future of Togoland, but it is not wholly clear why Tsekpo decided to have it printed by the West African Graphic Company in Accra.[6]

Both of the English-language texts considered here were published abroad. Theodore O. Asare's *The Case for a Reunited Togoland* was published in New York in 1953, where he was serving as a member of the bar (i.e. a lawyer). Asare was probably born in the Twi-speaking area of Worawora, approximately 30 miles NNE of the cocoa-marketing town of Hohoe.[7] He was unusual among Togolanders in qualifying as a lawyer, having studied at Lincoln University, Pennsylvania (Nkrumah's alma mater). He later served under the Convention People's Party (CPP) government as Ghana's first ambassador to Germany, but in 1953 he argued the reunificationist case.[8]

The best known of all the reunificationist texts, however, was *"Most Secret" Politics in Togoland*, edited by S. G. Antor and Paul Ecker, and published in New York with the assistance of the Movement for the Democracy of Content.[9] *"Most Secret"* achieved notoriety because within its pages Antor and Ecker claimed to have uncovered a British-CPP strategy for ensuring the integration of the trust territory with the Gold Coast. Brown comments on the significance of *"Most Secret"* in staving

[5] I found one copy of this newspaper in the Togolese national archives, Lomé, file Klouto 226. It appears that the commandant de cercle (whose position was equivalent to that of the district commissioner in the British zone) was monitoring the circulation of *Mia Denyigba* and thought it had subversive potential.

[6] G.K. Tsekpo, *Togo Nukae Hiawo?* (Accra, 1953). I am grateful to Richard Salifu for help with translating this text.

[7] Interview with Michael Senoo and Richard Banibensu, Dansoman, Greater Accra, 14 Aug 2000. According to Ivor Wilks, this area fell within the eastern frontier of the greater Asante empire, and much of it was controlled 'through the agency of a group of Kwawu colonists there, the Dokoman'. See *Asante in the Nineteenth Century: The Structure and Evolution of a Political Order* (Cambridge, 1975), 58. The Worawora Development Club, however, indicate that the people of Worawora in particular are the direct descendants of Asante migrants who came from Kuntanase via Nkonya in the mid-eighteenth century. See http://woradec.webs.com/historyofworawora.htm [last accessed 16 Dec 2013].

[8] See his entry in www.lincoln.edu/library/Yrbook-pdfs/Yearbook_1950.pdf [last accessed 30 Apr 2015].

[9] T.O. Asare, *The Case for a Reunited Togoland: Nkabum ne Biakoye* (New York, 1953) and *"Most Secret" Politics in Togoland: The British Government's Attempt to Annex Togoland to the Gold Coast*, ed. S. G. Antor and P. Ecker (New York, c.1954). The Twi expression *nkabɔmu ne biakoyɛ* literally means 'union and unity'. However, *nkabɔmu* also implies 'union in order to achieve something' and therefore the sense conveyed in this subtitle may be 'progress through unity'. I am grateful to Tom McCaskie for his comments on this.

off CPP attempts to win support in the trust territory in the 1954 election campaign. In quoting from the British-CPP strategy for achieving integration, Antor closed down any scope for local or regional CPP leaders to claim that the party had an open stance on the Togoland question or that the central committee would be prepared to negotiate with Togolanders who transferred their votes to the party.[10]

The CPP must have taken the publication of *"Most Secret"* seriously, because they retaliated with the publication of their own text, *Togoland and Gold Coast: 'Forward Together to Freedom'*. In distributing this text prior to the 1954 election campaign, the CPP signified that it was no longer attempting to delay or obfuscate on the Togoland question: voters should be clear that the party was for integration, and they needed to be persuaded that the alternatives (particularly Togoland reunification) would not serve their interests. *Togoland and Gold Coast* circulated the arguments that were made by S. Togbe Fleku, the CPP's regional secretary, when he appeared at the Trusteeship Council.[11] In addition to the reaction that it provoked from the CPP, however, *"Most Secret"* is particularly interesting because it reveals the diversity and the eclecticism of Antor's political networks.

The Movement for the Democracy of Content was (ironically) a secretive organisation. Despite some intriguing research by Marcel van der Linden, which revealed the identities of several key members, 'Paul Ecker' was among those who insisted on maintaining anonymity.[12] It is therefore difficult to establish exactly how Antor met Ecker or the circumstances in which they decided to co-author this pamphlet. A brief description of the movement, however, will suggest some likely points of contact and mutual interest. The movement's explicit activity began with the first publication, in June 1947, of the German magazine *Dinge der Zeit – Zeitschrift für inhaltliche Demokratie* (Contemporary Issues – Journal for a Democracy of Content).[13] This publication operated alongside an English counterpart, *Contemporary Issues*, and the magazines served as the basis of discussion group meetings in New York, Cologne, and Gelsenkirchen by 1951.

[10] Brown, 'Politics in the Kpandu Area of Ghana', 290, fn 57.

[11] See Nugent, *Smugglers, Secessionists and Loyal Citizens*, 195–6; Amenumey, *The Ewe Unification Movement*, 145.

[12] Marcel van der Linden, 'The Pre-History of *Post-Scarcity Anarchism*: Josef Weber and the Movement for a Democracy of Content (1947–1964)', *Anarchist Studies* 9 (2001), 127–45.

[13] I am grateful to Insa Nolte for assisting me with this translation.

The founder member of the movement was Josef Weber, who was born in the Ruhr, and worked as a 'bandmaster, composer and pianist' alongside his political activities before fleeing to France.[14] Many of the other early members were German émigrés who had shared Weber's trajectory of support for the Communist Party in the aftermath of the November Rising of 1918, followed by disillusionment with Stalinism and a shift towards the international Trotskyist movement. During the time he spent in France as an exile, Weber was one of founder members of the Fourth International in 1938, and he long continued to share both its concern about the authoritarianism of the Stalin regime and its belief that a revolutionary movement must be international in scope and membership. In the aftermath of the Second World War, however, Weber broke with the Trotskyists by formulating a distinctive utopian vision for the future, which also appealed to a younger group of Americans, including Paul Ecker and Murray Bookchin.

It is likely that Antor met Ecker in New York in December 1952 (when he appeared at the seventh session of the Fourth Committee of the General Assembly to debate the findings of the United Nations visiting mission to Togoland) and in November 1953 (when he attended the eighth session, which debated the implications of the White Paper issued by the Government of the Gold Coast on the future of Togoland). Under the intellectual leadership of Weber, the movement sought to mobilise people all over the world against 'internal bureaucratisation'. Members were deeply sceptical of political party organisation, and believed that party leaders, like those who led the trade unions, were susceptible to the particular dynamics of bureaucracy: '[they] gain influence, power, positions, privileges, high salaries, even fortunes; they get well embedded in bourgeois society, lower the intellectual level to zero and sacrifice everything ... except their positions.'[15]

The morally and intellectually degenerative effects of bureaucracy were to be challenged through 'a worldwide movement for a democracy of content', which was less concerned with disseminating ready-made tenets and agendas, and more with stimulating mobilisation across the world through 'democratic publication'. Weber's vision was a magazine that would 'state everything that needed to be said', thus contributing to a 'polis' – 'an assembly of citizens with equal rights who come voluntarily

[14] van der Linden, 'The Pre-History of *Post-Scarcity Anarchism*'.

[15] Josef Weber as cited in van der Linden, 'The Pre-History of *Post-Scarcity Anarchism*', 131.

together for common deliberation, everybody speaks as it is given to him [sic] and how he [sic] pleases'.[16] The wide range of issues that were highlighted within *Contemporary Issues*, and the discussions groups that formed around the magazine, were intended to underpin a utopian vision of an international participatory democracy.[17]

It is not difficult to understand why Antor might have been attracted to such a vision. As we saw in Chapter 3, extra-mural classes and the People's Education Association became popular in southern British Togoland partly because they tapped into enthusiasm for discursive forums in which individuals participated as equals and addressed the international context of local and territorial issues. But, given the frustrations of so many African petitioners at the United Nations, it is also likely that Antor shared some of the movement's scepticism with what we might call 'formal democracy', and a concern that, now they were in a power-sharing arrangement with the British, the apparent radicalism of the CPP had been easily diverted into consolidating and rendering permanent the integration of the trust territory with the Gold Coast.

D. E. K. Amenumey explains very well how African petitioners at the Trusteeship Council consistently found that structures which appeared to provide channels for protest, and thereby ensure accountability of the administering authorities, could in fact be used to limit the scope to express dissenting views.[18] Petitioners pressing for an ethnic Ewe homeland came up against the barrier that the Trusteeship Council could make recommendations only on matters pertaining to the two trust territories, and not to the Ewe-speakers of the Gold Coast. In effect, it was not possible for the All Ewe Conference (AEC) to have its 'whole' case for an Ewe homeland examined or resolved. Even petitioners who prioritised the reunification of the two trust territories found that the British and French administering authorities were loath to criticise one another. Petitioners, then, had to drum up support from the 'non-administering members' if they were to have any hope of getting the council to pass a favourable resolution.

[16] Josef Weber as cited in van der Linden, 'The Pre-History of *Post-Scarcity Anarchism*', 130 and 133.

[17] In 1956, New York groups of the movement launched a solidarity campaign with the rebels in the Hungarian Rising, whilst the Johannesburg group participated in the People's Transport Committees during the Alexandria bus boycott of 1957.

[18] Amenumey, *The Ewe Unification Movement*, 187–204.

After 1951, African petitioners preferred to press their case at the Fourth Committee of the General Assembly, where they expected to find a greater concentration of anti-colonial sentiment. But as the administering authority began to argue that British Togoland would benefit from continued administrative union with the Gold Coast, which was making rapid constitutional progress, and as the CPP began to position itself as the party of 'Self-Government Now!', the reunificationists sensed the potential for them to be outmanoeuvred there too. In this sense, print gave the reunificationists scope to set out their 'whole' case on their own terms – something they had always struggled to do in the more formalised and bureaucratic structures of the United Nations. And in bringing printed matter from America for sale at rallies in the trust territory, Antor was able to provide physical proof of his efforts to position the Togoland question as an international issue and to attract the kind of external support that would benefit a future independent Togoland state.

NATIONALS AND FOREIGNERS

In all the written texts, historical narratives were used to represent a prior state of unity, establish causes of disunity, and suggest the appropriate steps to eradicate conflict. Common to these narratives was a concern to establish the proper basis of nationhood, and all authors employed two methods: firstly, they sought to define categories of 'we' and 'they'; secondly, they argued that the social and economic development of the 'we' group would best be served by a particular political settlement. Reunificationists seized the initiative in shifting the argument away from ideals of unity that were based on an ethnic Ewe identity, emphasising instead the potential of colonial systems to bind Africans together into national processes of social and economic development whose character was determined by that of the mother country. For them, the 'we' group was not 'the Ewe', but rather those people whose first experiences of biomedicine, formal schooling, and infrastructural development had been shaped by a German tradition.

Asare therefore emphasised the rupture and disunity that had resulted from the partition of Togoland between Britain and France:

> As education began to develop and as new political institutions took shape ... It became quite clear to both groups of Togolanders that these policies, if they were continued, would make the two regions as different from each other as Great Britain and France and result in complete absorbtion [sic] of the two trust territories into their respective colonies and/or political systems.

> Recognising this eventuality, the leaders ... are seeking unification of the two regions making Togoland again one nation and one cultural group as they originally were.[19]

The non-ethnic basis of nationhood presented by the reunificationists was inclusive of the plethora of non-Ewe minorities living in the southern section, and indeed several leading members of the Togoland Congress (including Antor himself) originated from these areas. Hence Tsekpo, despite writing in Ewe, was not appealing to an exclusionist ethnic sentiment. His text rather claimed that differences of language and custom were less important than the role of Germany, the 'mother' country, in the construction of a national Togoland identity: 'If something hits and kills a hen, the chicks will gather together in one part of the hutch. They do not go to another chick's mother. They will stick together and help to feed one another ... White fowl, black fowl, red fowl or any fowl, are all towns of Togo.'[20] A corollary of this Togoland identity was the reunificationist portrayal of the Togoland Congress as a national liberation movement, and the CPP as a foreign and intrusive political party.[21] Thus, Asare complained: 'As a direct result of the New Constitution of the Gold Coast, the business of government in the Gold Coast has now become a game of party politics, and Togoland has been made a football in the game.'[22]

Although the Togoland Congress was being forced, rather than choosing, to play the CPP at its own game, after the debacle of the February 1951 elections it also committed itself to winning any future contests, and this meant countering the potential appeal of the CPP. The CPP was a slippery opponent in the Togoland question: on the one hand, it could claim to be the future Ghana's only nationwide anti-colonial party and the one with the best prospect of hastening the end of colonial rule; on the other hand, it also appealed to ethnic sentiment in British Togoland by arguing that a higher proportion of the trust territory's population would achieve unity with ethnic kin through integration. Thus in *Togoland and Gold Coast*, Fleku presented the following case:

[19] Antor, 'Preface' in *"Most Secret"*, 3; and Asare, *Case for a Reunited Togoland*, 10.
[20] Tsekpo, *Togo Nukae Hiawo?*, 6–7.
[21] The distinction between nationalist movement and political party was also made in Asante politics in the mid-1950s, although it was employed to a different end. See Jean Allman, *The Quills of the Porcupine: Asante Nationalism in an Emergent Ghana* (Madison WI, 1993), 110.
[22] Asare, *Case for a Reunited Togoland*, 17.

> The figures indicate that under the existing arrangement nearly three-fourths of the total number of the Ewe population live under British administration in the Gold Coast and British Togoland ... Would it not be misguided for more than three-fourths of the Ewe population to refuse or to be denied the attainment of self-government on the plea that the remaining one-fourth in French territory is not yet in a position to do so?[23]

Fleku tried to claim the legacy of the AEC for the integrationist position, reminding readers that the AEC had 'never envisaged that Ewe unification would take place except in association with the Gold Coast'.[24]

Antor, on the other hand, included in *"Most Secret"* a copy of a petition signed by I. K. Atiogbe, the acting general secretary of the AEC, which deprecated the tactics deployed by the CPP and the administering authorities in promoting the integrationist agenda.[25] The AEC had in fact divided. Although AEC founder-member Daniel Chapman was won over to the CPP, other AEC members – notably Albert Simpson – met with Antor and with representatives of the Comité de l'Unité Togolaise (CUT) at Denu in July 1954 to agree on a common strategy: they would press for a directly elected Joint Togoland Council and for a plebiscite that would cover both British and French Togoland.[26] This agreement was publicised in another pamphlet, which was sold in the trust territory for the price of 3d.[27] Both the reunificationists and the integrationists may have been seeking to capitalise on any remaining prestige or sympathy that attached to the AEC, but it was undoubtedly Fleku who laid the greatest emphasis on ethnicity in his propaganda. Fleku thus insisted that the Togoland Congress was 'afraid to be honest with the people' about how Togoland reunification would entail 'separation of the Buems, the Akans and the Krachis from their kinsmen in the Gold Coast' and 'the splitting in two of the Dagombas, the Gonjas, the Mamprusis and the Kusasis in the north'.[28]

[23] Fleku, *Togoland and Gold Coast*, 5–6. Fleku estimated that 476,000 Ewes were living under British administration.

[24] Fleku, *Togoland and Gold Coast*, 4.

[25] Petition from I. K. Atiogbe to the Secretary-General of the United Nations, 25 July 1953, cited in *"Most Secret"*, 8–9.

[26] Interview with Daniel Chapman, Nyaho Clinic, Airport Residential, Greater Accra, 21 Sept 2000. Chapman explained to me that he had become disillusioned with the CPP after Independence, but that he had never regretted the integration of British Togoland with Ghana.

[27] *The Togoland Re-Unification Problem* (n.d). A copy of this pamphlet was shown to me by E. K. Gavu of Dzogbofeme-Avatime.

[28] Fleku, *Togoland and Gold Coast*, 4.

The reunificationists attempted to shift the argument away from headcounts of the various 'tribes', to focus instead on the nature of self-government, and to explain why self-government as part of the Gold Coast was not self-government for Togoland at all: it was an annexation manoeuvred by a colonial stooge. Thus in his Introduction to *"Most Secret"*, Ecker condemned the CPP for supporting the integrationist agenda of the administering authority without securing a popular mandate for it:

> imperialism sooner or later in almost every case, must call upon a "native", properly educated in the ruler's "civilising mission", to assume the robes of government and supply the pretence of self-government for a hostile population ...
>
> ... he may appear to conduct a struggle against the very ruling forces whose interests in the last analysis he is on the scene to protect ... he is a figure deeply cynical, a Quisling, a Gottwald or a Chiang Kai-Shek.[29]

Ecker appears to have conceived of Nkrumah as a man in the grip of 'internal bureaucratisation', gradually abandoning his anti-colonial radicalism as he became engaged in the daily work of 'Leader of Government Business' and recognised the administrative convenience of integration. Ecker also castigated the United Nations for its failure to stand firm in the face of the administering authorities' attempts to effect an integrationist '*anschluß*'.[30] Asare, meanwhile, recalled the Italian invasion of Ethiopia in 1935, which he saw as an example of the international community failing to take stringent measures to defend small nations.[31]

This was not simply a rhetorical flourish designed to prick the consciences of United Nations delegates in New York. It spoke directly to the experiences of grassroots activists back at home. Whilst reunificationist spokesmen pressed the United Nations on the need for the administering authorities to convene, as a matter of urgency, a directly elected Joint Togoland Council, activists in the local and district councils came face-to-face with the integrationist implications of local government reform. In the Trans-Volta Togoland Regional Council and in the new local and district councils, which had been recommended by the Coussey Commission and established in 1952–3, Ewe-speaking areas belonging to the Gold Coast were mixed in with parts of the southern section of the trust territory.

Thus, whilst the administering authority presented the shift towards elected local government as a form of 'progress' for the trust territory,

29 Ecker, in 'Introduction', *"Most Secret"*, 4.

30 The term 'anschluß' is used in the original text, and refers to the annexation of Austria by Nazi Germany in 1938.

31 Ecker, in *"Most Secret"*, 24; Asare, *The Case for a Reunited Togoland*, 29.

within the Dzigbe Local Council, Councillor Kodzo Ayeke secured unanimous support for a resolution protesting against the inclusion of any part of the Gold Coast in the Ho District Council.[32] In 1954, Ayeke was elected to the Legislative Assembly on the reunificationist ticket. Exactly the same issue was debated in the Gbi-Hohoe Local Council, which objected to the inclusion of Peki-Guan (whose territory lay in the Gold Coast) in the Kpandu District Council and in the Akpini electoral district.[33] In June 1953, Antor, who had been elected to the East Dain Local Council, led a rancorous debate on whether the council should even send a representative to the Trans-Volta Togoland Regional Council. He was narrowly defeated on this matter – presumably because other councillors feared that unless they were represented they would not be able secure funding for local development projects.[34]

Chants and songs cast these issues in terms of a distinction between 'nationals' (Togolanders) and 'foreigners' (Gold Coasters) and implied that the latter could not legitimately lead or represent the former. Many of these Ewe-language chants and songs were invented by women, who sang them during the course of gender-segregated everyday work and at rallies which they attended together with men.[35] The CPP was often referred to as *Akokɔ* (meaning cockerel in Twi), which was the party's symbol. Ewe-language chants distinguished between 'natives' of Togoland, who were assumed to be supporters of reunification, and the 'foreigners' who backed the CPP: '*CPP-tɔwoe, Miyi afee, Togoviwo l'Ablɔḑe me!*' ('CPP people, go home, the children of Togo are living in freedom!').[36] Similar distinctions were also conveyed in interviews with party supporters. One man from Alavanyo (near Kpandu) explained, 'We did not want anyone coming here from that side to rule us', and another, from Hohoe, described Nkrumah as 'someone who came in the Gold Coast, he came in Accra and he wanted to extend his arm'.[37]

[32] PRAAD, Ho, DAO (D) 214, Dzigbe Local Council: minutes of 21 April 1953.

[33] PRAAD, Ho, DAO (D), 219, Gbi-Hohoe Local Council: minutes of 10 Sept 1953.

[34] PRAAD, Ho, DAO (D) 218, East Dain Local Council: minutes of 15 June 1953.

[35] Interview in Ewe with Mercy Akosua Tegbe, Hohoe, 19 Sept 2000 (translation by Lydia Osei-Brantuo).

[36] I am grateful to Gladys Akoli of Taviefe for providing me with a tape recording of this and other reunificationist songs and chants, and to Richard Banibensu (former tutor at the Institute of Adult Education, Legon) for translating them.

[37] Interview in Ewe with Cleophas Ntsri, Alavanyo-Agoxoe, 19 Sept 2000 (translations by Rose Ntsri and Lydia Osei-Brantuo), and interview with Rev E. T. Adiku, Hohoe, 13 Sept 2000. Both Hohoe and Alavanyo were Togoland Congress strongholds.

In principle, then, Togoland nationalism embraced the different peoples of both the northern and southern sections of the British trust territory, and aimed to separate it from the Gold Coast in order to reunite it with the French zone. In this respect, reunificationist demands in the mid-1950s were quite different from the demands that had been made by the AEC in the late 1940s for an ethnic Ewe homeland. In practice, however, differences between the northern and southern sections posed a problem to the reunificationists.

German-led infrastructural development was indeed impressive, but the construction of railways in the south and centre of Togoland relied heavily on labour extracted in lieu of cash payment of taxes, whilst German-owned companies – including those that established cotton plantations – also depended on government recruitment of labourers to work under long contracts, in gruelling conditions, and for pay that barely met their subsistence needs.[38] The extraction of labour in lieu of cash payment of taxes was common throughout Togo, and in this respect people everywhere paid the price for infrastructural development, but labour recruitment on behalf of companies was particularly vigorous in the northern districts. Arguably people in the south and centre subsequently derived greater benefit from the railways, as here conditions were more favourable for new cash crops, such as cocoa and coffee, which were embraced by independent African producers in the first half of the twentieth century, whilst the northern districts once again supplied labour. German missionary access to southern Togoland was much easier, and educational provision was therefore more abundant than was the case in the northern section, which also advantaged southerners in the exchange sector.

Thus, whilst the political boundaries on a map created vertical lines between the Gold Coast and the two Togolands, the trust territories were themselves divided on a socio-economic basis, with lines that were

[38] Donna Maier, 'Slave Labor and Wage Labor in German Togo, 1885–1914', in *Germans in the Tropics: Essays in German Colonial History*, ed. Arthur Knoll and Lewis Gann (New York, 1987), 73–92. See also Ulrike Schuerkens, *Du Togo allemand aux Togo et Ghana indépendants: changement social sous régime coloniale*, (Paris, 2001), 57. For a more general critique of German administration and the use of forced labour, see Manfred Nüßbaum, *Togo, Eine Musterkolonie?* (Berlin, 1962) and Arthur Knoll, *Togo Under Imperial Germany, 1884–1914: A Case Study in Colonial Rule* (Stanford, 1978). For a recent study of cotton in Togo see Andrew Zimmerman, *Alabama in Africa: Booker T. Washington, the German Empire, and the Globalization of the New South* (Princeton NJ, 2010).

horizontal, dividing north from south. Reunificationist propaganda, then, was not 'ethnic' in the sense that it referred exclusively to the Ewe, but the 'we' group that such propaganda most successfully mobilised was, in effect, 'we the southern Togolanders'. As we shall see at the end of this chapter, the north/south divide proved highly significant in the results of the plebiscite and in the United Nations' interpretation thereof, and thereby influenced the form that self-government would ultimately take.

'SEEK YE FIRST THE POLITICAL KINGDOM'

Having established the 'we' group which they hoped to mobilise, the authors of propaganda texts then proceeded to marshal the evidence that their own political solution would provide the path to more rapid and far-reaching socio-economic development. According to Paul Nugent, the Togoland Congress made a tactical error in aligning itself too closely with the 'natural rulers' (chiefs) and the commercial cocoa farmers, who were but a minority of the electorate, leaving the CPP ample space to promote its vision of developmentalist decolonisation, which had a wider appeal. Accepting that the British administration had done little in terms of amenity development or infrastructural improvement in the trust territory, the first CPP government awarded a special development grant to the Trans-Volta Togoland Region.[39] It thus held out the promise that the neglect experienced under British administration would not be repeated if the trust territory achieved its Independence as part of Ghana. In specific localities, such as Anfoega, which had been denied access to development funds throughout the 1940s as a result of its refusal to join one of the new amalgamated 'native states' initiated by the British, the CPP was able to appeal to local opinion leaders, including the commoners in the home-town improvement societies and those chiefs who positioned themselves as modernisers. Nugent thus concludes that the CPP was able to synchronise local dynamics with the 'modernist myth around which Ghanaian independence was built'.[40]

The reunificationist case was more complex, but Antor's concern with cocoa, and the financial support he received from farmers, should not be understood purely in terms of alignment with an interest group. Had this been the case, Antor would probably have pressed for a free market in cocoa for the trust territory, thereby enabling producers to openly sell

[39] Nugent, *Smugglers, Secessionists and Loyal Citizens*, 187. [40] Ibid., 197.

their crops across the border in French Togoland where prices were higher. In addition to his contacts with the Movement for a Democracy of Content in New York, however, Antor also followed up the older contacts that G. O. Awuma and Harry Anku Morny had initiated with the Fabian Colonial Bureau (FCB) in London. It is clear from the reunificationists' correspondence with the FCB that they were not seeking a free market in cocoa, but a separate Cocoa Marketing Board for the trust territory.[41]

Producers were certainly aware of price differentials, and given that not all of the producers were even Togolanders, their preference for selling in French Togoland, rather than to the (Gold Coast) Cocoa Marketing Board, might be interpreted, à la Polly Hill, in terms of the rational choice of *homo economicus*.[42] What Antor sought to highlight, however, was the specific connection between cocoa production and sale, and the relative infrastructural backwardness of the trust territory. Producers were sensitive not only to price differentials, but also to transport costs. This was raised at the Dzigbe Local Council meeting in March 1953, when councillors complained that 'people made great losses in the high transport rates by carting Dzigbe Local Council Area cocoa via Senchi-Accra at the rate of 9d on a load of 60lbs, whilst 3d a load was chargeable through Palime [Kpalimé in French Togoland]'.[43] A substantial proportion of the special development grant to the Trans-Volta Togoland Region had been earmarked for a highly visible infrastructural improvement in the form of a motorable bridge over the river Volta. This was intended both to counter the perception of neglect of the trust territory and to facilitate the transport of goods from the east to

[41] Clippings from the *Togoland Vanguard* were sent to the FCB and can be found at Rhodes House, Oxford, MSS.Brit.Emp.s.365, Box 89, file 3. They indicate that Coleman was incorrect in suggesting that British Togoland farmers wanted a free market in cocoa. Here, I agree with Nugent in suggesting that a separate Togoland marketing board was their preferred alternative, but I offer a different interpretation of the political implications of this preference. See J. S. Coleman, 'Togoland', *International Conciliation* 509 (1956), 2–91 at 36; and Nugent, *Smugglers, Secessionists and Loyal Citizens*, 186.

[42] There is a venerable scholarly tradition of analysing the Ghanaian cocoa farmer as a *homo economicus*, starting with Polly Hill, *Migrant Cocoa Farmers of Southern Ghana: A Study in Rural Capitalism* (Oxford, 1998 [1963]). For a more recent analysis see Gareth Austin, *Labour, Land and Capital in Ghana: From Slavery to Free Labour in Asante, 1807–1956* (Rochester NY, 2005).

[43] PRAAD, Ho, DAO(D) 214 Dzigbe Local Council, minutes of meeting on 17 March 1953. Nugent notes that in January of 1953 the same local council had sent a message to the Gold Coast CMB stating that farmers were no longer prepared to sell through the official channels. See *Smugglers, Secessionists and Loyal Citizens*, 187.

the west bank of the Volta and down to the ports of the Gold Coast. Many producers, however, still found it cheaper and more logical to transport goods to Kpalimé, where they could be taken down to the coast line of French Togoland via the Kpalimé-Lomé rail road.

Cocoa farmers' complaints over road infrastructure and the price of cocoa were directly connected to specific political grievances that the reunificationists pursued at the United Nations. When Theodore O. Asare pointed out that 'Togoland shares with the Gold Coast a common budget and common administrative and technical services', he was quoting directly from the Special Report of the Trusteeship Council on administrative unions, which had been published two years earlier.[44] This report reiterated the Trusteeship Council's earlier concerns that revenues from the trust territory were included without distinction in the budget of the Gold Coast, that revenues were not allocated to the trust territory on the basis of its overall needs, and that there were 'no adequate figures and data which would enable the Council to appraise the exact status or situation of the Trust Territory'.[45] Across the bodies of the United Nations there was recognition of the need for safeguards against the elision of administrative union with political union and the importance of data in monitoring the progress of trust territories.[46] By 1954, Asare and Antor were arguing that the administering authority was blurring the allocation of government resources to the trust territory with the allocation of a special development grant to the new Trans-Volta Togoland Region, and thereby circumventing the safeguards that the United Nations had tried to put into place. If in fact the trust territory was a net contributor Gold Coast government revenue, the inhabitants of the trust territory had no reason to feel grateful for any special development funds provided to the Trans-Volta Togoland Region. The grant was merely a fig leaf, designed to obscure a situation that was fundamentally exploitative and to undermine the argument that the trust territory could support a government of its own.

These arguments had resonance beyond the minority of commercial cocoa producers, because they rested on a more deep-seated and widely held conviction that the trust territory's relative lack of secondary schools,

44 United Nations, 'Special report of the Trusteeship Council on administrative unions affecting Trust Territories and on the status of the Cameroons and Togoland under French administration arising out of their membership in the French Union', (New York, 1952), 26.

45 Ibid., 26.

46 Trusteeship Council resolution 109 referred directly to these issues.

medical facilities, and motorable roads was directly attributable to the absence of a government of its own. Propaganda was peppered with images of the state as a parental figure, implying that a young nation, like a household, could only be built up through government's fair and prudent use of material and human resources. Reunificationist writers suggested that the defeat of the 'mother country' in the First World War had left Togoland in the position of an orphan. Not only had the partition of Togoland interrupted the processes of development initiated under German rule: it had also, in Asare's words, relegated the two Togolands to 'the position of a colonial "step-child" waiting in line until the Administering Nations could get to them'.[47]

In his Ewe-language text, Tsekpo used a similar metaphor to pursue this theme:

> It is true that someone who takes on the role of a father will not be as good as a real father. When orphans are with a group and it is time to eat, the orphans will be sent to the river to fetch water. By the time they come back, the rest of the group have finished the food, leaving a few crumbs in a bowl.

Neither the transfer of sovereignty from the British to Africans, nor the impressive plans for the future Ghana's economic development, could alter this basic dynamic. As a marginal member of another 'household', Togoland would always receive less favourable treatment, no matter how great its contribution or how prosperous the household became. By contrast, argued Tsekpo, if the towns of Togo could overcome their differences (as symbolised by the different coloured fowl), they could 'stick together and help to feed one another. They have one mouth and one stomach, so when one eats a little, all will be fed.'[48]

Whilst Antor was concerned with the immediate problems of the cocoa industry, Tsekpo further suggested that the trust territory actually contained valuable mineral resources, which the Germans had known about, but had tried to keep secret when they were forced to give up their colony in Togo:

> All of Togo's neighbours are older by far, and moreover, Togo's father has died. [In other words, the Gold Coast and Dahomey were more developed than Togoland, which had been 'orphaned' by the expulsion of the Germans in the First World War.] So Togo is the child stuck between two bigger people. These two people didn't inform him where his father kept his riches. But his father kept records. The bigger neighbours also know it.

[47] Asare, *The Case for a Reunited Togoland*, 27.

[48] Tsekpo, *Togo Nukae Hiawo?*, 6–7.

Working from a German map, Tsekpo compiled a list of what he referred to as Togo's 'hidden inheritance' (*domenyinu xaxla la*), buried under the ground. He insisted that Togo's mineral deposits included ferric oxide, silica, aluminium, manganese oxide, phosphoric oxide, sulphuric anhydride, and gold. In the 1970s, the Republic of Togo enjoyed an economic boom based on phosphate exports, so Tsekpo had a point.[49]

It is difficult to be sure how seriously his readers in the mid-1950s may have taken his claims about mineral wealth, but it was clear in my interviews with former activists and supporters that they sympathised with Tsekpo's argument that 'If Togo is very small, it does not mean that what is there is not for Togo [i.e. does not belong to Togo]. If a chief has a child and the child is not old before the chief dies, the stool is still for the child ... This is how issues in Togo are.'[50] M. K. Asase of Ho-Dome, speaking in English, indicated that Togoland had 'certain amenities' of its own, and thus, in order to avoid further exploitation and promote the development of resources, it was vital to reach a political settlement in which Togolanders would 'know our share'. The same phrase, 'know our share', was given as an English translation in an interview with E. K. Mfojoh of Sokode-Gbagble.[51] The most important 'amenity' in the trust territory was, of course, the river Volta, which both the British and the CPP wished to dam for the generation of hydro-electric power. Antor, and his threat to contest the Volta River Project at the International Court of Justice, thus represented a risk to this crucial element in Nkrumah's plans for Ghana's industrialisation, and this doubtless accounts for some of the urgency with which the CPP sought to win popular support for integration between 1953 and 1956.[52]

Chants and songs forcefully asserted that a reunified and independent Togoland state was the best safeguard for the people of the trust territory:

Tɔgbe Gabusu be:
Togo mayi Dahome o,
Yigbe!

[49] For a comparison with the language and imagery surrounding the discovery of crude oil reserves off the Ghana coast in the early twenty-first century, see Tom McCaskie, 'The United States, Ghana and Oil: Global and Local Perspectives', *African Affairs* 107 (428) (2008), 313–32.

[50] Tsekpo, *Togo Nukae Hiawo?*

[51] Interview with M. K. Asase, Ho-Dome, 18 May 1999; E.K. Mfojoh, Sokode-Gbagble, 2 June 1999 (translation by Lydia Osei-Brantuo).

[52] See also Nugent, *Smugglers, Secessionists and Loyal Citizens*, 184–5 and fn 155.

Tɔgbe Gabusu be:
Togo mayi le Ghana o,
Yigbe!

Eyata miele Togoa yi
Togo to enye Ablɔɖe
Ablɔɖe gbadzaa![53]

Chief Gabusu says:
Togo will not go to Dahomey,
[French Togoland will not integrate with Dahomey]
No way!

Chief Gabusu says:
Togo will not go to Ghana,
[British Togoland will not integrate with Ghana]
No way!

Therefore, we are going to Togo
[We will unite with Togo]
Togo's right is freedom,
Complete freedom! [54]

Ablɔɖe gbadzaa! was also used as a chant in its own right, and it conveyed the notion that freedom would be most meaningful when it was 'complete' and enjoyed 'everywhere' – in other words, when both British and French Togoland had achieved separation from neighbouring colonies and been reunited as an independent state.

Reunificationists clearly believed that the state had a unique power, not only in setting in motion social and economic processes that could bind citizens together in a national identity, but also in making decisions on investment and expenditure that would determine the pace and distribution of all future development. Although it was Nkrumah who coined the phrase 'Seek ye first the political kingdom', it would have resonated with Tsekpo, Asare, and Antor, who aligned themselves with the same kind of 'developmental decolonisation' which has more often been attributed

[53] I am grateful to Mercy Akosua Tegbe of Hohoe for providing me with a tape recording of this song. She was a wife of the late Chief Gabusu IV of Hohoe, who had supported the Togoland Congress in the 1950s. Following the passage of the Preventive Detention Act in July 1958, he went into exile in Kpalimé in French-speaking Togo. Tegbe had travelled with him, and both remained there until the fall of Nkrumah in 1966. Interview in Ewe with Mercy Akosua Tegbe, Hohoe, 19 Sept 2000 (translation by Lydia Osei-Brantuo).

[54] I am grateful to Richard Banibensu for translating this song from Ewe to English.

to the CPP.[55] Whatever Antor's relationship with Paul Ecker and the Movement for a Democracy of Content, this was a far cry from anarchist utopia. For Ecker, the divergences may not have mattered – the movement's aim was to stimulate debate and collective action, not simply to propagate a list of tenets. Thus, whilst Antor shared enough in common with the movement to take up its unique opportunity to publish his case, he did not share Ecker's suspicion of the capacity of state bureaucracy to limit collective endeavour and creativity. Rather, he shared with Tsekpo, Asare, and numerous supporters back at home a conception of the state which emphasised its unique role as a guarantor of security of persons and as an agent of socio-economic development. In this respect, the debate between the CPP and the reunificationists revolved not around pro- or anti-state positions, but around who should determine the boundaries of the state and whose interests it would serve.

In Ewe-language texts, the reunificationist preoccupation with the state was sometimes expressed through metaphors of food and eating, and it is tempting to interpret these metaphors in terms of a broader pattern of 'politics of the belly' in late colonial and post-colonial Africa.[56] However, although reunificationists sometimes referred to 'freedom' in terms of pleasure, satisfaction, and enjoyment, their ideas about Independence did not derive purely from a desire to stake out claims for individual and communal accumulation in a decolonised future – although their opponents certainly accused them of this.[57] There was also a strong defensive element: a reunified and independent Togoland state was also perceived as a necessary safeguard against a return to the suffering, exploitation, and servitude experienced in the past. This was alluded to in the following song:

Togoviwoe, mis'ablɔɖe gɔme,
Ablɔɖe gɔme nye bena
Ɖokuisinɔnɔ
Fukpekpewo nu ava yi.

[55] Nkrumah used this phrase in the 1951 CPP manifesto, *Towards the Goal*. See Dennis Austin, *Politics in Ghana, 1946–60* (London, 1964), 131.

[56] Jean-François Bayart, *The State in Africa: The Politics of the Belly* (New York, 1993).

[57] Daniel Chapman, a founder-member of the All Ewe Conference and later cabinet secretary to Nkrumah, informed me that Antor 'just wanted to be prime minister of an independent Togoland, but it was selfish because he was not qualified'. Interview with Daniel Chapman, Nyaho Clinic, Greater Accra, 21 Sept 2000.

Children of Togo, understand freedom
What freedom means is
Independence
All suffering will be over.[58]

Here, *ɖokuisinɔnɔ* (autonomy) is presented not as equivalent to 'freedom' (*ablɔɖe*), but rather as a means to achieve it. This emphasis on 'autonomy' captures not only the desire of reunificationists to end the disadvantageous association of British Togoland with the Gold Coast, but also a desire to protect Togolanders against the condition of being 'unfree', subservient, or dependent. Whilst the metaphor of Togo as an 'orphan' or 'step child' tapped into a theme that was instantly recognisable in popular theatre during this period and usually evoked a sympathetic response, the reunificationists' emphasis on becoming a marginal member of another household may also have alluded to forms of servitude.[59]

The Ewe word *ablɔɖe* translates roughly as 'freedom' and, in the context of mid-1950s politics, it was certainly used as a straightforward response to the CPP's equivalent English-language slogan. Missionary Westermann's dictionary, however, is suggestive of the historical implications of the Ewe term. While *ablɔɖenyenye* is translated as *das Freisein* ('the state of being free') and *ablɔɖenyinɔnɔ* as *Freiheit* ('freedom'), *ablɔɖe* itself is likened to *Stand des Freien* ('the free-born strata'). Similarly, Westermann indicated that an *ablɔɖemɛ* is a *Freigeborener* ('free-born person'), and he translated the term *ɖokuisinɔla* as *ein freier, selbständiger, unabhängiger mensch*. If the first of these two adjectives mean that the person was free and self-supporting, the third implies that the person was not dependent, encumbered, or bonded. A *ɖokuisinɔla* could be juxtaposed to both *awuba* (a pawn) and *kluvi* (a slave).[60] The choice of the slogan *Ablɔɖe!* and the use of the term *ɖokuisinɔnɔ* for political

[58] Tape recording of song provided by Gladys Akoli, Taviefe, 31 Aug 2000. Ewe-English translation by Richard Banibensu.

[59] For a discussion of the orphan-protagonist in popular culture, see Peter Bloom and Kate Skinner, 'Modernity and Danger: The Boy Kumasenu and the Work of the Gold Coast Film Unit', *Ghana Studies* 12/13 (2009); and Catherine Cole, *Ghana's Concert Party Theatre* (Bloomington IN, 2001), 133–58.

[60] Diedrich Westermann, *Wörterbuch der Ewe-Sprache I* (Berlin, 1905); *Wörterbuch der Ewe-Sprache II* (Berlin, 1906). I am grateful to John Peel for encouraging me to look for precise translations and for uses in the Ewe bible. Akosua Perbi, *A History of Indigenous Slavery in Ghana from the 15th to the 19th Century* (Accra, 2004), 1–12 provides a summary of scholarly debates over the definition and practice of slavery and servitude within Africa, and a comparison of Twi and Ewe terms corresponding to 'servant', 'pawn', 'slave', and 'war captive'.

autonomy may indicate that reunificationist calls for 'freedom' were invoking memories of being 'unfree' or 'subservient'.[61]

The point here is not that there is a direct correlation between voting patterns in 1954 or 1956 and an uncontested collective memory of capture during the Asante invasion of 1869 or the prolonged practice of enslavement under eighteenth-century Akwamu suzerainty. Clearly, there were some localities where pre-colonial experiences of enslavement did not result in votes for the Togoland Congress. The point is that the pre-colonial and early colonial experience of Krepe (later southern British Togoland) created references which influenced the presentation, interpretation, and evaluation of the political options that were available in the mid-1950s. (This connection is particularly clear in the case of Tsekpo, who wrote in Ewe the life history of Josef Famfantor of Wusuta, and described his enslavement by Asantes.[62]) Having a state of one's own provided a form of protection against the plundering of persons and resources by more powerful neighbours. Support for a restoration of the German borders – that is, for a reunified Togoland – did not stem from rose-tinted recollections of German administration.[63] Rather, reunificationists tapped into (but did not always monopolise) a broader, and sometimes unspoken, acknowledgement of previous marginality and servitude, and identified more openly the material benefits that had derived from finally having a state of one's own. As one man from Hohoe put it:

> I can't tell you the atrocities that the Germans did to our people who couldn't pay their taxes. We used to say ... "Death is better than a German prison." ... But one thing about the Germans ... in thirty years they developed the country so fast that they had put a telephone in Yendi.[64]

While reunificationists were persuaded of the need for an independent Togoland state, they were also aware of serious practical obstacles that might reduce individual and community prospects of accumulation. It may have been these obstacles that account for the achievement of some

[61] *Reconfiguring Slavery: West African Trajectories*, ed. Benedetta Rossi (Liverpool, 2009) for a recent discussion of the ways in which former slave status has been mobilised in political contests in a series of West African countries.

[62] Sandra Greene, *West African Narratives of Slavery: Texts from Late Nineteenth- and Early Twentieth-Century Ghana* (Bloomington IN, 2011), 121–35.

[63] As suggested in Brown, 'Politics in the Kpandu Area of Ghana', 240–1.

[64] Interview with Rev E. T. Adiku, Hohoe, 14 Sept 2000. Yendi was situated in the north of British Togoland and was the capital of the Dagomba kingdom.

degree of support for integration, rather than the CPP's appeals to ethnicity or their attempts to create synergies between localised disputes and a distinctive vision of developmentalist decolonisation. In the words of E. T. Adiku from Hohoe:

> The problem was that the other side of Togo [French Togoland] is two thirds and we [British Togoland] are only one third. When we join, which language are we to take? ... If you wanted to go to Nkrumah [support integration], people would say, "You are bad, you are unpatriotic, you want to throw your country to the Gold Coast!" But then, if you wanted to join with Togo [support reunification] others will say, "What? You want your children to go to school to learn French, to start from scratch while the French Togolanders are running ahead of you?"[65]

Adiku said that he had favoured reunification in spite of its potential inconveniences, but others told me that this was precisely the reason for which they had shifted their support towards the integrationist solution.[66] The point was made, apparently with some success, by Philip Key (CPP activist and member for Ho-Bankoe) in August 1952 when the Asogli Local Council debated what they should write in their petition to the forthcoming United Nations visiting mission: 'we must bear in mind that the Togoland under French administration is larger than the part under British administration, and if we do not take care in our decision ... it might be possible that the smaller area ... could be added to the larger area ... under the French Government.'[67] Key was thereby able to persuade the other councillors that their petition should focus on parity of representation for British and French Togoland in the Joint Togoland Council, and not on the need for immediate separation of British Togoland from the Gold Coast.

The complex and mutually exclusive nature of such calculations precluded any straightforward process by which reunificationist leaders in southern British Togoland could construct a national identity on behalf of their followers, either by lumping together at a territorial level a series of local disputes, or by presenting a clear-cut case based on material self-interest. Togoland reunification was not a neat or convenient solution.

[65] Interview with Rev E. T. Adiku, Hohoe, 13 Sept 2000.

[66] Interview with Fia Adzatakpor VI, Vane-Avatime, 22 and 23 July 2000. Adzatekpor VI was a young man when he became chief in the 1950s. He told me that his predecessor had initially supported Togoland reunification, but had been gradually won over to the integrationist agenda on the grounds that the educational progress of British Togoland would be severely retarded by reunification with French Togoland should French be adopted as the official language.

[67] PRAAD, Ho, DAO (D) 213, Asogli Local Council: minutes of 20 Aug 1952.

The study of propaganda renders the strength and prevalence of reunificationist feeling comprehensible because it reveals that the engagement between leaders and supporters was predicated, at least in part, on a historically created and widely shared suspicion of unfavourable incorporation into larger political units.

READING, WRITING, AND RESPONSIBILITY

Reunificationist authors, and indeed their CPP opponents, tended to portray the conflict arising over Togoland's future as an abnormal or unnatural state of affairs. Tsekpo suggested that, by personal example and through their writings, reunificationist authors could foster harmony within the Togoland nation and reduce the 'confusion' that had been introduced by the intrusions of the CPP.[68] As Tsekpo wrote:

> Our brains are divided into ten, and we are ten groups who are quarrelling. Every group is blaming the other. The author of this book will never blame any of these ten groups. We should advise and be patient with one another. We should discuss the problem, listening first to one, then to the other.[69]

He thus invoked an idealised picture of an author disseminating the consensus view that had emerged from a dignified discussion among elders.

Although Theodore O. Asare was writing in English, some features of his text tally with Kwesi Yankah's description of how oral appeals were presented to Akan chiefs and elders: by treating a chief and his office with respect, a petitioner could place upon the chief an obligation to justify this respect by finding a wise and just solution to the dispute at hand.[70] In criticising the administering authorities for failing to respond to the findings of the 1952 visiting mission (which had come to meet with Togolanders face-to-face), Asare also recalled the United Nations' ultimate responsibilities as an arbiter and a guarantor of justice.[71] Togolanders were thus implicitly likened to an unfortunate people suffering at the

[68] The term 'confusion' is widely used in Ghanaian English to describe situations of conflict and disagreement. It implies that harmony and consensus are more natural and achievable conditions.

[69] Tsekpo, *Togo Nukae Hiawo?*, 5.

[70] Kwesi Yankah, *Free Speech in Traditional Society: The Cultural Foundations of Communication in Contemporary Ghana* (Accra, 1998), 26. Yankah, however, has tended to suggest that the use of English in Ghanaian media and political institutions may exclude or inhibit the traditional restraints on speech.

[71] Asare, *The Case for a Reunited Togoland*, 11–13.

FIGURE 1: Pro-Integration Petitioners at the United Nations, 1954. Copyright / by permission of: United Nations.

hands of a malevolent sub-chief who was subverting the righteous recommendations of a higher authority.

Ironically, whilst Asare wanted to expose the administering authority's delaying tactics vis-à-vis a directly elected Joint Togoland Council, and the ineffectiveness of the Trusteeship Council, Fleku rather argued that it was the reunificationists who held an unfair advantage.[72] '[G]reater attention', he claimed, 'is paid to those petitioners who appear in person than to those who address the United Nations by post or through Visiting Missions.' His own participation in a delegation in 1954 was explained in terms of the need to 'correct the false impressions' made by delegates of the Togoland Congress, who, 'by frequent personal visits' had been able to 'mislead the United Nations'.[73] (See Figure 1.)

Reunificationists treated the face-to-face presentation at the United Nations as a culmination of, not an alternative to, the mastery of written English and of United Nations documents and procedure. These skills, and their conscientious deployment, were necessary for the preparation of a credible and authentic case: the petition was the document that would open the door for a truly compelling physical appearance. Authors thus made a conscious effort to engage with United Nations' delegates on the terms that they believed would best enhance understanding of and sympathy for the reunificationist cause. Asare, for example, made legalistic claims in citing large chunks of the United Nations Charter, and demonstrated his knowledge of world history in comparing the Togoland question with other cases in which the rights of small nations to self-determination had been

[72] Ibid., 13. Asare argued that 'the Trusteeship Council is dominated by the administering authorities'.

[73] Fleku, *Togoland and Gold Coast*, 109.

at stake. His educational achievements are further reflected in the academic format and tone of his work, which he structured into an introduction, six chapters, and a synopsis.[74] Similarly, Antor seized on an opportunity to attack his opponents' credibility and authenticity by pointing out that the Togolanders who put the case for integration at the United Nations had been coached for their appearances, whereas reunificationists had mustered their own intellectual resources.[75]

However, from the point of view of activists and supporters who had little formal schooling, and no opportunity to travel outside West Africa, the more highly educated leadership held an esoteric form of power – their influence was exercised in an inaccessible language in a faraway forum. Thus, M. K. Asase from Ho-Dome expressed his disillusionment with the reunificationists who had transferred to the CPP in 1951: '[F. Y.] Asare and them, they knew everything, and we sent them to the United Nations and everything. But leaders, you know, they just crossed the carpet, and that was why our Togoland politics was spoiled.'[76] Indeed, in interviews, reunificationist supporters sometimes cast themselves in the role of 'loyal foot soldiers' who, through the lottery of educational opportunities, had been forced into a dependent relationship with their more highly educated and yet unreliable peers.[77]

Political rallies back at home provided an occasion for a face-to-face encounter in which representatives' commitment and endeavour could be appraised by their supporters. During the mid-1950s, these rallies became central to the business of 'making politics'.[78] A former district commissioner who had been based in Kpandu in the mid-1950s recalled

[74] Asare sought to minimise his authorial voice: chapter headings took the passive form, and, even when explicitly introducing his own agenda, Asare opted for an academic vocabulary, using expressions such as 'Our thesis here'. As a member of the New York bar, Asare had significantly higher qualifications than all the other major reunificationist spokesmen and representatives.

[75] S. E. Olympio, S. G. Antor, and A. K. Odame, letter to the Chairman of the Fourth Committee, 4 Dec 1953, cited in *"Most Secret"*, 23.

[76] Interview with M. K. Asase, Ho-Dome, 20 July 2000. Asase's phrase, 'crossed the carpet', is used in British politics. When a parliamentarian leaves a governing party for an opposition party, or vice-versa, he or she physically crosses the stretch of carpet which divides the benches on which government and opposition members sit.

[77] The term 'loyal foot soldiers' is borrowed from Allman, who describes how the radicalism of the commoners or 'young men' in Asante was constrained by their leaders and by their sense of loyalty to the Golden Stool. See Jean Allman, 'The Young Men and the Porcupine: Class, Nationalism and Asante's Struggle for Self-Determination, 1954–57', *Journal of African History*, 31 (2) (1990), 263–79 at 275.

[78] Rallies and mass meetings in Asante are described in Allman, *Quills of the Porcupine*, 102–4.

that there would be a rally in one of Togoland's bigger towns every month.[79] The United Nations missions that visited the trust territory in 1952 and 1955 acknowledged the importance of rallies by attending competing events organised by both the Togoland Congress and the CPP in the major towns of the southern section (Ho, Kpandu, and Hohoe).[80] The visiting missions focussed on rallies as indicators of the strength of feeling over the Togoland question, but they were also significant as sites of exchange between educated representatives and their less educated supporters.

In particular, rallies were often called in order to collect funds to support reunificationist petitioners' travel to the United Nations in New York, and were also held to coincide with their return in order that progress could be reported back.[81] By publishing the cases they had presented, and distributing copies back at home, representatives sought to persuade their supporters that they were working hard on their behalf and had put forward a sophisticated and impressive case for reunification. But rallies also provided an occasion on which leaders and representatives were expected to demonstrate their continuing commitment to the reunificationist cause, not necessarily by elaborating in further detail on the cases articulated in their pamphlets, but rather by participating in and leading the popular chants and songs that emphasised loyalty and courage.

In print, authors positioned themselves as members of an intelligentsia that was enlightening its compatriots, but they were also willing participants in chants and songs at rallies. Antor had his own particular warm-up chants, while Tsekpo was also famous for setting popular reunificationist songs to music from the Ewe Hymn Book.[82] While the

[79] Interview with David Heaton, Wimbledon, London, 5 April 2000. Heaton is a former district commissioner who was based at Kpandu 1952–6, and then at Ho, 1956–7, where he served as assistant secretary to Krobo Edusei, the regional commissioner of the Trans-Volta Togoland Region.

[80] United Nations Visiting Mission to Trust Territories in West Africa, 1952, 'Report on Togoland under United Kingdom Administration together with related documents' (New York, 1954), 2; and United Nations Visiting Mission to the Trust Territories of Togoland under British administration and Togoland under French Administration, 1955, 'Report on Togoland under British Administration together with related documents' (New York, 1956), 1–3.

[81] Correspondence with E. K. Datsa of Amedzofe-Avatime, n.d. (but c. Nov 1999).

[82] David Heaton described how Antor would rouse the crowd by shouting '*Ablɔḍe*' with ever increasing volume, shifting the stress from the first syllable to the second and then the third. According to a former Togoland Congress activist, the most important *Ablɔḍe* song that was not invented by women was *Togo fe Ablɔḍe*, which was Tsekpo's adaptation of Ewe Hymn Book No. 340. Telephone conversation with Kofi Kodzi, Edmonton, London, 5 May 2003.

FIGURE 2: Togoland Congress Rally in Ho, 1956. Copyright / by permission of: United Nations.

United Nations visiting missions recognised the significance of rallies, their attendance was cut short on at least one occasion due to the risk of violence, while colonial administrators contended that the 'danger of disorder' was 'very great indeed'.[83] The potential for violence stemmed partly from the fact that rallies were typically held in towns that were party strongholds, and as support for the opposing party was often strong in the villages that lay in close proximity, a rally organised by one party would often prompt the other to call for a competing event.[84] Physical identifiers of party loyalties, such as flags and women's cloths, were means of demonstrating the numerical strength of support, while chants and songs emphasised that defeat of opponents could best be manifested through their ousting from public space. Thus the reunificationist chant, *Akokɔ, Suie Suie!* (Cockerel [CPP], Out Out!) was countered by a CPP song: 'I used to be *Ablɔḍe*, now I am CPP, *Eyɛ Eyɛ* (it is good).'[85] (See Figure 2.)

There were some basic similarities between the two parties' approaches to rallies, but the CPP was gradually able to bring its greater financial weight to bear and therefore make a show of strength even in towns where the majority of the inhabitants supported the Togoland Congress. Thus elderly women from Awudome – a CPP stronghold just outside Ho,

[83] United Nations Visiting Mission, ... 1952, 'Report on Togoland under United Kingdom Administration', 4. This occurred at Jasikan in the cocoa-growing area north of Hohoe. The visiting mission had intended to visit a co-operative but curtailed their itinerary 'when it observed that the two rival factions were beginning to demonstrate and grow rowdy'. Also, interview with David Heaton, London, 5 April 2000.

[84] For example, the town of Kpandu favoured the CPP, but many nearby villages (including those of Alavanyo) were Togoland Congress strongholds.

[85] Interview with David Heaton, London, 5 April 2000.

and not even in the trust territory itself – recalled that they were bussed to rallies in 'Ho, Kpandu, other places, plenty plenty', they had never paid for anything, and they had enjoyed considerable hospitality, in terms of food and drink, from the CPP branch in the town that was hosting the rally.[86] Togoland Congress supporters, on the other hand, usually had to travel at their own expense, and this tended to restrict the ability of the Congress to hold rallies in areas where they could not be confident of a pro-Ablɔɖe turnout.[87] Similarly, CPP women were often provided with flags bearing the red cockerel for use at rallies, whilst Congress women held flags bearing three stripes and a yellow star. As more funds became available, however, CPP women also wore a cloth that bore the head of Nkrumah. The same former district commissioner described the CPP women as 'Nkrumah's secret weapon': their presence was formidable as they marched or danced, chanting, down a town's main street in their matching cloths.

Recollections of rallies and the advantages of the CPP are entangled with late twentieth-century popular histories which emphasised a fundamental cleavage in Ghanaian politics between parties that could mobilise the masses and those whose composition and ethos was more elitist. This distinction between mass and elite parties was also a key element in the early scholarship on nationalist parties and decolonisation, and later we will return to the problem of categorising Ablɔɖe within Ghana's main political traditions.[88] For now, however, let us note the degree of ambivalence in recollections of the internal dynamics of both parties.

With the benefit of hindsight, the CPP's tactics and its perceived willingness to abuse the advantages of incumbency could easily have been presented as early indicators of intolerance and authoritarianism, and set in an unfavourable comparison to the more sophisticated approach of the Togoland Congress. But it was clear in some interviews that it was not always the tactics themselves to which the reunificationists objected: it was their inability to retaliate on an equal playing field. Michael Senoo recalled that it was not only the CPP which sought to squeeze the scope for dissent. On his own return from the teaching training college at

86 Interview with Mama Adomwa I, Queenmother, Awudome-Anyirawase, 19 July 2000, translation by Lydia Osei-Brantuo. Mama Admonwa stated: 'They provided the buses, the food, the drink, everything. Sometimes, when the people were plenty, they would even bring the food in a helicopter.'

87 Interview with anonymous informant at Taviefe, 31 Aug 2000.

88 Dennis Austin, *Politics in Ghana* (London, 1964) and Thomas Hodgkin, *Freedom for the Gold Coast?* (London, 1951).

St Augustine's to the trust territory in 1950, and particularly after his transfer to Hohoe in 1954, he witnessed the degree of pressure that was brought to bear on the chiefs to affiliate to the Togoland Congress: 'You dare not be out, you had to be in.'[89]

In order to overcome the legacy of distrust and division within the reunificationist camp, to attract voters to the Togoland Congress, and to secure financial contributions, Antor needed the type of mass forum provided by the rally. But this does not necessarily mean that he conceived of it as an unwelcome concession thrust upon a more educated leadership from the grassroots. The self-image of the leadership also demanded that their engagement with less educated supporters should contain a didactic element. Practices of quoting and critiquing within the propaganda texts challenged the separation of those who could access the constitutional arguments presented outside, in English, from those who were confined to arguments spoken at home, in Ewe. Rather, Antor deliberately published excerpts from the case that he and other reunificationist petitioners had presented outside, and made this work available alongside Tsekpo's Ewe texts at political rallies.[90] Literate supporters regarded the transportation, sale, and impromptu translation and discussion of these texts as a key part of their contribution to the movement.[91]

Despite the necessity of, and even enthusiasm for, this engagement between people of varying levels of literacy and formal education, there was a persistent sense that the nature, if not the degree, of an individual's contribution was determined by how far he or she had gone in school. Thus G. S. K. Adedeme of Amedzofe-Avatime, who transported and interpreted written propaganda, suggested that there were two forums of reunificationist activity: 'You can only go to meetings by invitation, but anyone can go to a rally.'[92] As the party leadership travelled through the trust territory, it would call private meetings with trusted activists and supporters. Some of the most highly educated individuals in the trust territory were consulted on tactics, even when their positions as church, local council, or government departmental employees deterred them from owning a party membership card. E. K. Datsa therefore recalled

[89] Interview with Michael Senoo, Hohoe, 13 Sept 2000.

[90] Tsekpo also produced some shorter Ewe pamphlets on the reunification issue (copies in author's possession). I am grateful to the late E. K. Gavu of Dzogbofeme-Avatime for providing me with examples of Tsekpo's work.

[91] Interviews with G. S. K. Adedeme, Amedzofe-Avatime, 24 July 2000 and 13 Aug 2000.

[92] Interview with G. S. K. Adedeme, Amedzofe-Avatime, 13 Aug 2000.

that although these 'cabinet' meetings were often held in private homes or empty school rooms, 'every thing was formal. Mr Antor was referred to as "Chairman", or "Our Leader", or as "Our Father". We referred to one another as "Comrades".'[93] Contributions to debate were supposed to be grounded in knowledge and experience. Thus although there was 'freedom of speech and freedom of expression, those who were more knowledgeable or better informed on the Togoland Congress matters were those who talked most'.[94] When discussion about tactics was in English, those who lacked formal education may have struggled to participate on an equal footing.

This semi-visible but persistent differentiation between the literate and the illiterate (and finer distinctions between levels of facility with written and spoken Ewe and English) was significant not simply for the nature of the Togoland Congress' internal organisation and its campaigning strategies. It also permeated subsequent explanations for the failure of the movement to achieve its goal. If 'tactics' and 'strategy' were best decided by a formally educated leadership, then it was also they who needed to explain why their chosen tactics had not delivered the desired result. In some cases, recriminations over strategic errors blended with the bitter personal disputes that had arisen in the disagreements between reunificationists prior to 1951. Thus, A. M. K. Dumoga (younger brother to E. O. Kofi Dumoga) was clear that the responsibility lay with Antor.[95] Others agreed that Antor had made strategic errors, but felt that this was understandable in the context of the extreme machinations of the French and British governments and the alliance of the latter with the CPP. The key point here is that the reunificationists believed that they had been outmanoeuvred. They did not believe that they had lost the argument, or that their case had been proved illegitimate or unfeasible. As we shall see in Chapters 5 and 6, this meant that when new opportunities arose in which the Togoland question might be pursued, Ablɔɖe proved to have very long legs indeed.

WARS OF WORDS

If "*Most Secret*" is taken at face value, the British administration believed in 1953 that a plebiscite on the future of the trust territory would have

[93] Letter from E. K. Datsa, in author's possession (n.d. but c. Nov 1999). [94] Ibid.
[95] Interview with A. M. K. Dumoga, Ho, 28 Aug 2000.

resulted in a victory for Ablɔɖe.[96] By October 1955, when the report of the third United Nations visiting mission recommended that a plebiscite be held, the administration believed that an integrationist victory was possible. Private 'cabinet' meetings of the Togoland Congress debated long and hard on the unsatisfactory terms of the plebiscite, and whether the party ought to participate in a contest that was tipped against them.[97] There were numerous bones of contention, but two were particularly significant.

Firstly, voter registration was based on residency rather than on birth. Technically, the payment of rates was not a requirement for voter registration, but in reality a rate receipt was the primary means by which potential voters could prove residency.[98] This meant that Gold Coasters who were posted in the trust territory by government departments or by private companies could register to vote on production of evidence that they had paid their rates. The same applied to traders, migrant farmers, and other 'strangers'. Meanwhile, Togolanders who were residing in the Gold Coast and had not paid rates at home could not vote. It was also possible for individuals who resided in the Gold Coast to simply to walk very short distances into the trust territory, and attempt to vote even if they lacked evidence of paying their rates. The United Nations plebiscite commissioner's report noted that in the northern section, where women did not pay tax and the rate receipt did not apply, having two children was accepted as evidence of meeting the age qualification.[99] Many reunificationists felt the scope for abuse was high given that the plebiscite commissioner brought a delegation of only twenty-four international observers, while the administering authority itself – which explicitly favoured integration – had nominated Sir John Dring as the plebiscite administrator (i.e. the primary organiser).[100]

Secondly, the plebiscite did not apply to French Togoland, and did not specifically mention the option of 'reunification of the two Togolands and their joint Independence'. Rather, the plebiscite applied only to British Togoland and asked whether its inhabitants preferred 'union' with the Gold Coast, which was soon to be independent, or separation from the Gold Coast pending a decision on its future status. This framing of the

96 Antor and Ecker, "*Most Secret*", 11.
97 Interview *with E. K. Datsa*, Amedzofe-Avatime, 3 June 1999; and interview with A. M. K. Dumoga, Ho, 28 and 29 Aug 2000.
98 United Nations, 'Report of the United Nations Plebiscite Commissioner for the Trust Territory of Togoland under British Administration', (New York, 1956), 66 and 144–5.
99 Ibid., 145.
100 United Nations, 'Report of the United Nations Plebiscite Commissioner', 66.

plebiscite question reflects the extent to which the reunificationists had lost – or had been excluded from – control of the mechanisms through which the future of the trust territory would be decided.[101]

Once again, however, texts provided an opportunity for reunificationists to articulate their case on their own terms. The Department of Information Services in Accra had some difficulties in finding an Ewe translator for its plebiscite information pamphlets because the Vernacular Literature Bureau seemed to have no-one qualified to do the work.[102] The drafts were therefore sent to the Regional Liaison Officer in Ho on 10 December 1955 with a request that he find a translator. In these drafts, voters were given a choice between 'integration of Togoland under British administration with an independent Gold Coast' and separation of British Togoland and its 'continuance under trusteeship, pending the ultimate determination of its future'.[103] Just a few days later, however, the United Nations General Assembly passed resolution 944 (X), which replaced the word 'integration' with the word 'union'.[104] The plebiscite commissioner himself noted that the real meaning of the term 'union' was contingent on the resolution of disputes raging through the Gold Coast as to whether the Independence constitution should be federal or unitary. The reunificationists were willing to consider joining a federal Gold Coast *after* they had achieved Independence with French Togoland. They were vehemently opposed to integration under a unitary constitution.[105]

The reunificationists thus circulated their own interpretation of the plebiscite question, emphasising that what voters were really being asked was whether they wanted their *own* Independence, in which case they should vote for separation, or whether they wanted to be 'under the Gold Coast'.[106] According to Brown, this interpretation was made in a 'Togoland Congress broadsheet distributed in Kpandu District', which is almost certainly a reference to G. K. Tsekpo's newspaper, *Mia Denyigba*.[107] Ironically, and perhaps in recognition of his extraordinary powers not only of translation but also of persuasion, Tsekpo was actually appointed

[101] Brown, 'Politics in the Kpandu Area of Ghana', 290, also notes that the reunificationists were outmanoeuvred in all their demands about the shape of the plebiscite.

[102] PRAAD, Ho, DAO(D) 114: Office of the Advisor to the Governor on Plebiscite Arrangements, Accra, to O. R. Blair, Regional Liaison Officer, Ho, 10 Dec 1955.

[103] PRAAD, Ho, DAO (D) 114. Draft pamphlet, first page.

[104] United Nations, 'Report of the United Nations Plebiscite Commissioner', 9.

[105] Ibid., 42–65.

[106] Brown, 'Politics in the Kpandu Area of Ghana', 290 and fn 58.

[107] The only copies of *Mia Denyigba* that I have been able to access come from the period immediately after the plebiscite, so I was not able to see this statement in its Ewe original.

as an Ewe translator when the Vernacular Literature Bureau was replaced by the Bureau of Ghana Languages after Independence.[108] The reunificationists' interpretation of the term 'union' as subordination to the larger political unit of the Gold Coast clearly had considerable resonance. As we saw earlier, Clephas Ntri, the former activist from Alavanyo, phrased his opposition to integration in precisely those terms: 'We did not want anyone from that side coming here to rule us.'

THE NORTHERN QUESTION

Within the leading ranks of the Togoland Congress, there was always debate about the prospects of securing a majority vote for reunification in the northern section of Togoland. The perception amongst many southern Togolanders – whichever political solution they preferred – was that political life in the north was underdeveloped due to the relative poverty of the area and the lack of schools. According to F. Y. Asare (the former reunificationist from Buem-Borada who defected to the CPP), Nkrumah's strategy was to construct temporary alliances with the most powerful chiefs in the expectation that they could deliver the necessary votes.[109] This was not necessarily easy, given that the major royal families of the North were associated with the Northern People's Party (which opposed the CPP in the Gold Coast parliament) and relations between the royal houses and the local CPP branches were often very sour.

In the case of Dagomba, the CPP were fortunate in that the Ya Na declared himself implacably opposed to any separation of northern British Togoland from the Gold Coast as early as 1953.[110] The Ya Na's position on the Togoland question can be explained in the following terms. During the period of German rule, the Dagomba population which fell within the British zone had been separated from the kingdom's capital, Yendi, which was taken by Germany. The new border that resulted from the Franco-British division of Togoland placed Yendi and the entire Dagomba population under British administration.[111] Alhaji Dawuda Yahaya, the former CPP branch secretary in Yendi, thus recalled that Nkrumah had warned him prior to the United Nations visiting

108 Interview with Mercy Tsekpo, Alavanyo-Abehenase, 7 June 2010.

109 Interview with F. Y. Asare, North Kaneshie, Greater Accra, 26 May 1999.

110 Paul Ladouceur, *Chiefs and Politicians: The Politics of Regionalism in Northern Ghana* (London, 1979), 134.

111 Ladouceur, *Chiefs and Politicians*, 34.

mission in 1955 about the need to demonstrate the level of popular support for integration. Yahaya promised that the local party organisation would be mobilised to this effect: 'He gave us motorbikes, and we make campaign.' Although there was no love lost between the local CPP members and the Dagomba chiefs ('who used their office to harass us'), on the question of integration they stood as one:

> By the time the United Nations visiting mission arrived, when they went to the meetings of chiefs and people, the chiefs had already prepared their memorandums against unification and rather for integration. They came to organise the registration for the plebiscite. The DC Yendi recommended me as a registration officer . . . and I acted as an interpreter. I did that work with them, and then I came back to my party to campaign . . . when the voting opened, we did not have any trouble.[112]

Such calculations of chiefly support, however, could also be complicated by the fact that the larger states in the Northern Territories (Dagbon, Mamprugu, Gonja, and Nanumba) had taken the opportunity of the Native Authority (Northern Territories) Ordinance 1932 to reassert, reshape, or exaggerate their control over groups which were either acephalous or in which chieftaincy operated on too small a scale to be deemed practical by a British administration seeking to implement indirect rule (Konkomba, Bimoba, Chakosi, and Bassari). This raised the possibility that subordinated groups might look to Togoland reunification as a means of escaping their oppression.

In his interpretation of the northern plebiscite results, which consists largely of a tribal head count, James Coleman suggested that only one quarter of the total Dagomba population actually lived in the trust territory, and that in the plebiscite they were outnumbered by Chakosi and Konkomba, whom he believed to be inclined towards their 'ethnic kin' in the French zone.[113] It is unfortunate that, in his recent study of the Konkomba struggle against Dagomba and Nanumba domination, Benjamin Talton does not offer any explanation for Konkomba voting behaviour in the plebiscite.[114] Very little is known about the motivations of A. A. Chambaas (a member of the Nanumba royal family) in backing

[112] Interview with Alhaji Dawuda Yahaya, Nima, Greater Accra, 21 Sept 2008.

[113] Coleman, 'Togoland', 13.

[114] Benjamin Talton, *Politics of Social Change in Ghana: The Konkomba Struggle for Political Equality* (New York, 2010). Talton is, however, much more informative as to how the Konkomba were unrepresented in native tribunals and had to pay tribute to Dagomba and Nanumba chiefs.

the reunificationists, although one possibility is that he knew the Dumoga family from the time he spent working on the *Ashanti Pioneer* newspaper. In the event, the reunificationists made a reasonable showing in Chereponi and Sunsun, but did not achieve a majority in either.[115]

A little more information is available for Mamprugu, although even here there is considerable scope for further research. According to F. Y. Asare, Nkrumah suspected that the king of the Mamprusi – the Nayiri – was less committed on the Togoland question than his Dagomba counterpart, the Ya Na. In view of the Nayiri's association with the Northern People's Party and his opposition to Nkrumah's proposals for a unitary constitution, it may have seemed plausible to Nkrumah that the Nayiri would throw in his lot with Antor in 1956 in order to delay Gold Coast Independence. According to Asare, then,

> I went to Mamprusi to talk. The first time I went, they didn't like me at all because they had been told that I was a strong Nkrumahist ... [But] their faces were changing, they were changing because they had believed Antor's propaganda and now I was telling them something different ... So the chief asked [his advisors], 'Is Asare saying the truth or not?' and, in fact, it was true [that if the Nayiri were to back unification, he risked losing control over some of his subjects] ... Then the chief has told me that now he has understood the case, he would ... travel from village to village and when it came to voting day I should watch for the results ... And, in fact, East Agolle, those who voted for separation were three ... those who voted for separation in West Agolle were six.[116]

However, the heavy vote for integration in the two Agolle areas identified by Asare may have been as much the result of Kusasi and Frafra campaigns as it was the work of the Nayiri. In the 1954 general election, two organisations (the Frafra Youth Association and the South Mamprusi Youth) had channelled voters towards the CPP in order to gain the support of the Ministry of Local Government for their separation from the Mamprusi District Council.[117] Despite the repeated assertions of southern activists on both sides of the reunification/integration divide that political life in the north was underdeveloped, the pattern in the case

[115] Chereponi and Sunsun were the two Local Council areas where Konkomba and Chakosi (respectively) accounted for a high proportion of the population. Both these areas fell under the Dagomba District Council. Coleman, 'Togoland', 72.

[116] Interview with F. Y. Asare, North Kaneshie, Greater Accra, 26 May 1999. Asare seems to have exaggerated the figures as, according to Coleman, 'Togoland', 72, there were 394 votes for separation in the two Agolle areas, and 14,431 votes for integration. Nonetheless, the integrationists won a resounding victory.

[117] Coleman, 'Togoland', 124–6.

of the Kusasi and Frafra bears some resemblance to that identified by Nugent for Anfoega (in the southern section of the trust territory).[118] Once the CPP had secured control of the Ministry of Local Government after 1951, it was in a position to win voter support by rectifying the numerous grievances generated by the British implementation of indirect rule. By contrast, the Togoland Congress had a limited presence in northern British Togoland, and it is thus unsurprising that disgruntled groups did not see the party as a powerful organisation that could provide solutions to their problems.

Another perspective on this phenomenon can be gleaned in the memoirs of Mumuni Bawumia. Describing his experiences as secretary to the Mamprusi Native Authority, a member of the Legislative Assembly, and a founder member of the Northern People's Party, Bawumia insisted that the Nayiri 'never at any time threatened to support the separation of the mandated territory', and elaborated his own role in delivering the desired results.[119] In Bunkprugu Local Council area, the Bimoba Youth Association, led by J. P. Kona, campaigned vigorously for Togoland reunification, seeing it as a means of liberating the Bimoba from Mamprusi control.[120] According to Bawumia, Kona 'organized his supporters to stone my group', but in response

> I succeeded in telling the people that the Bimobas were migrants from the French mandated Territory and the land on which they had settled belong to the Nayiri and Mamprugu. I further warned that if they voted for separation they would leave their settlements and move back into the French mandated territory.[121]

These threats apparently fell on deaf ears. In the event, Bunkprugu was one of only two local council areas in the northern section which actually turned out a majority in favour of separation.[122]

Not everyone was convinced that the 'backwardness' of northern voters and their willingness to follow their chiefs accounted for the integrationist victory in northern British Togoland. Some argued that it was the nature of state-sponsored development, and the location of the amenities that the state had provided, which rendered a choice for integration far more

[118] Nugent, *Smugglers, Secessionists and Loyal Citizens*, 195–7.

[119] Mumuni Bawumia, *A Life in the Political History of Ghana: Memoirs of Alhaji Mumuni Bawumia* (Accra, 2004), 53. Interestingly, F. Y. Asare believed that Antor had persuaded Bawumia into the reunificationist camp.

[120] Ladouceur, *Chiefs and Politicians*, 135. [121] Bawumia, *A Life*, 52.

[122] In Bunkprugu, the votes were 1,593 for integration and 1,625 for separation; in Kworli the votes were 170 for integration and 1,104 for separation.

likely.[123] Formal schooling came considerably later to the northern parts of the Gold Coast and Togoland than it did to the south, primarily as a result of a deliberate British policy of deterring Christian missionaries from the largely Muslim and animist areas of the north. The White Fathers, however, managed to open the first mission school in the north at Navrongo in 1907, and the first government primary school opened in Tamale two years later.[124] In 1922, a Junior Trade School was opened at Yendi, and in 1927, it was transferred to Tamale and fused with the Government Senior Boarding School. This was the only institution in either the Northern Territories or northern British Togoland that offered education up to standard VII.[125]

Paul Ladouceur argues that this school fostered a strong 'sense of solidarity and common identity' among the pupils who walked literally hundreds of miles to Tamale at the beginning of each term. 'Many of those who went to Tamale [in the 1930s and 1940s] were, in line with early British policy towards recruiting for the schools, sons or grandsons of chiefs, although few of them actually became chiefs. Despite the limited scope of the education available to them, many of these men became leaders of the North in the 1950s.'[126] Each year, a handful of the Tamale standard VII graduates would be selected to attend teacher training courses at Achimota. This was the only route for further study that was open to most Northerners. Fearing the 'detribalising' effect of study in the south, the colonial administration finally opened a teacher training college in Tamale in 1944. Of the twenty-six northern Members of the Legislative Assembly elected in 1954 and in 1956, twelve and nine respectively were 'Certificate A' middle-school teachers, and six and seven respectively were 'Certificate B' primary-school teachers.[127]

On the face of it, then, there were some similarities between the northern and southern sections: a sense of relative disadvantage vis-à-vis the Gold Coast Colony area in terms of educational provision; the dominance of a single standard VII provider; intense competition to enter teacher training institutions in the Colony area due to lack of educational opportunities in the home region; solidarity among a group of teachers who wanted to provide regional leadership; and a fear that public sector posts in the home region would become dominated by more advantaged individuals from other parts of the country. But, despite these similarities,

[123] Interview with E. K. Datsa, Amedzofe-Avatime, 3 June 1999.
[124] Ladouceur, *Chiefs and Politicians*, 49. [125] Ibid., 51. [126] Ibid., 53.
[127] Ibid., 86.

the Togoland Congress leadership could not easily tap into and mobilise local networks, or bring the Tamale 'graduates' into the heart of the reunificationist project.

Ladouceur argues that, until the 1954 election, the senior school/training college graduates essentially co-operated with the chiefs (to whom they were frequently related and whom they had often served as Native Authority clerks) in order to act as a pressure group for 'the north' within the new organs of government that resulted from the Coussey Commission.[128] It was only by accident of the abysmal performance of the Ghana Congress Party in 1954 that the Northern People's Party entered into the role of official opposition to the CPP government.[129] Whilst in southern British Togoland, there was considerable awareness of and investment in the distinctive constitutional status of the trust territory, in northern British Togoland this proved less important than the socio-economic divide, which, until 1954, enabled the Northern People's Party to claim to be the authentic representative of northern interests, including those of northern British Togoland.

Arguably, the Togoland Congress leadership could have done more to persuade the northerners that they would not be economically and politically marginalised within an independent Togoland. The widespread use of the Ewe word, *Ablɔɖe*, to denote both the Togoland Congress itself and the objective of Togoland reunification was unlikely to have fostered confidence that northern Togolanders would enjoy equal participation in a reunified and independent Togoland. After 1954, the CPP, despite its origins as a southern party, worked to convince clusters of northern voters that it could use its power to increase the pace of socio-economic development in the north – and indeed, in policies such as the Accelerated Plan for Educational Development in 1951, the CPP had already made significant gestures in this direction. The Togoland Congress, like the CPP, could not disguise its southern origins, but nor was it able to mobilise the advantages of incumbency to offer tangible evidence of a commitment to northern development.

LOSING THE PLEBISCITE

On the day the results came in, none of this actually mattered. The reunificationists might have been surprised by the extent of their defeat

[128] Ibid., 83–88 and 107–110. [129] Ibid., 128–130.

in the northern section, where 79 per cent of the votes were cast for integration, and only two local council areas showed a majority for separation. In the southern section of the trust territory, however, 55 per cent of the votes cast were for separation. In the Ho and Kpandu districts, the reunificationists achieved substantial majorities (72 per cent and 66 per cent), and this doubtless reinforced their sense that they had won the argument by demonstrating the legitimacy and the feasibility of their cause. In the southern section as a whole, the majority for separation was slightly lower at 55 per cent, because in the Buem-Krachi district, 60 per cent of the votes were for integration.[130] Thus despite their attempts in print and song to mobilise a Togoland national identity, and not an exclusionist Ewe sentiment, the reunificationist vote was mainly concentrated in the areas where Ewe was an accepted vehicular or majority language. Nonetheless, and as Nugent has explained, ethnicity does not provide a wholly satisfactory explanation for the voting patterns in Buem-Krachi or indeed elsewhere in the southern zone.[131] In the local council area of Buem, which was linguistically diverse as a result of pre-colonial migrations and more recent influxes of 'stranger' cocoa farmers, there was a small majority for separation. The local council area of Krachi, which had lobbied long and hard to be transferred into the Trans-Volta Togoland Region, showed overwhelming support for integration, perhaps because they saw their relationship to the CPP government as the best way of protecting their access to the regional development fund.

The analysis of the plebiscite results in Tsekpo's newspaper, *Mia Denyigba*, suggests that, at least initially, the reunificationists were pleased with their victory in the southern section.[132] The 1955 visiting mission had originally recommended that the plebiscite votes should be counted in four separate zones, but as this had been overturned in the General Assembly, there was flexibility in the interpretation of results.[133] The reunificationists believed that the results would be interpreted in the light of the long-established practice of administering the northern and southern sections of British Togoland separately, thus creating scope for the separation of the southern section. Over the next six months,

[130] Nugent, *Smugglers, Secessionists and Loyal Citizens*, 190 – table based on the results provided in United Nations, 'Report of the United Nations Plebiscite Commissioner'.

[131] Nugent, *Smugglers, Secessionists and Loyal Citizens*, 189–98.

[132] *Mia Denyigba*, 15 June 1956.

[133] United Nations, 'Report of the United Nations Plebiscite Commissioner', 13.

however, the integrationists worked hard to prevent this outcome. Recognising the importance of the question posed by the plebiscite commissioner about what in practice 'union' would mean, the British administration suggested that the plebiscite be interpreted in the light of the results of the July 1956 general election. Arguably, these results confirmed the popularity of the CPP and its proposals for a unitary constitution.[134] The Trusteeship Council concluded that, although parts of the trust territory had exhibited a preference for separation from the Gold Coast, the overall majority in favour of integration must prevail. On 31 July 1956, the council voted through the draft resolution of the Indian delegate, which recommended the termination of trusteeship.[135] This resolution still had to be ratified by the General Assembly, which was due to meet in November.

Whilst Antor continued to hope for a partition of the trust territory, he recognised that the General Assembly would probably accept the Trusteeship Council's decision. The impending reality of integration compelled the Togoland Congress to consider the exact means by which it was to be effected. Leaders, advisors, and activists believed that, even if they could not prevent integration, they would be entitled to negotiate the terms and conditions under which 'union' with the Gold Coast would occur.[136] They were dismayed to discover that the British administration and the CPP treated the plebiscite result as a mandate for automatic and total integration: southern British Togoland would simply become part of the Trans-Volta Togoland Region of an independent Ghana, and would be governed according to a unitary constitution.

Recognising the likelihood of such a decision, the reunificationists had used the time between July and November 1956 to strengthen their relationships with the Gold Coast opposition parties, which opposed CPP plans for a unitary constitution. This process had begun as early as July 1955, when Antor had participated at a conference held in Kumasi by 'Movements and Parties other than the CPP'. There he had signed a document entitled 'Proposals for an Independent Gold Coast and Togoland', which demanded nothing short of a federal constitution.[137]

[134] Coleman argues that the 1956 election results were critical in convincing the Trusteeship Council that the plebiscite results should be accepted as a mandate for the integration of the whole of southern British Togoland into Ghana. Coleman, 'Togoland', 77.

[135] Amenumey, *The Ewe Unification Movement*, 268–75.

[136] Interview with A. M. K. Dumoga, Ho, 28 Aug 2000; interview with Kofi Kodzi, Edmonton, Greater London, 13 Dec 2000.

[137] Allman, *Quills of the Porcupine*, 113–14.

Confronted by the Trusteeship Council's decision in favour of terminating the Trusteeship Agreement, Antor decided to participate in a delegation to London in September 1956, alongside leading members of the (Asante) National Liberation Movement and the Northern People's Party. It is difficult to believe that he was not disappointed with the visit. The delegation's demands stopped far short of the federal constitution advocated in July 1955, but, in spite of the reduced demands, the delegation as a whole did not win any significant concessions.[138]

Antor now faced a dilemma. He continued to believe that southern British Togoland had a distinctive status as a trust territory. Until the United Nations had reached its final decision in November, Antor was unwilling to compromise arguments based on the constitutional distinctiveness of Togoland by joining too closely with the NLM and NPP. On the other hand, the resolution to terminate trusteeship had already been accepted by the Trusteeship Council, and the likelihood that this would be overturned was very slim. It was thus in the interests of the Togoland Congress to co-operate more closely with bodies that were trying to ensure that some degree of power would be devolved to the regions of an independent Ghana. Antor therefore issued careful instructions to the London solicitors hired in a joint enterprise with the Nayiri of Mamprusi and the Asanteman Council.

On 30 November 1956, Coward, Chance and Co. wrote to the Secretary of State for the Colonies on behalf of its clients in the Northern Territories, Asante, and British Togoland. All three clients agreed that the CPP government's 'Revised Constitutional Proposals for Gold Coast Independence' failed to provide 'those checks, balances and safeguards essential to the preservation of individual liberty and the rights of minorities and regions in a nascent state'.[139] The Togoland Congress, however,

[138] In July 1955, the Gold Coast opposition parties had hoped to achieve a bicameral parliament for each region, as well as a bicameral federal parliament in which chiefs would dominate the second chamber. The regional parliaments would have a wide range of powers, leaving only foreign policy, commerce, higher education, and communications to the federal government. After the Bourne Report of December 1955, however, the leadership of the NLM and NPP began to focus on gaining regional assemblies within a unitary framework.

[139] The National Archives (TNA), Kew, UK. CO 554/827 West Africa Department: Gold Coast Opposition Parties: Legal Measures in the UK, Coward, Chance and Co., London, to Secretary of State for the Colonies, 30 Nov 1956, including Antor's notes from his speech at the Fourth Committee, United Nations. The three clients complained that if the proposed constitution could be altered by a two-thirds majority in a single chamber, the CPP would be able to alter it very easily; that the promised regional assemblies should be

appeared to believe that it had additional, or better, grounds for dissatisfaction with the Ghana constitution because the latter did not meet the criteria that the United Nations had laid down for itself in deciding to terminate the Trusteeship Agreement. Coward, Chance and Co. thus included the text of Antor's speech to the Fourth Committee.

Firstly, Antor argued that the plebiscite was not a 'valid and effective method of determining the *wishes* of the people of Togoland' and that the Trusteeship Council should have allowed for plurality by recognising separate voting zones and the long-standing administrative distinction between the northern and southern section. Secondly, Antor argued that the plebiscite had offered voters a choice between union with, or separation from, the Gold Coast, but Togolanders would not have voted for union had they realised that the new Ghanaian constitution would provide so few guarantees of the rights of minorities, regions, or individuals. Indeed, Antor claimed that, as far as the trust territory was concerned, Independence as part of the Gold Coast did not really constitute Independence at all. The administering authority had failed to ensure 'progressive development towards self-government or independence', as specified under article 76 of the United Nations Charter, and the General Assembly should therefore refuse to terminate its supervision over British Togoland.[140]

Antor suggested that the Ghanaian constitution should be subjected to the approval of the United Nations, or that the International Court of Justice should be called upon to prevent the 'precipitate merger of British Togoland into Ghana'. Coward, Chance and Co. informed the Secretary of State that if a satisfactory constitution could not be achieved, he should appoint 'a Partition Commission to divide assets and liabilities between the Colony, Ashanti, the Northern Territories and Togoland'. Neither the Secretary of State for the Colonies nor the Fourth Committee at the United Nations was prepared to accept Antor's arguments. Influenced again by the Indian representative, the Fourth Committee voted to terminate the Trusteeship Agreement.[141]

established before Independence and not after; that the proposed regional houses of chiefs should have more than advisory functions; that the police should be organised into regional forces, not controlled by central government; that measures should be taken to ensure that all groups would be represented in the civil service and judiciary; and that human rights provisions should be inscribed in the Ghana constitution. See also Allman, *Quills of the Porcupine*, 162–75.

140 Antor's notes from his speech at the Fourth Committee of the United Nations in CO 554/827 West Africa Department: Gold Coast Opposition Parties., p. 12.

141 Amenumey, *The Ewe Unification Movement*, 273. According to Amenumey, the Indian representative emphasised that a unit as small as southern British Togoland was

THE DENIAL OF DUE RECOGNITION

By the time the termination of trusteeship had been finally decided, Ablɔḍe's allies in the NLM and NPP had begun to divide among themselves. Jean Allman argues that whilst there was considerable secessionist sentiment within both the NLM and Asante as a whole, Kofi Busia and the Asantehene led a movement in favour of compromise with the CPP. By January 1957 they had backed well away from the original demand for a federal constitution and were willing to accept minor concessions.[142] Once Secretary of State for the Colonies Alan Lennox-Boyd succeeded in obtaining an invitation from Nkrumah, his visits to Accra, Kumasi, and Tamale between 24 and 30 January 1957 were critical in allowing key opponents of the CPP to save face in the negotiations that preceded Independence. Lennox-Boyd, however, declined to visit Ho, and according to a statement by Antor and Ametowobla to the *Ashanti Pioneer*, he also refused to meet with a Togoland Congress delegation in Accra.[143]

This was deeply humiliating to Antor and Ametowobla, because it implied a refusal to recognise not only that they had a case to make, but also that they were legitimate representatives of popular opinion. It also implied that Antor and Ametowobla were persons of lesser importance than the Asante or northern leaders who opposed Nkrumah. Whether a face-saving visit would have been enough to persuade Antor to accept Ghana's Independence constitution is a matter for speculation. The failure of Lennox-Boyd to meet with the Togoland Congress, however, may explain why it was only the reunificationists who protested against Independence in March 1957, when, for much of the previous three years, it was Asante that had seen more violence. By the end of February, Busia, the Asantehene, and the Nayiri had all accepted the British government's White Paper, and had agreed that Independence celebrations would take place.[144] In the debate on the White Paper in the Gold Coast parliament, Busia was conciliatory, leaving the only real condemnation of Ghana's Independence constitution to Antor.[145]

unviable – although it is possible that his views were also shaped by the bitter experience of the India-Pakistan partition of 1947.

142 Allman, *Quills of the Porcupine*, 168–78.

143 *Ashanti Pioneer*, 28 Feb 1957, front page.

144 *Daily Graphic*, 18 Feb 1957, 7 and *Ashanti Pioneer*, 27 Feb 1957, 5.

145 Allman, *Quills of the Porcupine*, 180–182.

Meanwhile, Antor had mobilised the chiefs of southern British Togoland into an official boycott of all Independence celebrations. The Howusu, Mote Kofi II, collected the signatures of twenty-three chiefs and presented a resolution to the Regional Officer, Ho (T. A. Mead), declaring their intentions. According to the *Daily Graphic*, Mead had adopted a conciliatory approach, promising that although 'any attempt ... to interfere with peaceful celebrations in the region would be quickly and firmly dealt with ... he would [also] do his best to ensure that persons celebrating independence offered no unnecessary provocation'.[146] Antor and Ametowobla, however, informed the *Ashanti Pioneer* that Mead had in fact deliberately provoked them by appointing Togbe Apede Asor of Ho-Bankoe (Mote Kofi's long-standing rival and a CPP loyalist) to take care of the arrangements for celebrations.[147]

A few days after Independence, the Minister of the Interior, Ako Adjei, released a statement that appeared in major Ghanaian newspapers on 11 and 12 March.[148] The statement claimed that, between 15 and 20 February, the government had received information about two camps where opponents of integration were being trained for the disruption of Independence celebrations. On the basis of this information, the Governor of the Gold Coast, Sir Charles Arden-Clarke, signed two Peace Preservation Orders, requiring the inhabitants of Alavanyo and Hodzo to give up all weapons and ammunition except those that were covered by a special licence. On 1 March, police found evidence that telephone wires had been cut, and the two camps, with small cachés of weapons and evidence of recent occupation, were discovered. Two hundred extra police were sent to the area, whilst military companies were stationed at Ho, Hohoe, and Kpandu in order to act as 'reserve security forces'.

According to the Minister of the Interior, on 3 March, sixteen individuals were arrested for refusing to give up their weapons. On 4 March, sixty people travelled by lorry to Kpandu, where they tore down Independence decorations and broke the windows of the post office. A riot ensued in which sixty-nine people were arrested. On the same day, 150 people demonstrated outside the office of the Government Agent, Jasikan, and a riot ensued when they were attacked by local advocates of integration. In this riot, eight were arrested, four were injured (one of whom died in hospital), and one person was killed outright. On 5 March, 'minor incidents' occurred in 'many scattered localities' and the total

[146] *Daily Graphic*, 20 Feb 1957, 16. [147] *Ashanti Pioneer*, 28 Feb. 1957, 7.
[148] *Daily Graphic*, 11 March 1957, 5 and *Ashanti Pioneer*, 12 March 1957, 2 and 7.

number of arrests now reached eighty. On 6 March, a major incident occurred at Kpandu-Konda. A platoon of police reserves, leaving the town by lorry, was surrounded and fired upon. Reinforcements of police arrived, and in the ensuing riot, three reunificationists were killed and six were wounded. Supporters of reunification, on the other hand, remembered the sequence of events rather differently, emphasising the extent to which they were provoked, harassed, and attacked by members of the army and police force.[149]

The Togoland Congress must have been disappointed by the failure of other leading opponents of the CPP to organise a Gold Coast–wide boycott of Independence celebrations. However, the government's decision to post companies of troops to southern Togoland during the Independence celebrations generated an immediate issue around which anti-CPP parties could rally. The government statement insisted that troops were 'at no time ... engaged in operations' and had simply been posted to the region to demonstrate that reinforcements were available in the event of any serious insurrection.[150] The *Ashanti Pioneer*, however, ran an article entitled 'Police or Army' in which the posting of troops to southern Togoland was likened to the approach of the colonial government to the servicemen's riots of 1948.

> If, therefore, Mr Nkrumah's Government, after ousting the imperialist government, now wants so cheerfully to go the way of the imperialists, then it has far too soon betrayed the very struggle for independence. In the sacred name of independent Ghana, will the Government please put the army in its true place in a true democracy, by discouraging it from vying with the police in its inalienable role of maintaining law and order.[151]

As we shall see in Chapter 6, the CPP's treatment of its opponents continued to provide issues around which reunificationists could re-establish co-operation with other elements of the Ghanaian opposition, and thus overcome their disappointment at their isolation in March 1957.

[149] See for example the account in E. K. Datsa, *Doing My Duty: Memoirs of a Ghanaian Educationalist*, 117–18.

[150] *Ashanti Pioneer*, 12 March 1957, 7.

[151] *Ashanti Pioneer*, 14 March 1957, 4.

5

Activists in Exile

Political Possibility in the Post-Colony

In January 2013, the Western Togoland Assembly issued 'Circular 2013', which recalled the violence that had accompanied Ghanaian Independence and accused the government of Ghana of engaging in a 'triumphant annexation, subjugation and . . . continued programme of enslavement' of the people of the former trust territory of British (Western) Togoland.[1] The authors of the circular pointed out that the British government had presented the plebiscite result to the United Nations as evidence of popular support for the 'union' of Togoland with Ghana. However, as the term 'union' implied an agreement achieved by dialogue between equals, the actual manner by which integration had been effected in 1956 and 1957 rendered it closer to an illegal occupation. The Western Togoland Assembly produced a membership handbook which explained these arguments in greater detail, whilst the Association of Homeland Study Groups (based in Kpandu) wrote to the United Nations secretary-general in the hope of reopening an international debate on the Togoland question. More than half a century after the trusteeship agreement was terminated, a core of activists in the former British Togoland seek to remind residents of the special status of the area and to challenge the means by which integration with Ghana was achieved. The efforts of these activists do not, in and of themselves, prove that the Togoland question is still of pressing importance to the majority or that secession is imminent. What the efforts of these activists certainly do indicate, however, is that the Togoland question has had a surprisingly long post-colonial tail, and a persistence which has hitherto gone unremarked by historians.

[1] Copy in author's possession.

The remaining chapters of this book, then, are concerned with the reformulation and survival of Ablɔḍe in the post-colonial era. We shall begin with the period immediately after Independence, when Ghana and Togo, like many other sub-Saharan states, were characterised by shifts towards authoritarian single-party regimes, coups d'état, and phases of military rule. David Brown concluded that, in the town of Kpandu, the Ablɔḍe 'faction' was dissolved during this period of repression and that 'the goal of Togoland Unification ceased to be an immediately practical possibility'.[2] Paul Nugent argued that, during the Nkrumah years, Ablɔḍe became 'a foreign country' to the people of the former trust territory as they developed a stronger sense of Ghanaian identity, and he pinpoints the late 1970s as 'the end of the story' for Togoland reunification.[3] The gap between these conclusions and the story that I tell here requires us to rethink our approaches to post-colonial history, and to find alternative means of understanding the nature of political mobilisation and dissent in Africa's new states.

Case study approaches, which rely heavily on district level records and interview individuals as representatives of a particular place, have generated voluminous evidence of political interactions that were intended to advance highly localised agendas. But this abundance of evidence for the instrumentalist logic of political affiliation in rural Africa results, at least in part, from the record-keeping practices of the state. District commissioners in post-colonial Ghana, and their counterparts (the *commandants de cercle*) in Togo, were political appointees, chosen partly on the basis of their record of support for the ruling party. Like their colonial equivalents, these district level representatives of the state worked by identifying local allies and marginalising actual and potential opponents, usually by resolving chieftaincy disputes in favour of candidates who pledged support to the regime, and by directing developmental resources away from opposition strongholds. It is unsurprising, therefore, that district level records generate evidence of individual and communal calculations as to the benefits to be gained from co-operation. In order to recover evidence of dissent, the historian may need to look elsewhere.

Recent scholarship on struggles for Independence and on the management of dissent in new nations has therefore paid attention to physical movements of political activists across borders, and to the mechanisms by which radical, left-leaning, and anti-colonial movements sought

[2] David Brown, 'Politics in the Kpandu Area of Ghana', 309.
[3] Paul Nugent, *Smugglers, Secessionists and Loyal Citizens*, 218 and 230.

intellectual, diplomatic, and economic support from newly independent nations. Meredith Terretta, Klaas van Walraven, and Jeff Ahlman all point to Kwame Nkrumah's Ghana as a nodal point in these radical networks. The Conference of Independent States and the All-African Peoples' Conference held in Accra in 1958 debated the means by which Ghana and other independent states might support anti-colonial nationalist movements in other parts of Africa and mobilise international opinion against racist settler regimes. The Bureau of African Affairs in Accra went on to provide direct support to defeated and persecuted 'freedom fighters', including those seeking refuge from the emerging neo-colonial or 'puppet' regimes which enjoyed the support of the French in Niger and Cameroon.[4] These studies highlight the movement of radical and left-leaning anti-colonial activists into Accra, and the projection from Accra of an evolving vision of pan-Africanism.

For Terretta, this activity throws into question the extent to which the 1950s can be regarded as a period in which a preoccupation with territorial nationalism displaced older ideals of solidarity between African peoples.[5] In this chapter, I shall demonstrate that the political traffic in post-Independence Ghana travelled in more than one direction, and that it was not confined to the capital, Accra. In other words, as Accra welcomed in those whose stance was endorsed by the Nkrumah regime, those who found themselves on the wrong side of the political divide were making their way out across Ghana's eastern border. This chapter therefore focusses on a community of approximately 5,700 political refugees who left Ghana between 1958 and 1961, and who remained across the border in French Togoland (from 1960, Republic of Togo) until the coup that toppled the Ghanaian government in 1966. The experiences of this relatively small number of refugees are revealing as to the nature of cross-border political mobilisation in rural areas in the immediate aftermath of Independence.[6] The problematic status of the refugee population and

[4] Meredith Terretta, 'Cameroonian Nationalists Go Global: From Forest *Maquis* to Pan-African Accra', *Journal of African History* 51 (2) (2010), 189–212; Klaas van Walraven, *Yearning for Relief: A History of the Sawaba Movement in Niger* (Leiden, 2013); Jeff Ahlman, 'Road to Ghana: Nkrumah, Southern Africa and the Eclipse of a Decolonizing Africa', *Kronos* 37 (1) (2011), 23–40.

[5] Terretta, 'Cameroonian Nationalists Go Global', 204.

[6] According to the 1958/9 census, the population of Togo was approximately 1.3 million. Têtêvi Godwin Tété-Adjalogo, *Histoire du Togo: le regime et l'assassinat de Sylvanus Olympio*, vol. 3 (Paris, 2002), 24. According to the 1961 census, the population of Ghana was approximately 6.7 million.

disagreements about the ways in which they might be assisted also speak to wider debates about the challenges of new nations and their relationships to their former colonial powers.

Three types of sources will be brought to bear. Firstly, in interviews, former refugees and their relatives asserted their continuing commitment to Togoland reunification in this period, and presented their relationship with Togo's first president, Sylvanus Olympio, as a new opportunity to rectify their grievances about the integration of the former British Togoland with Ghana. The experience of exile in a francophone country interrupted some of the claims to authority and spokesmanship that had been made within the Ablɔɖe movement in British Togoland in the mid-1950s: the ability to formulate and present a legalistic case in English counted for rather less by 1960 than it had just a few years before. Interviews with former refugees suggest that the relative paucity of references to them in Togolese district records does not reflect a lack of activity on their part, so much as a shift towards conducting their political activity in the Ewe-language and in oral and literary domains which sometimes fell outside of the record-keeping remit of the state.

Secondly, underutilised diplomatic records indicate that, in the complex and precarious process of decolonisation in French Togoland, the presence of Ghanaian refugees acted as a focal point in a series of related disputes over the relationships of new states with their former colonial powers, with the international community and, most importantly, with each other. As the Ghanaian and Togolese governments put forward competing and incompatible solutions to the Togoland problem, each became aware that the refugee population represented a test of their capacity to deal with dissent both within and across national borders. In their responses to activists in exile, the newly independent states confronted the limits of their powers and attempted to extend their range. The former colonial powers, on the other hand, were confronted with a diplomatic dilemma which challenged their categorisations of African governments into neo-colonial 'friends' and radical 'foes'.

Finally, an Ewe-language newspaper, produced in Kpalimé, from 1958 through the 1960s, permits an insight into the idiom of political debate in the border area and in towns where refugees had settled. *Ablɔɖe Safui* (*Key to Freedom*) consistently addressed the Togoland question, deploying a range of images and metaphors in support of reunification, and vilifying the Ghanaian president, Kwame Nkrumah, and his Convention People's Party (CPP) regime. Following the instrumentalist logics that are emphasised in case studies, we might expect this kind of newspaper to formulate national political issues in culturally specific terms and hitch them to local agendas in order to influence the party affiliations of its rural readers. In the closing section of this chapter, I highlight the ways in which *Ablɔḍe Safui* confounds such expectations: readers in rural areas had access to a range of competing interpretations of the border issue, and newspapers had to work hard to convince readers of the truthfulness of their coverage. Rather than privileging highly localised agendas, Ewe-language publications were also used to cast political issues in an international and historical framework, and to hold leaders accountable. In these respects, vernacular print was one of the mechanisms through which Ewe-speaking Togolese, and the Ghanaian refugees who lived among them, debated what it meant to be a citizen of a newly independent state and how an individual should go about the business of 'making politics'.[7]

'KEEP QUIET, GO UNDERGROUND, OR CROSS THE CARPET': OPTIONS FOR THE VANQUISHED

In the immediate aftermath of Ghanaian Independence, the prospects for Ablɔḍe activists looked bleak. The CPP had defeated the Togoland reunificationists in the plebiscite of May 1956 and secured a unitary constitution in the negotiations that led to Independence in March 1957. Opportunities for further agitation were restricted by the arrest of two leading members of the Togoland Congress and the imposition of a Peace Preservation Order on the areas in which riots had occurred during Ghana's Independence celebrations. The Avoidance of Discrimination Act of December 1957, which prohibited political parties organised on a 'tribal', regional, or religious basis, prevented the Togoland Congress from operating publicly as a separate organisation and pushed its remaining members of parliament into the new Ghana-wide United Party.[8]

In the spring and summer of 1958, however, the CPP experienced several setbacks. Firstly, the local council elections of April 1958 produced evidence of intransigence in key Ablɔḍe strongholds. Brown thus noted that although the CPP took a clear majority of seats across the Trans-Volta Togoland Region (which included the Anlo- and Peki-Ewe areas in addition to the southern section of the former British Togoland), 'in the

[7] I am currently working with Wilson Yayoh on further translations of *Ablɔḍe Safui* and we hope to publish an extended commentary on its significance as a source for African history. The volume is provisionally entitled *Ablɔḍe Safui (the Key to Freedom): Writing the New Nation in a West African Border Town.*

[8] Dennis Austin, *Politics in Ghana 1946–60* (London, 1964), 377.

three Local Council areas of the Kpandu North Constituency, the CPP was heavily defeated'.[9] This indicates that one of the CPP's primary strategies for winning over its opponents since 1952 had reached its limits: despite the direction of development funds towards the areas that were prepared to play ball with the ruling party, despite the resolution of chieftaincy disputes in favour of candidates who pledged to support the CPP, and despite the 'conversion' of several high profile Ablɔɖe activists, certain areas persisted in their opposition.

Secondly, the nationalists in French Togoland won the critical elections of 27 April 1958. The Comité de l'Unité Togolaise (CUT) and its allied movement, Juvento, took 61.1 per cent of the valid votes, and twenty-nine of forty-six seats in the new legislative assembly.[10] The CUT leader, Sylvanus Olympio, became prime minister with a clear mandate to reject the limited autonomy that France had offered in 1956 and to hold out instead for fuller measure of self-government. His party was also committed to the reunification of the two Togolands. In the same month, then, the CPP was confronted with the evidence that, not only had Ablɔɖe refused to die in parts of the former British Togoland, but it now had a powerful ally just a short distance across the border in French Togoland. Finally, two Togoland Congress leaders, S. G. Antor and Kodzo Ayeke, were released from detention on appeal and returned to their parliamentary duties.[11]

It was in the aftermath of these setbacks that the CPP began to close the net around its opponents, in the former British Togoland and indeed elsewhere in Ghana. The Preventive Detention Act of July 1958 gave the government the power to detain an individual for up to five years without the right of appeal.[12] The effect of this legislation was not felt in the former British Togoland until C. H. Chapman was replaced as Regional Commissioner, first by Krobo Edusei (renowned for his handling of opposition to the CPP in Asante), and subsequently by Ferdinand Koblavi Goka and F. Y. Asare.[13] In the early part of 1960, as the Independence of French Togoland approached, the police presence was doubled in the former British trust territory area and preventive detention

[9] Brown, 'Politics in the Kpandu Area of Ghana', 316.

[10] Amenumey, *The Ewe Unification Movement*, 319–20.

[11] Godwin Têtêvi Tété-Adjalogo, *Histoire du Togo: la palpitante quête de l'Ablode (1940–1960)* vol. 2 (Paris, 2000), 444.

[12] Austin, *Politics in Ghana*, 380–1.

[13] Edusei was appointed to TVT in September 1958. Brown, 'Politics in the Kpandu Area of Ghana', 317.

orders were issued against individuals who were suspected of plotting disturbances aimed at a revision of the decisions made in 1956 and 1957.[14] In particular, the government claimed that former Ablɔɖe activists were cultivating subversive links with French Togoland, as can be seen in the grounds for detention that were issued to Moses Kofi Asase of Ho-Dome and thirteen other Ablɔɖe activists in March 1960.[15] Further preventive detention orders were issued through the spring and summer of 1960, prompting an exodus of Ablɔɖe activists who feared that they would also be arrested.

Describing his experience in the People's Education Association in this period, the former adult educationist Richard Banibensu summarised the options that were open to individuals who opposed the CPP: 'In those days, if you wanted to have your peace, it was better to ally with the CPP. Keep quiet, go underground, or cross the carpet – those were your options.'[16] Brown argues that, in Kpandu, it was the stick of preventive detention, rather than the proverbial political carrot, that ultimately proved more effective in removing visible opposition to the CPP in 1960. Nugent, on the other hand, maintains that the process of 'cipipification' was more far-reaching across the former trust territory area. Noting the rise of a new generation of opinion leaders who had benefitted from the expansion of educational opportunities in Nkrumah's Ghana, he points to the failure of the older Ablɔɖe leadership to reassert itself even after the coup of 1966, and concludes that that the co-operation of individuals and communities with the CPP represented not only acquiescence, but also a 'belated acceptance of the CPP vision of modernity'.[17] Missing from these interpretations, however, is an exploration of the experiences of the individuals who chose to 'go underground'.

'HE WANTED TO DIE WITH POLITICS': ACTIVISM IN EXILE

As an increasing number of arrests were made throughout Ghana, including the former trust territory area, Ablɔɖe activists began to flee across the eastern border to avoid preventive detention. By October 1961, the Togolese government informed the United Nations that 5,700 Ghanaians (belonging to various ethnic groups and former opposition parties) had taken refuge in

[14] Ibid., 319. [15] A copy of the text of the detention order is in the author's possession.

[16] Interview with Richard Banibensu and Michael Senoo, Dansoman, Greater Accra, 14 July 2000. It was Richard Banibensu who made this observation. By 'crossing the carpet' he was referring to a change of party loyalty – in the British House of Commons, parliamentarians who are elected on one party ticket but subsequently join a different party may literally walk across the strip of carpet which divides the government from the opposition benches.

[17] Nugent, *Smugglers, Secessionists and Loyal Citizens*, 217.

Togo. Those from the former British Togoland clustered around the towns of Lomé and Kpalimé, and in the area of Akposso-Badou.[18] As we shall see, the status of these individuals was problematic. The Nkrumah government regarded them as living in self-imposed exile, whilst the British also suggested that they had chosen to move across the border for economic reasons and were not bona fide political refugees. Given that the threat of preventive detention loomed large in the accounts of all the individuals to whom I spoke, I shall refer to them here as 'refugees' – a status that was also tacitly acknowledged by the United Nations High Commission for Refugees in its somewhat piecemeal and belated assistance programme.

On the basis of his field work in the late 1980s, Nugent indicated that the refugees appear to have been deterred from maintaining an active interest in unification politics.

> The Togolese authorities did not wish to add credence to Ghanaian claims that they were encouraging subversion, and specifically informed the refugees that they could only stay if they desisted from engaging in political activity. It is easy to see that a highly politicised refugee population might pose a threat to the power base of the Olympio regime itself. The fact that they were also widely dispersed across rural Togo was a further barrier to regular interaction.

Nugent therefore concluded that, for the majority of refugees, 'enforced exile was a rather solitary experience' characterised more by material hardship than by political activism. Individuals 'took to farming to subsist, awaiting the day when they could return to their homes'.[19]

When I interviewed former refugees and their families in 1999, 2000, and 2010, however, almost everyone I spoke to maintained that the refugees had been politically active throughout their time in Togo. Edward Kojo Mfojoh, a goldsmith from Sokode-Gbagble, and a friend of Moses Kofi Asase, crossed the border in June 1960 to avoid arrest. He described Kpalimé as a hive of activity: refugees were drawn to it in the knowledge that they would find their fellow activists. He stated that he travelled regularly between Kpalimé and Lomé in order to attend meetings with Olympio: 'I met him plenty of times, sitting down next to him and talking to him, just like I am with you now.'[20] Mercy Akosua Tegbe, one of the wives of the late Togbe Gabusu IV of Hohoe, also

[18] The National Archives (TNA), Kew, UK. DO 195/75 Ghana-Togo Relations: United Nations High Commissioner for Refugees, Geneva, to Secretary of State for Foreign Affairs, London, 13 Feb 1962.

[19] Nugent, *Smugglers, Secessionists and Loyal Citizens*, 215–6.

[20] Interview with E. K. Mfojoh, Sokode-Gbagble, 19 July 2000. I am grateful to Lydia Osei-Brantuo for acting as interpreter.

FIGURE 3: Mercy Akosua Tegbe in Ablɔḍe Cloth. Copyright: Kate Skinner.

recalled that her husband had spent much of his time attending political meetings, along with the Howusu, Mote Kofi.[21] Tegbe remembered numerous political songs from her time in Togo, and she had also kept her 'Ablɔḍe cloth'.[22] (See Figure 3.) When I asked Agnes Tachie Adzraku, a trader, farmer, and wife of the late chief Komlateng of Kpandu-Aloi, whether she and her husband had ever talked with Olympio about the reunification issue, she responded: 'Ha! We talked about nothing else!'[23] Edward Wuanka remembered that his father, Komla Foli, a cocoa farmer

[21] Mote Kofi had been paramount chief of the Asogli state during the 1940s, but was forced to cede this position after several bitter disputes (some of which related to the Togoland unification issue). He therefore reverted to the title 'Howusu' which was given to him in the town of Ho Dome.

[22] Interview with Mercy Akosua Tegbe, Hohoe, 19 Sept 2000. I am grateful to Michael Senoo for arranging this interview and to Lydia Osei-Brantuo for acting as interpreter.

[23] Interview with Agnes Tachie Adzraku, Kpandu-Aloi, 7 June 2010. I am grateful to Cecilia Dusi for introducing me to this elderly lady and acting as interpreter during the interview. Brown, 'Politics in the Kpandu Area of Ghana', 316, describes Komlateng as 'the effective leader of the Togoland Congress in Kpandu'.

from Dzolo-Gbogame, 'did not stop doing politics. He wanted to die with politics! [Laughter]'.[24]

In the final chapter, I examine why former refugees were prepared to discuss their experiences with me. First, however, let us learn a little more about their experiences. At the level of political imagination, the refugees who came across the border into French Togoland were hardly in a 'foreign country'. The main focus of their political efforts over the past decade had been the separation of British Togoland from the Gold Coast in order to preserve the possibility of reunification with French Togoland. In this sense, a move from Hohoe to Kpalimé could be conceived as nothing more than a physical shift from the western to the eastern part of the same imagined nation. As the language of everyday interaction remained the same, and as many extended families were spread out through towns and villages on either side of the border, the refugees were easily dispersed within the host communities. Ironically, however, the very individuals who espoused the political project of Togoland reunification experienced their time in French Togoland as a period of dislocation.

When former refugees emphasised their material hardships, they described this not simply as a short-term loss of status or comfort: it was a serious setback to longer-term family strategies to achieve economic security. As we have seen in previous chapters, the social composition and the activities of the Ablɔɖe movement were shaped by the economic opportunities that were available to the people of the trust territory. Cocoa farmers made important contributions to the expenses of the reunificationists who petitioned the United Nations, and were well-represented among the founder members of the Togoland Congress. But the spokespersons, both in the Gold Coast/Ghana legislature, and at the United Nations in New York, were chosen on the basis of their formal education: it was deemed essential that they could master a legalistic case, and present it fluently and convincingly, in English, both on paper and in person. It was this petitioning activity that generated some of the major sources on which historians and political scientists have come to rely in their accounts of political protest in the trust territories.[25] The experience

24 Interview with Edward Komla Danquah Wuanka, Dzolo-Gbogame, 12 June 2010. I am grateful to Seth and Albert Yayoh for introducing me to this elderly man and arranging the interview.

25 See Meredith Terretta, *Petitioning for Our Rights, Fighting for Our Nation: the History of the Democratic Union of Cameroonian Women, 1949–1960* (Oxford, 2013).

FIGURE 4: Refugees from Dzolo. Copyright holder unknown.

of exile, however, disrupted both of these patterns within the Ablɔɖe movement, and therefore gave rise to different types of records.

Whilst many refugees fled their homes abruptly, travelling in the night after receiving a tip-off from a friend about their imminent arrest, they also retained a sense of themselves as a cohort with a particular purpose. In March 1960, eight men from the villages of Dzolo-Dzave and Dzolo-Kpuita received requests to attend an interview and respond to allegations that they were involved in a conspiracy. Just two days after the arrest of Moses Kofi Asase on 14 March, these eight men decided that rather than attending the interview, and risking being sent to preventive detention (as happened to Asase), they would cross the border to French Togoland. In order to mark this, they later donned their cloth, erected a signboard explaining the reason for their departure, and posed for the photograph in Figure 4.[26]

Among the group of eight (sitting in the front row, third from the left) was the ardent reunificationist and cocoa farmer Komla Foli. His son, Edward Wuanka, recalled that whereas in British Togoland Foli had produced cocoa on his own farm, in exile he struggled to find a new means of subsistence. Foli received some food and clothing through the United Nations relief efforts, but, like most of the refugees, he arranged his own accommodation, choosing a village on Mount Agu, near Kpalimé, where one of his daughters was living with her husband. It was fortunate that Foli was 'a talented man' who

[26] I am grateful to Edward Komla Danquah Wuanka of Dzolo-Gbogame for giving me a copy of this photograph. He was not able to specify who had taken the photograph or when. Wuanka thought it possible that it had been taken shortly after the refugees' arrival in French Togoland by a local photographer, rather than at home in Dzolo, where a photographer would probably have been known to his family.

could turn his hand to various types of craft work. According to his son, he learned to weave baskets and make palanquins, and this enabled him to get by until May 1966, when he returned home to Dzolo. Edward Kojo Mfojoh also remembered that what saved him was having a trade: 'I had some goldsmith friends and luckily they were passing me work. The people who did not have a trade, well, that one was a real problem.' People who had previously been farmers in their own right now 'had to go and labour in the fields of other people'.[27] Similarly, Mercy Akosua Tegbe recalled that refugees were restricted to growing their own food crops rather than participating in the cash-cropping economy.[28] Agnes Tachie Adzraku was more fortunate: she and her husband had a substantial farm on the Togo side of the border, and were able to live comfortably from this, and from her trading activities, during their time in exile.[29]

The disruption of livelihoods that were based on cocoa farms on the Ghana side of the border had a knock-on effect on the children who were left behind. Among these children was Emmanuel Dzeletsu, whose father, Manfred Dzeletsu, was among the group of eight represented in the photograph (he sits in the front row, second from the left).[30] Separated from his cocoa farm on Mount Awakpale, Manfred had little choice but to turn his hand to subsistence agriculture during the six years that he spent at Akpadapé, near Kpalimé. He received some farming inputs through the United Nations relief effort, as well as some food and clothing. 'He suffered,' recalled his son, 'and even I had to cut short my secondary-school education because he was not in a position to take over responsibility for that.' Emmanuel left the West Africa Secondary School in Accra and undertook a fee-free teacher training course at Jasikan. These personal accounts complicate Nugent's argument that as individuals and families benefitted from the expansion of educational opportunities in Nkrumah's Ghana, their identity as 'Togolanders' was eroded. For Emmanuel Dzeletsu, the threat of preventive detention, and his father's subsequent exile, resulted in a reduction of opportunity at a key stage of his secondary education.

The family crises that followed on from the unanticipated departure of a father were quickly brought to his attention. Both Wuanka and Dzeletsu

27 Interview with Edward Kojo Mfojoh, Sokode-Gbagble, 19 July 2000.
28 Interview with Mercy Akosua Tegbe, Hohoe, 19 Sept 2000.
29 Interview with Agnes Tachie Adraku, Kpandu-Aloi, 7 June 2010.
30 Interview with Emmanuel Dzeletsu, Dzolo-Gbogame, 12 June 2010. I am grateful to Seth Yayoh for arranging this interview.

recalled that they had crossed the border on several occasions in order to visit their fathers. Dzeletsu's mother came under suspicion as a result of her frequent trips to the border, and she eventually joined her husband in exile. Richard Banibensu recalled that *wɔ* (flour, ground from roasted corn) became a staple food for men seeking to avoid arrest: it can be preserved for long periods when dry, and can also be kept for several days after it has been cooked into a dumpling (*akplɛ*), so women could prepare it and carry it across the border or into the bush, if their husbands were in hiding.[31] These recollections are important because they suggest that the refugees did not survive in a state of isolation: people, supplies, and news from home found their way across the border on a fairly regular basis, which raises the possibility that political reports and commentaries could do so too.

In earlier chapters, we have seen how formal education and fluency in English gradually became prerequisites for reunificationist spokespeople. Ironically, for those living in exile in a francophone country, a manual skill, a plot of land, a friend, family member, or indeed a chief who was willing to help, all became much more useful assets than the formal qualifications that British Togolanders had struggled so hard to acquire for most of the 1940s and 1950s. The chiefs, whose role in the delegations and petitions to the United Nations in the 1950s had often been limited by their low levels of formal education, now found themselves in leadership roles. Mercy Akosua Tegbe recalled that her husband, Togbe Gabusu IV of Hohoe, received donations from supporters back home.[32] One former refugee suggested to Brown that approximately fifty people from Kpandu-Aloi had clustered in Kpalimé and that they looked to their chief, Komlateng, to give them work on his farms.[33] Several former refugees also mentioned Henri Kofi Apetor, chief of Kpalimé, who was instrumental in persuading residents to accept refugees into their households when no other accommodation was available. (See Figure 5.) Tegbe concluded that her time in Togo was bearable partly because the local population 'received us nicely'.[34]

Those refugees who, by virtue of their educational achievements, had been selected as Ablɔɖe spokespersons now found themselves excluded from their former political positions and disqualified from professional

[31] Interview with Richard Banibensu and Constant Senoo, Medina, Greater Accra, 11 July 2000.
[32] Interview with Mercy Akosua Tegbe, Hohoe, 19 Sept 2000.
[33] See Brown, 'Politics in the Kpandu Area of Ghana', 319 for details of his interview with Paul Badasu of Kpandu-Aloi.
[34] Interview with Mercy Akosua Tegbe, Hohoe, 19 Sept 2000.

FIGURE 5: Refugees at Chief's House in Kpalimé. Courtesy of Koku Avortri. Copyright holder unknown.

opportunities. Thus Bernice Ametowobla, wife of the former parliamentarian Reverend Francis Ametowobla, recalled, 'When we were in Togo, Pa was not able to work properly because he could not speak good French. He did some small work translating things from Ewe to English. Then Sylvanus Olympio put him in touch with some people in Liberia … and that is how Pa became principal of the Presbyterian College there.'[35] Written English was of relatively little use in a situation where French was a prerequisite to public sector employment (including most teaching posts) and where communication across the border took place primarily in Ewe. By contrast, the Ewe-language author G. K. Tsekpo was able to carry on working during his time in exile. According to his daughter Mercy, Tsekpo retired from teaching and in 1960 was working at the Bureau of Ghana Languages (formerly the Vernacular Literature Bureau) in Accra as an Ewe expert. However, 'he was on the Ablɔɖe side so he went into exile', taking Mercy with him.[36] Whereas Ametowobla had been obliged to leave for an anglophone country in order to continue practising his profession, Tsekpo 'got work from the church and also from government'. He reopened his Mawuli Press in Lomé, publishing *Togo Ŋutinya Akpa II* (*Togo History Part II*), and was also given

[35] Interview with Bernice Ametowobla, Ho, 12 Aug 2000, translation by Lydia Osei-Brantuo. During his time in Togo, Reverend Ametowobla was an assistant to Hans Debrunner, who was then researching the history of the Evangelical Presbyterian Church (successor to the Bremen mission). Ametowobla took up his position in Liberia after Olympio's assassination in 1963.

[36] Interview with Mercy Yawa Tsekpo, Alavanyo-Abehenease, 7 June 2010. I am grateful to Cecilia Dusi for arranging this interview, acting as interpreter and arranging copies of some of Tsekpo's Ewe-language publications.

responsibility for the Ewe-language page in the government newspaper, *Togo Presse*, from 1962.[37]

These oral testimonies suggest that as the refugees found new ways of making a living in exile, the Ablɔɖe movement did not disappear so much as assume new characteristics. The refugees believed that they mattered to Olympio and that they could make claims upon him for material assistance and for a continued commitment to Togoland reunification. In neither respect did Olympio fully deliver. In order to understand, then, why the refugees believed that Olympio was so committed to their cause, we need to know more about the situation that greeted them when they crossed the border into French Togoland.

CROSSING BORDERS: SOURCES FOR A TRANSNATIONAL HISTORY OF THE POST-COLONY

In August 1956, a new statute was promulgated in the trust territory of French Togoland, renaming it (misleadingly) the Autonomous Republic of Togo. Although the principle of universal suffrage had been accepted for French colonies as a result of the *loi cadre* in June, the primary beneficiaries of the enlargement of powers in the new legislative assembly were not the nationalists, who were committed to the reunification of the two Togolands, but the Parti Togolais du Progrès (usually known simply as 'Progrès') and the northern-based Union des Chefs et Populations du Nord (UCPN). Sylvanus Olympio's party, the CUT and its allied movement, Juvento, had protested since 1952 against electoral irregularities, which they claimed were deliberate attempts by the French to ensure the success of more malleable African politicians in the Progrès and the UCPN.[38]

Whilst in British Togoland the period between the plebiscite of May 1956 and the achievement of Ghanaian Independence in March 1957 was characterised by a frantic debate over the interpretation of the plebiscite results and whether Ghana should adopt a federal or unitary constitution, in French Togoland an equally frantic debate was taking place around a related issue. The French proposed to hold a referendum in October 1956. With the Progrès and the UCPN both supporting a settlement based

[37] G. K. Tsekpo, *Togo Ɖutinya Akpa II* (Lomé, 1961); see also Raymond Guillaneuf, 'La presse au Togo (1911–1966)', (Mémoire présenté pour le diplôme d'études supérieures, Université de Dakar, 1967, appendix 60/2).

[38] Amenumey, *The Ewe Unification Movement*, 64–80.

FIGURE 6: Elections in French Togoland, 1958. Copyright / by permission of: United Nations.

on limited autonomy within the French Union, the French anticipated that the results of this referendum would persuade the United Nations that French Togoland had achieved an acceptable measure of self-government and that its trusteeship status could be terminated.[39] In the event, however, French hopes were thwarted. Following a special mission to French Togoland in 1957, the United Nations decided in favour of holding fresh elections and sent their own observer.[40] (See Figure 6.)

According to Amenumey, the primary issue in the elections of April 1958 was not Togoland reunification per se, but the measure of self-government that the Togolese wished to obtain and the leaders that they trusted to conduct the negotiations.[41] However, the reunificationists on the Ghanaian side of the border also had an important stake in this election: with British Togoland already integrated into a unitary Ghana, the settlement of French Togoland for limited autonomy along the lines of that proposed in 1956 would curtail any prospects of reunification in the future, because the Togolese legislature would not have full control over defence, foreign affairs, security, external trade, or customs.[42] The success of Olympio, the CUT, and the Juvento, on the other hand, appeared to offer Togoland reunification a second chance. We now know that the CUT's stated commitment to

[39] Ibid., 285–99.

[40] Ibid., 299–319. See also Brian Digre, 'The United Nations, France, and African Independence: A Case Study of Togo', *French Colonial History* 5 (2004), 193–205.

[41] D. E. K. Amenumey, 'The General Elections in the "Autonomous Republic of Togo", April 1958: Background and Interpretation', *Transactions of the Historical Society of Ghana* 16 (1) (1975), 47–65.

[42] Ibid., 54 – secondary and higher education, public freedom and finance were also excluded from the powers of the Togolese legislature.

reunification did not translate into the desired result, but in April 1958 Olympio's victory, and his popular mandate to negotiate the terms under which French Togoland would become self-governing, was greeted with jubilation. From the perspective of the Ablɔɖe activists from the former British Togoland, the period 1958 to 1963 represented a new and decisive chapter.

The history of modern Togo has been written in the shadow of Olympio's assassination in 1963. The colonial period has received considerable attention, including analyses of the broad social composition and the innovative methods of the nationalist movement, but these studies have tended to conclude with the achievement of Independence in 1960.[43] The small number of scholars who have written about the early post-colonial period are divided in their interpretations. Wen'saa Ogma Yagla emphasised the ethnic divisions of the Olympio period, and the perception of bias towards the Ewe-speakers of the south, thereby offering an implicit justification for the coup d'état that brought the northerner Gnassingbé Eyadéma to power in 1967 and ushered in Africa's longest single-party regime.[44] Têtêvi Godwin Tété-Adjalogo, on the other hand, has argued that Olympio's unpopular austerity measures were designed to secure Togo's economic future, and that French anger at Olympio's intention to take Togo out of the franc zone was the primary factor in his assassination.[45] In this chapter, I do not intend to attribute responsibility for Olympio's assassination, or to cast doubt upon the considerable evidence for French neo-colonial intentions and interventions in Africa. My concern is that, in foregrounding Olympio as a nationalist martyr and a victim of French neo-colonial treachery, Togolese nationalist historiography should not underestimate the extent to which the terms of the

[43] Ginette Ayéle Kponton, 'La décolonisation au Togo (1940–1960)' (doctoral thesis, Université de Provence, 1977). Benjamin Lawrance has also commented on the intensive study of anti-colonial nationalism in Togo, and argues for more attention to twentieth-century social history. See *Locality, Mobility and "Nation:" Periurban Colonialism in Togo's Eweland 1900–1960* (Rochester NY, 2007), 6–9.

[44] Wen'saa Ogma Yagla, *L'édification de la nation togolaise: naissance d'une conscience nationale dans un pays africain* (Paris, 1978).

[45] Têtêvi Godwin Tété-Adjalogo, *Histoire du Togo: le regime et l'assassinat de Sylvanus Olympio (1960–1963)* (Paris, 2002). Tété-Adjalogo acknowledges that the assassination is usually attributed to two other factors: 1. a conspiracy amongst Olympio's opponents, particularly those residing in Ghana; 2. an angry response on the part of troops who, having been demobilised from French campaigns in Algeria and Vietnam, could not be re-employed in a Togolese national army because Olympio had decided that a large army was a luxury that a small African nation could not afford.

country's Independence, the government's subsequent relationship with the French, and the domestic opposition that the government encountered, were all shaped by its struggle with the neighbouring state of Ghana.

As we have seen, by the terms of the statute of 1956, the enlarged powers of Togo's legislative assembly did not include defence, security, foreign affairs, external trade, or customs. Control of these and other areas of policy was reviewed between 1958 and 1960, but under the terms of the trusteeship agreement, the administering authority (France) remained responsible for defence of the territory, until such time as the United Nations agreed that a satisfactory measure of self-government had been achieved and that trusteeship status could be terminated. Togo achieved Independence on 27 April 1960, but within three months, the government had entered into a defence pact with France, and often communicated with the Ghanaian government via the French ambassador in Accra. Ironically, then, it is in the French diplomatic archive at Nantes, rather than the state archives in Accra or Lomé, that a detailed record of Ghanaian-Togolese relations can be most easily accessed.[46]

This diplomatic record attests to a complex web of transnational negotiations in anglophone and francophone West Africa. On the basis of his interviews with former diplomats and his review of the West African press, Thompson concluded in the late 1960s that no state had been more important to Ghana than Togo in the years that followed Independence.[47] The same might also be said in reverse. Whilst French policy certainly aimed to develop a framework that would favour French interests, the existing sources of tension between West African states also shaped their responses to French initiatives and the types of relationship that they ultimately forged with the former colonial power. As we shall see, the community of 5,700 political exiles occupied a key position in the struggles that took place between Britain, France, Togo, and Ghana against the background of the Cold War. The outcome of these struggles determined, at least in part, the ways in which newly independent states learned to deal with their opponents. In this respect the refugee experience was one of lasting significance, despite their failure to achieve their immediate aim of Togoland reunification.

[46] I am grateful to Sandrine Mansour Merien for all her assistance in locating and copying relevant files at the Centre des Archives Diplomatiques de Nantes.

[47] W. Scott Thompson, *Ghana's Foreign Policy 1957–66* (Princeton NJ, 1969), 10.

'THE ARROGANCE OF A BLACK AND THE ACUMEN OF A WHITE': NEGOTIATING WITH NATIONALISTS

Since the First World War, relations between the French administration and its Togoland nationalist opponents had usually been bitter and sometimes violent.[48] The contempt with which the French had regarded Olympio through the 1950s did not disappear at Independence. Henri Francis Mazoyer, France's long-serving ambassador in Lomé, was particularly sceptical of Olympio, apparently struggling to comprehend how a 'bourgeois gentleman' of mixed race could claim to be an African nationalist.[49] He thus wrote in 1961, 'Although the president of the republic is not entirely African in colour, most of his reactions are African. From his race, he has acquired a susceptibility to pride and arrogance. The white contribution has conferred in him business sense, a taste for order and a certain self-discipline.'[50] Despite the ambassador's personal animosity and his propensity for racial stereotypes, attitudes within the different institutions of the French government underwent significant changes after Olympio's victory in the elections of April 1958.

Within Togo, Olympio faced pressure from his allies in the Juvento to bring Togo to Independence as quickly as possible. Less than three weeks after the Togolese elections, a political crisis in Algeria triggered an upheaval in France which brought General Charles de Gaulle back into power, and thus paved the way for him to present his constitutional proposals for the Fifth Republic. Voters in the colonies were given a choice between immediate Independence and membership of the French Community. Nkrumah had no desire to see France's African colonies joining in an arrangement that would maintain their ties with their former

[48] See, for example, Benjamin Lawrance's account of the 1933 riots in Lomé, *Locality, Mobility and "Nation"*, 69–89, including photographic evidence.

[49] All translations from the French diplomatic records are my own.

[50] Centre des Archives Diplomatiques à Nantes (CADN), Lomé Ambassade 134, Relations Togo-Ghana 1961: 'Polemique de la presse ghanéen contre M. Olympio', H. F. Mazoyer, Ambassade de France au Togo, Lomé, to Ministre des affaires étrangères, Paris, 22 Dec 1961. The same comments are repeated in Accra Ambassade 61, Togo-Ghana 1957–1961: H. F. Mazoyer to Secrétaire d'état aux affaires étrangères, 5 Jan 1962. Mazoyer was providing his own commentary of Sylavnus Olympio's reaction to an article in the CPP's *Evening News*, which described him as the offspring of a Kabré slave mother and her slave-trading master, Epiphanio Olympio. The publication of such comments in a CPP newspaper represented a serious transgression of the social norm in Ghana that prohibits open discussion of slave ancestry, and this is indicative of the intense hostility with which Nkrumah regarded Olympio at this time.

colonial power and inhibit his own pan-African vision, hence his support for the option of immediate Independence for Guinea in the referendum held there in September 1958.[51] Olympio and his team of Togolese negotiators were in Paris as the Guinean drama unfolded.[52] As France severed its ties with Guinea, and swiftly withdrew all economic assistance, Nkrumah offered a loan to bridge the budgetary chasm, and Sekou Touré agreed to a Ghana-Guinea Union. Olympio was alert to the consequences of following the Guinean path. Whilst the other French colonies initially voted in favour of de Gaulle's proposals for a French Community, apparently leaving Guinea in isolation, during the course of 1959 one colony after another attempted to negotiate an Independence settlement and the French Community concept unravelled.

It was against this background that Togo's negotiations were completed, and it was in this period that French concern about the pan-African ambitions and activities of Nkrumah's Ghana intensified. This culminated in the spring of 1960, when Louis de Guiringaud, the French ambassador in Accra, expressed his concern that Ghana would use the Togolese Independence celebrations, planned for 27 April 1960, as an opportunity to annex Togo.[53] His immediate anxiety was provoked by the printing and distribution of a draft Togolese constitution, which indicated that illiterates would not be allowed to vote, that polygamy would be made illegal, and that an independent Togo would reclaim from Ghana the territory that had been taken in 1956 [i.e., the former British Togoland]. The ambassador believed that this document was a forgery produced by the CPP in order to provoke a crisis that would result in annexation. Justifying his concerns, the ambassador compiled a record of all the actions taken by Ghana in regard to the territories of the former French West Africa.[54] Togo was the first country to be considered in this list, but the embassy also commented on Nkrumah's advocacy of Sanvi secession from the Ivory Coast, the creation of a workers' camp on

[51] See Elizabeth Schmidt, *Cold War and Decolonization in Guinea, 1946–1958* (Athens OH, 2007).

[52] Tété-Adjalogo, *Histoire du Togo* vol. 2, 448.

[53] CADN, Accra Ambassade 61, Togo-Ghana 1957–1961: Louis de Guiringaud, Ambassade de France au Ghana, Accra, to Ministre des affaires étrangères, Paris, and representatif français à l'Organisation des Nations Unies, New York, 12 March 1960; see also memorandum by Ako Adjei, Ghana's foreign minister, 4 April 1960.

[54] CADN, Accra Ambassade 61: 'Révendications territoriales du Ghana sur les Etats de l'ex AOF.' This document is not dated. I surmise from its contents that it was compiled in early April 1960.

Ghana's border with Upper Volta for the purpose of monitoring popular participation in the campaign against French nuclear testing in the Sahara, the CPP's assistance to the Sawaba party in Niger, and a series of recruitment campaigns organised in Ghana and other parts of West Africa to recruit volunteers into the Front de la Libération Nationale in Algeria.[55]

Studying the actions and backgrounds of those who advocated the integration of the Republic of Togo into Ghana, the French ambassador identified two groups that had emerged within the CPP between 1958 and 1960. Firstly, he believed that there was still a group of Ewe-speakers within the party who could be mobilised behind the old Ewe unification agenda advanced by Daniel Chapman in the late 1940s. According to numerical logic, the easiest way to effect the unification of the Ewe-speaking peoples under a single government was to bring the southern half of francophone Togo into Ghana. As the northern half of Togo would lack either an export crop or a port, it too would be forced to join with Ghana in an economic and political union. De Guiringaud argued that the 'anglo-saxons' had no problem with Ghana swallowing up a small and poor state such as Togo, which they deemed vulnerable to communist infiltration.[56] The ambassador thus characterised Nkrumah as the heir of British expansionist intentions in West Africa and as the newest entrant to a longer-term anglophone conspiracy to limit the reach of the French government and French language in Africa.[57]

[55] French embassies in West African continued to track Ghana's activities and interventions – see for example CADN, Lomé Ambassade 134, Relations Togo-Ghana 1961: 'L'envoyé exceptionnel et plenipotentiaire de la république francaise et de la communauté aupres de la république de la Haute Volta', to French ambassador in Lomé, 17 Jan 1961. This period is now being researched intensively, and the connections between West African states are becoming better understood. See, for example, Jean Allman, 'Nuclear Imperialism and the Pan-African Struggle for Peace and Freedom: Ghana 1959–62', *Souls: A Critical Journal of Black Politics, Culture, and Society* 10 (2) (2008), 83–102; and Klaas van Walraven, 'Decolonization by Referendum: The Anomaly of Niger and the Fall of Sawaba 1958–1959', *Journal of African History* 50 (2) (2009), 269–92.

[56] Togo, Dahomey, and Niger were all in a similar position, which the ambassador deemed comparable to that of Poland vis-à-vis Nazi Germany in 1939. CADN, Accra Ambassade 61, Togo-Ghana 1957–1961: Louis de Guiringaud, Ambassade de France au Ghana, Accra, to Ministre des affaires étrangères, Paris, 12 March 1960.

[57] Elizabeth Schmidt makes a similar point about French anxieties vis-à-vis Nkrumah in 'Pan-Africanism, People's Power and Decolonization in Ghana and Guinea: The Uneven Legacy of Kwame Nkrumah and Sekou Touré', in *Africa, Empire and Globalization: Essays in Honor of A. G. Hopkins*, ed. Toyin Falola and Emily Brownell (Durham NC, 2011), 525–53. I am grateful to Elizabeth Schmidt for sending me an advance copy of this publication.

In addition to Nkrumah's bellicose public statements about Togo becoming a 'seventh region of Ghana', the ambassador believed that subtler strategies were also at work.[58] A special committee, led by a reunificationist convert, John Quarshie, had been formed within the CPP in September 1959. Quarshie was working with the recently appointed regional commissioner, Ferdinand Koblavi Goka, to stimulate support for the old Ewe unification agenda within the Republic of Togo, including reminding Olympio of his own enthusiasm for this ethnic project more than a decade earlier.[59] The French chargé d'affaires in Accra was particularly interested in a series of Ewe-language articles that appeared in the CPP newspaper, *Evening News*, in November 1959. Investigating their origins, he discovered that the author, who wrote under a pseudonym, was Georges Djokotoe, who had attended primary school in Kpalimé before becoming employed by the Ministry of Foreign Affairs in Accra. These Ewe-language articles described the border as an attempt by colonial outsiders to meddle in family affairs, and urged Olympio to unify Togo with Ghana. The ambassador estimated that the *Evening News* was selling 300 copies per day in Lomé, and that it sold out completely whenever it featured controversial articles or editorials on Ghana-Togo relations.[60] The publication of Ewe-language texts aimed at a Togolese readership was therefore interpreted by the ambassador as an attempt to undercut Olympio's domestic support base in the Ewe-speaking south of Togo.

The CPP justified this tactic of undermining Olympio at home by claiming a special responsibility to represent the voice of the people against neo-colonialism. Thus, Komla Gbedemah (Nkrumah's Ewe-speaking minister of finance) addressed a meeting at Aflao on the border on 5 March 1960. He recalled that, as a result of French oppression during the Second World War, women traders had been forced to undress every time they had travelled between Lomé and Keta to trade. Invoking this 'abominable' practice against market women (who were, of course,

[58] CADN, Accra Ambassade 61: Ambassade de France au Ghana, Accra, to Ministre des affaires étrangères, Paris, 12 March 1960. The ambassador noted that Nkrumah himself had used this exact phrase in speech at Keta on 30 October 1959, as well as speaking openly about his intentions in Ho on 29 October 1959 and in the Ghana parliament on 16 December 1959.

[59] CADN, Accra Ambassade 61: G. Spenale, Haut-Commissaire de la République Française au Togo, Lomé, to Premier Ministre de la Republique Française, Paris, 2 Nov 1959.

[60] CADN, Accra Ambassade 61: Pierre Justinard, Chargé d'affaires au Ghana, Accra, to the Haut-Commissaire de la République Française, 4 Nov 1959.

among Olympio's key financial supporters throughout the 1950s), Gbedemah warned that he could not stand by as a Ghanaian and watch Olympio take his brothers and cousins in Togo into any form of French Community. If Olympio could not grasp this, there were people in Anécho and Kpalimé who would 'set him straight'.[61]

Whilst the CPP's first strategy, then, depended on invoking an older ethnic Ewe agenda to win support within Togo for integration with Ghana, the second strand depended on the mobilisation of opposition to Olympio among Togolese living in Ghana, and this had a more ideological dimension. The French embassy in Accra had long been interested in the Juvento branches formed in the larger Ghanaian towns of Kumasi, Takoradi, Tamale, Accra, and Koforidua. These branches included labour migrants from French Togoland, tailors, catechists, United Africa Company clerks, and members of prominent reunificationist families from British Togoland, including the Anku Mornys of Hohoe and the Ametowoblas of Amedzofe. Juvento meetings were also attended by S. G. Antor and Kodzo Ayeke (the Togoland Congress parliamentarians).[62] Before Olympio's victory in the 1958 elections, the French regarded these branches as part of Olympio's support network in the former British Togoland, but in February 1959 they noted a new development. Amos Klutse Sosu from the Akepe branch of Juvento travelled to Accra where he gave an interview to the *Ghanaian Times* stating that the Juvento drew inspiration from the 'socialist ideology' of the CPP: as a consequence it advocated immediate Independence for Togo followed by participation in a Ghana-Togo union and support for Nkrumah's broader vision for West Africa.[63]

This was alarming to the French government. In Paris, the ministers for French foreign affairs and for la France d'Outre-Mer had been following for over a year the activities of Messan Aithson, a founder member of the Juvento who was both a committed socialist and a supporter of the CPP.

[61] CADN, Accra Ambassade 61: Louis de Guiringaud, Ambassade de France au Ghana, Accra, to the Ministre des affaires étrangères, Paris, 10 March 1960. On women in the CUT, see Ginette Ayélé Kponton, 'La femme dans la lute pour la decolonisation (1946–1960)', in *Les Togolais face à la colonisation*, ed. Nicoué Gayibor (Lomé, 1994), 173–93.

[62] CADN, Accra Ambassade 61: Pierre Justinard, Chargé d'affaires au Ghana, Accra, to Haut-Commissaire de la République Française, Lomé, 3 Jan 1958.

[63] CADN, Accra Ambasaade 61: Louis de Guiringaud, Ambassade de France au Ghana, Accra, to Haut-Commissaire au Togo, Lomé, 21 Feb 1959, referring to *Ghanaian Times*, 21 Feb 1959.

They regarded Aithson as a threat to their interests, 'not only in Togo but across the whole coast of West Africa.'[64] At the All-African Peoples' Conference of December 1958, the Juvento's official representatives had entered a bitter dispute with Messan Aithson, whose membership they claimed to have revoked.[65] This signalled a rift within the Juvento between those who identified themselves with a socialist agenda, and those who continued to back Olympio. The increasing tension between the CUT and the Juvento culminated in the resignation of the Juventist Anani Ignacio Santos from Olympio's government in May 1959, and in the elections and referendum of April 1961, the Juvento entered a pact with its erstwhile opponents against Olympio and the CUT. As we shall see, the fracturing of the nationalist CUT-Juvento alliance caused Olympio great anxiety: the Togolese president claimed that Nkrumah would use Togolese opponents across the border in Ghana to bring about his assassination.

ABLƆƉE SAFUI (THE KEY TO FREEDOM): MAKING POLITICS WITH WORDS

The diplomatic record, then, suggests that the period between 1958 and 1960 was characterised by an intense and complicated struggle over the type of Independence that Togo would obtain, and how this would fit with the competing visions put forward by Nkrumah on the one hand, and the French on the other, for the broader West African sub-region. This struggle was well-documented by the embassies of former colonial powers who followed very closely any potential splits in the nationalist parties of Ghana and Togo. It would be a mistake, however, to think that this struggle took place only in the capital cities, behind the closed doors of power, or above the heads of the grassroots activists in the Ablɔɖe movement. The war of words that had accompanied the struggle for the future of British Togoland in the mid-1950s was now pursued with equal vigour in relation to the future of French Togoland. In both cases, grassroots activists undertook to write in Ewe about the past and the future of their country, and they saw the production of a credible record of events as an essential element of their political work. These texts indicate that

[64] CADN, Accra Ambassade 61: Ministre de la France d'Outre-Mer, Paris, to Ministre des affaires étrangères, Paris, 16 June 1958.

[65] CADN, Accra Ambassade 61: Haut-Commissaire de la République Française au Togo, Lomé, to Premier Ministre, 26 Oct 1959.

people in the small towns and villages of the border area were not deprived of information or left to decide their political affiliations mainly through calculations as to how best to advance highly localised agendas, because in this part of West Africa at least, rural people certainly had access to a range of competing interpretations of national and indeed pan-African and global affairs. The challenge for the historian is to understand the idioms in which these were discussed and the impact that they might have had.

Interesting insights can therefore be gleaned from an Ewe-language newspaper, *Ablɔɖe Safui* (*Key to Freedom*), copies of which were deposited regularly at the office of Sam Klu, the new commandant de cercle for the Klouto district of French Togoland, from 1959. In 2000, I interviewed the editor of this newspaper. Holiday Komedja (b. 1922) was a cobbler by trade. He was brought up in Nyogbo on Mount Agu, an area which, rather like Mount Gemi on the Ghana side of the border, had attracted nineteenth-century German-speaking missionaries looking to build stations and schools in comparatively cool areas where malaria was less endemic. Komedja, like most of his neighbours, was a committed member of the Eglise Evangélique (the successor church of the Bremen mission). He attended primary school in his home village and 'cours moyen' (middle school) in the nearby town of Kpalimé, but did not complete his education due to 'a lack of means'. Instead, he went to stay with an older brother in Kadjebi, on the British side of the border, and became an apprentice cobbler. When he returned to French Togoland, he set up his own shoe-making and shoe-repairing workshop in Kpalimé.[66]

Komedja started producing *Ablɔɖe Safui*, acting as owner, editor, and reporter.[67] The early issues of 1958 and 1959 were produced in batches of 500, and Komedja recalled that he had boys who sold them for him in the town of Kpalimé, in surrounding villages, and further afield, including across the border in Ghana.[68] Komedja identified himself as a Juventist, but, importantly, he added that he had been part of the faction that remained loyal to Olympio. From the outset, his paper followed events

[66] Interview with Holiday Komedja, Agu Nyogbo, 29 June 2000.

[67] The earliest issues in my possession date from 1959, but it is clear there were approximately twenty earlier issues, which leads me to believe that the newspaper was founded around the time of the April 1958 elections.

[68] The British High Commissioner in Accra noted: 'The Ghana government also found it necessary in October 1960 to ban the import into Ghana of an Ewe-language newspaper published in Togo.' TNA, DO 195/75 Ghana-Togo Relations. Doc 1A, UK High Commission, Accra, to Secretary of State for Commonwealth Relations, London 4 May 1961.

on both sides of the border, and, in particular, Komedja summarised, responded to, and corrected public statements made by Nkrumah and other members of the CPP about the former British Togoland. Thus, interrogating Goka's speech at Ho in September 1959, he formulated a series of questions (*biabia*) that were intended to highlight for his readers the inaccuracies in Goka's historical account. Komedja rejected Goka's claim that British Togoland belonged to Ghana, and challenged him to look at a German map of Togo in order to see how that country had been divided by the British and the French.[69] The following month, he reported on Nkrumah's speech at Ho, in which Nkrumah had denounced persistent rumours that when French Togoland became independent in 1960, Olympio would erect a Togolese flag in the former British Togoland, thereby reclaiming the territory from Ghana. Komedja warned his readers of the annexationist implications of Nkrumah's statement that 'Togo and Ghana are one'.[70]

Several issues released in rapid succession in April and May 1960 depicted Togo's Independence in pictures whose meaning was carefully explained to readers. The first of this series depicted Togo as an object between the hands of two men. One man (Nkrumah) was relinquishing the object to the other (Olympio), stating, 'BMT [British Mandated Togoland] is not mine. I was only taking care of it for you.'[71] On the front page of the next issue was a picture of one person grasping a rectangular object in both hands and holding it up high in the air. This, Komedja explained, symbolised 'the whole of Togo in the hands of a new government'.[72] Next came a picture of a man sat down rubbing his head. This was humorously entitled 'Aaaah, look at that', and it represented Nkrumah trying to figure out how he could explain to the people of Ghana and the followers of the CPP that 'Togo BMT has slipped from my hands'.[73] For Komedja, Togo's achievement of Independence was only one of two stages that were required to achieve real freedom: the second stage would be the reclamation of the former British Togoland from Ghana, and its reintegration with the Republic of Togo.

Komedja was in touch with the refugee population in and around Kpalimé and he received news about CPP treatment of Ablɔḍe supporters

[69] *Ablɔḍe Safui* 21 (27 Oct 1959), 2. Translation by Daniel Adadjo and Wilson Yayoh.
[70] *Ablɔḍe Safui* 22 (26 Nov 1959), 2. Translation by Daniel Adadjo and Wilson Yayoh.
[71] *Ablɔḍe Safui* 25 (13 April 1960), 1. Translation by Tina Dugbazah and Wilson Yayoh.
[72] *Ablɔḍe Safui* 26 (2 May 1960), 1. Translation by Edem Adotey and Wilson Yayoh.
[73] *Ablɔḍe Safui* 26 (2 May 1960), 2. Translation by Edem Adotey and Wilson Yayoh.

across the border in Ghana. In July 1960, he wrote about an event that had taken place the previous month in Kpandu-Aloi. Komedja claimed that CPP 'thugs', dressed as 'general police', had assaulted Ablɔḍe supporters, including one Kwame Kuma, who was beaten so badly that 'he defecated on himself and blood oozed from his nostrils'.[74] Speaking in 2000, Komedja said that he had started producing *Ablɔḍe Safui* because 'I wanted people to be able to read the news, so that they would know what was happening in the world'. In many cases, however, there was a gap of a fortnight or more between the events that Komedja wrote about and the publication of the next issue of *Ablɔḍe Safui*. This suggests that he was motivated not simply by a desire to report on events as they happened, but also to assess their implications and formulate his own critique. Ablɔḍe supporters being beaten in Kpandu-Aloi was probably not 'news', because, as we have seen, people, supplies, and therefore all sorts of oral information, found their way across the border on a regular basis. What is important, then, is that Komedja found it necessary to record this, in writing, for people to read and discuss. The description of Kwame Kuma was doubtless intended to elicit sympathy and outrage. The personal detail was significant because Komedja questioned Nkrumah's assertion of the need for unity and solidarity between Ghana and Togo: how could the Ghanaian president talk about 'brotherliness' (*nɔvinyenye*), asked Komedja, when this was how he treated 'brothers' who disagreed with him?[75] Publicising individual instances of distress was thus a rhetorical means of challenging Nkrumah's metaphors of the African household and extended family in his appeals for a particular type of political and economic union.[76]

Komedja also deployed metaphors of his own. The name *Ablɔḍe Safui* was imbued with historical meanings, which Komedja rendered explicit in February 1960. Drawing on a theme similar to that of G. K. Tsekpo in *Togo Nukae Hiawo?* (*Togo, What Do You Need?*), Komedja described Togo as a small land (*anyigba*) wedged between Ghana to the west and French Dahomey to the east. Togo was thus conceptualised as a door, but 'the key is one of the most important accessories of the door and one has no faith in the security of a door without a key'.[77] Referring to the 1869

[74] *Ablɔḍe Safui* 28 (13 July 1960), 1–2. Translation by Edem Adotey and Wilson Yayoh.
[75] The Ewe word *nɔvi* is not gender specific. It simply means 'sibling'. *Nɔvinyenye* therefore refers to the relationship between siblings.
[76] *Ablɔḍe Safui* 26 (2 May 1960), 3. Translation by Edem Adotey and Wilson Yayoh.
[77] *Ablɔḍe Safui* 23 (26 Feb 1960), 1. Translation by Edem Adotey and Wilson Yayoh.

Anlo-Asante invasion of Krepe (which later became the southern section of British and French Togoland), Komedja explained that, because the door did not have a key, a series of other outsiders (Danish, German, British, and French) were also able to enter the country. It was only with the emergence of capable leaders such as Olympio that Togo's door became fully equipped with a key. Although the metaphors are different, and although Komedja wrote more explicitly about the Anlo-Asante invasion and thus made allusions to experiences of domination and enslavement, his historical narrative shares a central feature with the history constructed by G. K. Tsekpo in *Togo Nukae Hiawo?*: both emphasised the vulnerability of the people living along the thin strip of Togolese territory, and both conceived of political Independence in essentially defensive terms. National sovereignty was portrayed as a bulwark against intrusion and plunder, and leaders were entrusted with a role of protection.

Ablɔɖe Safui certainly presented 'news' in ways that were intended to vilify Nkrumah, insist upon Togo's national sovereignty, reject any proposal to take Togo into a union with Ghana, and stimulate support for the reunification of the former British Togoland with the newly independent Republic of Togo. Komedja was well aware, however, that there were other texts circulating in both Ghana and Togo which presented the situation very differently, and he did not assume that the people reading *Ablɔɖe Safui* would accept his interpretation simply because it was written in Ewe. Indeed, according to Tété-Adjalogo, under the previous Progrès administration, another Ewe-language newspaper, entitled *Kekeli kple Nyatefe (Light and Truth)*, had also circulated in the Klouto district, while in 1959 the *Evening News* was also publishing selected articles in Ewe in order to promote Nkrumah's preferred solution to the Togoland problem.[78] Komedja therefore employed textual strategies that were designed to enhance his own credibility and convince his readers that what they read between the pages of *Ablɔɖe Safui* was more truthful and accurate than the interpretations that they might come across elsewhere. In other words, it was not the local language that conferred authenticity so much as the sincerity of the author. This poses an interesting counter-example to anthropological theories of writing as an 'autonomous mode of communication' in which the message becomes detached from the relationship between the people who formulate and receive it, and may

[78] Têtêvi Godwin Tété-Adjalogo, *Histoire du Togo: La palpitant quête de l'Ablodé (1940–1960)* (Paris, 2000), 617.

be indicative of the relative intimacy of print publics in rural areas.[79] For Komedja, however, there was a more urgent imperative: as an author who embraced a particular political stance, he sought to combat what he believed were the falsehoods – and indeed the outright forgeries – that were produced and circulated by his political opponents. He became a spokesperson engaged in a war of words.

Like the reunificationist authors featured in Chapter 4, Komedja's primary strategy for enhancing his credibility was to incorporate advice to his readers and thus to make himself and his paper a regular and reliable point of reference. Indeed, one of his early issues of *Ablɔḍe Safui* explicitly warned readers to consult 'many newspapers in order to better inform yourselves as to the truthfulness of the information'.[80] Those who did not read widely were more vulnerable to being deceived.

Komedja did not restrict his advice to national politics but pronounced on a wide range of contemporary issues. Parents, for example, were cautioned not to teach their children how to drink 'poisonous' local gin for this would only turn a child into 'a friend of the bottle and the brewing pot'.[81] Picking up on another theme that is explored extensively in West African popular culture, Komedja wrote about the materialistic tendencies of the modern woman. The cautionary tale of Afua and Adzoavi warned women of the fate of those who identify potential husbands on the basis of the degree of wealth that they appear to exhibit, and concluded with the following advice: 'work, be submissive to a man, listen to your husband so you shall live long which is better than all things in life.'[82] In order not to appear one-sided, he promised that his advice to the men would follow shortly, and indeed his habit of making references to other articles that had appeared or would appear in his paper also served to emphasise to readers that *Ablɔḍe Safui* could be relied upon for regular and consistent advice and commentary.

Cultivating this status of trustworthy advisor, Komedja took it upon himself to use *Ablɔḍe Safui* not simply to stimulate support for the Olympio government amongst his readership, but also to draw attention to issues that he thought deserving of governmental intervention. Often,

[79] This argument was first advanced by Jack Goody in *Literacy in Traditional Societies* (Cambridge, 1968) but has since been subjected to numerous critiques. On the particularities of early African print publics, see Barber, *The Anthropology of Texts, Persons and Publics*, 137–61.

[80] *Ablode Safui* 21 (27 Oct 1959), 2. Translation by Daniel Adadjo and Wilson Yayoh.

[81] *Ablɔḍe Safui* 28 (13 July 1960), 4. Translation by Edem Adotey and Wilson Yayoh.

[82] *Ablɔḍe Safui* 28 (13 July 1960), 4. Translation by Edem Adotey and Wilson Yayoh.

Komedja was acting as an advocate for villages, individuals, or groups whom he saw as the victims of political bias in the period that the Progrès had dominated local administration. But in other cases, he also reminded the new government of its obligations. Thus, in his own area on Mount Agu, he pointed out that several roads had been constructed through self-help projects and unpaid labour. The fact that these roads had not been tarred by the previous administration was attributed to political bias, but Komedja also reminded the new government (which promoted self-help as a means of improving infrastructure and amenities without burdening the public finances) that the villagers of Agu-Nyogbo were still waiting for the 'caterpillar' to come and finish their roads.[83] He also expressed his concern over public sector redundancies, asked what could be done about the rising cost of living, and reminded the government of the needs of the farmers of the Klouto district by drawing an unfavourable comparison between governmental provision of insecticide in Togo and the cocoa-spraying efforts of 'Agric' [the 'extension' officers of the Department of Agriculture] in Ghana.[84]

In positioning himself as an honest and reliable witness to the social and political issues of the day, Komedja formulated a framework for political action that used Christianity to justify the expression of dissent. He thus went to considerable lengths to explain to his readers what activities should be described as 'politics'. He noted that, 'if someone expresses a different opinion regarding the position of any leader, the person is seen as ... hindering the work of the government ... if somebody decides to speak his mind according to his Christian principles, someone will exclaim that the person ... is practising bad politics.'[85] He therefore insisted that 'every citizen has the right to make politics', but they must do so from the correct moral position, which privileged love of country and commitment to nation building.[86] This was mirrored by a similar exhortation to leaders. Thus, Komedja defined politics as 'the wisdom with which one rules a country'. This wisdom (*adanu*) was characterised as 'a unique intelligence seen in the outcome or work achieved by such wisdom', which itself entailed a further series of laudable qualities of integrity, self-sacrifice, and perseverance.

[83] *Ablɔḍe Safui* 23 (26 Feb 1960), 3. Translation by Edem Adotey and Wilson Yayoh. The 'caterpillar' is a mechanised roller used for flattening roads.
[84] *Ablɔḍe Safui* 28 (13 July 1960), 3. Translation by Edem Adotey and Wilson Yayoh.
[85] *Ablɔḍe Safui* 25 (13 April 1960) 2 (continuation of article). Translation by Tina Dugbazah and Wilson Yayoh.
[86] Ibid.

The choice of *Ablɔḍe Safui* as the name for the newspaper, and the likening of Olympio to a key, was of course propaganda aimed at glorifying the leader. But it also served to attribute to Olympio a special, almost God-given responsibility to protect Togo's sovereignty – a responsibility for which he would ultimately be held accountable, if not in this life then in the next. The imagery of the door and key, deployed in Komedja's historical account, also invoked John's gospel, chapter 10: 'I am the door of the sheep ... The thief commeth not, but for to steal, and to kill, and to destroy; I am come that they might have life, and that they might have it more abundantly.'[87] Komedja thus returned to necessity of a newspaper such as his that would speak the truth, not only in correcting the falsehoods propagated by opponents, but also in keeping the government on the right path and ensuring that the promises attached to Independence were delivered.

Within this Christian framework for politics, Komedja suggested that an individual's good conscience and commitment was open to public scrutiny and judgement. Importantly, the willingness of individuals to 'suffer' at the hands of the previous regime was deemed a test of their conscience and of their fitness to occupy leadership positions under the new dispensation. Narratives of suffering were thus serialised and dramatised in the pages of *Ablɔḍe Safui*. Chief Adzini, for example, described in three parts how he had been forced under the previous Progrès administration to walk westwards across the border to Hohoe. His misery came to an end only when he was greeted there by the allies of Ablɔḍe, who supported him through his period of exile in British Togoland. Thus, in the same period that refugees were about to start arriving from Nkrumah's Ghana, Komedja was recalling the periods of exile that Togolese nationalists had been forced to spend in British Togoland in order to avoid the persecution of the French administration and its allies in the Progrès. Notably, Togbe Gabusu IV of Hohoe, who at the time of publication was living in exile in Kpalimé, was listed as one of those who had generously hosted Adzini.[88] Komedja also wrote about how much he himself had to suffer in order to produce the newspaper at all. The front page of each issue reminded readers that Komedja was the reporter, the editor, and the owner all at the same time, and he periodically inserted pleas for financial support that would enable him to continue

[87] King James Bible, John 10:7 and John 10:10.
[88] *Ablɔḍe Safui* 27 (20 May 1960), 4. Translation by Tina Dugbazah and Wilson Yayoh.

the newspaper.[89] Apologies to readers about the lack of phonetic characters in the Ewe text also provided Komedja with an opportunity to expound upon the struggles he had in getting his paper printed, and indeed he returned to this theme of suffering and struggle forty years later when I turned up in Agu-Nyogbo asking for an interview.

Whilst these narratives were partly intended to vindicate the claims of those who had been on the wrong end of the previous administration, they also contained an implication about the trustworthiness and legitimacy of those who had not endured comparable suffering. In other words, those who were now seeking positions as chiefs or as civil servants, and those enjoying benefits of contracts and salaried employment, were deemed to be acting from selfish motives, getting fat at the expense of the grassroots activists of the nationalist movement in French Togoland. Those who had suffered and struggled under the Progrès administrations, on the other hand, had proven themselves to be individuals of conscience, who were prepared to make sacrifices for the common good. Looking back on Olympio's election victory in April 1958, and anticipating the final achievement of Independence in April 1960, Komedja cast shame on those 'sceptics and unbelievers' in the Progrès and Juvento who had shown so little faith in the future of Togo as an independent sovereign state, and 'could not now partake of freedom'.[90] Thus, whilst a Christian framework was used to assert the rights of individual citizens to express dissenting views, it was also used to make judgements about individuals' characters and to decide who was undeserving of the fruits of freedom.[91] If Komedja is representative of the idiom in which politics was being discussed on the eve of Independence in April 1960, Olympio's austerity measures were dangerous indeed.

DEFENDING VICTORY: ABLƆḌE IN THE DOMESTIC AND INTERNATIONAL ARENA

France's permanent representative at the United Nations complained formally to the secretary-general in March 1960 about Ghana's annexationist

[89] *Ablɔḍe Safui* 25 (13 April 1960), 3 and 4. Translation by Tina Dugbazah and Wilson Yayoh.

[90] *Ablɔḍe Safui* 23 (26 Feb 1960), 1. Translation by Edem Adotey and Wilson Yayoh.

[91] Brown makes this point about the CPP in Kpandu: whilst the central party wanted to see opposing villages won over to the CPP, local activists thought that the district commissioner should focus on rewarding those who had shown loyalty to the party through the 1950s. Brown, 'Politics in the Kpandu Area of Ghana', 331–4.

intentions towards Togo.[92] At Togo's Independence on 27 April 1960, a Ghanaian military intervention did not materialise, but once the celebrations were over, Ghanaian efforts to erode Olympio's domestic support intensified. It was against this background that the French embassies interpreted the rise of the Ghana-Togo Union Movement in July 1961. The French ambassador in Accra explained that the movement's explicit aim was to end the artificial barriers between Ghana and Togo and to encourage the formation of an economic and political union between the two states. He added, however, that the movement had been formed 'at the instigation of the CPP and the Bureau of African Affairs', and that it intended to mobilise support by forming branches within Togo as well as in Ghana.[93] The ambassador regarded this as a deliberate provocation, and linked it to an editorial in the *Ghanaian Times* on 13 July 1961, which challenged Olympio to hold a referendum and allow the inhabitants of Togo to decide whether they wanted to unite with Ghana.

The CUT (known from 1960 as 'Unité Togolaise') mounted a two-pronged response. First, within Togo's own borders, it sought to demonstrate the strength of domestic support not simply for the survival of Togo as a separate sovereign nation-state, but also for its historic claim to reunification with the former British Togoland. In effect, the refugees who arrived in 1960 and 1961 experienced two 'Independences' – one in Ghana and the other in Togo – and if the former was something to be mourned, the latter called for celebration. In Ghana, '*Ablɔɖe!*' was the slogan of the defeated Togoland Congress, whereas in (francophone) Togo, '*Ablɔɖe!*' was the slogan of the victorious CUT. Whilst Nkrumah described Togo as a 'seventh region of Ghana', in Togo the terms 'Eastern Togo' and 'Western Togo' were adopted to emphasise that the former British trust territory rightfully belonged in the new sovereign republic of Togo. Unité Togolaise regularly reaffirmed its commitment to Togoland reunification, using rallies and congresses in order to build public displays of commitment.[94] Whereas women in Ghana wore Kwame Nkrumah

92 CADN, Accra Ambassade 61: Armani Bérard, French ambassador and permanent representative at the United Nations, to Dag Hammarskjold, United Nations secretary-general, 12 March 1960.

93 CADN, Accra Ambassade 61: Ambassade de France au Ghana, Accra, to Ministre des affaires étrangères, Paris, 14 July 1961.

94 CADN, Accra Ambassade 61: Secretary General of Unité Togolaise to Ambassade de France, Lomé, 23 Sept 1961. Six months later, at a two-day congress in Kpalimé in March 1962, the party passed a motion urging that the government should 'do everything possible to obtain by peaceful means the reunification of the two Togos'. *West Africa*,

cloth to display their loyalty to the CPP, those in Togo, including the Ghanaian refugees, bought Sylvanus Olympio cloth to display their loyalty to Unité Togolaise.[95] And on both sides of the border, women sang the victory songs which proclaimed the aims of the ruling party and extolled the virtues of its leader. In Togo, then, the refugees were on the winning side of a very similar kind of politics to that of which they had been the victims in Ghana. The district records for Klouto (Togo) attest to much the same series of claims and counter-claims that one can find in the Ho archive (Ghana): chieftaincy disputes were now believed to be settled in favour of candidates who had supported the victorious political party. Coercion and intimidation were used to punish activists who had been on the losing side.

The second prong of Togo's response was directed outwards, to the international community. In October 1961, Paulin Freitas, Togo's minister for foreign affairs, broached at the United Nations General Assembly in New York the exodus of Ghanaian citizens to Togo as refugees. The French embassy in Lomé sent a telegram to Paris to warn the government of Freitas' intentions: under the cover of a social and humanitarian appeal, Freitas was drawing attention to the political dimension of the refugee problem and seeking thereby to reopen the Togoland question.[96] The following day, the French ambassador in Lomé received a telegram reporting what had transpired at the General Assembly in New York. Freitas' agenda, according to the French representative, was scarcely hidden: he had spoken directly about the problems that stemmed from the manner in which the former British Togoland had been integrated into Ghana.

Freitas argued more specifically that, contrary to the modalities later implemented in Cameroon, the United Nations had approved the integration of British Togoland with Ghana on the basis of the overall majority achieved in the plebiscite of May 1956. Had the United Nations accepted

17 March 1962. Similarly, the national assembly, which, after 1958, was dominated by Unité Togolaise, continued to pass motions in favour of reunification. TNA, DO 195/75 Ghana-Togo Relations: doc. 24, Corbett, British Embassy, Lomé, to British embassy, Dakar, UK High Commission, Accra and Lagos, and Foreign Office, London, 7 June 1961.

95 Interview with Mercy Akosua Tegbe, Hohoe, 19 Sept 2000.

96 CADN, Lomé Ambassade 59: C. Mantel, Ambassade de France au Togo, Lomé, to Diplomatie, Paris, 6 Oct 1961. 'L'empressement avec lequel le Gouvernement togolais a soulevé cette question à l'Assemblée Générale dissimule mal ses arrières pensées et ses desseins. A propos d'un examen d'une affaire de caractère social et humanitaire, les implications politiques ne manqueront pas d'être soulevées. Ainsi, les Togolais espèrent-ils que, par ce biais, la question de la reunification du Togo serait indirectement posée.'

the need to count the votes of the northern and southern sections of British Togoland separately, the southern section could have been reunited with French Togoland, as the majority there had clearly wished. Freitas concluded that it was this misguided approval of a single counting zone that had encouraged the Ghanaian leadership in thinking that it would be possible for them to annex the remainder of Togo after Independence. Whilst Freitas indicated that it was the sheer volume of refugees entering Togo that had prompted him to ask the United Nations for assistance, the Ghanaian representative wanted to know why Freitas had not brought this matter directly to Accra.[97] Mazoyer concluded that the refugee question had provided Olympio with a perfect opportunity to internationalise his quarrel with Nkrumah.[98]

The United Nations High Commission for Refugees sent a mission to Togo by the end of October 1961, but by the time it issued its preliminary report in July 1962, Ghana-Togo relations had taken a turn for the worse. In Ghana, the discovery of a 'conspiracy' in October 1961 generated a further wave of departures from Ghana by activists and parliamentarians associated with the opposition United Party. Similarly, the discovery of a 'plot' to assassinate Olympio in December 1961 prompted Théophile Mally, minister of the interior, to take into detention all members of the opposition. On 14 January 1962, all opposition parties in Togo, including the Juvento, were banned.[99] Just as the CPP government silenced the *Ashanti Pioneer* newspaper in December 1960, so the December 1961 'conspiracy' was used by Unité Togolaise to justify silencing newspapers such as *Togo Observateur*.[100] (Komedja, on the other hand, continued to produce *Ablɔḍe Safui*.) It was in a public statement of denial about complicity in the plots against Nkrumah and the Ghanaian government that Olympio pronounced that the refugees were given asylum in Togo only on the condition that they refrained from political activity, but this can scarcely be taken at face value.[101]

[97] CADN, Lomé Ambassade 59: Diplomatie, Paris, to Ambassade de France au Togo, 7 Oct 1961.

[98] CADN, Accra Ambassade 61: H. F. Mazoyer, Ambassade de France au Togo, Lomé, to Ministre des affaires étrangères, Paris, 6 Dec 1961, 'Les relations avec le Ghana depuis la levée de tutelle'.

[99] TNA, DO 195/75 Ghana-Togo Relations. Doc 82, British Embassy, Lomé, to JHA Watson, H.M. Ambassador, Dakar, 18 Jan 1962.

[100] Ibid.

[101] CADN, Lomé Ambassade 134: Olympio's open letter to the Government of Ghana, 19 Dec 1962.

EATING THE CONSEQUENCES OF NEO-COLONIALISM

Ironically, both the British and the French found their instincts to be at odds with their calculations of self-interest by the beginning of 1962. In their Togo Annual Review for 1960 (written before Freitas had brought the refugee situation directly to the attention of the United Nations), the British had been emphatic in their support both for Olympio's leadership and for the survival of Togo as a separate country. Contrary to the French ambassador's anxiety about an expansionist anglo-saxon conspiracy, British diplomats described the Togolese government as administering the country 'in a more enlightened, honest and moderate way than most West African Governments ... And we ourselves have a particular interest in Mr Olympio's survival in that, alone among the leaders of non-Commonwealth West Africa, he both knows and likes England.'[102] The British were perturbed, however, by the Togolese government's decision to bring the refugee question to the United Nations, and therefore suggested that whilst the 'good offices' of the High Commissioner for Refugees could be used to ease the situation, there was a question mark over the 'status of many of the so-called "refugees". Our own information was that the majority were in fact people, mainly Ewes, who moved at the time of the plebiscite in 1956–7, preferring to live in what was then French Togoland rather than remain in the Gold Coast, and others who left Ghana for Togo after Togo's Independence in April 1960.'[103]

This disingenuous representation of the refugee community in Togo was probably related to the British government's desire to minimise friction with Nkrumah in the run-up to the Queen's visit to Ghana in November 1961, and to avoid giving Nkrumah a pretext on which he could withdraw Ghana from the Commonwealth.[104] By February 1962, the Foreign Office was prepared to concede that those arriving in Lomé

[102] TNA, DO 195/75 Ghana-Togo Relations: Togo Annual Review for 1960, JHA Watson, Dakar, to Foreign Office, London, 23 Jan 1961.

[103] TNA, DO 195/75: GTP Marshall, Foreign Office, London, to D.M. Edward, UK mission to the United Nations, Geneva, 28 Feb 1962. This letter describes, retrospectively, the position that the British government had taken when Freitas first raised the refugee question in Oct 1961.

[104] The British High Commissioner in Accra was concerned by the hostility towards Nkrumah that was being displayed in the British press in October 1961. TNA, DO 195/39 Preventive Detention in Ghana: UK High Commissioner, Accra, to Commonwealth Relations Office and Cabinet, London, 7 Nov 1961.

in the wake of the Sekondi-Takoradi workers' strike were bona fide political refugees, but argued that as 'their number is very small ... it may be difficult to justify helping them out on a purely refugee basis'. Their preferred alternative was that 'assistance to the Togolese should be given under some other umbrella'.[105] The British were worried by Nkrumah's shift to the left, and they regarded Olympio as a valuable counterweight, who would provide a 'link between the moderate Nigerian leaders and the French-speaking States'.[106] But the Foreign Office could not bring itself to support Olympio or his government in any move that might ultimately lead to the reopening of the Togoland question. This would have entailed an implicit admission that their insistence on a single counting zone in interpreting the results of the 1956 plebiscite had been a mistake.

The French ambassador to Togo, on the other hand, disliked Olympio intensely. But whilst the French government may have had little interest in preserving a Unité Togolaise government led by Olympio, they certainly wished to maintain Togo as a separate country and resist what they perceived as Nkrumah's annexationist intentions. Mazoyer was sceptical about the amount of assistance that would actually reach the refugees, and believed that the Olympio regime was using them primarily for political capital at the United Nations, but he also reminded the French foreign minister that 'for political reasons, which have lost none of their significance' it was in the French interest to support the Ghanaian refugees in Togo. Mazoyer therefore recommended expenditure of approximately six million francs for the provision of tools and equipment to those who could support themselves as artisans.[107]

As Ghana-Togo relations deteriorated, the French government's commitment was tested further. Olympio had long made it known to both the British and French ambassadors that he feared that he would be

[105] TNA, DO 195/75: GTP Marshall, Foreign Office, London, to D. M. Edward, UK mission to the United Nations, Geneva, 28 Feb 1962.

[106] TNA, DO 195/75: Togo Annual Review for 1960, JHA Watson, Dakar, to Foreign Office, London, 23 Jan 1961.

[107] CADN, Lomé Ambassade 59: H. F. Mazoyer, Ambassade de France au Togo, Lomé, to Ministre des affaires etrangères, Paris, 8 Aug 1962. The French ambassador in Lomé explained his position: He suggested that the Red Cross was shocked by 'l'indifférence et la mauvaise volonté' displayed by the Togolese government over the question of the refugees. Nonetheless, he reminded the French foreign minister that 'nous avions pour les raisons politiques qui n'ont pas perdu leur valeur, commencé à aider ce groupe de refugiés', and he argued that the government could, at minimal cost, meet the request for equipment for refugee artisans and thereby gain positive publicity.

undermined by opponents who were being sheltered by the Nkrumah regime. Towards the end of 1962, however, he held a series of meetings to plan for the possibility of his assassination: his primary concern was that in the event of a Ghanaian invasion of Togo, the French would act upon their defence pact with Togo to maintain its territorial integrity, even in the absence of a formal presidential request.[108] It is clear that there was little love lost between Olympio and the French ambassador, but again, broader West African interests were brought to bear: 'If Togo should be attacked, it is essential for us that the military pact is seen by other African heads of state to be effective.'[109]

In so far as I can tell from the refugees' petitions and the correspondence of the Red Cross with potential donor governments, the refugees did not benefit from any large-scale concerted assistance from the Togolese government between their mass arrivals in 1960 and their departure in 1966.[110] The United Nations High Commissioner for Refugees did not bring his final report to the General Assembly until April 1963, by which point most of the refugees had been in Togo for two to three years.[111] In July 1962, the UNHCR representative, M. E. Ettmueller, produced a preliminary report and made recommendations as to how the refugees should be assisted.[112] Much of the implementation, however, was left to the Red Cross International. In August 1963, the Red Cross expressed concerns about the small amount of piece-meal assistance that the refugees had actually received.[113] And as late as 1965, the Western Togo

[108] Telegramme, Diplomatie, Paris, to Ambassade de la France au Togo, Lomé, 12 Dec 1962. This is followed by several pages of handwritten notes discussing what Olympio had told President Maga of Dahomey, what he most feared, and what the French thought that they might be able to do about it.

[109] 'Si le Togo est attaqué, il est essential pour nous que notre pacte militaire fasse aux yeux des autres chefs d'Etat africains la preuve de son efficacité.' Handwritten note, author unclear, dating from Dec 1962 – see previous footnote.

[110] A few months after Olympio's assassination, Mazoyer commented that his regime had made political capital out of the refugee situation whilst leaving the relief efforts to the United Nations and the Red Cross International. CADN, Lomé Ambassade 59: H. F. Mazoyer, Ambassade de France au Togo, to M. le Ministre des affaires étrangères, Paris, 9 May 1963.

[111] CADN, Lomé Ambassade 59: High Commission for Refugees, Rapport final sur l'assistance aux refugies au Togo, 9 April 1963, intended for the UN General Assembly, original in English.

[112] CADN, Lomé Ambassade 59: M. E. Ettmueller, chargé de mission, Lomé, to the High Commissioner for Refugees, 12 July 1962.

[113] CADN, Lomé Ambasaade 135: Petition for Review of Attitudes of UNHCR, Lomé, 16 June 1963.

Refugees' Union petitioned the Togo government on a variety of matters regarding their material welfare.[114]

Dispersed within host communities, and benefitting only from belated and piecemeal assistance, the 'western Togo refugees' bear little resemblance to the 'modern, postwar refugee' who emerged as a 'knowable and nameable figure' and an 'object of social-scientific knowledge' through the spatial concentration and bureaucratic processes that were key features of the camps of post-war Europe.[115] In many contexts, the category 'refugee' has the effect of reinforcing 'the national order of things', by defining as problematic people living outside of 'the supposedly normal condition of being attached to a territorial polity and an identifiable people'.[116] The definition of the 'western Togo refugees', however, was contested and paradoxical. Ironically, in self-identifying as 'refugees', people from the former British Togoland were also defining francophone Togo as a 'foreign' or 'host' country, rather than part of the reunified and independent Togoland nation for which they continued to struggle. The British and the Ghanaian governments had a vested interest in denying them the label of 'refugee' in order to emphasise that the integration of the former trust territory of British Togoland with Ghana was normative: from this perspective, the inhabitants of the former trust territory held Ghanaian citizenship, and were residing outside of the nation-state of Ghana on a temporary basis and by their own choice. The Togolese government, on the other hand, sought to define these same people as 'refugees' in order to access international assistance and draw attention to the problematic status of the border and the repressive character of the Ghanaian regime. The refugees thus became a valuable constituency at a time when Olympio's domestic support base was fracturing along ideological lines. Whilst it is beyond the remit of this book to attribute responsibility for the assassination of Olympio on 13 January 1963, the evidence assembled here adds a new layer to Tété-Adjalogo's account of

[114] ANT, Lomé, Series: Klouto, Dossier 110, Affaires Politiques: Western Togo Refugees' Union, Kpalimé, to Ministre de l'intérieur, 26 Oct 1965; and petition from the Western Togo Refugees' Union, Kpalimé to the President of the Republic, Lomé, 11 Aug 1965. The union elected Ebeneezer Dumoga as its secretary. The younger refugees formed their own organisation, which also restated its commitment to the reunification of East and West Togo. See in the same file W. K. Prempeh, Secretary of the Committee of the Youths for the Refugees, Kpalimé, to Adjoint Commandant, Cercle de Klouto, Kpalimé, n.d.

[115] Liisa Malkki, 'Refugees and Exiles: From "Refugee Studies" to the National Order of Things', *Annual Review of Anthropology* 24 (1995), 495–523 at 498.

[116] Ibid., 516.

neo-colonial treachery, and points to the significance of the refugee community and the border issue in determining relations between Nkrumah and Olympio, between each of these new presidents and the former colonial powers, and between ruling parties and their domestic opponents.

THE PATH NOT TAKEN

Writing on the fifty-year anniversaries of Independence for many African colonies, Frederick Cooper urged historians to resist the determinism implied in quests to define the legacies of colonial rule, and to concentrate instead on recovering the alternatives that were posited and the paths that were not taken during the period of decolonisation.[117] This chapter contributes to a growing literature on the years surrounding Independence, and argues for a framework that combines transnational approaches to political history with a more fine-grained exploration of the experiences and perceptions of grassroots activists. In recovering the activities of a community of political refugees, I demonstrate that dissent was alive and well in this period of authoritarian single-party rule, assuming new forms that were not always captured in the types of governmental records on which researchers have usually relied. In the longer term, it is true that Africa's colonial borders proved surprisingly stable. The story I tell here, however, suggests that in the years surrounding Independence, it was the perceived contingency, and not stability, of national borders which underpinned the reformulation of older political movements and projects, threw up new diplomatic dilemmas, and shaped the ways in which West African states engaged with each other and with their former colonial powers. Investigations of the nature and extent of political activity across national borders is a prerequisite to understanding the limits of the powers of post-colonial states over their citizens. Having examined in this chapter some of the diplomatic work in which grassroots activists and the leaders of new states were engaged, let us now return to the repressive tools that ruling parties could use at home to bring domestic opponents into line.

[117] Frederick Cooper, 'Possibility and Constraint: African Independence in Historical Perspective', *Journal of African History* 49 (2) (2008), 167–96 at 196.

6

'No-One Will Hear Your Name Again'

The Terms of the Union

From the vantage point of the early twenty-first century, Ablɔɖe is an anomaly in Ghanaian politics. At various moments since Ghanaian Independence, the movement appears to have been silenced and suppressed by governments, abandoned by frustrated and marginalised supporters, and ignored by younger generations. Today, the Togoland question is clearly less pressing than it was in the 1950s, but it stubbornly refuses to die. It would be easy to attribute the recent wave of activity around the Togoland question to the efforts of a small minority of elderly activists who are out of touch with the mainstream of Ghanaian politics and fail to recognise the futility of their own endeavours. I suspect, however, that Ghana's current status as a successful two-party democracy has required particular issues and individuals to 'get disappeared', in a process not dissimilar to that identified by Jean Allman vis-à-vis the construction of a nationalist meta-narrative.[1] In this chapter, then, I piece together a narrative which offers an alternative means of understanding the persistence of the Togoland question and thereby challenges some of the main explanatory frameworks that have been brought to bear on the politics of post-colonial Ghana.

In Chapter 5, we saw how the threat of preventive detention served to uproot many Togoland reunificationists from Ghanaian soil in the aftermath of Independence. Under the protection of the Togolese president, Sylvanus Olympio, these individuals reconstituted themselves as a refugee community on the Togolese side of the border, and, in the context

[1] Jean Allman, 'The Disappearing of Hannah Kudjoe: Nationalism, Feminism, and the Tyrannies of History', *Journal of Women's History* 21 (3) (2009), 13–35.

of Olympio's struggles with his former allies in the Juvento, the reunification issue developed considerable salience in Togo's domestic and foreign affairs. The assassination of Olympio in January 1963 was a watershed moment which, from the perspective of the reunificationists, entailed the tragic loss of their most important ally. This chapter takes us back across the border to Ghana, where the toppling of Kwame Nkrumah in the coup of 1966 was also a watershed moment. This time, however, the outlook for the reunificationists was rather brighter: the demise of the Nkrumah regime was perceived as the end of victimisation and an opening up of new opportunities.

In retrospective analyses of Ghanaian politics, the coup of 1966 was but the first in a series of dramatic about-turns: the military interregnum of the National Liberation Council was ended in 1969 by elections which brought Dr Kofi Busia and his Progress Party to power. Busia was removed by a coup in 1972, after which Ghana witnessed an extended period of military rule through the remainder of the 1970s, dominated by the figure of General I. K. Acheampong. Flight Lieutenant Jerry Rawlings' first coup of June 1979 paved the way for fresh elections and a brief period of civilian rule under Dr Hilla Limann, but Rawlings' 'second coming' in December 1981 returned Ghana to an authoritarian system until 1992. These milestones are familiar to most adult Ghanaians, but there are few scholarly analyses which treat the period 1966 to 1992 as a subject of interest in its own right. For many historians, this was the unhappy postscript to the rise of anti-colonial nationalism and the achievement of Independence, whilst for many political scientists it is the unfortunate prelude to the elections of 1992 and the subsequent consolidation of one of contemporary Africa's most successful multi-party democracies.

In both scholarly and popular analyses of Ghanaian politics, there are three main ways of imposing order upon the bewildering series of events between 1966 and 1992, and each of these is underwritten by normative assumptions about national sovereignty and/or democratic governance. The first way of making sense is to categorise governments according to whether they were civilian or military, multi- or single-party, and to extrapolate from these labels the level of 'democracy' pertaining in the country since Independence. Ghana's downward trajectory through the 1960s, 70s, and 80s is deemed typical of the continent as a whole, but since 1992 it has been singled out as a success story which might serve as a model for other African countries. Those who are more interested in the particularities of the Ghanaian experience have brought two further explanatory frameworks to bear. One is concerned with the cyclical nature of Ghanaian politics and the emergence of a two-party system built around an 'elite'/'Danquah-Busia' tradition and a 'populist'/ 'Nkrumahist' tradition. The other is concerned with the association of each of the two main party traditions with distinctive ethno-regional support bases, and particularly the association of the 'Danquah-Busia' tradition with Ghana's Akan heartlands.

In none of these three frameworks is there space for Ablɔɖe. It is tempting to conclude, as others have done, that these frameworks offer satisfactory explanations for the political affiliations and behaviours of most Ghanaians over the past half century, and that Ablɔɖe has ceased to be an effective movement precisely because it failed to establish a solid base for itself in either of the main party traditions or their associated ethno-regional voting blocks. My contention here is that whilst these frameworks do indeed make a good deal of sense, they work retrospectively, to explain the present situation, and not historically to identify processes or agents of change. There are still relatively few scholarly efforts to explore the rhetorical, performative, and political effort which was required to establish the two main party traditions out of a much messier reality, to build the connections of each main party tradition with its distinctive ethno-regional support base, and to marginalise movements that could not be 're-homed' within the new order.[2]

The relative lack of attention to this rhetorical and performative work has the effect of making today's ethno-regional voting patterns appear axiomatic – a reflex on the part of voters that successful politicians have simply learned to manipulate or navigate. One of the most ubiquitous contemporary stereotypes of the Ewe-speakers of Ghana's Volta Region is that they are 'tribalists' who have turned out en masse in every election since 1992 to vote for the party established by their fellow Ewe, Jerry Rawlings. The voting patterns in the Volta Region at the turn of the twenty-first century do indeed indicate consistent and numerically overwhelming support for this party. But today's Volta Region also encompasses the southern section of the former trust territory of British Togoland and numerous linguistic minorities. It will by now be obvious

[2] The best available study is still Paul Nugent's *Big Men, Small Boys and Politics in Ghana: Power, Ideology and the Burden of History, 1982–1994* (London, 1995). See also *Le Ghana de J. J. Rawlings: Restauration de l'état et renaissance du politique*, ed. Comi Toulabour (Paris, 2000); and Kevin Shillington, *Ghana and the Rawlings Factor* (London, 1992).

to any reader of this book that the people who spoke Ewe, either as their first language or as a useful vehicular, did not act as a single political unit before or during the period of British administration, and they were bitterly divided over the nature and form of Independence in the mid-twentieth century. The fact that the people of this area are now acting as an ethno-regional voting block still requires historical explanation.

The task is complicated by issues of methodology and interpretation. Precisely because the nation-state has cohered against the odds in most parts of sub-Saharan Africa, it has become a default unit of analysis. The study of politics thus revolves around explaining the outcomes of competition for control of the state and identifying the logics that determine the uses of state resources. The gaping holes in the Ghana national archives between 1966 and 1992 certainly pose a challenge to anyone who wishes to engage in a detailed analysis of the day-to-day functioning of the post-colonial state, but this is scarcely the only period in which the nature of African states, and the opposition they encountered, has to be inferred from problematic and incomplete sources.[3] The very recentness of the post-colonial period provides exciting opportunities to understand how 'politics' was constituted, not only in institutions and organisations, but in the lived experiences of individuals.

For Achille Mbembe, an understanding of how politics is constituted in everyday life necessitates an engagement with indigenous imaginaries of power. For him, tyrannical leaders and their subjects share the same epistemic field, and 'power compels its subjects ritualistically to perform, within and through the mundane practices of everyday life, a ratification of its own theatricality and excess'.[4] Paradoxically, this convivial participation in the rearticulation of power serves both to ratify and to de-legitimise it. For the period and places with which I am concerned here, state power was not associated with the levels of excess or obscenity which Mbembe seeks to explain. Nonetheless, my attempts to build relationships with former activists generated a series of accounts of being 'on the losing side', and a series of reflections upon the form and meanings of this loss. In Mbembe's analysis, imageries of loss are inherently sexual, because, in the post-colony, 'power dons the face of virility'.[5] Thus when

[3] Jean Allman, 'Phantoms of the Archive: Kwame Nkrumah, a Nazi Pilot Named Hanna, and the Contingencies of Post-Colonial History Writing', *American Historical Review* 118 (1) (2013), 104–29.

[4] Achille Mbembe, 'On the Postcolony: A Brief Response to Critics', *African Identities* 4/2 (2006), 143–178 at 161.

[5] Ibid., 163.

he speaks of the principle of the manducation of power, he is referring to 'the practice, in political and social struggles, that consists in stripping the enemy of everything that constitutes the emblems of his virility, and consuming him'.[6] I am not convinced that the political activists with whom I spoke imagined the Ghanaian state as an erect penis which cast itself beyond its limits, but it is also highly unlikely that they would have discussed with me any sexualised images of power and loss, even if these had been intensely meaningful to them. What is useful in Mbembe's analysis is his emphasis on the *intimacy* of power, because it is in this realm – in the undermining conduct of the powerful towards their opponents – that the continuing significance of the Togoland question is to be explained.

The story that I tell here does not necessarily constitute an authoritative account of what happened to Ablɔɖe, nor can it provide a definitive explanation for the emergence of an ethno-regional voting block in an area formerly characterised by party-political competition. This chapter contributes to the rather underdeveloped literature on the post-Nkrumah and post-Olympio periods in two respects. Firstly, it explores the terms in which reunificationists described and explained their political cause and its failure, and their responses to the means deployed by post-colonial governments to curtail dissent. Secondly, it highlights the opportunities that spaces behind prison bars and beyond the nation-state have offered to citizens wishing to organise around agendas that were cast beyond the pale of national politics. In the final chapter, we will examine existing observations about the 'cyclical' nature of Ghanaian politics and the two dominant party traditions, and thereby render intelligible the periodic bursts of interest in the Togoland question – an issue that might otherwise appear anachronistic or anomalous.

'NO-ONE WILL HEAR YOUR NAME AGAIN': SECURITY, STATUS, AND THE INTIMACY OF POWER

Following the coup that ousted Nkrumah in 1966, and the military interregnum of the National Liberation Council, multi-party elections were held throughout Ghana in 1969. In the Volta Region, including the former British Togoland, Komla Gbedemah's National Alliance of Liberals (NAL) proved more popular than Kofi Busia's Progress Party,

[6] Ibid., 167.

but the latter won the elections on the basis of its stronger support in other regions. The Volta Region electorate of 1969 included a cohort of individuals who were too young to vote in the plebiscite of 1956, whilst the oldest of the voters in 1956 would have passed away by 1969, and in this sense the electorate of 1969 is not strictly comparable with that of 1956. Nonetheless, the level of support for the NAL in the former trust territory area indicates that there must have been numerous individuals who had voted for Togoland Congress in 1956 but transferred their votes to the NAL in 1969. Paul Nugent and David Brown both interpret this as a failure on the part of the old Togoland Congress leadership to re-establish itself as a political force even within its former strongholds. Brown suggests that this was partly due to accusations of corruption amongst individual reunificationists in local political committees during the 1966–9 interregnum.[7] Nugent, on the other hand, emphasises that former supporters were reluctant to reassociate themselves with the reunificationist leadership because the consequences of previous political failure were still too fresh, both for the individuals who had experienced persecution and for the communities which had lost out on development projects as a result of their identification with the reunificationist cause.[8]

Some former political detainees certainly indicated in interviews that they had withdrawn from party politics on the grounds that it was too risky. Thus, Moses Kofi Asase concluded: 'I don't support anything anymore ... I was tortured and I have suffered, so why would I now indulge myself in politics?' Mr Asase explained that in his younger days he had taken risks, and he felt that he had seen some benefits in the immediate aftermath of the overthrow of Nkrumah in 1966:

> It was Kotoka who released us in 1966. Kotoka, he is my man. I will praise him. It was him who helped me to start in the cement-selling business. I had a special authorisation from the government, so I was selling cement. By and by, I saw that other people, who were buying the cement, were building. And me, who was selling it, was not building anything. So, after a while, I started to use my money to buy materials. I was living a small small life, just taking my chop money and using the rest for materials, and that is how I got this house.[9]

Mr Asase was proud of his large house, with its electricity, running water, and metal roofing, and he drew two conclusions from his success in

[7] David Brown, 'Borderline Politics in Ghana: The National Liberation Movement of Western Togoland', *Journal of Modern African Studies* 18 (4) (1980), 575–609 at 596.
[8] Nugent, *Smugglers, Secessionists and Loyal Citizens*, 212–3.
[9] Interview with M. K. Asase, Ho, 20 July 2000.

building it: firstly, that it was careful management of limited resources, and not conspicuous consumption or excess, that enabled individuals to attain the more secure and enduring measures of social status; and secondly, that politics, rather like gambling, only paid off if you quit whilst you were ahead:

> That is how government is. If you don't get your money before your government is gone, well, you will just have nothing . . . The day your government falls, no-one will hear your name again. Unless you are a big big man, like Busia or Danquah, or those people. But the rest of us, no-one will hear your name again.[10]

Politics, he concluded, was a high-risk strategy, entailing abrupt reversals of fortune that ordinary individuals were ill-equipped to handle. Mr Asase no longer wanted the trouble, and believed that the energies of the young would be better focussed on safer means of acquiring social status and financial security. Success, in this view, came not from Mbembe's convivial participation in the simulation of power, but by accumulating just enough resources to be able to place a safe distance between oneself and politics. 'Politics,' he concluded, 'is a dirty game, and I have told my children never to do it. You too should not do it. Better to finish your studies and become a university lecturer.'[11]

The desire to withdraw into a secure space was sometimes expressed by other former exiles and detainees too, but it was by no means the only reaction to the experience of political failure and persecution. Amongst the Togoland Congress leadership, the tendency towards the Progress Party was strong. E. O. Kofi Dumoga and S. G. Antor were both invited on to the political committee established by the National Liberation Council following the overthrow of Nkrumah in February 1966. In 1969, Antor stood (albeit unsuccessfully) as a Progress Party candidate in the Dayi East constituency, which was roughly equivalent to his old constituency of Kpandu North.[12] Kodzo Ayeke, who was then abroad studying to become a lawyer, chaired the London branch of the Progress Party in 1969.[13] At the grassroots level, Brown indicates that the core of Ablɔɖe activists in Kpandu lined up behind the Progress Party. Mathias

[10] Interview with M. K. Asase, Ho-Dome, 20 July 2000. 'No-one will hear your name again' is a direct translation of the Ewe saying, 'Ameaɖeke ma ga se wo ŋkɔ azɔ o.'

[11] Interview with M. K. Asase, Ho, 11 Aug 2000.

[12] Nugent, *Smugglers, Secessionists and Loyal Citizens*, 219.

[13] Pamphlet produced and printed for private distribution at the funeral of Kodzo Afelete Ayeke, Taviefe, 15 June 1995. I am grateful to G. Y. M. Ayeke, Kodzo's brother, for giving me a copy of this pamphlet.

Agbodza of Santrokofi was so proud of his Progress Party membership card that he photocopied it and posted me a copy so that I could see the signature of B. J. da Rocha (the party secretary).[14] Edward Wuanka in Dzolo-Gbogame also commented on the tendency towards the Progress Party among those who were returning from exile in Togo: 'that was our father's party.'[15] Ironically, then, some of the individuals who had been the strongest advocates of Togoland reunification in the 1950s – looking east to French Togoland, rather than west to the Gold Coast, when they envisaged Independence – were also those who appeared at the end of the 1960s to identify most strongly with the Ghana-wide party led by Busia. How did this reorientation come about?

'WE WERE ALL IN THE SAME TROUBLE': PREVENTIVE DETENTION AND THE GHANA-WIDE OPPOSITION

The Togoland reunificationists forged connections with two of the major figures in Gold Coast/Ghanaian politics: Dr J. B. Danquah and Dr Kofi Busia. The earliest of these connections was forged in the pre-Independence era, whilst other relationships emerged as a consequence of the Preventive Detention Act of 1958. Busia and Danquah were rooted in different regional and professional networks: the former was an academic sociologist who originated from Wenchi (now in Ghana's Brong-Ahafo Region), whilst the latter was a lawyer from Akyem (now in the Eastern Region). It was not until the mid-1950s that they came together in their opposition to Nkrumah's CPP. In 1950, chief Mote Kofi II had asked Danquah to represent him during his bid to retain the paramountcy of the amalgamated Asogli state.[16] Danquah also represented S. G. Antor during the latter's first period in preventive detention and helped to secure his release in June 1958.[17] The relationships of Togoland Congress leaders with Busia, on the other hand, were forged in 1956, when Antor hitched his objections to the integration of British Togoland with the Gold Coast to the wider attempt by the (Asante) National Liberation Movement and the Northern Peoples' Party to challenge Nkrumah's plans for a unitary constitution. The relationship between these opposition parties

[14] Letter from M. K. Agbodza to the author, 31 Jan 2001.
[15] Interview with E. K. Wuanka, Dzolo-Gbogame, 12 June 2010.
[16] PRAAD, Ho. VRG 2/110, Asogli Native Affairs: J. B. Danquah to Assistant District Commissioner, Ho, 8 March 1950.
[17] Interview with Robert Antor and S. G. Antor Jr, Logba-Alakpeti, 15 Sept 2000.

was reinforced by the Avoidance of Discrimination Act of 1957, which prohibited political parties from organising along regional, religious, or 'tribal' lines. Thus, the members of parliament elected by the various opposition parties were forced to join together in the United Party.

Antor's status within the United Party was reinforced by accusations of subversion against the Nkrumah government, particularly during the Awhaitey Affair of December 1958.[18] Major Awhaitey was court martialled under suspicion of receiving arms from M. K. Apaloo and R. R. Amponsah with the intention of assassinating Nkrumah. The Commission of Enquiry reported in May 1959, with the majority report indicating that Antor, together with Joe Appiah and Victor Owusu (both formerly of the National Liberation Movement), had conspired to install Busia as Nkrumah's successor. As we saw in Chapter 5, Ablɔɖe activists were detained in waves through the spring and summer of 1960, including Alex Odame, E. O. Kofi Dumoga, Kofi Daniel Dumoga, Albert Simpson, Christian Baxter Attah, and Moses Kofi Asase. Again, they looked to Danquah to represent them, but this time he was not able to procure the desired results. On 2 September 1961, Ghana's supreme court ruled that the Preventive Detention Act was constitutional. This paved the way for further waves of arrests in the wake of the Sekondi-Takoradi workers' strike and the discovery of new 'conspiracies' which Nkrumah believed to emanate from the community of United Party refugees across the border in Lomé.[19] Antor was now detained for a second time, along with Appiah and Owusu, whilst Busia went into exile, first in Togo and then in the Netherlands.[20] The British high commissioner estimated that there were 700 people detained under the Preventive Detention Act by the end of February 1962, and the *Daily Express* reported that a new higher-security detention centre was built at Ussher Fort.[21]

[18] Antor was actually posted as a teacher to Wenchi in 1945, but I am not certain that he established a relationship with Busia during that time.

[19] The National Archives (TNA), Kew, UK. DO 195/39 Preventive Detention in Ghana: press clippings on page 62 of file. I also discussed the issue of preventive detention with Nkrumah's former cabinet secretary. Interview with Daniel Chapman, Nyaho Clinic, Airport Residential, Greater Accra, 21 Sept 2000.

[20] TNA, DO 195/75 Ghana-Togo Relations: U. K. High Commission, Accra, to Commonwealth Relations Office (CRO), London, 22 Nov 1961. Busia went with Olympio on a tour of the United States in November and December 1961. Nkrumah believed that Busia was using the tour to undermine American support for the Volta River Project. See also DO 195/39 Preventive Detention in Ghana, clippings from *The Times* 22 Dec 1961.

[21] TNA, DO 195/39 Preventive Detention in Ghana: press clipping on page 66 of file.

This may have been a tactical error on the part of Nkrumah. Although the United Party had been forged by parliamentarians whose grassroots support was based around different issues in various parts of Ghana, the experience of preventive detention bound together a much more diverse range of politicians and activists. In the words of Christian Baxter Attah:

> We were all in the same trouble. Major Awhaitey used to tell us a story about how, when he was in East Africa, he had been inside a cave. So many different animals were in, all afraid, and none of them knowing what was really happening. And that is how we were in detention. We were just together.[22]

This enforced proximity over periods of several years prompted detainees to find ways of passing the time. Christian Baxter Attah taught himself some French as well as picking up Twi and Ga from fellow detainees. According to Joe Appiah, the self-improving adult education tradition was reinvigorated and the experience of detention became something akin to a 'barbed-wire university':

> To relieve our boredom we decided to set up daily classes for ourselves. I lectured on the science of fingerprints and identification, while others lectured on different interesting topics. I must say that our keepers rather enjoyed these free tutorials and often pleaded with us that we bring our lectures [down] to their level; this we did.[23]

Some of the detainees made sense of their dire circumstances by anticipating the cyclical nature of politics. Appiah therefore claimed in his autobiography that he had confidently predicted the downfall of the Nkrumah regime, and indeed used such predictions as a restraint on the prison guards' behaviour. He recalled that, in the aftermath of the attempt on Nkrumah's life at Kulungugu, he was transferred to Ussher Fort (Ghana's 'Alcatraz') where conditions were far less comfortable:

> Once in a while, some of us [the detainees] reminded them [the guards] that we were, after all, political detainees who someday could become ministers of state in whose hands their destinies would lie. This did seem to have some salutary effect ... [24]

Appiah was confident that detention was merely a temporary setback – and indeed an experience that might even serve to authenticate his status

[22] Interview with C. B. Attah, Ho, 20 Sept 2000.

[23] Joe Appiah, *Joe Appiah: The Autobiography of an African Patriot* (New York, 1990), 259. The term 'barbed-wire university' was not used by Appiah, but has recently been popularised by Midge Gillies, *Barbed-Wire University: The Real Lives of Allied Prisoners of War in the Second World War* (London, 2012).

[24] Appiah, *Joe Appiah*, 262.

and enhance his prospects after the demise of the Nkrumah regime. Despite a keen awareness of their diminished circumstances in the cells, the detainees still believed that they were, quite literally, 'respectable' individuals, deserving of a respectful manner in their interactions with the prison guards who were tasked with keeping them in confinement. One of the things that made detention bearable, then, was engagement in self-improving activities, which reinforced their collective identity as 'political detainees' and reminded themselves and the prison guards that they were a category apart from the majority of Ghana's prison population.

Appiah's confidence about the imminent reversal of fortunes, however, was not necessarily shared by all of the detainees. He was released in 1964, before the majority of the Togoland Congress activists, who had to wait until the fall of Nkrumah in the coup of February 1966. Their final year in detention was overshadowed by the death of Danquah in February 1965. Through his efforts to challenge the constitutionality of the Preventive Detention Act, Danquah had become a heroic figure to all the detainees. Moses Kofi Asase told me with pride that 'he was our lawyer' and it was painful for Asase to recall, more than forty years later, the 'wicked' treatment meted out to the ageing lawyer by the prison guards, who apparently poured buckets of water on to the floor of his cell in order to aggravate his rheumatoid arthritis.

During their time in detention, then, the Ablɔḍe activists were forced into close proximity with other elements of the Ghana-wide opposition to Nkrumah: they interacted closely with these detainees, enduring bitter moments, finding ways of making detention bearable, and seeking to make sense out of their current circumstances. Preventive detention could be an experience which chastened individuals and made them wary of the risks attached to political activism. But in other cases, it drew a hard core of Togoland Congress activists into new relationships, binding them first to the United Party and then to its late twentieth-century reincarnations. Preventive detention, however, was experienced at first-hand by only a small minority. Now then, let us turn to some of the other means by which the Nkrumah regime sought to marginalise its Togoland opponents, and assess the implications for future political affiliations.

SCHOOLBOY SPIES: REPUTATION AND HUMILIATION IN THE CONTROL OF DISSENT

In Chapter 3, we saw that the opening of Mawuli secondary school in 1950 was an important moment in the history of the trust territory because, for a whole generation of middle-school leavers, it reduced the financial barriers that had previously precluded them from acquiring secondary education in the Gold Coast. Beyond the immediate beneficiaries in the student body, Mawuli was more widely recognised as the institution which would enable the trust territory to produce its first substantial cohort of secondary-school graduates, who could then move on to university and penetrate the professions and the senior ranks of the civil service, in which Togolanders had previously felt under-represented. Staffed largely by graduate teachers, Mawuli became home to the tiny handful of Togoland graduates who had managed to obtain a university education during the late 1940s and early 1950s. Among these teachers were E. K. Datsa of Amedzofe-Avatime and A. K. Tse of Kpandu-Bame (who had both gained their degrees in Scotland), along with S. K. Ohene of Abutia-Teti (who was a Legon graduate). Whilst the primary- and middle-school teachers we encountered in Chapter 2 were persons of status in their own localities, and rendered valuable services in terms of organising community development projects and teaching mother-tongue literacy, the graduate teachers at Mawuli represented a pinnacle of achievement for their generation. Their political affiliations were thus a matter of interest to colleagues, students, and a wider public, and it was no secret that most of them had opposed the integration of Togoland with Ghana in 1956 and were personally acquainted with numerous Ablɔɖe leaders and activists both around the school campus, in Ho, and across the wider trust territory area.

In his memoirs, Mr Datsa recalled two incidents which culminated in his departure from Mawuli. The first, in February 1957, entailed the arrival of 'a big truck loaded with policemen in the forecourt of the Administration Block'. The policemen descended and proceeded towards the bungalows in which Datsa, Tse, Ohene, and another colleague, V. O. Anku, resided. The policemen produced their search warrants, and each of the teachers in turn asked the policemen to turn out their pockets. Mr Datsa explained 'to the senior officer ... that much as I had no reason to resist a search authorized by a recognized authority, I had to be sure that the policeman sent to search me did not have on him any contraband items like diamonds or seditious document that he could plant anywhere in my room'.[25]

[25] E. K. Datsa, *Doing My Duty: Memoirs of a Ghanaian Educationist* (Accra, 2006), 116.

Mr Ohene's daughter, Elizabeth, therefore watched the somewhat bizarre spectacle of the teachers inspecting the policemen's pockets and the policemen searching the teachers' rooms. The incident yielded no evidence that could be used to bring a prosecution, and the policemen soon went away. 'Looking back on it now,' explained Elizabeth Ohene, 'I think that the police were embarrassed to come and do this because in those days, Ewedome [i.e., the inland, as opposed to coastal, Ewe-speaking area], you could count the number of graduates on one hand, so they were the crème de la crème.'[26] The significance was symbolic: the search was intended to undermine the teachers, not, as Mbembe would have it, by stripping them of the 'emblems of their virility', but by stimulating gossip and rumours on the campus, thereby denying them the recognition and respect that their status and qualifications would normally confer. In asking the policemen to turn out their pockets, the teachers were able to reassert an element of control over the situation and thus maintained some dignity in front of students and colleagues, but this won them only a temporary reprieve.

A few weeks later, the teachers were once again under scrutiny. Mr Datsa thus recalled: 'There were strong rumours on Mawuli School campus that some of us, the supporters of the Togoland Congress, had assembled weapons in our bungalows for shooting and killing our colleague teachers, who were members of the CPP ... on Independence Day.'[27] When Independence Day came, no-one was killed on the campus, and the Independence parades went ahead in Ho (although the children of the Tse, Ohene, Datsa, and Anku households were deterred from participating).[28] Finally, in 1958, the situation came to a head. The minister of education, the regional education officer, and the district commissioner (S. W. Kuma, a CPP activist from Kpandu and a former member of staff at the school) arrived in a delegation at the campus. They informed Tse, Ohene, Datsa, Anku, and another colleague, J. K. B. Adzotor, that 'because of their political activities calculated to undermine the authority of the government of Ghana, their continued stay in the Volta Region' was no longer 'conducive to the security and the success of the work of the government'.[29]

[26] Interview with E. Ohene, Airport Residential, Accra, 22 June 2010.
[27] Datsa, *Doing My Duty*, 115.
[28] Interview with E. Ohene, Airport Residential, Greater Accra, 22 June 2010.
[29] Datsa, *Doing My Duty*, 119.

In the event, the teachers managed to find posts elsewhere, but this was beside the point. In the strictly hierarchical environment of a prestigious boarding school, they had experienced a frontal assault on their reputations. More than forty years later in their recollections of their departure from Mawuli, Mr Tse and Mr Datsa described it as a part of a world turned upside-down, in which junior people who attached themselves to the CPP no longer gave due recognition to the hard-earned professional status of their seniors. According to Mr Datsa, 'Professors were dismissed! Judges were dismissed! Pupils were spying on their teachers and reported all kinds of nonsense. Someone can just come for you in the night and put you in preventive detention for six years'.[30] Mr Tse recalled that teachers who attended Togoland Congress meetings were closely monitored by 'typists, secretaries, people working in the school office' as well as by their own students who would in turn report on them to their pro-CPP colleagues.[31] In establishing Young Pioneer branches in schools throughout Ghana, the CPP had provided a means by which students could undercut the status and authority of their teachers by conveying information directly to the local party machinery.

From these experiences, the elite of graduate teachers appeared to have developed a deep suspicion of 'populist' politics and its capacity to unsettle the status order through which they had risen. Elizabeth Ohene thus recalled her late father's regular admonishment that 'ruling a country was too serious to be reduced to the waving of handkerchiefs' and his irritation that Nkrumah used his honorary title 'Dr' when he had not actually completed a PhD.[32] The public humiliation of the graduate teacher elite may, on the face of it, seem like a minor irritation in comparison with a six-year stretch in preventive detention. But it was experienced as a denial of due recognition: the graduate teachers believed that CPP activists refused to respect educational qualifications and professional status acquired through effort and merit. Mr Tse connected these experiences to his decision to support the Progress Party in 1969: 'I trusted the person of Busia because he was educated.'[33]

If the politicisation of school campuses provoked a sense of outrage amongst some of the most highly qualified reunificationist teachers, it also had far-reaching effects among the students. In July 2003 Robert Antor

[30] Interview with E. K. Datsa, Amedzofe-Avatime, 3 June 1999.
[31] Interview with A. K. Tse, Achimota, Greater Accra, 21 Sept 2000.
[32] Interview with E. Ohene, Airport Residential, Greater Accra, 22 June 2010.
[33] Interview with A. K. Tse, Achimota, Greater Accra, 21 Sept 2000.

(son of S. G. Antor) told a public hearing in Accra how he and his siblings had suffered as a result of their father's detention from 1961 to 1966: 'the bursaries of two of his brothers, then at Mawuli School were revoked and he was together with them sacked from the School. He said he sought employment as a pupil teacher to look after his younger siblings.'[34] As was the case for the refugees whom we encountered in Chapter 5, one of the worst consequences of being on the losing side in politics was disruption at key points in one's children's education. Moses Kofi Asase was making a similar point when he explained to me that although all of his children were educated, 'the mother could not get the money for secondary school' for the ones who were growing up during the period that he had been in preventive detention.[35] Teacher training and nursing training opened up cheaper alternatives that were very respectable but not particularly well paid.

The historical position of the trust territory area as an exporter of skilled labour, the absence of an urban commercial centre comparable with Accra or Kumasi, and the constrained possibilities for cocoa cash cropping, all pointed towards formal education as a key mechanism for social mobility and for intergenerational wealth transfer. Those who had benefitted from early mission or church initiatives in schooling almost invariably sought further educational opportunities for their children, and these opportunities constituted the primary means by which individuals and families could attain economic security and the social recognition that came with their particular abilities to represent or otherwise assist a community. In disrupting the education of the children of political detainees, the CPP regime visited significant damage on families' longer-term security and prosperity, as well as threatening the very basis on which their continued social status depended. It seems unlikely that this was anything other than an intentional strategy on the part of those who occupied positions in the district and party administration. If the CPP and its opponents shared an epistemic field, it was one that was operationalised not at the symbolic level, in a fantasised economy of power, but in much more mundane strategies aimed at curtailing the ability of political opponents to reproduce the social status and financial security that they had achieved through formal education.

[34] www.modernghana.com/news/37843/1/sg-antors-son-testifies-at-nrc.html [accessed on 12 May 2011].

[35] Interview with M. K. Asase, Ho, 20 July 2000.

APOLLO AND THE ALIENS: THE AKAN-EWE CLEAVAGE IN GHANAIAN POLITICS

In the three-year interregnum that followed the demise of Nkrumah, reunificationists reflected on experiences of exile, detention, and being on the losing side. The Ablɔɖe movement thereby fractured according to a range of conclusions about the risks and opportunities that pertained to activism in Ghana. Thus, in 1969, some of its supporters cast their votes for Gbedemah and the NAL, others aligned themselves with Busia and the Progress Party, and some of the core grassroots activists engaged in a tactical withdrawal. The Togoland question had clearly lost its purchase as 'the' issue around which voters in the former trust territory would unite or divide. New cleavages emerging within the military and the National Liberation Council gave rise to new characterisations of Ghanaian politics which insisted on the centrality of an Akan-Ewe ethnic divide and thereby downplayed the distinctive trajectory of the former trust territory and the historic cleavages between the various speakers of Ewe in Ghana.

In the period 1966 to 1969, the ethnic composition of the Ghanaian military, and the potential impact of ethnic cleavages on the National Liberation Council, were widely discussed. Baynham later noted that 'Ewe officers [led by Kotoka] had formed the core of the conspiratorial group against Nkrumah' in 1966, and at the end of 1967 Ewes 'commanded the three wings of the armed forces as well as the First Brigade and the Police'.[36] During the run-up to the 1969 elections, there was a well-observed division between military members of the National Liberation Council (General Afrifa and Lieutenant-Colonel Yeboah) who allied themselves with Busia and police members (Commissioner Harlley and his deputy, A. K. Deku) who allied themselves with Gbedemah. After his victory in the elections of 1969, Busia was anxious to protect himself from further military interventions in politics, and through 1969–71, a series of changes in personnel had the effect of marginalising Ewe-speakers from 'strategically significant command posts' and replacing them with Akans who appeared more politically reliable.[37]

Although the Akan-Ewe cleavage within the military has received considerable attention in analyses of the downfalls of both Nkrumah and Busia, there is no obvious connection between the key Ewe military

[36] Simon Baynham, 'Civilian Rule and the Coup d'Etat: the case of Busia's Ghana', *The RUSI Journal* 123 (3) (1978), 27–33.

[37] Ibid., 30.

personnel and the former Togoland Congress leadership. General Kotoka was an Anlo, while Brigadiers Amenu and Kattah (who were both replaced by Akans under Busia) were from Peki and Anlo, respectively. In other words, they came from areas which had never belonged to the trust territory and had no tradition of support for the Togoland Congress. Whether or not they intended to replace Busia with Gbedemah (or indeed any other Ewe-speaking politician), it is unlikely that they were doing so in cahoots with the former Togoland Congress leadership, which, as we have seen, had thrown in its lot with Busia and the Progress Party. In its first year in office, however, the Busia government undertook two key measures which contributed to the disillusionment of other Ablɔɖe supporters who had backed the Progress Party and stimulated a resurgence of interest amongst the new leadership in the Republic of Togo.

The former Ablɔɖe activists and supporters whom I interviewed were less concerned with ethnic cleavages in the military than they were with the notorious 'Apollo 568' which affected the civil service. Under the transitional provisions of the 1969 constitution, the Busia government dismissed 568 civil servants who had served under the Nkrumah administration. Within the Volta Region, there was a widespread perception that Ewe-speakers were over-represented among the 568 individuals who lost their positions, and that the measure was motivated by ethnic bias. The issue had political legs because when E. K. Sallah (manager of the Ghana National Trading Corporation) challenged the government's right to dismiss him, and won a favourable judgement from the Supreme Court, Busia responded that no court could 'compel the government to employ or re-employ anyone'.[38] This undercut Busia's own rhetoric about the failure of populist politicians to respect the rule of law, and gave rise to a deep suspicion of anti-Ewe bias even among people in the former trust territory who had been willing to support Busia in the 1969 elections. According to Mr Tse, who had trusted Busia in 1969 'because he was educated', Apollo 568 was a turning point, and he had since retained a suspicion that Akan politicians 'like Akan'.[39]

If Apollo 568 had consequences for political affiliations within Ghana, it ran alongside another measure which had diplomatic and international repercussions. In mid-November 1969, the Ghana government announced an Aliens' Compliance Order, which required all non-Ghanaians living in the country to acquire a residence permit by 2 December. Of a total

[38] Ibid., 28. [39] Interview with A. K. Tse, Achimota, Greater Accra, 21 Sept 2000.

population of 8 million, it was estimated that 1.5 million were not Ghanaian nationals. Busia insisted that this was not a 'quit order' but a 'compliance order' whereby the formally employed could acquire residence permits and thereby regularise their status.[40] Nonetheless, it provoked a significant exodus amongst those who did not expect to obtain a residence permit and preferred to leave quickly rather than await forcible expulsion. Although some of these 'aliens' came from Ivory Coast to the west, or from Upper Volta to the north, all those who came from Nigeria, Dahomey, or Togo had to cross Ghana's eastern border. Between 2 and 4 December 1969, over 50,000 people arrived at the Aflao border crossing, some of them utterly penniless, others lacking sufficient funds to reach their countries of origin, and many with no formal means of identification. On 6 December the border was closed to anyone who was not a Togolese national or could not guarantee that they had transport to take them directly to another country. The French ambassador to Togo, Henri Langlais, emphasised the risk of a humanitarian crisis if the flow of refugees continued apace.[41] By 13 December, the Togolese minister for foreign affairs informed the French ambassador in Lomé that, in addition to the 300,000 who had already crossed the border (some of whom were Togolese nationals), they now estimated that a further 700,000 people might cross into Togo en route to their respective countries of origin.[42]

Following the establishment of a Comité d'Aide aux Refugiés by the Togolese government, and donations from France, Britain, the United States, and the Federal Republic of Germany, the French embassy in Lomé co-operated with representatives of the neighbouring African governments and the International Red Cross to hire transport for those seeking to reach Niger, Dahomey, and Nigeria.[43] Faced with urgent representations from the governments of neighbouring countries, the

[40] Ousman Kobo, '"We Are Citizens Too": The Politics of Citizenship in Independent Ghana', *Journal of Modern African Studies* 48 (1) (2010), 67–94.

[41] CADN, Lomé Ambassade 135, 1969–83 Refugiés du Ghana: Langlais, French embassy in Lomé, to Paris, 'Problème des expulses du Ghana' 9 Dec 1969 and 'Exode au Togo des refugiés du Ghana' 6 Dec 1969. All translations from French are my own.

[42] CADN, Lomé Ambassade 135: Togolese minister of foreign affairs to the French embassy in Lomé, 13 Dec 1969.

[43] CADN, Lomé Ambassade 135: News despatch from French embassy in Lomé to Direction des Affaires Africaines et Malagaches, Paris, 23 Dec 1969; Togolese minister for foreign affairs to French embassy in Lomé, 26 Jan 1970, acknowledges a contribution of 2 million CFA to meet the costs of supporting refugees; telegram from French embassy in Lomé to Paris, 20 Dec 1969, outlined how the ambassador had hired four lorries in order to transport 1,200 individuals back to Niger.

Ghana government agreed to establish camps for those who were attempting to leave the country but lacked transport, money, or food, and the pace of the departures into Togo and neighbouring countries began to slow. A large-scale humanitarian crisis was thus averted, but, amidst numerous individual and press accounts of intimidation and spoliation of Togolese citizens and other 'aliens' in Ghana, the newly established Rassemblement du Peuple Togolais (RPT) across the border in Togo was able to make political capital. Thus, in addition to the concrete measures that were taken to assist the refugees, the RPT regime also issued press releases about the need for the Togolese population to show solidarity with the refugees and to live up to their national reputation for hospitality in the face of the most inhospitable behaviour of the government next door.[44]

STRANGE BEDFELLOWS: THE RE-EMERGENCE OF 'THE EWE QUESTION'

On the face of it, the new regime established in the Republic of Togo by General Gnassingbé Eyadéma was an unlikely ally of Ablɔɖe. As a Kabyé from northern Togo who had seized power in the 1967 military coup, Eyadéma had no obvious reason to support either an ethnic reunification of the Ewe-speakers or to take on the Togoland reunification agenda espoused by Sylvanus Olympio prior to his assassination in 1963. Nonetheless, in February 1970, the French ambassador to Togo sent a secret report to the Ministry of Foreign Affairs in Paris, detailing the nature of his recent discussions with Eyadéma.[45] The ambassador suggested that Eyadéma's policy of 'national reconciliation' required him to make gestures towards the Ewe-speakers of southern Togo at precisely the same time that he became aware of the disgruntlement of the Ewe-speakers of Ghana with the Busia government. According to the ambassador, then, contacts between Ghanaian Ewes and the Togolese regime were being established as early as December 1969 in a clandestine meeting at Ho, and were further developed at the annual Agbogbozã festivals (which commemorate the historic departure of the Ewe-speakers from the walled town of Notsé, and thus their freedom from the tyrannical reign of King

[44] CADN, Lomé Ambassade 135: 'Communiqué à la population du minister de l'information', n.d.

[45] CADN, Accra Ambassade 62, Togo-Ghana 1968–1972: Langlais, French embassy, Lomé to Direction des Affaires Africaines et Malagaches, Paris, 2 Feb 1970.

Agokoli).[46] In the ambassador's own meetings with Eyadéma, he had concluded that the Togolese leader saw things 'from the perspective of a soldier' and was therefore anxious about the defence of a country whose western border lay 'in the suburbs of its capital city'. Eyadéma thus emphasised to the ambassador that the river Volta was Togo's 'natural and historical border' and that if the current border was to be pushed westwards to the river, this would provide a 'zone of protection' between the Togolese capital, Lomé, and the neighbouring state of Ghana.[47]

In July 1970, E. O. Kofi Dumoga was appointed as Ghana's ambassador to Dahomey, and S. G. Antor was appointed as Ghana's ambassador to Togo, in a move that the French ambassador interpreted as a conciliatory gesture on the part of the Busia government towards Ewe opinion in Ghana.[48] Ostensibly, Antor was working with Victor Owusu (Busia's minister of foreign affairs) to effect a thaw in relations between the Ghana government and the Eyadéma regime, and a high profile delegation visited Eyadéma in Lomé the same month. But Busia's courtesy call had no lasting effect on Eyadéma. In October 1971, the French ambassador contacted Paris with some alarm, warning the minister that during the visit of the European Economic Community's director of development assistance, Eyadéma had asked quite openly, 'How can we re run the plebiscite so as to restore the Ewe area to Togo?' The Togolese leader proceeded to explain that the 1956 plebiscite question was badly phrased, that the Ewes in Ghana wanted to be reattached to Togo, and that the Ghanaian government knew this, hence its blatant lack of interest and investment in the area. The ambassador predicted that Eyadéma would raise exactly the same questions in his forthcoming meeting with the French president, Georges Pompidou, and regarded this as a matter of concern.[49]

If the diplomatic records are to be believed, then, it seems that as early as 1969, Eyadéma was interested in claiming areas of Ghana for

[46] The political opportunities arising from the Agbogbozã festivals are also mentioned in Sandra Greene, *Sacred Sites and the Colonial Encounter: A History of Meaning and Memory in Ghana* (Bloomington IN, 2002), 24.

[47] CADN, Accra Ambassade 62: Henri Langlais, French embassy, Lomé to Directions des Affaires Africaines et Malagaches, Paris, 2 Feb 1970.

[48] CADN, Accra Ambassade 62: French ambassador in Lomé to Ministre des Affaires Etrangères, Paris, 15 July 1970.

[49] CADN, Accra Ambassade 62: Campredon, French embassy, Lomé to Direction des Affaires Africaines et Malagaches, Paris, 'Confidences du Président Eyadéma', 26 Oct 1971.

the Republic of Togo, and had expressed this desire fairly openly by late 1971 in the anticipation of French support.[50] The demise of the Busia regime in the Acheampong coup of January 1972 did not therefore mark the onset of Eyadéma's irredentist agenda. But the coup was significant in two respects. In terms of the organisation of reunificationist sentiment, the coup posed an important challenge to those reunificationists who had joined the Progress Party. In taking up positions as ambassadors for Ghana, both Antor and Dumoga had implied their acceptance of the territorial status quo and their willingness to work within the framework of the Republic of Ghana. Under the new regime of General I. K. Acheampong, both individuals were once again out in the cold in terms of Ghanaian politics. This meant that they were liberated to pursue alternative opportunities in the Republic of Togo, where they took up long-term residence, but that in doing so, they laid themselves open to accusations of inconsistency and opportunism.

The coup was also significant because, despite periodic efforts to convene meetings of border commissions, the potential for a diplomatic thaw was undermined by a number of violent incidents which occurred when members of the Ghana police crossed into Togolese territory – usually in pursuit of suspected smugglers.[51] When confronted with persistent questions from Eyadéma about the possibilities for revising the border, the French ambassador attempted to disentangle the former colonial power by insisting that Ghana-Togo relations were a problem for those two countries to resolve and did not involve France. Eyadéma quickly responded by reminding the ambassador that the Republic of Togo had signed a defence agreement with France in 1960 and this was directly relevant in the case of any Ghanaian threat to Togolese territorial integrity – a stance not dissimilar from that held by Olympio prior to his assassination. Eyadéma, however, had greater confidence in his personal relationship with the French president. In November 1972, the ambassador once again warned Paris that Eyadéma was likely to use his personal meetings with the French president to air his grievances over the border.[52]

[50] Brown, 'Borderline Politics in Ghana' suggests that it was not until after 1972 that Eyadéma became an active supporter of reunification, but this is not strictly accurate.

[51] CADN, Accra Ambassade 62: Retransmission from French embassy in Lomé to French embassy in Accra, 28 Nov 1972.

[52] CADN, Accra Ambassade 62: telegram from Campredon, French embassy in Lomé to 'DiploParis' 16 Nov 1972.

There is an interesting difference between the accounts of Togolese irredentism produced by the French ambassadors in Lomé and Accra, and the reunificationist texts that were produced by activists from the border area during the early and mid-1970s. The French ambassadors frequently referred to the border issue as 'the Ewe problem'. If the establishment of a defensive zone between Lomé and the river Volta was Eyadéma's main objective, it was indeed Ewe unification (and not Togoland reunification) that he was seeking. The southern coastal area to the west of Lomé was populated by the Anlo-Ewe, who had been part of the Gold Coast colony since 1874. The coastal strip was never part of the mandated or trust territory of British Togoland. The reunification of the two Togolands, then, would not have recuperated the coastal Anlo-Ewe area that Eyadéma needed in order to create a substantial buffer between Lomé and the Ghana border – although it might still have been useful to Togo in claiming greater rights over the electricity that was now being produced by the hydro-electric dam on Lake Volta further inland. In line with his appreciation of the Mobutu-ist policy of *autenticité*, Eyadéma was an enthusiast for cultural festivals, including Agbobozã. This annual event had long provided opportunities for cross-border contacts between Ewe-speakers, and Eyadéma's irredentist rhetoric emphasised the illegitimacy of Acheampong's moves to close the border to 'natural' cultural and economic linkages between the Ewe-speakers.[53]

This perception of the border question as an ethnic, Ewe issue was reinforced by the use that Acheampong made of cultural festivals on the Ghana side of the border. Thus, in November 1973, he delivered an address at the Hogbetsotso in Anlo, promising the inhabitants that his regime was willing to address their difficulties with poor roads, diseased coconut plantations, and sea erosion, but cautioning them to desist from land litigation and from smuggling their shallots across to Togo. The shallots were of small importance in comparison to the large volumes of cocoa that were being smuggled across to Togo further up the border, or indeed the numerous imported items (such as tinned sardines, sugar, and petrol) that were subsidised by the Ghanaian government at a time when it was under pressure from its creditors, but persistently found their way across to Togo where they were sold at a higher price. Acheampong's choice of occasion thus appeared to be building a connection between the practice of smuggling and 'Ewe' habits. As Nugent notes, the propaganda

[53] CADN, Accra Ambassade 62: Campredon, French ambassador in Lomé to Direction des Affaires Africaines et Malagaches, Paris, 17 Oct 1972.

of the Acheampong regime increasingly linked smuggling with other forms of subversion, including secessionism, particularly in Operation Counterpoint of 1976.[54]

In the texts produced by individuals from the former British Togoland, the border question was presented rather differently, and in terms much more consistent with the 1950s propaganda that was examined in Chapter 4. In October 1971, the French embassies in Accra and Lomé shared copies of a petition drawn up by an organisation known as the 'Former British Togoland Youth', which had its headquarters in Kadjebi. This document made no reference to 'the Ewe' or indeed to any cultural or commercial ties that straddled the border. The petitioners explicitly accepted the results of the 1956 plebiscite, and the signatories claimed that they had, 'no trouble with being called Ghanaians'. Instead, the emphasis was placed on the need for a legal instrument which specified the terms on which the former trust territory had been integrated into Ghana in 1957.

> Up until now all motorable roads in the territory are left in poor conditions which are only serving as death traps ... There are no electricity facilities in the territory; No railway transportation for the peoples. No properly galvanised agricultural revolution is set up in the land. No higher educational institution on university level is provided for the people. No industry is built in the land for the provision of jobs for the inhabitants. Instead, many citizens of the former trust territory serving in many departments in Ghana were dismissed arbitrarily and government stated that they formed the majority of working personnel and therefore had to sustain the larger sack.[55] This is a clear indication that the citizens of the former British Togoland are less regarded Ghanaians.[56]

The petitioners must have known that there was no legal instrument regarding the terms of the integration of British Togoland with Ghana. By requesting it, then, they may have been implicitly condemning the manner in which integration was effected, whilst also protecting themselves against potential accusations of secessionism. Their grievance was clear: they were not being treated on a basis of equality with other Ghanaians. What is interesting, in the context of their experiences over the past decade, is their belief that a legal instrument would have provided an effective safeguard.

[54] See Nugent's description of Operation Counterpoint propaganda, in *Smugglers, Secessionists and Loyal Citizens*, 251.

[55] This refers to Apollo 568.

[56] CADN, Accra Ambassade 62: Former British Togoland Youth's demand for the Integration Instrument of their Land with Ghana. (Date of 26 Oct 1971 added in pencil to typed petition.)

SECESSIONISM AND THE SUSPICIONS OF SPOKESMEN

In 1972, the National Liberation Movement of Western Togoland began a sustained campaign on the border question. Rather like the Togoland Congress in the mid-1950s, the movement made its case in two arenas: it produced newsletters and other forms of propaganda that aimed to influence opinion at home, and it directed petitions abroad, first to the newly established Organisation of African Unity and then to the United Nations. Whilst the tone of this propaganda varied according to the intended readership, its argumentative core retained some key features that are recognisable from the 1950s. Firstly, like the youths in Kadjebi, the movement avoided the term 'Ewe' and presented its case not in terms of a desire for ethnic unity, but in terms of the unfair treatment of the former trust territory under successive Ghanaian governments. Thus, in its newsletter of 16 December 1972, it challenged its readership with a series of questions:

Is there any Western Togolander on the NRC?
Is there any Western Togolander amongst the Commissioners (Ministers) of the NRC?
Is there any Western Togolander among the Regional Commissioners?
Is there any Western Togolander who is made a Chairman of any of the Public Boards / Corporations?
The answer to these four questions above is "No".
How many envoys have the NRC appointed? – There is only one Western Togolander amongst them.
Is this a fair share?[57]

Reminding its readers of an Ewe proverb, 'The orphan does not eat liver, he is given a bone,' the newsletter deployed an emotive image that was familiar from the reunificationist propaganda of the mid-1950s (see Chapter 4), and indeed suggestive of the ways in which earlier fears had been borne out by bitter experience.

The movement was also fond of religious language, and in presenting contemporary injustices as an affront both to God and to modern democracy, it followed one of the strategies used by Holiday Komedja in *Ablɔḍe Safui* (as discussed in Chapter 5). The Movement's Christmas message of December 1972 thus referred to the position of the former

[57] CADN, Accra Ambassade 62: National Liberation Movement of Western Togoland, News Letter vol. 1 no. 4 (16 Dec 1972).

trust territory as a 'colony' of Ghana, weaving an abbreviated quotation from the United States Declaration of Independence into an image of Acheampong's NRC offending the Holy Father at the birth of his only child. The regime was thus urged to

> advise themselves properly on this matter and in the true Christmas spirit lest your singing of Christmas Carolls [sic] jam the ears of the Mosthigh [sic] and your Christmas Offerrings [sic] will smell foul to the Divine Father of all men before whom all men are created equal and none has a right to hold another in bondage.[58]

The Christmas message claimed that the government had 'no legal standing to include our part of West Africa in the Republic of Ghana' and had been acting as 'a colonial power' for the past sixteen years. The movement thus hoped that the New Year would bring 'Joy and peace and freedom from colonial bondage to us the people of Western Togoland'.

The petition presented to the Organisation of African Unity in November 1972 reached the same conclusion, albeit through a more elaborate argument. Firstly, it detailed the perfidious means by which the British and Nkrumah had effected the wholesale 'integration' of the trust territory into Ghana in 1957 on the basis of a plebiscite which indicated only partial support for 'union'. The absence of a process of negotiation between equals on the nature and form of that union had effectively rendered the former trust territory a present-day colony of Ghana. The latter's treatment of its colonised peoples was exposed through references to the violent suppression of protests at Alavanyo in the aftermath of Ghanaian Independence, the attempted and actual detention of reunificationist leaders, the mass exile of people from British Togoland across the border into the French-speaking zone, and the disregard for the health and welfare of the people living around Lake Volta who saw less benefit from the hydro-electric dam than Ghanaian citizens in faraway Accra.[59]

A month later, the movement wrote again to the Organisation of African Unity, this time clarifying that not only was the wording and conduct of the 1956 plebiscite unsatisfactory, but that the very use of a plebiscite as a means of resolving the Togoland question was itself highly questionable. The plebiscite stemmed from the measures taken by one coloniser (Britain) in order to bequeath a legacy to another coloniser

[58] CADN, Accra Ambassade 62: National Liberation Movement of Western Togoland, News Letter vol. 1 no. 5 (23 Dec 1972).

[59] Copy available in CADN, Accra Ambassade 62.

(Ghana) in the form of territory (British Togoland). As the inhabitants of the trust territory had never been consulted about the drawing of the border at the end of the First World War, or indeed during the Anglo-German partition, the voting in May 1956 gave nothing more than a veneer of democratic process to what was, fundamentally, a colonial situation. This time, the movement explained to African Heads of State that it wanted them to support its appeal to the United Nations to admit the illegitimacy of the entire plebiscite process and to press the Ghana and Togo governments to restore the former British Togoland to the Republic of Togo. Whilst the first petition had more in common with that of the 'youth' in Kadjebi, the second moved to a more explicitly secessionist position.[60]

Again, it is surprising in view of their past experiences that the reunificationists still appeared to believe that well-made arguments would actually induce the United Nations to revoke the plebiscite, or that pressure from African Heads of State would be effective in persuading Acheampong to negotiate either on the border itself or on the terms by which integration had been achieved. Nonetheless, these appeals to external arbiters and attempts to internationalise the border question continued through the 1970s, with petitions to United Nations Secretary General Kurt Waldheim in 1974, demonstrations upon his visit to Lomé in 1975, an appearance on the BBC's Focus on Africa programme in 1976, and a delegation to the United Nations in September 1977.[61]

In one of the only first-hand studies of the National Liberation Movement of Western Togoland, Brown suggests that the efforts of the movement to publicise its cause abroad provided but a thin cover for its failure to achieve significant grassroots support at home.[62] He attributed this to two fundamental problems. Firstly, the movement was unable to capitalise on the undoubted disillusionment of 'the Ewes' in Ghana with their economic and political marginalisation at the hands of the Akan, because its leadership and its propaganda were too closely associated with the Togoland reunification agenda of the 1950s. This inhibited the geographical reach of the movement into the Anlo- and Peki-Ewe areas (which had never belonged to British Togoland) and it reinforced the

[60] Petition submitted to the Secretary General, Organisation of African Unity, Addis Ababa, by the National Liberation Movement of Western Togoland, 9 Dec 1972. Copy available in CADN, Accra Ambassade 62, Togo-Ghana 1968–1972.

[61] These activities are all detailed in a lengthy report on Ghana-Togo relations since Independence, in CADN, Accra Ambassade 63, Togo-Ghana 1981–89.

[62] Brown, 'Borderline Politics in Ghana'.

association between attempts to revise the border and being on 'the losing side' of Ghanaian politics. Secondly, the movement became overly dependent on Eyadéma's patronage, which included the use of his conference and rally facilities in Kpalimé, the financing of trips to the Organisation of African Unity and the United Nations, and the payment of allowances to the movement's leadership (or their appointment to nominal public sector positions in order that they could be paid a salary).[63] Not only did this render the movement vulnerable to Eyadéma's vacillation between his irredentist ambitions and his episodic attempts to reconcile with Ghana, but it also meant that leaders were perceived to be deriving personal benefits from their positions as exiles in Togo whilst failing to distribute significant patronage to potential supporters in Ghana (who were much more vulnerable to any coercive measures taken by the Acheampong regime).[64]

Brown suggested that these two underlying problems manifested themselves in 1975, when the dominant figures in the movement – G. O. Awuma, E. O. Kofi Dumoga, and Albert Simpson, who had been 'prominent in the old Togoland Congress' – were marginalised in favour of other individuals such as I. B. Bawa and C. K. Denyo, who were more directly accountable to Eyadéma. It was in this later period that the anglicised abbreviation TOLIMO (Togoland Liberation Movement) replaced the rather wordy National Movement for the Liberation of Western Togoland. Whilst the TOLIMO achieved some international attention in 1976 and 1977, when Eydéma's irredentism was at its most strident, it also meant that once the Togolese leader pulled back from this position (following an assassination attempt in October 1977), the movement had little independent support to fall back upon, and its fundamental weakness was thus revealed.

Brown is probably correct in his conclusion that the TOLIMO was not able to capture the dissatisfaction of Ghanaian Ewe-speakers with the Acheampong regime and channel it into an effective campaign to renegotiate either the border itself or the terms on which integration had occurred. In my own field work, I found little evidence of proactive engagement with the TOLIMO, and only two people whom I interviewed on the Ghana side of the border were prepared to admit

[63] The payment of salaries was confirmed in interviews with the children of some of the movement's leaders, e.g. Interview with A. Odame and L. Odame (daughters of A. K. Odame), Buem-Borada, 17 Sept 2000.

[64] Brown, 'Borderline Politics in Ghana', 606–8.

to participation. Repression of the movement during the 1980s may have had something to do with this silence, because in my interviews on the Togolese side of the border, at a time when Gnassingbé Eyadéma was still in power, instances of active participation were much more readily discussed. Some of the same individuals who had told me in Ghana that they were not involved were in fact named as activists during my discussions with other people across the border in Togo.[65] Nonetheless, the numbers involved are too small to prove that there was significant grassroots support for the TOLIMO in the former trust territory.

If Brown's conclusions about the TOLIMO's relative lack of popularity remain intact, his explanations could be refined. In essence, Brown looked at the TOLIMO as a secessionist movement: he took as a given that within the nation-state of Ghana, politics during the 1970s revolved around Akan-Ewe antipathy, whilst across the border in the nation-state of Togo, politics was defined by a North-South or Kabyé-Ewe divide. Brown thus measured the TOLIMO's effectiveness according to its capacity to capture Ewe sentiment, which was not necessarily what the movement's leaders set out to do. The examples of petitions and newsletters quoted above are strikingly consistent with arguments and imagery in the propaganda produced by S. G. Antor, G. K. Tsekpo, and Theodore O. Asare back in the mid-1950s, and in the texts of present-day activists who seek to reopen debate on the Togoland question. They do not address an ethnic Ewe readership, nor are they primarily concerned with ethnic unity. Their primary concerns are the perfidy of the British vis-à-vis their trust territory, a historic grievance over the conduct and interpretation of the 1956 plebiscite, and the lack of consultation or agreement on the terms by which British Togoland was integrated with the Republic of Ghana. The arguments of the TOLIMO, then, may have held greater legitimacy than the leaders who articulated them. In other words, it was not so much that people no longer sympathised with the Ablɔɖe case, but rather that they doubted the feasibility of the TOLIMO proposals and the sincerity of some of their leading advocates.

In view of his own familiarity with the politics of the 1950s, it is surprising that Brown refers straightforwardly to Awuma, Dumoga, and Simpson as 'prominent in the old Togoland Congress' and skates over their problematic status. Awuma, as we saw in Chapter 2, was indeed an

[65] This happened during an interview with Togbe Tsally X of Agome-Yoh near Kpalimé, 12 May 2000. Agomé was sometimes described as 'the TOLIMO village' and Awuma was based there through to at least 1980.

important early advocate of Togoland reunification in the Ho/Asogli area, but defected in the early 1950s, much to the chagrin of the young men who had supported him. Dumoga quarrelled bitterly with Antor in the early 1950s, whilst Albert Simpson also defected to the CPP, albeit after the plebiscite and doubtless under pressure.[66] Ironically, it was in the context of Nkrumah's Preventive Detention Act that all three figures were 'rehabilitated' as 'anti-CPP' during the early 1960s: Dumoga went into exile in Togo, whilst Awuma and Simpson were detained. Nonetheless, the rift between Antor and Awuma ran particularly deep. According to his son, Robert, Antor maintained his distance from Awuma throughout the years that they both resided in Togo:

> The very same people who were standing in the TOLIMO were the ones who were undermining him previously ... I can say that Awuma was my father's bitterest enemy. As soon as he saw that Awuma was in it, he wouldn't join this TOLIMO thing. My father said to Awuma: 'You just want the money. You saw the money before, and you chopped it. Now you see more money, and you want to chop it again. You go, chop it!'[67]

In 1976, the United Association of Ghana Rationalists made some similar points in an open letter sent to the TOLIMO leadership, President Eyadéma, the diplomatic missions in Ghana and Togo, and all African heads of state. The association demanded to know why secessionist words had not escaped the lips of the TOLIMO leaders when the Ghana government was controlled by their allies. It referred to Awuma as a seventy-five-year-old Rip Van Winkle, and suggested that Bawa (who had served as a district commissioner in Konkomba under Nkrumah) was hiding in Togo primarily because he had backed the losing side in the Yendi chieftaincy dispute. It is difficult to be sure whether the Ghana Rationalists was a grassroots organisation or a fiction of the Acheampong regime – certainly the association's emphasis on the 'unimpeachable' conduct of the plebiscite seems unlikely to have flowed from any former Togoland Congress supporter's pen.[68]

The broader point, however, is that by the end of the 1970s, little had happened to persuade former reunificationists of the illegitimacy of their

[66] It is curious that Brown did not mention this in his article because in his PhD dissertation he indicates that Albert Simpson defected in 1958 around the same time as Regina Asamany. See Brown, 'Politics in the Kpandu Area of Ghana', 318.

[67] Interview with Robert Antor and S. G. Antor Jr, Logba-Alakpeti, 15 Sept 2000.

[68] CADN, Nantes, Accra Ambassade 63, Togo-Ghana 1976–1980: Letter from United Association of Ghana Rationalists, to G. O. Awuma, I. B. Bawa, and E. O. Kofi Dumoga, Oct 1976.

case. It was not difficult to find evidence for the relative poverty of the former trust territory or its position as the 'step child' in a political household dominated by Akan soldiers and politicians. Nor was it difficult to remind people of flaws in the conduct and interpretation of the plebiscite. The obstacles to channelling these sentiments into political action lay in the issues of feasibility and good faith: the TOLIMO leadership was no longer able to draw on a track record of service to individuals and communities in the former trust territory; nor was it able to persuade them in sufficient numbers that it had a privileged insight into the intentions of external actors so as to devise feasible solutions to the problem. In these respects, the TOLIMO leadership struggled to meet the criteria for spokesmanship, and its activities therefore mark the limits of Togoland reunification as an achievable agenda commanding mass support.

Brown indicates that some of the TOLIMO participants were well aware of the improbability of success: their activities were essentially aimed at keeping the issue alive until the day when the circumstances for action were more propitious.[69] In this respect, the TOLIMO might have been more effective than Brown gave them credit for. He could not have known this when he published his account in 1980, and indeed, for much of the 1980s and 1990s, the reunification issue appeared to have been laid to rest. The Akan-Ewe cleavage, which had dominated perceptions of Ghana's national politics in the 1960s and 1970s, was gradually replaced with a new framework emphasising the cyclical nature of politics and the emergence of a two-party tradition. In Chapter 7, then, we shall examine one final surprising manifestation of the reunification issue. The recent surge of interest does not demonstrate that secession is imminent, or even that the reunification question is of pressing importance for the majority. What it demonstrates is that, even now, there are individuals who believe that the legacy of Ablɔɖe is worth fighting for. This is revealing of the means by which political histories are produced in contemporary Ghana, and it is to this question, and to the 'invention' of Ghana's political traditions that we must turn by way of conclusion.

[69] Brown, 'Borderline Politics in Ghana', 599.

7

Of Elephants and Umbrellas

Ablɔḍe in Ghana's Political Traditions

Almost every scholarly or popular account of post-colonial politics in Ghana emphasises its division into two major traditions. The 'elite tradition' is usually described as originating in the United Gold Coast Convention of the 1940s, developing through the United Party and its opposition to Nkrumah in the 1960s, and enjoying a brief hiatus in Dr Kofi Busia's Progress Party government when Ghana returned to multi-party parliamentary democracy in 1969. This tradition is associated with a liberal-democratic approach to politics, suggesting that multi-party parliamentary democracy should be the system of choice, state intervention in the economy should be reduced, and supportive relationships should be cultivated with Western countries. The 'populist tradition' is somewhat more difficult to define, but it is usually thought to originate with Nkrumah, to espouse a greater level of state intervention in both society and economy, and to favour a non-aligned foreign policy. In view of the large swathe of literature on the invention or imagining of customs and identities in colonial Africa, surprisingly little attention has been paid to the emergence of these two traditions, which are ubiquitous features of popular analyses of post-colonial politics in Ghana and are taken as a given in much of the political science literature.[1] Here I shall argue that the two traditions do not simply describe the organisation and ideologies of the major political parties: the traditions emerged from rhetorical and performative work, and they continue to influence the positioning and

[1] For further detail on the two traditions, see Naomi Chazan, *An Anatomy of Ghanaian Politics: Managing Political Recession, 1969–1982* (Boulder CO, 1983), 119–134.

claims of contemporary politicians and activists – including those in the former British Togoland.

Whilst scholars have disagreed over the strengths and weaknesses of Nkrumahism as a body of political ideas, the origins of the term itself are not difficult to establish.[2] Ghana's first president, anxious to establish a reputation as a political thinker, wrote prolifically about his ideas and encouraged the use of the term 'Nkrumahism' to describe them. The juxtaposition of an 'Nkrumahist tradition' with a 'Danquah-Busia tradition' requires more explanation. Until the mid-1980s, commentators did not generally use the term 'Danquah-Busia tradition', but they did note that during public debates on constitutional reform in 1977, General I. K. Acheampong located his preference for 'Unigov' within more general claims to be upholding the legacy of Nkrumah.[3] According to Mike Oquaye, Acheampong recognised that the 'Busiaists' whom he had overthrown in 1972 would never back his regime, and he thus tried to win over and use the 'Special Aides, the Society of Friends, the Ideological Institute graduates and a host of other "Nkrumahist comrades" ... in his campaign for Unigov'.[4]

Two years later, the 1979 elections provided commentators with another opportunity to assess the role of Nkrumahism and anti-Nkrumahism in both the ideology and organisation of the emerging parties. The People's National Party (PNP), led by Dr Hilla Limann, clearly held the Nkrumahist mantle. Oquaye pointed to the PNP's adulation of the personality of Nkrumah (embodied in its revival of the Young Pioneers' Movement), whilst Chazan declared that the PNP 'was unabashedly constructed on the remnants of the old CPP organisation, with the careful superimposition of a new guard of youngmen (who tended to romanticize Nkrumah ...)'. In describing the anti-Nkrumahists, however, commentators still did not speak of a Danquah-Busia tradition. Indeed, according to Chazan, the division between the two main anti-Nkrumahist organisations – the

[2] Nugent refers to the 'vacuity' of Nkrumahism, whilst Chazan emphasises that it was a 'change-oriented ideology' whose inclusiveness was its greatest strength. Thompson encourages a 'periodisation' of Nkrumahism, and sees the 1962 assassination attempt at Kulungugu as a turning point. Paul Nugent, *Big Men, Small Boys and Politics in Ghana: Power, Ideology and the Burden of History, 1982–1994* (London, 1995), 243; Chazan, *An Anatomy of Ghanaian Politics*, 121–3; W. Scott Thompson, *Ghana's Foreign Policy 1957–66: Diplomacy, Ideology and the New States* (Princeton NJ, 1969), 265–70.

[3] Unigov was a non-partisan system in which soldiers, police, and civilians would share power. For greater detail, see Mike Oquaye, *Politics in Ghana (1972–1979)* (Accra, 1980), 67–105.

[4] Oquaye, *Politics in Ghana*, 174.

Popular Front Party (PFP) and the United National Convention (UNC) – reflected distinctions between Busia and Danquah, and differences in the type of support that they had commanded two decades earlier.[5]

It was not until the late 1980s that Ghanaian politicians and academics set about popularising the notion of a Danquah-Busia tradition. In an influential lecture series in February 1988, Adu Boahen offered an interpretation of Ghana's twentieth-century history that traced 'a direct linear progression from Kojo Thompson and the Mambii Party and Nanka-Bruce and the Ratepayers' Association [of the 1920s] to the Kwame Nkrumah/CPP and Danquah/UGCC groups'.[6] In his analysis of Ghanaian politics since the 1950s, Boahen implied that the Busia administration of 1969–72 was the direct descendant of the UGCC. Skating over some of the more unpopular aspects of the Busia administration, he suggested that the Acheampong coup deprived Busia of the time that was necessary for sound economic policies to translate into improved standards of living. Boahen also stated that the Acheampong era was catastrophic in almost every respect, and that Flight Lieutenant Jerry Rawlings' first 'house-cleaning' coup of 4 June 1979 'was not only absolutely necessary and justifiable, but was also most opportune'.[7] In the elections that followed, Boahen noted that among those whom he regarded as the descendants of Busia and the Progress Party, a division had emerged between the PFP, led by Victor Owusu, and the UNC, led by William Ofori-Attah. He concluded that this 'truly regrettable and highly reprehensible' division was directly responsible for the victory of Limann's PNP, and thus indirectly responsible for the unhappy situation that provoked Rawlings' 'second coming' on 31 December 1981.[8]

When Boahen delivered these lectures in 1988, the implications of his analysis could not have been clearer. At precisely this time, the possibility of the re-establishment of multi-party democracy prompted political activists across the spectrum to reactivate their organisational networks. Nugent notes that whilst a plethora of organisations were to claim the Nkrumahist mantle in 1990 and 1991, the Danquah-Busia Memorial Club, based in Kumasi, had already secured a head-start in regrouping former politicians from the Progress Party, the PFP, and UNC.[9] While

[5] Chazan, *An Anatomy of Ghanaian Politics*, 287–8.

[6] Boahen's lecture series was published the following year, and it is from the published volume that quotations are drawn. Albert Adu Boahen, *The Ghanaian Sphinx: Reflections on the Contemporary History of Ghana 1972–1987* (Accra 1992, [1989]), 60.

[7] Boahen, *The Ghanaian Sphinx*, 27. [8] Ibid., 26–7.

[9] Nugent, *Big Men, Small Boys*, 221.

Boahen's political ambitions achieved a focus through the Memorial Club, his academic energies were directed into the exhumation of Danquah's correspondence and its collation into a volume that would reassert the doyen's role as the 'principal architect of Ghana's independence'.[10] According to Boahen, Danquah had developed his own system of political thought, 'Ghanaianism', which emphasised 'the worth of the individual, individual initiative and individual enterprise'.[11] Boahen contrasted Ghanaianism with Nkrumahism, arguing that the former prioritised 'the freedom and dignity of the individual and not [the] sordid materialism, regimentation and state ownership of property' that had been witnessed under Ghana's First Republic.[12]

It was through the J. B. Danquah Memorial Lectures that Boahen publicised his analysis of Ghanaian politics. The message was unmistakable: in order to avoid a repetition of the errors of 1979, everyone associated with the Progress Party, PFP, or UNC must come together in one organisation, which would exercise its claims to legitimacy on the basis of its supposed historical relationship with both Danquah and Busia. As the New Patriotic Party (NPP) 'emerged out of the cocoon of the Danquah-Busia Memorial Club', it seemed that Boahen, who was elected as presidential candidate in August 1992, had successfully united the elite tradition.[13]

In comparison to Boahen's strategic work in the NPP, which adopted the symbol of the elephant, his opponents appeared to be in disarray, and Nugent notes that it was not immediately clear that the former military leader, Jerry Rawlings, would actually contest a presidential election in 1992. Commentators initially predicted a three-way contest in which Rawlings' chosen candidate would be soundly defeated in the first round, clearing the way for the real fight between Boahen and the Nkrumahist candidate in the second round. This prediction soon proved wrong.[14] Both Hilla Limann and Kwabena Darko persisted in their separate Nkrumahist candidacies, whilst Rawlings' reorganised National Democratic Congress, with its umbrella symbol, mounted a surprisingly

[10] Although this book was not published until 1997, the preface explains that the work had been in progress for at least a decade. See J. B. Danquah (with editorial work by Albert Adu Boahen), *The Ghanaian Establishment: its Constitution, its Detentions, its Tradition, its Justice and Statecraft and its Heritage of Ghanaianism* (Accra, 1997).

[11] Ibid., 4. [12] Ibid., 4. [13] Nugent, *Big Men, Small Boys*, 222.

[14] For an explanation of the divisions that arose between the former Nkrumahists, and the association of key Rawlings supporters with the National Co-ordinating Committee of Nkrumahists, see Nugent, *Big Men, Small Boys*, 221–2.

effective campaign. The real contest, then, was between Boahen and Rawlings, the elephant and the umbrella, with the latter procuring 58.3 per cent of the national vote and thus winning the presidency in the first ballot. The NPP attributed this result to electoral irregularities, and referred to it as the 'stolen verdict', but they still had to wait another eight years before John Agyekum Kufuor was finally able to return the elite tradition to power in 2000.[15] It was in the run-up to these critical elections that I conducted my initial interviews with former Togoland reunificationists, and although it took me some time to figure out exactly how and why, the anticipation of these elections shaped the narratives they recounted and the explanatory frameworks that they brought to bear on their past experiences.

'WE THE DIE-HARDS ... HAVE SUCH A STRONG TRADITION'

Rawlings presided over the inauguration of a democratic constitution for Ghana in 1992, but having won elections in 1992 and 1996, he was not eligible in 2000 to stand for a third term. During my first period of field work in 1998 and 1999, there was widespread speculation, first that Rawlings might seek to amend the constitution to allow himself a third term, and then that he might simply refuse to go. But there was also anticipation that, after almost two decades, Ghana might have a new president. In the event, the elections of 2000 were a two-horse race: John Atta-Mills became the new 'flag bearer' for the NDC – a party which many continued to regard as Rawlings' personal creation – whilst his main opponent, John Agyekum Kufuor, led the NPP. It was in the context of this imminent choice between the umbrella and the elephant that I first spoke to former reunificationists and their family members, and within these interviews, I was offered two main interpretations of how the issues of the 1950s and 1960s were feeding through into the party affiliations of the year 2000.

The clearest and boldest explanation was put forward by Alfred Dumoga, a graduate maths teacher at Mawuli school and younger brother to the late E. O. Kofi Dumoga. According to Alfred Dumoga, the former Ablɔɖe activists and their descendants would find their 'natural home' in the NPP. There was no doubt in his mind that the Togoland Congress was part of the liberal-democratic tradition which had endured

[15] The NPP lost another election in 1996.

almost three decades in the political wilderness, first under Acheampong and then under Rawlings. Dumoga indicated that some of those who had taken shelter under the NDC umbrella had done so 'because of the stomach', or, more forgivingly, because it was so hard to be always in opposition. He was proud of his own family's tradition of resistance, including another brother, a journalist, who had been detained under Rawlings. 'We the die hards,' he concluded, 'we will never join the NDC. We will die of hunger before we join the NDC ... We have such a strong tradition.'[16]

Those who were backing the NDC did not necessarily agree that they were doing so 'because of the stomach'. But some of them nonetheless seemed to sense that support for the NDC might be seen as inconsistent with their earlier reunificationist stance, and this sometimes prompted them to offer explanations. The villages of Alavanyo, as we saw in Chapter 4, were Ablɔɖe strongholds through the 1950s, and the site of an anti-integration protest in March 1957. Looking back on this in the year 2000, the chief at Alavanyo-Kpeme, Togbe Tsedze Atakora VII, who had studied history and politics at Legon, explained the loyalties of his area in the following terms:

> There was, and there is, the U. P. [United Party] tradition, the Busia-Danquah tradition. The people in this area were thinking of uniting with French Togoland, and they were also dissatisfied with Kwame Nkrumah, so they found strong allies in the U. P. ... [17] Because we have been in opposition for so long, we have been neglected ... In the old days we wouldn't get anything. Even a government official didn't want to come here because, apart from the road, the people wouldn't receive him. They will just go to farm and hide. Hohoe people, they had the same thing, and it affected them greatly ... [People] decided that ... the most important thing [is] to be on the side of the government. In 1996, this was an NDC stronghold, and now we have a sec tech [secondary technical] school. When government grants come out, we get our share. We have radio-phone and electricity. Hohoe is a district capital under Rawlings. What other district capitals have, Hohoe will also have it ... So now it would be difficult to persuade people to go back to the Busia-Danquah tradition.[18]

In other words, communities of voters had taken pragmatic decisions, having learned through bitter experience that opposition came at a high

[16] Interview with Alfred M. K. Dumoga, Ho, 29 Aug 2000.

[17] As we saw in Chapter 5, the Avoidance of Discrimination Act proscribed parties that were organised on a 'tribal', religious, or regional basis, and thus prompted those who opposed the CPP to form the United Party.

[18] Interview with Togbe Tsedze Atakora VII, Alavanyo-Kpeme, 16 Sept 2000.

price. In order to have access to amenities, and to avoid discrimination when scarce and finite resources were being distributed, many voters were prepared to give their support to the party in power, and throughout the recent past, that had been the NDC. According to this logic, then, voting was not really about competition between the ideologies that parties claimed to represent: a vote for the incumbent was primarily a vote for local development.

A somewhat similar logic also operated at the individual level, particularly among those whose political careers seemed to consist of lessons learned the hard way. Christian Baxter Attah, who had been detained for six years under Nkrumah, refused to be drawn on the upcoming election: 'I will never oppose the government again. I don't want to be involved in any opposition. I will support the government in power.'[19] According to both these interpretations, support for the NDC could be construed as essentially apolitical: rather than reflecting imaginaries of power in which the holder may gorge himself at the expense of the vanquished, this was a pragmatic strategy aimed at protecting oneself and one's home town.

However, whilst no former activist explicitly contradicted Dumoga's association of Kufuor and the NPP with the Danquah-Busia tradition, some expressed doubts about where to place Rawlings and the NDC in this schema. On the one hand, Rawlings was a 'man of the people', and this placed him in the populist tradition that supposedly ran counter to the elitism of Danquah and Busia. In the words of Michael Senoo:

> It has always been a problem in our politics that the most highly educated people cannot relate to the rest. People liked Nkrumah partly because he had the popular touch. He could mix with the common man. Rawlings is also like that. Busia and Danquah and those people were never able to do it.[20]

In terms of his charisma, then, Rawlings was often likened to Nkrumah, but there was some scepticism about how far the analogy could be carried in terms of his government's policies. Edward Mfojoh clearly had his doubts about the association: 'People think that Rawlings is Nkrumah's child, that the NDC is just a new CPP. But if you to listen to his [Rawlings'] speeches, it seems that he is trying to do something different.'[21] Mfojoh, in other words, disagreed that there was any fundamental inconsistency in having supported Ablɔḍe in the 1950s and 1960s, and supporting the NDC

[19] Interview with C. B. Attah, Ho, 20 Sept 2000.
[20] Interview with M. Senoo and R Banibensu, Dansoman, Greater Accra, 14 July 2000.
[21] Interview with E. K. Mfojoh, Sokode-Gbagble, 19 July 2000, translation by Lydia Osei-Brantuo.

in 2000. He suggested that the NDC was a new organisation, born of different circumstances, and was not the heir to Nkrumah's CPP. As Rawlings had been forced to take Ghana through a Structural Adjustment Programme during the 1980s, it is unsurprising that some people were sceptical of the supposed commonality between his regime and the socialist industrialising ambitions of Nkrumah.[22]

Whilst former activists had reached different positions by the year 2000, some of their reflections on Ghana's recent political history seem broadly consistent with Nugent's analysis of how the NDC had managed to win elections in 1992 and 1996. In both cases, the NPP and a cluster of smaller opposition parties had been preoccupied with examining their historical antecedents and establishing their claims to represent either the Danquah-Busia or the Nkrumahist traditions. Rawlings, on the other hand, had made a notable public gesture towards Ghana's first president during his opening of the Kwame Nkrumah Mausoleum in Accra in 1992, and certainly enjoyed the popular touch during campaign tours for the NDC, but for the most part, the NDC campaigns paid comparatively little attention to Ghana's political history. Instead, the party preferred to mobilise the advantages of incumbency and placed 'greater faith in manipulating its control over material resources'.[23] Less cynically, one might say that, in 1992 and 1996, the NDC succeeded in maintaining voter confidence in its capacity to deliver 'development' at the local level. In 2000, however, things turned out differently.

'KUFUOR IS MY MAN!'

The NPP won the parliamentary elections in 2000 mainly by improving its performance in Brong-Ahafo, Eastern Region, Greater Accra, and, to a lesser extent, in the Central and Western Regions.[24] The presidential campaign also benefitted from additional votes in the Eastern, Western, Central, and Brong-Ahafo Regions, supplemented by the switch of a cluster of northern constituencies during the second round.[25] The Volta

[22] For an analysis of the impact of the programme, see Lynne Brydon and Karen Legge, *Adjusting Society: The World Bank, the IMF and Ghana* (London, 1996).

[23] Paul Nugent, 'Living in the Past: Urban, Rural and Ethnic Themes in the 1992 and 1996 Elections in Ghana', *Journal of Modern African Studies* 37 (2) (1999), 287–319 at 289.

[24] Paul Nugent, 'Ethnicity as an Explanatory Factor in the Ghana 2000 Elections', *African Issues* 29 (1 and 2) (2001), 2–7.

[25] Paul Nugent, 'Winners, Losers and Also Rans: Money, Moral Authority and Voting Patterns in the Ghana 2000 Election', *African Affairs* 100 (400) (2001), 405–28.

Region bucked the trend. Of the region's nineteen constituencies, two elected independent candidates to parliament and the remainder elected NDC candidates. In the presidential election, voter turn-out was down, suggesting some disillusionment amongst NDC supporters who recognised the imminence of defeat.[26] Nonetheless, every single constituency showed a majority in favour of the NDC's Atta-Mills, and although the Kufuor campaign gathered momentum in other areas of the country during the second round, the electorate of the Volta Region was unmoved.

Although there was no significant change in voting patterns in the Volta Region in 2000, the elections had a significant impact on recollections and representations of the Togoland question, both in Ghana and in its global Ewe-speaking diaspora. In London, these efforts were led by an elderly medical doctor, Kofi Kodzi, who sought to revitalise the Movement for a Resurgent Togoland (MORETO).[27] Kodzi expected that the new NPP government would agree to re-examine the Togoland question and negotiate a constitutional settlement which would recognise the special historical status of the former trust territory and acknowledge its developmental needs. Whilst I was doubtful that the NPP government would do this, Kodzi was confident: 'Kufuor,' he told me, 'is my man!' It was only a few years later that I realised why Kofi Kodzi had developed such expectations of the NPP.

During the election campaign, the NPP had promised that it would hold a National Reconciliation Commission to investigate human rights abuses under previous regimes.[28] After the opening of the new parliamentary session in January 2001, the government acted upon its promise, presenting a National Reconciliation Bill. The subsequent legislation conferred on a National Reconciliation Commission the responsibility of establishing 'an accurate, complete and historical record of human rights violations and abuses'.[29] Clause 3 of the bill provoked an intense and angry debate, both within and beyond parliament.[30] This clause

[26] Ibid., 420–1.

[27] See Kate Skinner, 'Local Historians and Strangers with Big Eyes: the Politics of Ewe History in Ghana and its Global Diaspora', *History in Africa: A Journal of Method* 37 (2010), 125–58.

[28] Robert Kwame Ameh, 'Uncovering Truth: Ghana's National Reconciliation Commission Excavation of Past Human Rights Abuses', *Contemporary Justice Review* 9 (4) (2006), 345–68 at 348.

[29] National Reconciliation Commission, Final Report, October 2004, 5.

[30] Ameh, 'Uncovering Truth', 351.

mandated the commission to investigate killings, abductions, disappearances, detentions, torture, ill-treatment, and seizures of property under periods of 'unconstitutional' rule (defined as 1966–9, 1972–9, and 1981–93). Sceptics believed that clause 3 revealed the true agenda behind the National Reconciliation Commission: they argued that the NPP wanted the commission to rake over the violence that occurred in aftermath of Rawlings' 'second coming', thereby discrediting the former president and the NDC in advance of the next round of presidential and parliamentary elections.

Following a walk-out by NDC MPs, the bill was passed along with an amendment which allowed the commission, upon application, to investigate abuses that may have occurred under other regimes. This did not satisfy all opponents, because whilst cases relating to some periods would be heard 'automatically' others would be heard only 'on application'. In practice, however, the commission interpreted its mandate broadly. It recorded over 4,000 statements, and, as noted by Robert Kwame Ameh, among the first to file their statements were those reporting abuses that occurred during the Nkrumah era. Approximately, half the total cases brought to the commission were listed for public hearings, which took place in the regional capitals as well as in Accra, and were widely reported in the media.[31]

At its sitting in Ho, the commission provided residents with the opportunity to air a wide range of grievances relating to abuses against their persons and property. Samuel Kwame Adablah, for example, gave voice to his family's objection to the siting of a public toilet on their land twenty-four years earlier, and requested compensation from the Ho district assembly. But the commission also received and considered petitions of a more explicitly political nature, including those relating to Ablɔɖe. Kwaku Ansah Tsiagbe thus described how his father, Lawrence Kumatse Tsiagbe of Taviefe, was forced into exile in Kpalimé through fear of arrest under the Preventive Detention Act, having been reported upon by a Young Pioneer.[32] Statements were also filed by, or on behalf of, those who had been detained, including Moses Kofi Asase, E. O. Kofi Dumoga, Daniel Kumasi Dumoga, and S. G. Antor.[33]

31 Ameh, 'Uncovering Truth', 346.

32 http://mail.ghanaweb.com/GhanaHomePage/NewsArchive/artikel.php?ID=50491 [last accessed on 9 Aug 2014].

33 Lists of petitioners are available in the National Reconciliation Commission, Final Report, October 2004.

In his analyses of the National Reconciliation Commission, Ameh points out that whilst in principle victims of abuses under previous regimes had access to justice through the courts, many of them had never brought a case to court (even after several changes of government) and yet were anxious to testify at the commission. For Ameh, this is indicative of the benefits of 'restorative justice': whereas a court case requires the victim to have confidence in the justice system, and the financial means to access it, in order to meet a high standard of proof, a reconciliation commission can operate according to a more flexible standard because its primary aim is not to indict a criminal but to hear the experiences and meet the needs of all parties who have experienced harm.[34] Thus, when Ameh notes that 89 per cent of those who petitioned the commission indicated that their reason for doing so was to claim compensation, he does not necessarily regard this as cynical. Indeed he sees it as a means of breaking the cycle of 'vengeance and vendetta' by acknowledging the longer-term impact of human rights abuses on victims and their families and providing them with a means of improving their situations.[35]

As we have seen, one of the major challenges faced by individuals in exile and in detention was their reduced earning capacity and their attendant difficulties in meeting the costs of their children's education, particularly at the secondary level. The testimony of Robert Antor at a public hearing in Accra in July 2003 (see Chapter 6) resonated with the experiences of disruptions to education that were endured by the sons and daughters of numerous former activists, exiles, and detainees, and it provided a focal point around which families associated with the Togoland Congress might metaphorically reassemble. The loss of educational opportunities at a key point in an individual's life had long-term consequences for their earning capacity, and thus the payment of compensation to the families of detainees and refugees could be seen as a belated recognition by the Ghana government of the longer-term disadvantages inflicted by previous regimes upon the families of political activists.

However, when the attorney-general announced in April 2006 that the government had budgeted 13.5 billion cedis for the purposes of implementing the recommendations of the commission and paying

[34] Robert Kwame Ameh, 'Doing Justice After Conflict: The Case for Ghana's National Reconciliation Commission', *Canadian Journal of Law and Society* 21 (1) (2006), 85–109 at 108.

[35] The phrase 'vengeance and vendetta' comes from Nana Akuffo-Addo, as cited in Ameh, 'Doing Justice', 97.

compensation to over 2000 individuals, this gesture was also open to other interpretations.[36] According to Edward Wuanka (whom we encountered in Chapter 5), 'They were trying to win us over.' Others also believed that the compensation payments had been released with the 2008 election campaign in mind. It is tempting to conclude, then, that the process of 'national reconciliation' encouraged an essentially instrumentalist reassertion of a minority core of the Danquah-Busia tradition in a region where most voters, possibly for equally instrumentalist reasons, had demonstrated solid support for the NDC through the 1990s. But of course, nothing in Ghanaian politics is ever that simple.

KOSI KEDEM AND THE DEATH OF A NATION

Any attempt to integrate the Togoland Congress within the Danquah-Busia tradition, and thereby imply support for the NPP, was contested. Among those who presented petitions to the National Reconciliation Commission in 2003 was Kosi Kedem, who was then the NDC member of parliament for Hohoe South. In 2005, Kedem wrote up and published his petition in order to clarify his position: he insisted that, contrary to media speculation, he was not a secessionist intent on taking the former British Togoland out of Ghana; his aim was to draw attention to a historic grievance over the manner in which the integration of British Togoland with Ghana had been achieved.[37]

In his petition, Kedem made the following arguments: the early British insistence on administrative union between the Gold Coast and the neighbouring trust territory indicated their bias towards an integrationist solution; the timing of the 1956 plebiscite in British Togoland and the question posed to voters were dictated more by the timetable for Gold Coast Independence than by the interests of the inhabitants of the two trust territories; the use of residence rather than birth as a qualification for voting meant that Gold Coasters working in British Togoland could vote, whilst Togolanders working outside the territory could not; by rejecting separate counting zones for the northern and southern sections in their interpretation of the plebiscite results, the British government and the United Nations effectively denied the people of southern British Togoland

[36] http://mail.ghanaweb.com/GhanaHomePage/NewsArchive/artikel.php?ID=125571 [last accessed 9 Aug 2014] and www.ghanaweb.com/GhanaHomePage/features/artikel.php?ID=116121 [last accessed 9 Aug 2014].

[37] Kosi Kedem, *British Togoland: An Orphan or the Death of a Nation* (Accra, 2005).

their right to self-determination; and in treating the plebiscite as a mandate for the integration of British Togoland with Ghana, rather than establishing a process of negotiation between equals on the terms of the union, the British and the United Nations had condemned the people of the former trust territory to live under a new form of imperialism at the hands of the Ghana government.

Kedem in fact put forward similar arguments to those that I had heard in interviews with Alfred Dumoga and Kofi Kodzi, both of whom were self-proclaimed NPP supporters. The significance of the petition, then, lies not simply in what it said, but in who said it, and how. Kedem, who was clearly associated with the NDC, positioned himself explicitly as a spokesperson for the dying generation of Ablɔɖe activists. He entitled his publication *British Togoland: An Orphan or the Death of a Nation*, deploying similar imagery to that used by G. K. Tsekpo during the 1950s (see Chapter 4). The petition was 'solemnly dedicated to S. G. Antor and his gallant colleagues of the Togoland Congress (TC). The men, women and the freedom fighters who were exiled, lost their lives and property, detained, imprisoned and suffered serious violation of their human rights during the struggle.'[38]

In her work on Cameroon, Meredith Terretta has suggested that the trusteeship system provided a key means by which African political activists engaged with and 'vernacularised' international discourses of human rights.[39] In the case of British Togoland, I would suggest that whilst spokespersons and activists were certainly aware of the Universal Declaration of Human Rights, in petitions and propaganda in the 1950s the main emphasis was placed on the specific constitutional status of the trust territory vis-à-vis the neighbouring Gold Coast. Similar documents in the 1970s highlighted grievances about the manner and legacies of integration. It is in the twenty-first century publications, and in accounts at the National Reconciliation Commission, that the language of human rights was most explicitly and consistently deployed. Kedem therefore mobilised human rights discourses to describe the bitter experiences of arrest, preventive detention, and exile, which were endured by Ablɔɖe activists – as indeed by members of other opposition parties – under the Nkrumah regime.[40]

[38] Ibid., iii.

[39] Meredith Terretta, '"We Had Been Fooled into Thinking that the UN Watches over the Entire World": Human Rights, UN Trust Territories and Africa's Decolonization', *Human Rights Quarterly* 34 (2) (2012), 329–60.

[40] Arrest, detention, and exile, and the right to be heard by an independent tribunal, are addressed in articles 9 to 12 of the 1948 Universal Declaration of Human Rights.

In the Togoland case, human rights may also have been invoked at a more metaphorical level: in writing of *The Death of a Nation*, Kedem may have been suggesting that Togolanders were deprived of their right to their nationality, whilst another Togoland campaigner, Koku Avortri once described the Togoland case to me as an example of 'stolen citizenship'.[41]

Thus in 2007, on the fifty-year anniversary of Ghana's Independence, Kedem produced another volume which expanded upon the points he had initially raised in 2003. He detailed his unsuccessful efforts to petition the British embassy and the German government on the Togoland question, indicating that whilst the National Reconciliation Commission had recognised injustices inflicted upon specific individuals within the Togoland Congress, neither the Ghana government nor the former colonial powers had engaged in any serious reconsideration of the status of the former trust territory. Kedem made no explicit reference to recent or forthcoming elections, but his status as an NDC parliamentarian was widely known, and indeed highlighted in his other publications.[42] In the first volume of his memoirs, published in 2008, Kedem explained that he was brought up in households whose male members were implacably opposed to the integration of British Togoland with the Gold Coast. As an infant, Kedem lived in Logba-Tota with his paternal grandfather. As Antor was also from Logba, Kedem had a reunificationist pedigree. Kedem's great uncle was a 'German scholar', a senior presbyter in the Ewe Church, and a member of the Bund der Deutschen Togoländer, while his father was a teacher-catechist and staunch reunificationist.

Through his forceful and prolific writings, Kedem demonstrated that it was not only those in the region's small NPP minority who retained an interest in the Togoland question. Whilst Kedem did not repackage the Togoland question as an NDC issue, his prominence in public debates worked against a straightforward absorption of the memory of Ablɔɖe into the Danquah-Busia tradition of Ghanaian politics. It would be very difficult to explain this level of effort in purely instrumentalist terms. Elections in 2004 and 2008 had demonstrated to both the main parties that the overwhelming majority of voters in the Volta Region persisted

[41] The right to a nationality is addressed in article 15 of the International Universal Declaration of Human Rights. Arguably, people in the former British Togoland do have the right to a nationality, but it is a Ghanaian nationality, rather than one that reflects the specific status of the former trust territory, and this is the nub of the grievance set out in Koku Avortri, *Togoland Ghana Relationship Explained (Volta Region at a Glance)* (Accra, 2010), 54.

[42] Kosi Kedem, *What I Said in Parliament* (Accra, 2005).

in their preference for the NDC. Atta-Mills received over 80 per cent of region's votes in both presidential elections, and whilst the number of constituencies in the region increased slightly, the NPP managed to take only one, in comparison to the NDC's twenty-one, in both parliamentary elections. Put simply, the NDC did not need to appeal to the legacy of Ablɔɖe to win votes in the Volta Region.

In the run-up to the 2000 elections, Kufuor made some appeals to the legacy of Ablɔɖe, including a reference at a delegates' conference in Ho to the 'historic contributions' of S. G. Antor and the Reverend Ametowobla. Nugent interpreted this as part of a wider concern on the part of the NPP campaign to rein in its image as a party of the Akan, and to gain a foothold in regions with a strong track record of support for the NDC.[43] As we have seen, however, this did not achieve the desired result in 2000, nor in 2004 or 2008, despite any publicity or compensation payments generated by the National Reconciliation Commission. Gestures which attempted to claim the legacy of Ablɔɖe for the NPP could not shift the persistent pattern of support for the NDC in the Volta Region.

If, however, the region's voters proved unreceptive to arguments based on a supposed historical connection to the Danquah-Busia tradition, they were also unmoved by the advantages of incumbency, which from 2000–8 pertained to the NPP. From the perspective of the small core of NPP activists, it was the very lack of instrumentalist logic that made their task so difficult. At the grassroots level, NPP activists would point to the poor record of the NDC in upgrading roads in the inland areas of the Volta Region and insist that this was the unhappy consequence of becoming 'a banker' for an incumbent party. Now that democratic government was more securely established, they suggested, the most advantaged constituencies were those that contained traditions of support for both of the major parties: no party could afford to ignore or penalise the 'swing' seats, and thus the voters in such constituencies had the least to fear from any change of government.

This kind of reasoning sought to relegitimise the presence of a Danquah-Busia minority tradition within the Volta Region: the minority of NPP activists were essentially arguing that they should cease to be regarded as a threat to their communities' interests, because their presence would actually prompt both the main parties to work harder at securing votes in

[43] Paul Nugent, *African Issues* 29 (1 and 2) (2001), 4, fn 12.

the region, thus procuring benefits for all the inhabitants. The problem for the NPP was that, like the 'historic legacy' argument in 2000, these kinds of instrumentalist arguments had an insignificant impact on voting behaviour. Elizabeth Ohene, who was appointed minister for tertiary education under Kufuor, commented wryly that despite the completion of several important road projects in the region, few people were switching their votes in favour of the NPP.[44]

By end of first decade of the twenty-first century, there was a cluster of individuals on both ends of the political spectrum who sought to reopen the Togoland question. All of them raised similar objections to the conduct and interpretation of the 1956 plebiscite. Most of them were reluctant to be labelled as secessionists and insisted that they were seeking due recognition for the trust territory by negotiating proper terms for an ongoing relationship between Ghana and British Togoland. There were also prominent individuals within each of the major parties who argued that the Togoland question should not now be revisited, whatever injustices may have been committed in the past, and regarded efforts to reopen debate on the terms of the union as a waste of everyone's time.

Perhaps, as Nugent suggested in 2003, the Togoland question was at best a secondary issue among the older voters, and possibly entirely absent from the calculations of younger voters who had grown up as Ghanaians. The electorate in Ghana, as in other parts of sub-Saharan Africa, is overwhelmingly young, and this, coupled with migration to urban areas, would seem to increase the likelihood of radical shifts in political priorities on the part of new generations grappling with changing economic circumstances and modes of communication. Here, however, I have suggested that issues which cannot be comfortably located in organisational or ideological spaces on the contemporary political spectrum are not necessarily dead. The demise of Ablɔɖe was less rapid and less complete than earlier analyses would have us believe. This does not necessarily mean that the Togoland question is still of pressing importance for the majority, but it does highlight the need to acknowledge and explain the persistence of phenomena that are inadequately accounted for, or deliberately marginalised, in the dominant frameworks that are brought to bear on post-colonial history.

[44] Interview with E. Ohene, Airport Residential, Greater Accra, 22 June 2010.

ABLƆĐE IN WIDER PERSPECTIVE

This book has told a particular story about Ablɔɖe. It is not the only version of the story, for people in and from the former British Togoland have demonstrated a remarkably persistent commitment to documenting the history of the trust territory and to memorialising the efforts of those activists who sought to protect its distinctive political status.[45] Primarily, then, this book is a work of historical recovery – a contribution to a field of enquiry which was first established in the small towns and villages of the former British Togoland, and which continues to flourish among Togolanders and their descendants, at home and in the global diaspora. Nonetheless, Ablɔɖe can also be read as one part of a larger history of the contingencies of decolonisation, and as such the story that I have recounted here engages with three wider debates in African Studies.

Firstly, I have emphasised the centrality of literary practices to the formulation of the Ablɔɖe project and to the work of African political activism. Stressing the creative possibilities of literacy, and its uses in petitioning and propaganda, does not imply a denial of its other uses, including as a tool of oppression which sought to categorise oral peoples and appropriate them as subjects of alien bureaucratic regimes. In his recent work on nineteenth-century Madagascar, however, Pier Larson has cast doubt on the utility of a creative/oppressive binary in studies of literacy, pointing instead to the difficulties faced by any group (African or European) who sought exclusive control over its uses. Instead he traces the rapid emergence of a plethora of literary and linguistic practices among fractured publics, both on the island itself and throughout its Indian Ocean diasporas.[46]

For the twentieth century, scholars who are animated by the possibilities of writing – in stimulating and expressing new subjectivities, and in convening new publics – have often focussed on regions which experienced a dramatic expansion of formal education. With the emergence of much larger African readerships in the first half of the twentieth century, writers could work across established, experimental, and hybrid genres, engaging rural and urban readers in debates about the morality of

[45] For example, the Homeland Study Group Foundation and the Western Togoland Assembly.

[46] Pier Larson, 'Literacy and Power in Madagascar', paper presented at the Wits Institute for Social and Economic Research, 12 Aug 2013, available at: http://wiser.wits.ac.za/system/files/seminar/Larson2013.pdf [last accessed 13 Aug 2014].

individual conduct in the context of rapid social and economic change, and invoking particular versions of the past and present in order to mobilise readers behind collective, future-oriented projects.[47] Literary practices were thus diverse in themselves (deploying African as well as colonial languages, in different genres, and for a range of purposes) and they diffused among a wider range of people (who could shift between the roles of private, contemplative reader and active translator, interlocutor, or opponent).

In the case of British Togoland, however, as in the southern Gold Coast and Nigeria, it is very clear that the emergence of a critical mass of literates depended on the expansion of a system of formal schooling, and that it was on the graduates of this school system that other efforts to universalise literacy would later depend. In former British colonies, where primary schooling in particular was so often initiated by or dependent upon Christian missionaries, there has been considerable attention to the ethos of educational institutions and the training of African teachers.[48] The standardisation and transcription of African languages, and the promotion of their use in primary schools, were often motivated by missionary and colonial concerns about the perceived clash of 'traditional societies' with 'modernity', and by their need to assert their own expertise in using education to navigate social change. The Togoland case is suggestive of the difficulties faced by missionary and colonial educationists in determining the interpretation and future uses of mother-tongue literacy and studies in local history, culture, and environment. Missionary emphasis on building Christian nations, and on the Ewe-speakers as a *volk*, might have been expected to stimulate ethnic nationalism, particularly amongst the cohort of teachers whom the missionaries trained. But this was cross-cut by the systemic features of formal schooling, which shaped a different and unanticipated political project.

[47] Derek Peterson, *Creative Writing: Translation, Bookkeeping and the Work of Imagination in Colonial Kenya* (Portsmouth NH, 2004); *Africa's Hidden Histories: Everyday Literacy and Making the Self*, ed. Karin Barber (Bloomington IN, 2006); Stephanie Newell, *Literary Culture in Colonial Ghana: How to Play the Game of Life* (Manchester, 2002); Stephanie Newell, *The Power to Name: A History of Anonymity in Colonial West Africa* (Athens OH, 2013), Isabel Hofmeyr, Preben Kaarsholm, and Bodil Fredericksen, 'Introduction: Print Cultures, Nationalisms, and Publics of the Indian Ocean', *Africa: Journal of International African Institute* 81 (1) (2011), 1–22.

[48] For Ghana, see Cati Coe, *Dilemmas of Culture in African Schools: Youth, Nationalism, and the Transformation of Knowledge* (Chicago IL, 2005); for a comparison see Isabel Hofmeyr, *The Portable Bunyan: A Transnational History of the Pilgrim's Progress* (Princeton NJ, 2003), particularly chapter 5.

Schools had their own internal hierarchies of age and achievement through which individual students might progress or on which they might stumble. But these hierarchies were also projected outward, into relationships between genders and generations, and into labour markets which were characterised by the dominance of particular cash crops and small but significant exchange sectors. Schooling introduced new measures of individual achievement: it facilitated or denied access to other opportunities, contributed to gendered and regional patterns of economic activity, and generated new solidarities amongst those who considered themselves disadvantaged.[49]

By bringing these older perspectives from the sociological literature on education into explicit dialogue with newer perspectives on the creative possibilities of literacy in Africa, I have sought to explain why teachers in particular assumed the role of political spokespersons, and how they were able to achieve legitimacy amongst a wider public. Skills in written and spoken English became a basic qualification for political spokesmanship. But such skills also had to be demonstrated in a range of other activities (including the unpaid provision of social services), and in particular literary practices (including the production, translation, and public explication of political texts), in order to confer legitimacy on their practitioners. Whilst there are many intriguing particularities in the origins, objectives, and characteristics of the Ablɔḍe movement, the teacher-politician was a widespread phenomenon in the era of decolonisation, in Africa more than any other continent, and the approach that I have pursued here may be fruitfully applied in other contexts.[50]

Secondly, I have emphasised the geographical mobility and intellectual range of Ablɔḍe activists, and pursued an approach comparable with the 'layering' methodology that Meredith Terretta has advocated in studies of anti-colonial movements – that is, research which allows local, territorial, and international activities and ideas to be considered in 'the same analytical plane' as interrelated phenomena.[51] My findings do not mirror

[49] Philip Foster, 'Secondary Schooling and Social Mobility in a West African Nation', Sociology of Education 37 (2) (1963), 150–71; and 'Education and Social Inequality in Sub-Saharan Africa', *Journal of Modern African Studies* 18 (2) (1980), 201–36. For a discussion of how formal education shaped new masculinities, see Stephan Miescher, *Making Men in Ghana* (Bloomington IN, 2005), particularly chapters 3 and 4.

[50] Linda Dove, 'Teachers in Politics in Ex-Colonial Countries', *Journal of Commonwealth and Comparative Politics* 17 (1979), 176–91.

[51] Meredith Terretta, *Nation of Outlaws, State of Violence: Nationalism, Grassfields Tradition, and State-Building in Cameroon* (Athens OH, 2013), 20–1.

exactly those of Terretta for Cameroon, where evidence of interest in, and efforts to 'vernacularise', the emerging international discourse of human rights is particularly striking from the 1950s. But I have demonstrated that debates about the rights and responsibilities of citizenship, the nature and form of self-government, and the place of trust territories in the international order, spread well beyond a tiny elite of university graduates, and could be encountered in new forums and public spaces across the small towns and villages of British Togoland, from the adult education class to the political rally. Contra older models of mass nationalism, urban experiences were not a prerequisite to individual activism, and politics was not simply a matter of harnessing parochial rural voters to anti-colonial party organisations that originated in the towns.[52] Political activism in rural areas was a work of persuasion, which required meaningful engagement with local issues and ideas, and the forging of plausible connections with competing versions of nationhood and with the opportunities and constraints of international trusteeship.

Thirdly, although this study of Ablɔḍe is only one amongst several recent efforts to unpeel the 'layers' of mass politics in the era of decolonisation, it offers a rather different perspective on the transnational dimensions of political dissent since Independence. Scholars are understandably attracted to the radicalism of Kwame Nkrumah's pan-African project, and have recovered convincing evidence of his support to individuals and organisations which challenged racist settler regimes in southern Africa and the neo-colonial leadership of several former French colonies. In these analyses, Nkrumah's Accra served as lynchpin in radical networks which emphasised solidarity between Africans and the obligations of independent African states towards oppressed and colonised peoples.[53]

But if Accra served as a place of refuge for activists fleeing neo-colonial or racist regimes, it is also clear that the political traffic moved in more

[52] Thomas Hodgkin, *Nationalism in Colonial Africa* (London, 1956). More recent research has sought to explore the specific dynamics of urban nationalism. See James Brennan, *Taifa: Making Nation and Race in Tanzania* (Athens OH, 2012).

[53] Meredith Terretta, 'Cameroonian Nationalists Go Global: From Forest *Maquis* to Pan-African Accra', *Journal of African History* 51 (2) (2010), 189–212; Klaas van Walraven, *Yearning for Relief: A History of the Sawaba Movement in Niger* (Leiden, 2013); Jeff Ahlman, 'Road to Ghana: Nkrumah, Southern Africa and the Eclipse of a Decolonizing Africa', *Kronos* 37 (1) (2011), 23–40; Jean Allman, 'Nuclear Imperialism and the Pan-African Struggle for Peace and Freedom: Ghana, 1959–1962', *Souls: A Critical Journal of Black Politics, Culture, and Society* 10 (2) (2008), 83–102.

than one direction. The threat of preventive detention drove thousands of Nkrumah's opponents across Ghana's national borders to seek refuge in neighbouring states. The artisans, farmers, school teachers, local councillors, and religious ministers who fled to francophone Togo cannot all have been misguided victims of false consciousness or members of a comprador bourgeoisie poised to undermine the greater pan-African project in exchange for a few concessions from their former colonisers. The Ablɔɖe refugees who found their way to francophone Togo were thoroughly disillusioned with the British government, and neither expected nor received its assistance. And if the Olympio government that hosted them was protective of its own national sovereignty and sceptical of Nkrumah's pan-African project, it was certainly no friend of France. People were forced out of Nkrumah's Ghana as well as welcomed in, and the case of Ablɔɖe suggests that the ideological lines between friend and foe were not always clear cut.

The nation-state in post-colonial Africa has indeed cohered in a surprisingly large majority of cases, but there were periods in which this depended as much on the deployment of coercion as it did on the manufacturing of acquiescence or the achievement of legitimacy. Even in Ghana, where the level of state violence was relatively attenuated, authoritarian measures bequeathed particular legacies. Preventive detention was intended to stamp out political dissent at home, but it created new communities of dissenters through experiences in exile and behind prison bars. Grievances that the new nation refused to address therefore found their way into the foreign policy of a neighbouring state or into a wider platform of political opposition at home, and reasserted themselves in new guises after successive changes of regime. Ablɔɖe is one of many paradoxes born of the contingencies of decolonisation in Africa: a project that has not been realised and yet refuses to die.

Bibliography: Primary Sources

National, Regional and Public Archives

Public Records and Archives Administration Department, Accra, Ghana

Files from the following series:
ADM 5, 11, 13, and 39
CSO 21
RG 3 and 11
SC/BAA (now RG 17)

Public Records and Archives Administration Department, Ho, Ghana

Files from the following series:
DAO, RAO, VRG (all partially catalogued)

Archives Nationales Togolaises, Lomé, Togo

Files from the following series:
Atakpamé APA
Klouto APA
Recherches scientifique – moeurs, coutumes et langues

Centre des Archives Diplomatiques, Nantes, France

Files from the following series:
Accra Ambassade 61, 62, and 63
Lomé Ambassade 59 and 135

The National Archives, Kew, United Kingdom

Files from the following series:
CO 96, 554, and 1045
DO 195

Rhodes House, Oxford, United Kingdom

Files from the Fabian Colonial Bureau Papers MSS.Brit.Emp.s.365
Files from the Africana Collection:
Lalage Bown, MSS.Afr.s. 1877
K. G. Glueck, MSS.Afr.s.508
Muchmore, MSS.Afr.s.414
A. J. Newall, MSS.Afr.s.967
E. H. Nichollson, MSS.Afr.s.532
Pope, MSS.Afr.s.1275
Sir George Sinclair, MSS.Afr.s.1622
Tordoff, MSS.Afr.s.1825

Printed Sources

United Nations Official Records

United Nations. 'Charter of the United Nations'. San Francisco, CA: United Nations, 1945.

United Nations, General Assembly. 'Trusteeship Agreement for the Territory of Togoland under British Administration: as approved by the General Assembly on 13 December 1946'. Lake Success, NY: United Nations, 1947.

United Nations, General Assembly. 'Trusteeship Agreement for the Territory of Togoland under French Administration: as approved by the General Assembly on 13 December 1946'. Lake Success, NY: United Nations, 1947.

United Nations, Trusteeship Council. 'Special Report of the First Visiting Mission to the Trust Territories of Togoland … On the Ewe Problem'. New York: United Nations, 1950.

United Nations, Trusteeship Council. 'Special Report on Administrative Unions Affecting Trust Territories and on the Status of the Cameroons and Togoland under French administration Arising out of their Membership of the French Union'. New York: United Nations, 1952.

United Nations, Trusteeship Council. 'Special Report on the Ewe and Togoland Unification Problem'. New York: United Nations, 1950–2.

United Nations, Trusteeship Council. 'United Nations Visiting Mission to Trust Territories in West Africa'. New York: United Nations, 1952.

United Nations, Department of Public Information. 'A Year of Progress in British Togoland'. New York: United Nations, 1954.

United Nations, Trusteeship Council. 'Visiting Mission to the Trust Territories of Togoland under British Administration and Togoland under French Administration'. New York: United Nations, 1955.

United Nations, Visiting Mission to Trust Territories in West Africa. 'Special Report on the Togoland Reunification Problem and the Future of the Trust Territory of Togoland Under British Administration Together with Related Documents'. New York: United Nations, 1956.

United Nations, Plebiscite Commissioner for the Trust Territory of Togoland under British Administration. 'The Togoland Unification Problem and the Future

of the Trust Territory of Togoland under British Administration: Report'. New York: United Nations, 1956.
United Nations, Trusteeship Council. 'The Future of the Trust Territory of Togoland under French Administration'. Geneva: United Nations, 1956.
United Nations, Trusteeship Council. 'Report of the United Nations Commission on Togoland under French Administration'. Geneva: United Nations, 1958.

Publications of the United Kingdom Government

Colonial Office, Advisory Committee on Education in the Colonies. 'Memorandum on the Education of African Communities'. London: HMSO, 1935.
Colonial Office, Advisory Committee on Education in the Colonies. 'Mass Education in African Society'. London: HMSO, 1943.
Colonial Office, Advisory Committee on Education in the Colonies. 'Education for Citizenship in Africa'. London: HMSO, 1948.
Colonial Office. 'Record of the Conference on Adult Education in the Colonies held at Sidney Sussex College, Cambridge, August 17–24 1951'. London: HMSO, 1951.

Publications of the Gold Coast/Ghana Government

Gold Coast, Department of Social Welfare. 'Welfare and Mass Education in the Gold Coast, 1946–1951'. Accra: Government Printer, 1951.
Gold Coast, Department of Social Welfare and Community Development. 'Plan for Mass Literacy and Social Welfare'. Accra: Scottish Mission Book Depot Printing Department, 1951.
Gold Coast, Department of Social Welfare and Community Development. 'Literacy Campaign, 1952'. Accra: West African Graphic Company, 1952.
A. W. Cardinall, Chief Census Officer. 'The Gold Coast 1931: A Review of Conditions in the Gold Coast in 1931 as Compared with Those of 1921, Based on Figures and Fact Collected by the Chief Census Officer of 1931, Together with a Historical, Ethnographical and Sociological Survey of the People of that Country'. Accra: Government Printer, 1932.
Gold Coast. 'The Gold Coast Census, 1931: Appendices, Containing Comparative Returns and General Statistics of the 1931 Census'. Accra: Government Printer, 1932.
Gold Coast. 'Census of the Population, 1948'. London: Crown Agents, 1950.
Gold Coast, Department of Social Welfare. 'Welfare and Mass Education in the Gold Coast, 1946–1951'. Accra: Government Printer, 1951.
Gold Coast, Department of Social Welfare and Community Development. 'Plan for Mass Literacy and Social Welfare'. Accra: Scottish Mission Book Depot Printing Department, 1951.
Gold Coast, Department of Social Welfare and Community Development. 'Literacy Campaign, 1952'. Accra: West African Graphic Company, 1952.

National and Local Newspapers

The Daily Graphic, Accra
Ewe Newsletter, Accra
Legon Observer, Accra
Mia Denyigba, Hohoe
Ablɔḍe Safui, Kpalimé
Ashanti Pioneer, Kumasi
The Liberator, Kumasi
Le Guide du Togo, Lomé
Le Progrès, Lomé
Les Echos du Togo, Lomé
West Africa, London

Mission/Church Reports (accessed at the Akrofi-Christaller Institute, Akropong, Ghana)

The Scottish Mission. 'Gold Coast Colony, Reports, 1925'. Edinburgh: Lorimer and Chalmers, 1925.
The Presbyterian Church of the Gold Coast. 'Gold Coast Colony and Ashanti, Reports, 1926'. Edinburgh: Lorimer and Chalmers, 1926.
'Gold Coast Colony and Ashanti, Reports and Accounts for 1928, and Synod Minutes for 1929'. Edinburgh: Lorimer and Chalmers, 1929.
Reports, Accounts and Statistics for 1929, 1930, 1931, 1933–40. Edinburgh: Lorimer and Chalmers.
'Summary Reports, Accounts and Statistics for the Period 1941–1948'. Edinburgh: Lorimer and Chalmers.

Adult Education Reports

University of Oxford Delegacy for Extra-Mural Studies. 'Adult Education in the Gold Coast: A Report for the Year 1948–49 by the Resident Tutor'. Achimota: Achimota Press, 1949.
University College of the Gold Coast Department of Extra-Mural Studies. 'Progress in Adult Education by David Kimble, Director of Extra-Mural Studies'. Achimota: Achimota Press, 1950.
Annual Reports of the Department of Extra-Mural Studies, 1951–5.
Annual Reports of the People's Education Association of Ghana, 1955–6, 1956–7, 1959–60, 1961–2, 1975–6.
University of Ghana. 'Report of the Advisory Committee for the Review of the Institute of Public Education'. Legon, 1966.
Institute of Adult Education, University of Ghana. 'Portrait of a Movement (1948–1973): A Commemorative Album'. Accra: Liberty Press, 1973.

Adult Education Newsletters

The Outlook, 1952 and 1956
Kpodoga, 1976
PEA News, 1976

Adult Education Discussion Pamphlets

'West African Affairs' series, published London, Staples Press, all n.d.:
Apeadu, K. K., *The Co-operative Movement*
Baldwin, Kenneth, *New Industries*
Boateng, E. A., *Tomorrow's Map of West Africa*
Busia, K. A., *Education for Citizenship*
Busia, K. A., *Self-Government*
Chadwick, E. R., *Community Development*
Colbourn, Dr M., and Hamilton, J., *Health in the Village*
Danquah, J. B., *Obligation in Akan Society*
Dumpleton, C. W., *Colonial Development Corporation* (London: Fabian Colonial Bureau, 1957)
Jones-Quartey, K. A. B., *Problems of the Press*
Kimble, David, *Outlook for Adult Education*
Kimble, David, *Public Opinion and Government*
Lerner, L. D., *The Language We Speak*
Milburn, S., *The Growing Cost of Education*
Price, J. H., *The Gold Coast Election 1951*
Roper, J. I., and Davison, R. B., *The Labour and Trade Union Ordinances of the Gold Coast*

Funeral Pamphlets

Ametowobla, Rev. Dr Francis Richard, Gbadzeme-Avatime, 1995
Ayeke, Kodzo Afelete, Taviefe, 1985
Batse, Michael Kosikumah, Hohoe, 2010
Dumoga, Emmanuel Obed Kofi, Anfoega-Akukome, 1993
Dumoga, Hamedada Regina Afua, Anfoega-Akukome, 2000
Commemorative Brochure on the late Togbe Tepre Hodo III, Aged 73 Years (printed for private circulation by Commercial Associates, Accra, 1998)

Interviews, Correspondence, and Private Papers

Ghana

Most interviews were conducted in English. Those marked with parentheses were conducted in Ewe with the assistance of an interpreter.
Abortta, Y., Taviefe, 31 Aug. 2000 (Lydia Osei-Brantuo)
Adedeme, G. S. K., Amedzofe-Avatime, 24 July 2000, 13 Aug. 2000 and 22 April 2004
Adiku, Rev. E. T., Hohoe, 13 and 14 Sept. 2000

Adinyra, J., Ho, 26 Feb. 1999
Adom, E., Hohoe, 13 Sept. 2000
Adom, E., Hohoe, 14 Sept. 2000
Adzraku, Agnes Tachie, Kpandu Aloi, 7 June 2010
Agbodza, M. K., Santrokofi-Benua, 19 Sept. 2000 and 23 April 2004
Akoli, G., Taviefe, 29 Aug. 2000 (Lydia Osei-Brantuo/Richard Banibensu)
Akoli, G., Taviefe, 31 Aug. 2000 (Lydia Osei-Brantuo/Richard Banibensu)
Amehame, V., Amedzofe-Avatime, 14 July 1999
Ametowobla, B., Ho, 12 Aug. 2000 (Lydia Osei-Brantuo)
Anku Morny, J. K., Hohoe, 14 Sept. 2000
Anonymous, Taviefe, 31 Aug. 2000 (Lydia Osei-Brantuo)
Anonymous member of Asamany family, Kpandu, 7 June 2010
Antor, R., and Antor, S. G. Jr., Logba-Alakpeti, 15 Sept. 2000
Apedu, S., Dzogbofeme-Avatime, 22 July 2000
Apedu, S., Dzogbofeme-Avatime, 13 Aug. 2000
Asare, F. Y., North Kaneshie, Greater Accra, 24, 25, 26, 27, and 28 May 1999
Asase, M. K., Ho, 24 March 1999, 18 May 1999, 20 July 2000, 11 Aug. 2000
Atikpui, K. D. G., and Dagadu, K., Amedzofe-Avatime, 3 June 1999 (Lydia Osei-Brantuo)
Attah, C. B., Ho, 20 Sept. 2000
Awuma, F. Y., Ho, 21 July 2000
Ayeke, G. M. Y., Goka, G. G., Togbe Krodo II and Rev. O.K. Abiwu, Taviefe, 29 Aug. 2000 (G. G. Goka)
Banibensu, R., Legon, 11 July 2000
Bukari, T., Yendi, 20 June 2010
Chapman, D. N., Airport Residential, Greater Accra, 21 Sept. 2000
Datsa, E. K., Amedzofe-Avatime, 3 June 1999
Dawuda Yahaya (Alhaji), Nima, Greater Accra, 21 Sept. 2008
Dumoga, A. M. K., Ho, 28 Aug. 2000 and 29 Aug. 2000
Dzeletsu, E., Dzolo-Gbogame, 12 June 2010
Dzidza, Rev. A. K., Ho, 24 March 1999 (Victor Dzidza)
Dzobo, Prof. N. K., Ho, 20 July 2000
Fia Adzatekpor VI, Vane-Avatime, 22 July 2000 and 23 July 2000
Gavu, E. K., Dzogbefeme-Avatime, 6 Aug. 2000 and 13 Aug. 2000
Hevi, E. J. (Jonnevi), Hohoe, 15 April 2013
Kludze, Prof. A. K. P., Hohoe, 13 Sept. 2000 and 14 Sept. 2000
Kuka, J., Ho, 31 Aug. 2000
Mfojoh, E. K., Sokode-Gbagble, 2 June 1999 and 19 July 2000 (Lydia Osei-Brantuo)
Ntsri, C., Alavanyo-Agoxoe, 19 Sept. 2000 (Lydia Osei-Brantuo/Rose Ntsri)
Nyonufia Mama Adomwa I, Tsiame Mama Wusia, Anyirawase-Awudome, 10 May 1999 (Lydia Osei-Brantuo/Edna Nkudede)
Nyonufia Mama Adomwa I and elders:
S. Y. Adatsi, O. Otoo, T. K. Kumah, L. K. Dakpey, A. Edem, S. Ansah L. Dzami, K. Agbagba, S. Dzani, E. Otoo, G. Tibu, P. Attram, V. Tepe, Anyirawase-Awudome, 19 May 1999 (Lydia Osei-Brantuo/S. Y. Adatsi)
Nyonufia Mama Adomwa I, Anyirawase-Awudome, 19 July 2000 (Lydia Osei-Brantuo)

Odame, A. and Odame, L., Buem-Borada, 17 Sept. 2000 (Lydia Osei-Brantuo)
Ohene, E., Airport Residential, Greater Accra, 22 June 2010
Senoo, C. and Banibensu, R., Madina, Greater Accra, 11 July 2000
Senoo, Michael, Hohoe, 13 Sept. 2000
Senoo, Michael and Banibensu, R., Dansoman, Greater Accra, 14 July 2000
Senoo, Modestus, Hohoe, 15 April 2013
Sewiah, F., Avatime-Amedzofe, 15 Aug. 2000 (Richard Salifu)
Tegbe, M. A., Hohoe, 19 Sept. 2000 (Lydia Osei-Brantuo)
Togbe Odoom Kumato and anonymous elders, Anfoega-Akukome, 24 Aug. 2000
Togbe Odoom Kumato, Legon, 1 Sept. 2000
TogbeTsedze Atakora VII, Alavanyo-Agome, 16 Sept. 2000
Tse, A. K., Accra, 21 Sept. 2000
Tsekpo, M. Y., Alavanya-Abehenase, 7 June 2010
Wuanka, E. K. D., Dzolo-Gbogame, 12 June 2010

Togo

All interviews were conducted in French except those marked (A), which were conducted in Ewe with the assistance of translators who preferred to remain anonymous.

Acolatse, A., Lomé, 24 June 2000
Acolatse, J. K., Lomé, 1 and 4 July 2000
Adda, A., Kpalimé, 12 May 2000
Adigbli, K. A., Kpalimé, 11 May 2000
Adjago, F., Tsévié, 24 June 2000 (A)
Agbedanu, S. K., Tsévié, 24 June 2000 (A)
Anonymous, Kpalimé, 10 May 2000
Anonymous, Kpalimé, 11 May 2000
Ayevor, Ebenezer, Agu-Nyogbo, 20 Feb. 2010
Bedu, K. K., Amedzro and Adadjo, Kpalimé, 26 June 2000
Bedu, K. K., Kpalimé, 28 June 2000
Dogbe, Kpele-Agbano, 14 May 2000
Gassou, E. A., Lomé, 19 May 2000, 19 June 2000 and 21 June 2000
Komedja, K. V. H., Agu-Nyogbo, 29 June 2000 (A)
Togbe Agboli Agokoli IV, Notsé, 2 July 2000
Togbe Adobole Amega Yao Gassou IV, Kpalimé, 14 and 18 May 2000
Togbe Kpegba Tegli II, Danyi-Apéyémé, 13 May 2000
Togbe Kpegba Tegli II, Notsé, 2 July 2000
Togbe Mlapa, Togoville, 20 June 2000
Togbe Tenu Koku Senyo Tsally X and Apécho, A., Agome-Yoh, 12 May 2000
Yewu, S. K. and Yewu, P., Kpalimé, 10 May 2000 (A)

United Kingdom

All interviews were conducted in English.

Bown, L., Shrewsbury, 30 April 2000 and 12 July 2004
Ensor, M., London, 25 Feb. 2000

Heaton, D., Wimbledon, London, 5 April 2000
Kimble, H., Oxford, 15 Oct 2003
Kodzi, Dr B. K., Edmonton, Greater London, 13 Dec. 2000
Kodzi, Dr B. K., Edmonton, Greater London, 27 Jan. 2001
Kodzi, Dr B. K., Edmonton, Greater London, 19 July 2001
Mead, T., Cheltenham, 16 March 2000
Olympio, G., London, 13 Dec. 2000
Tordoff, W., Chapel-en-le-Frith, 13 April 2004
Wilks, I., Cribyn Ceredigion, 30 Sept. 2004

Correspondence

Letters from M. K. Agbodza, 10 Oct. 2000, 20 Nov. 2000, 31 Jan. 2001, 11 Feb. 2002
Letter from Togbe Akoto I, Divisional Chief of Liati, 9 Oct. 2000
Letters from E. K. Datsa, n.d. (c. Nov. 1999), 26 Oct. 2001
Letter from T. Mead, 3 April 2000

Private Papers Belonging to Individuals

Acolatse, A., Lomé
Acolatse, J. K., Lomé
Adedeme, G. S. K., Avatime-Amedzofe
Adiku, Rev. E. T., Hohoe
Adom, E., Hohoe
Agbodza, M. K., Santrokofi-Benua
Apedu, S., Avatime-Dzogbofeme
Asase, M. K., Ho
Gavu, E. K., Avatime-DzogbofemeKimble, D., Chagford, Devon
Tsekpo, M. Y., Alavanyo-Abehenase

Bibliography: Secondary Sources

Adiku, E. T. and Adom, E. G. *Nufiame-ŋutinyawo*. London: T. Nelson, 1949.
Adinyra, W. E., Adinyra, A. and Datsa, E. K. *Amedzofe fe E. P. Hame ŋutinya 1889–1964*. Accra: Presby Press, 1965.
Aduayom, M. A. 'Un prélude au nationalisme togolais: la révolte de Lomé, 24 – 25 janvier 1933'. *Cahiers d'études africaines* 24, no. 1 (1984), 39–50.
'Lomé, une capitale-frontière: implications socio-économiques et politiques'. *Le centenaire de Lomé, capitale du Togo (1897–1997)*. Collection Patrimoines, no. 7 (1997), 289–302.
Agblemagnon, F. N'Sougan. *Sociologie des sociétés orales d'Afrique Noire: les Evé du Sud-Togo*. Paris: Mouton et Co., 1969.
Agbodeka, Francis. *Ghana in the Twentieth Century*. Accra: Ghana Universities Press, 1972.
Handbook of Eweland: The Ewes of Southeastern Ghana. Accra: Woeli, 1997.
Agbodza, M. K. *Kesinɔnu Kple Yayra*. London: T. Nelson, 1948.

Agyeman, Fred. *Amu the African: A Study in Vision and Courage*. Accra: Asempa/Christian Council of Ghana, 1988.

Ahlman, Jeff. 'Road to Ghana: Nkrumah, Southern Africa and the Eclipse of a Decolonizing Africa'. *Kronos* 37, no. 1 (2011), 23–40.

Akyeampong, Emmanuel. *Between the Sea and the Lagoon: An Eco-Social History of the Anlo of Southeastern Ghana, c.1850 to Recent Times*. Athens, OH: Ohio University Press, 2001.

Alexander, Jocelyn and McGregor, JoAnn. 'War Stories: Guerrilla Narratives of Zimbabwe's Liberation War'. *History Workshop* 57, no. 1 (2004), 79–100.

Alexander, Jocelyn, McGregor, JoAnn and Ranger, Terence. *Violence and Memory: One Hundred Years in the 'Dark Forests' of Matabeleland*. Oxford: James Currey, 2000.

Aligwekwe, I. E. *'The Ewe and Togoland Problem: A Case Study in the Paradoxes and Problems of Political Transition in West Africa'*. PhD thesis, University of Ohio, 1960.

Allman, Jean. 'The Youngmen and the Porcupine: Nationalism and Asante's Struggle for Self-Determination, 1954–57'. *Journal of African History* 31, no. 2 (1990), 263–79.

The Quills of the Porcupine: Asante Nationalism in an Emergent Ghana. Wisconsin, WI: University of Wisconsin Press, 1993.

'Be(com)ing Asante, Be(com)ing Akan: Thoughts on Gender, Identity and the Colonial Encounter'. In *Ethnicity in Ghana: The Limits of Invention*, edited by C. Lentz and P. Nugent, 97–118. London: Macmillan, 2000.

'Nuclear Imperialism and the Pan-African Struggle for Peace and Freedom: Ghana 1959–62'. *Souls: a Critical Journal of Black Politics, Culture, and Society* 10, no. 2 (2008), 83–102.

'The Disappearing of Hannah Kudjoe: Nationalism, Feminism and the Tyrannies of History'. *Journal of Women's History* 21, no. 3 (2009), 13–35.

'Phantoms of the Archive: Kwame Nkrumah, a Nazi Pilot Named Hanna, and the Contingencies of Post-Colonial History Writing'. *American Historical Review* 118, no. 1 (2013), 104–29.

Allman, Jean and Tashjian, Victoria. *'I Will Not Eat Stone': A Women's History of Colonial Asante*. Portsmouth, NH: Heinemann, 2000.

Alsheimer, Rainer. *Zwischen Sklaverei und christlicher Ethnogenese: die vorkoloniale Missionierung der Ewe in Westafrika (1848 – ca 1890)*. Münster: Waxmann Verlag, 2007.

Amedzro, Albert. 'University-Based Adult Education in Ghana 1948–2000'. In *The Practice of Adult Education in Ghana*, edited by Kobina Asiedu, Kate Adoo-Adeku, and Albert Amedzro. Accra: Ghana Universities Press, 2004.

Ameh, Robert Kwame. 'Uncovering Truth: Ghana's National Reconciliation Commission Excavation of Past Human Rights Abuses'. *Contemporary Justice Review* 9, no. 4 (2006).

'Doing Justice After Conflict: the case for Ghana's National Reconciliation Commission'. *Canadian Journal of Law and Society* 21, no. 1 (2006).

Amenumey, D. E. K. 'The Pre-1947 Background to the Ewe Unification Question: A Preliminary Sketch'. *Transactions of the Historical Society of Ghana* 10 (1969), 65–85.

'German Administration in Southern Togo'. *Journal of African History* 10, no. 4 (1969), 623–39.

'The General Elections in the "Autonomous Republic of Togo", April 1958: Background and Interpretation'. *Transactions of the Historical Society of Ghana* 16, no. 1 (1975), 47–65.

'The Plebiscite in Togoland under British Administration and Ewe Unification'. *Universitas* 5, no. 2 (1976) (new series), 127–39.

The Ewe in Pre-Colonial Times: A Political History with Special Emphasis on the Anlo, Ge and Krepi. Accra/Ho: Sedco Publishing, 1986.

The Ewe Unification Movement: A Political History. Accra: Ghana Universities Press, 1989.

Amonoo, Ben. *Ghana 1957–1966: The Politics of Institutional Dualism*. London: George Allen and Unwin, 1981.

Amos, Alcione. 'Afro-Brazilians in Togo: The Case of the Olympio Family, 1882–1945'. *Cahiers d'études africaines* 162, XLI-2 (2001), 293–314.

Ansre, Gilbert, ed. *Evangelical Presbyterian Church: 150 Years of Evangelization and Development 1847–1997*. Ho: E. P. Church, 1997.

Antor, S. G. and Ecker, Paul, eds. *'Most Secret' Politics in Togoland: The British Government's Attempt to Annex Togoland to the Gold Coast*. New York: Contemporary Press, c. 1954.

Apter, David. 'Political Religion in the New Nations'. In *Old Societies and New States: The Quest for Modernity in Asia and Africa*, edited by C. Geertz, 57–104. London: Free Press of Glencoe/Collier Macmillan, 1963.

Ghana in Transition. Princeton, NJ: Princeton University Press, 1972 [2nd revised edition].

Appiah, Joe. *Joe Appiah: The Autobiography of an African Patriot*. New York, NY; Westport, CT; London: Praegar, 1990.

Asamoa, A. K. *The Ewe of South-Eastern Ghana and Togo on the Eve of Colonialism: A Contribution to the Marxist Debate on Pre-Capitalist Socio-Economic Formations*. Accra: Ghana Publishing Corporation, 1986.

Asare, Theodore O. *The Case for a Reunited Togoland: Nkabum Ne Biakoye*. New York, NY: Trade Council Allied Printers, 1953.

Attignon, H. 'Lomé'. *Le Mois en Afrique (Revue française d'etudes politiques africaines)* 81 (September 1972), 47–57.

'Le Togo du congrès de Berlin à la conférence de Brazzaville'. *Le Mois en Afrique (Revue française d'études politiques africaines)* 82 (October 1972), 29–57.

Austin, Dennis. 'The Uncertain Frontier: Ghana-Togo'. *Journal of Modern African Studies* 1, no. 2 (1963), 139–45.

Politics in Ghana 1946–1960. London, New York, Toronto: Oxford University Press, 1964.

'Et in Arcadia Ego: Politics and Learning in Ghana'. *Minerva* 13, no. 2 (1975), 236–69.

Austin, Dennis and Luckham, Robin. *Politicians and Soldiers in Ghana, 1966–1972*. London: Cass, 1975.

Austin, Gareth. *Labour, Land and Capital in Ghana: From Slavery to Free Labour in Asante, 1807 to 1956*. Rochester, NY: Rochester University Press, 2005.

Avortri, Koku. *Togoland Ghana Relationship Explained (Volta Region at a Glance)*. Accra: Koku Avortri, 2010.

Ayeke, K. A. *Asitsu Atɔawo*. Accra: Bureau of Ghana Languages, 1969.

Azamede, Kokou. *Transkulturationen? Ewe-Christen zwishcen Deutschland und Westafrika, 1884–1939*. Wiesbaden: Franz Steiner Verlag, 2010.
Barber, Karin, ed. *Africa's Hidden Histories: Everyday Literacy and Making the Self*. Bloomington, IN: Indiana University Press, 2006.
'Introduction: Africa's Hidden Innovators'. In *Africa's Hidden Histories: Everyday Literacy and Making the Self*, edited by Karin Barber, 1–24. Bloomington, IN: Indiana University Press, 2006.
The Anthropology of Texts, Persons and Publics. Cambridge: Cambridge University Press, 2007.
Barbier, J.-C. 'Jalons pour une sociologie électorale du Togo: 1958, 1985'. *Politique africaine* 27 (1987), 6–15.
Bartels, C. *Ghana Who's Who 1972–73*. Accra: Bartels Publications, 1972.
Bawumia, Mumumi. *A Life in the Political History of Ghana: Memoirs of Alhaji Mumuni Bawumia*. Accra: Ghana Universities Press, 2004.
Bayart, Jean-François, Mbembe, Achille and Toulabour, Comi. *Le politique par le bas: contributions à une problématique de la démocratie*. Paris: Karthala, 1992.
Bayart, Jean-François. *The State in Africa: the Politics of the Belly*. New York: Longman, 1993.
Baynham, Simon. 'Civilian Rule and the Coup d'Etat: The Case of Busia's Ghana'. *The RUSI Journal* 123, no. 3 (1978), 27–33.
Bendix, Reinhard. *Force, Fate and Freedom: On Historical Sociology*. Berkeley, CA: University of California Press, 1948.
Bening, R. B. *A History of Education in Northern Ghana*. Accra: Ghana Universities Press, 1990.
'Evolution of Electoral Constituencies in Ghana, 1950–1982'. *Research Review, Institute of African Studies* 6, (1993), 1–44.
Berman, Bruce and Lonsdale, John. *Unhappy Valley: Conflict in Kenya and Africa, vols. 1 and 2*. London: James Currey, 1992.
Berry, Sara. *Fathers Work for Their Sons: Accumulation, Mobility and Class Formation in an Extended Yoruba Community*. Berkley, CA: University of California Press, 1985.
Chiefs Know Their Boundaries: Essays on Property, Power and the Past in Asante, 1896–1996. Oxford: Heinemann, 2001.
Bing, A. 'Popular Participation versus People's Power: Notes on Politics and Power Struggles in Ghana'. *Review of African Political Economy* 31, (1984), 91–104.
Bloom, Peter and Skinner, Kate. 'Modernity and Danger: The Boy Kumasenu and the Work of the Gold Coast Film Unit'. *Ghana Studies* 12, (2009), 121–54.
Boahen, Albert Adu. *The Ghanaian Sphinx: Reflections on the Contemporary History of Ghana 1972–1987*. Accra: Sankofa, 1992 [1989].
Bocco Yao, E. I. 'Peuples et nationalisme, les partis Ewe et l'Eglise Evangélique du Togo: Aspiration Unitaire 1919–1955' . Thèse de doctorat de 3è cycle, Université de Poitiers, Faculté des Sciences Humaines.
Branch, Daniel. *Defeating Mau Mau, Creating Kenya: Counterinsurgency, Civil War, and Decolonization*. Cambridge: Cambridge University Press, 2009.
Brennan, James. *Taifa: Making Nation and Race in Tanzania*. Athens, OH: Ohio University Press, 2012.

Brown, David. 'Politics in the Kpandu Area of Ghana, 1925–1969: A Study of the Influence of Central Government and National Politics upon a Local Factional Competition'. PhD thesis, University of Birmingham, 1977.
'Borderline Politics in Ghana: The National Liberation Movement of Western Togoland'. *Journal of Modern African Studies* 18, no. 4 (1980), 575–609.
'Sieges and Scapegoats: The Politics of Pluralism in Ghana and Togo'. *Journal of Modern African Studies* 21, no. 3 (1983), 431–60.
Brydon, Lynne. 'Women Chiefs and Power in the Volta Region of Ghana'. *Journal of Legal Pluralism and Unofficial Law* 28, no. 37–8 (1996), 227–47.
'Religious Encounter in Amedzofe: Women and Change Through the Twentieth Century'. In *Christianity and Social Change in Africa: Essays in Honour of J. D. Y. Peel*, edited by Toyin Falola, 471–88. Durham, NC: Carolina Academic Press, 2005.
'Extensions of Extended Families: A Case Study from Avatime, Ghana'. Working Paper No. 1 of the Missione Etnologica in Bénin e Africa Occidentale (2007). Available at: www.mebao.org/uploads/wps/mebao_wp01.pdf [last accessed 14 February 2013].
'Constructing Avatime: Questions of History and Identity in a West African Polity, c. 1690s to the Twentieth Century'. *Journal of African History* 49, no. 1 (2008), 23–42.
'After Slavery? Productive Relations in Krepi'. In *The Changing Worlds of Atlantic Africa*, edited by Toyin Falola and Matthew Childs. Durham, NC: Carolina Academic Press, 2009.
Lives and Livings. Unpublished book manuscript.
Brydon, Lynne and Legge, Karen. *Adjusting Society: The World Bank, the IMF and Ghana*. London: Tauris Academic Studies, 1996.
Callahan, Michael. *Mandates and Empire: The League of Nations and Africa 1914–31*. Brighton: Sussex Academic Press, 1999.
Calloway, Barbara. 'Local Politics in Ho and Aba'. *Canadian Journal of African Studies* 4, no. 1 (1970), 121–43.
Cell, John. 'On the Eve of Decolonization: The Colonial Office's Plans for the Transfer of Power in Africa, 1947'. *Journal of Imperial and Commonwealth History* 8, no.3 (1980), 235–57.
Chapman, D. A. *Our Homeland: A Regional Geography, Book 1, South-East Gold Coast*. Achimota: Achimota Press, 1943.
Chazan, Naomi. *An Anatomy of Ghanaian Politics: Managing Political Recession, 1969–1982*. Boulder, CO: Westview Press, 1983.
Christian Council of the Gold Coast. *Christianity and African Culture: A Series of Lectures*. Accra: Christian Council of the Gold Coast, 1955.
Coe, Cati. 'Educating an African Leadership: Achimota and the Teaching of African Culture in the Gold Coast'. *Africa Today* 49, no. 3 (2002), 23–44.
Dilemmas of Culture in African Schools: Youth, Nationalism and the Transformation of Knowledge. Chicago, IL: Chicago University Press, 2005.
Cohen, D. L. 'Convention People's Party of Ghana: Representational or Solidarity Party?'. *Canadian Journal of African Studies* 4, no. 2 (1970), 173–94.
Cole, Catherine. *Ghana's Concert Party Theatre*. Bloomington, IN: Indiana University Press, 2001.

Coleman, James S. 'Togoland'. *International Conciliation*, 509 (September 1956), 2–91.

Comaroff, Jean and Comaroff, John. *Of Revelation and Revolution: Christianity, Colonialism and Consciousness in South Africa*. Chicago, IL: University of Chicago Press, 1991.

Of Revelation and Revolution: The Dialectics of Modernity on the South African Frontier. Chicago, IL: University of Chicago Press, 1997.

Cooper, Frederick. *Africa Since 1940: The Past of the Present*. Cambridge: Cambridge University Press, 2002.

'Possibility and Constraint: African Independence in Historical Perspective'. *Journal of African History* 49, no. 2 (2008), 167–96.

'Alternatives to Nationalism: The Political Imagination of Elites in French West Africa, 1945–1960'. In *Elites and Decolonization in the Twentieth Century*, edited by Jost Dülffer and Marc Frey, 110–37. Basingstoke: Palgrave Macmillan, 2011.

Cornevin, Robert. *Histoire du Togo*. Paris: Editions Berger-Levrault, 1969 [3è édition].

'La politique extérieure de Togo. *Le mois en Afrique (Revue française d'études politiques africaines)* 82 (October 1972), 59–71.

Dakubu, Mary Kropp and Ford, K. C. 'The Central Togo Languages'. In *The Languages of Ghana*, edited by Mary Kropp Dakubu, 119–54. London: Kegan Paul, 1988.

Danquah, J. B. (with editorial work by Albert Adu Boahen). *The Ghanaian Establishment: Its Constitution, Its Detentions, Its Tradition, Its Justice and Statecraft and Its Heritage of Ghanaianism*. Accra: Ghana Universities Press, 1997.

Darkoh, M. B. K. 'Note on the Peopling of the Forest Hills of the Volta Region of Ghana'. *Ghana Notes and Queries* 11 (1970), 8–13.

Datsa, E. K. *Doing My Duty: Memoirs of a Ghanaian Educationist*. Accra: Woeli, 2006.

Debrunner, Hans. *The Church in Togo: A Church Between Colonial Powers*. London: Lutterworth Press, 1965.

Decalo, Samuel. *Coups and Army Rule in Africa: Studies in Military Style*. New Haven, CT: Yale University Press, 1976.

de Surgy, Albert. 'Les Puissances du Désordre au Sein de la Personne Evhé'. *Colloques internationaux du CNRS* 544 (1973), 99–118.

'Le sacrifice à la lumière des conceptions mwaba-gurma et evhé (nord et sud du Togo)'. *Anthropos* 84 (1989), 63–80.

Der, Benedict. 'Church-State Relations in Northern Ghana, 1906–1940'. *Transactions of the Historical Society of Ghana* 15, no. 1 (1974), 41–61.

The Slave Trade in Northern Ghana. Accra: Woeli Publishing Services, 1998.

Dickson, A. G. 'Mass Education in Togoland'. *African Affairs* 49, no. 195 (1950), 136–50.

Didier, J. 'L'économie togolaise'. *Le mois en Afrique (Revue française d'études politiques africaines)* 82 (October 1972), 73–9.

Digre, Brian. 'The United Nations, France, and African Independence: A Case Study of Togo'. *French Colonial History* 5 (2004), 193–205.

Douglas, R. M. 'An Offer They Couldn't Refuse: The British Left, Colonies and International Trusteeship, 1940–1951'. In *Imperialism on Trial: International*

Oversight of Colonial Rule in Historical Perspective, edited by R. M. Douglas, Michael Callahan and Elizabeth Bishop, 139–66. Lanham, MD: Lexington Books, 2006.

Douglas, R. M., Callahan, Michael, and Bishop, Elizabeth, eds. *Imperialism on Trial: International Oversight of Colonial Rule in Historical Perspective*. Lanham, MD: Lexington Books, 2006.

Dove, Linda. 'Teachers in Politics in Ex-Colonial Countries'. *Journal of Commonwealth and Comparative Politics* 17 (1979), 176–91.

Dülffer, Jost and Frey, Marc, eds. *Elites and Decolonization in the Twentieth Century*. Basingstoke: Palgrave Macmillan, 2011.

Dunn, John and Robertson, A. F. *Dependence and Opportunity: Political Change in Ahafo*. Cambridge: Cambridge University Press, 1973.

Duthie, A. S. and Vlaardingerbroek, R. K. *Bibliography of Gbe (Ewe, Gen, Aja, Kwala, Fon, Gun, etc.): Publications on and in the Language*. Basel: Basler Afrika Bibliographien, 1981.

Dzathor, P. K. *The Ewe Nation and Sasadu: A Brief History*. Accra: Berkadams, 1998.

Dzobo, N. K. *African Proverbs: The Moral Value of Ewe Proverbs; Guide to Conduct Vol. II*. Accra: Bureau of Ghana Languages, 1975.

Eckert, Andreas. 'Julius Nyerere, Tanzanian Elites, and the Project of African Socialism'. In *Elites and Decolonization in the Twentieth Century*, edited by Jost Dülffer and Marc Frey, 216–40. Basingstoke: Palgrave Macmillan, 2011.

Ellis, Stephen. *External Mission: The ANC in Exile, 1960–1990*. London: Hurst, 2012.

'Writing Histories of Contemporary Africa'. *Journal of African History* 43, no. 1 (2002), 1–26.

Equagoo, Rose Y., ed. *First Justice, then Peace: In Connection with the Ewe and Togoland Unification Problem*. Accra: West African Graphic Company, 1952.

Feierman, Steven. *Peasant Intellectuals: History and Anthropology in Tanzania*. Madison, WI: University of Wisconsin Press, 1990.

Fieldhouse, Roger. *Adult Education and the Cold War: Liberal Values under Siege, 1946–51*. Leeds: University of Leeds, 1985.

Fitch, Bob and Oppenheimer, Mary. *Ghana: End of an Illusion*. London and New York, NY: Monthly Review Press, 1966.

Fleku, S. Togbe. *Togoland and Gold Coast: 'Forward Together to Freedom'*. Accra: West African Graphic Co., c.1954.

Foster, Philip. 'Secondary Schooling and Social Mobility in a West African Nation'. *Sociology of Education* 37, no. 2 (1963), 150–71.

Education and Social Change in Ghana. London: Routledge, 1965.

'Education and Social Inequality in Sub-Saharan Africa'. *Journal of Modern African Studies* 18, no. 2 (1980), 201–36.

Fred-Mensah, B. K. 'Bases of Traditional Conflict Management Among the Buems of the Ghana-Togo Border'. In *Traditional Cures for Modern Conflicts*, edited by I. W. Zartman, 31–47. Boulder, CO: Lynne Reinner, 2000.

Fynn, J. K. *Asante and its Neighbours 1700–1807*. London: Longman, 1971.

Gavua, Kodzo. *A Handbook of Eweland: The Northern Ewes in Ghana*. Accra: Woeli, 2000.

Gayibor, T. N. *'Migrations-Sociétés-Civilisations: Les Ewe du Sud-Togo'* . Thèse de Doctorat en Histoire, Université de Paris I, 1975.
ed. *Les Togolais face à la colonisation*. Lomé: Presses de l'UB, 1994.
ed. *Le peuplement due Togo: état actuel des connaissances historiques*. Lomé: Presses de l'UB, 1996.
Geertz, Clifford. 'The Integrative Revolution: Primordial Sentiments and Civil Politics in the New States'. In *Old Societies and New States: The Quest for Modernity in Asia and Africa*, edited by Clifford Geertz, 105–57. London: Free Press of Glencoe/Collier Macmillan, 1963.
ed. *Old Societies and New States: The Quest for Modernity in Asia and Africa*. London: Free Press of Glencoe/Collier Macmillan, 1963.
Geiger, Susan. *TANU Women: Gender and Culture in the Making of Tanganyikan Nationalism, 1955–1965*. Portsmouth, NH: Heinemann, 1997.
Genoud, Roger. *Nationalism and Economic Development in Ghana*. New York, NY: Frederick A. Praeger Publishers, 1969.
Gillies, Midge. *Barbed-Wire University: The Real Lives of Allied Prisoners of War in the Second World War*. London: Aurum Press, 2012.
Goldman, Lawrence. *Dons and Workers: Oxford Adult Education Since 1850*. Oxford: Clarendon Press, 1950.
'Education as Politics: university adult education in England since 1870'. *Oxford Review of Education* 25, nos.1 and 2 (1999), 89–101.
'Intellectuals and the English Working Class 1870–1945: The Case of Adult Education'. *History of Education* 29, no. 4 (2000), 281–300.
Goody, Jack, ed. *Literacy in Traditional Societies*. Cambridge: Cambridge University Press, 1968.
Grau, Eugene E. 'The Evangelical Presbyterian Church (Ghana and Togo) 1914–1946: A Study in European Mission Relations Affecting the Beginning of an Indigenous Church'. PhD thesis, Hartford Seminary Foundation, 1964.
Greene, Sandra. *Gender, Ethnicity, and Social Change on the Upper Slave Coast: A History of the Anlo-Ewe*. Portsmouth, NH and London: Heinemann and James Currey, 1996.
'Notsie Narratives: History, Memory and Meaning in West Africa'. *South Atlantic Quarterly* 101, no. 4 (2002), 1015–41.
Sacred Sites and the Colonial Encounter: A History of Meaning and Memory in Ghana. Bloomington, IN: Indiana University Press, 2002.
'Modern "Trokosi" and the 1807 Abolition in Ghana: Connecting Past and Present'. *William and Mary Quarterly* LXVI, no. 4 (2009), 959–74.
West African Narratives of Slavery: Texts from Late Nineteenth and Early Twentieth-Century Ghana. Bloomington, IN: Indiana University Press, 2011.
Guillaneuf, Raymond. 'La presse au Togo (1911–1966)'. Mémoire présenté pour le diplôme d'études supérieures, Université de Dakar, 1967.
Habermas, Jürgen. *The Structural Transformation of the Public Sphere: An Inquiry into a Category of Bourgeois Society*. Cambridge: Polity Press, 1989.
Hagan, Kwa. *Oxford University and an Adult Education Experiment in Ghana, 1947–1950*. Legon: Institute of Adult Education, IAE monographs series 9, 1974.
Hawkins, Sean. *Writing and Colonialism in Northern Ghana: The Encounter Between the LoDagaa and 'The World on Paper,' 1892–1991*. Toronto: University of Toronto Press, 2002.

Hill, Polly. *Migrant Cocoa Farmers of Southern Ghana: A Study in Rural Capitalism*. Oxford: James Currey for the International African Institute, 1998 [1963].

Hobsbawn, Eric and Ranger, Terence, eds. *The Invention of Tradition*. Cambridge: Cambridge University Press, 1983.

Hodgkin, Thomas. *Freedom for the Gold Coast?* London: Union of Democratic Control, 1951.

Nationalism in Colonial Africa. London: Frederick Muller, 1956.

Hofmeyr, Isabel. *The Portable Bunyan: A Transnational History of the Pilgrim's Progress*. Princeton, NJ: Princeton University Press, 2003.

Hofmeyr, Isabel, Kaarsholm, Preben, and Fredericksen, Bodil. 'Introduction: Print Cultures, Nationalisms, and Publics of the Indian Ocean'. *Africa: Journal of International African Institute* 81, no. 1 (2011), 1–22.

Honneth, Axel. *The Struggle for Recognition: The Moral Grammar of Social Conflicts*. Cambridge: Polity Press, 1995.

Hopkins, Tony. *An Economic History of West Africa*. Harlow, ND: Longman, 1973.

Hyam, Ronald. 'Africa and the Labour Government, 1945–1951'. *Journal of Imperial and Commonwealth History* 16, no. 3 (1988), 148–72.

Jeffries, Richard. *Class, Power and Ideology in Ghana: The Railwaymen of Sekondi*. Cambridge: Cambridge University Press, 1978.

'Ghana: Jerry Rawlings ou UN populisme à deux coups …'. *Politique africaine* 8, (1982), 8–20.

Jézéquel, Jean-Hervé. '"Collecting Customary Law": Educated Africans, Ethnographical Writings, and Colonial Justice in French West Africa'. In *Intermediaries, Interpreters and Clerks: African Employees in the Making of Colonial Africa*, edited by Benjamin Lawrance, Emily Osborn and Richard Roberts, 139–58. Madison, WI: University of Wisconsin Press, 2006.

Johnson, Marion. 'Ashanti East of the Volta'. *Transactions of the Historical Society of Ghana* 8 (1965), 33–59.

'M.Bonnat on the Volta'. *Ghana Notes and Queries* 10 (1968), 4–17.

'Ashanti, Juaben and M. Bonnat'. *Transactions of the Historical Society of Ghana* 12 (1971), 17–41.

Kea, Ray. 'Akwamu-Anlo Relations, c. 1750–1813'. *Transactions of the Historical Society of Ghana* 10, (1969), 29–63.

Kedem, Kosi. *British Togoland: An Orphan or the Death of a Nation*. Accra: Stailof Services on behalf of Kosi Kedem, 2005.

What I Said in Parliament, 1993–2005. Accra: K. Kedem, 2005.

How Britain Subverted and Betrayed British Togoland. Accra: Governance and Electoral Systems Agency on behalf of Kosi Kedem, 2007.

2010 Constitutional Review and the Rectification of the Ghana-British Togoland Union. Accra: Governance and Electoral Systems Agency on behalf of Kosi Kedem, 2010.

Kimble, David. *A Political History of Ghana: The Rise of Gold Coast Nationalism 1850–1928*. Oxford: Clarendon Press, 1963.

Kirk-Greene, Anthony. 'The Thin White Line: The Size of the British Colonial Service in Africa'. *African Affairs* 79, no. 314 (1980), 25–44.

Knoll, Arthur. *Togo under Imperial Germany, 1884–1914: A Case Study in Colonial Rule*. Stanford, CA: Hoover Institution Press, 1978.

Kludze, A. K. P. 'Family Property and Inheritance among the Northern Ewe of Ghana'. In *Domestic Rights and Duties in Southern Ghana: Legon Family Research Papers*, 199–229. 1974.
Kobo, Ousman. '"We Are Citizens Too": The Politics of Citizenship in Independent Ghana'. *Journal of Modern African Studies* 48, no. 1 (2010), 67–94.
Kodzi, Kofi. *Worse than South Africa: Hypocrisy in African Politics*. London: Moreto Publishers, 1991.
The Ewe Language in Danger. Unpublished manuscript, 2002.
Kponton, Ginette. 'La décolonisation au Togo (1940–1960)' . Thèse de Doctorat en Histoire, 3è cycle, Université de Provence, 1977.
'Rôle et activités politiques des femmes du sud du Togo pendant la décolonisation (1946–1960)'. *Cahiers du CRA* 8, (1994), 53–68.
'La femme dans la lute pour la decolonisation (1946–1960). In *Les Togolais face à la colonisation*, edited by Nicoué Gayibor, 213–44. Lomé: Presses de l'UB, 1994.
Kratz, A. 'Le Togo au début de notre siècle: I'. *Le mois en Afrique (Etudes politiques, économiques et sociologiques africaines)* 211–12 (1983), 144–65.
'Le Togo au début de notre siècle: II'. *Le mois en Afrique (Etudes politiques, économiques et sociologiques africaines)* 213–14 (1983), 125–42.
'Le Togo au début de notre siècle: III'. *Le mois en Afrique (Etudes politiques, économiques et sociologiques africaines)* 217–18 (1984), 153–72.
Kwaku, Ken. 'Tradition, Colonialism and Politics in Rural Ghana: Local Politics in Have, Volta Region'. *Canadian Journal of African Studies* 10, no. 1 (1976), 71–86.
Kwakumé, H. *Précis d'historie du peuple Ewe (Evhé)*. Lomé: Imprimerie Ecole Professionelle, 1948.
Ladouceur, Paul. *Chiefs and Politicians: The Politics of Regionalism in Northern Ghana*. London and New York, NY: Longman, 1979.
Lange, Marie-France. *L'école au Togo: processus de scolarisation et institution de l'école en Afrique*. Paris: Karthala, 1998.
Larson, Pier. *Ocean of Letters: Language and Creolization in an Indian Ocean Diaspora*. Cambridge: Cambridge University Press, 2009.
'Literacy and Power in Madagascar'. Paper presented at the Wits Institute for Social and Economic Research, 12 August 2013, available at: http://wiser.wits.ac.za/system/files/seminar/Larson2013.pdf [last accessed 13 Aug 2014].
Law, Robin. *The Slave Coast of West Africa, 1550–1750: The Impact of the Atlantic Slave Trade on a West African Society*. Oxford: Clarendon Press, 1991.
Ouidah: The Social History of a West African Slaving 'Port', 1727–1892. Athens, OH: Ohio University Press, 2004.
Lawrance, Benjamin. 'Most Obedient Servants: The Politics of Language in German Colonial Togo'. *Cahiers d'études africaines* 159, XL-3 (2000), 489–524.
'Bankoe v. Dome: Traditions and Petitions in the Ho-Asogli Amalgamation, British Mandated Togoland, 1919–39'. *Journal of African History* 46 (2005), 243–67.
'En proie à la fièvre du cacao: Land and Resource Conflict on an Ewe Frontier, 1922–1939'. *African Economic History* 31 (2005), 135–81.

A Handbook of Eweland: The Ewe of Togo and Benin. Accra: Woeli, 2005.
Locality, Mobility and 'Nation': Peri-Urban Colonialism in Togo's Eweland 1900–1960. Rochester, NY: Rochester University Press, 2007.
Lawrance, Benjamin, Osborne, Emily and Roberts, Richard. *Intermediaries, Interpreters and Clerks: African Employees in the Making of Colonial Africa*. Madison, WI: University of Wisconsin Press, 2006.
Lentz, Carola. *Ethnicity and the Making of History in Northern Ghana*. Edinburgh: Edinburgh University Press for the International African Library, 2006.
'SWDK Gandah (1927–2001): Intellectual and Historian from Northern Ghana'. *Africa* 82, no. 3 (2012), 342–55.
Lentz, Carola and Nugent, Paul. 'Introduction'. In *Ethnicity in Ghana: The Limits of Invention*, edited by C. Lentz and P. Nugent, 3–18. London: Macmillan, 2000.
eds. *Ethnicity in Ghana: The Limits of Invention*. London: Macmillan, 2000.
Lohrmann, Ullrich. *Voices from Tanganyika: Great Britain, the United Nations and the Decolonization of a Trust Territory, 1946–1961*. Münster: Lit Verlag, 2007.
Lonsdale, John. 'States and Social Processes in Africa: A Historiographical Survey'. *African Studies Review* 24, nos. 2 and 3 (1981), 139–225.
Maier, Donna. 'Asante War Aims in the 1869 Invasion of Ewe'. In *The Golden Stool: Studies of the Asante Center and Periphery*, edited by Enid Schildkrout. New York, NY: American Museum of Natural History, 1987.
'Slave Labor and Wage Labor in German Togo, 1885–1914'. In *Germans in the Tropics: Essays in German Colonial History*, edited by Arthur Knoll and Lewis Gann, 73–92. New York, NY: Greenwood Press, 1987.
Malkki, Liisa. 'Refugees and Exiles: From "Refugee Studies" to the National Order of Things'. *Annual Review of Anthropology* 24 (1995), 495–523.
Mamdani, Mahmood. *Citizen and Subject: Contemporary Africa and the Legacy of Late Colonialism*. Princeton, NJ: Princeton University Press, 1996.
Manoukian, Madeleine. *The Ewe-speaking People of Togoland and the Gold Coast*. London: International African Institute, 1952.
Marriott, Stuart. *Extramural Empires: Service & Self-Interest in English University Adult Education, 1873–1983*. Nottingham: University of Nottingham Department of Adult Education, 1984.
Mauny, R. 'Etat actuel de nos connaissances sur la préhistoire du Dahomey et du Togo'. *Etudes Dahoméenes* 4 (1950), 5–11.
Mbembe, Achille. *On the Postcolony*. Berkeley, CA: University of California Press, 2001.
'On the Postcolony: A Brief Response to Critics'. *African Identities* 4, no. 2 (2006), 143–78.
McCaskie, Tom. *State and Society in Pre-Colonial Asante*. Cambridge: Cambridge University Press, 1995.
Asante Identities: History and Modernity in an African Village. Edinburgh and Bloomington, IN: Edinburgh University Press and Indiana University Press, 2000.
'Writing, Reading, and Printing Death: Obituaries and Commemoration in Asante'. In *Africa's Hidden Histories: Everyday Literacy and Making the Self*, edited by Karin Barber, 341–84. Bloomington, IN: Indiana University Press, 2006.

'The United States, Ghana and Oil: Global and Local Perspectives'. *African Affairs* 107, no. 428 (2008), 313–32.

Meyer, Birgit. 'Christian Mind and Worldly Matters: Religion and Materiality in Nineteenth-Century Gold Coast'. *Journal of Material Culture* 2, no. 3 (1997), 311–37.

Translating the Devil: Religion and Modernity Among the Ewe in Ghana. London and Edinburgh: International African Institute and Edinburgh University Press, 1999.

'Christianity and the Ewe Nation: German Pietist Missionaries, Ewe Converts and the Politics of Culture'. *Journal of Religion in Africa* 32, no. 2 (2002), 167–99.

Miescher, Stephan. *Making Men in Ghana.* Bloomington, IN: Indiana University Press, 2005.

'"My Own Life": A. K. Boakye Yiadom's Autobiography – the Writing and Subjectivity of a Ghanaian Teacher-Catechist'. In *Africa's Hidden Histories: Everyday Literacy and Making the Self*, edited by Karin Barber, 27–51. Bloomington, IN: Indiana University Press, 2006.

Miescher, Stephan and Tsikata, Dzodzi. 'Hydro-Power and the Promise of Modernity and Development in Ghana: Comparing the Akosombo and Bui Dam Projects'. *Ghana Studies* 12, no. 13 (2009/10), 15–55.

Morrell, Gordon. 'A Higher Stage of Imperialism: The Big Three, the United Nations Trusteeship Council and the Early Cold War'. In *Imperialism on Trial: International Oversight of Colonial Rule in Historical Perspective*, edited by R. M. Douglas, Michael Callahan and Elizabeth Bishop, 111–38. Lanham, MD: Lexington Books, 2006.

Müller, K. *Histoire de l'Eglise catholique au Togo.* Lomé: Editions Librairie Bon Pasteur, 1968.

Newell, Stephanie. *Ghanaian Popular Fiction: 'Thrilling Discoveries in Conjugal Life' and Other Tales.* Oxford: James Currey, 2000.

Literary Culture in Colonial Ghana: How to Play the Game of Life. Manchester: Manchester University Press, 2002.

The Power to Name: A History of Anonymity in Colonial West Africa. Athens, OH: Ohio University Press, 2013.

Nkrumah, Kwame. *The Autobiography of Kwame Nkrumah.* Edinburgh: T. Nelson, 1957.

Nugent, Paul. 'National Integration and the Vicissitudes of State Power in Ghana'. PhD thesis, SOAS, London, 1992.

'A Regional Melting Pot: The Ewe and Their Neighbours in the Ghana-Togo Borderlands'. In *The Ewe of Togo and Benin*, edited by Benjamin Lawrance, 29–43. Accra: Woeli, 2005.

Big Men, Small Boys and Politics in Ghana: Power, Ideology and the Burden of History, 1982–1994. London and New York, NY: Pinter, 1995.

'Living in the Past: Urban, Rural and Ethnic Themes in the 1992 and 1996 Elections in Ghana'. *Journal of Modern African Studies* 37, no. 2 (1999), 287–319.

'"A few lesser peoples": The Central Togo Minorities and Their Ewe Neighbours'. In *Ethnicity in Ghana: The Limits of Invention*, edited by Carola Lentz and Paul Nugent, 162–82. London: Macmillan, 2000.

'Ethnicity as an Explanatory Factor in the Ghana 2000 Elections'. *African Issues* 29, nos. 1 and 2 (2001), 2–7.

'Winners, Losers and Also Rans: Money, Moral Authority and Voting Patterns in the Ghana 2000 Election'. *African Affairs* 100, no. 400 (2001), 405–28.
Smugglers, Secessionists and Loyal Citizens on the Ghana-Togo Frontier: The Lie of the Borderlands since 1914. London and Athens, OH: James Currey and Ohio University Press, 2002.
'Putting the History Back into Ethnicity: Enslavement, Religion, and Cultural Brokerage in the Construction of Mandinka/Jola and Ewe/Agotime Identities in West Africa, c.1650–1930'. *Comparative Studies in Society and History* 50, no. 4 (2008), 920–48.
Nukunya, G. K. *Kinship and Marriage Among the Anlo Ewe*. London: Athlone Press, 1969.
'Some Underlying Beliefs in Ancestor Worship and Mortuary Rites Among the Ewe'. *Colloques internationaux du CNRS* 544 (1973), 119–30.
Tradition and Change in Ghana: An Introduction to Sociology. Accra: Ghana Universities Press, 1992.
Nüßbaum, Manfred. *Togo, Eine Musterkolonie?* Berlin: Rütten und Loening, 1962.
Obianim, S. J. *Eve Kɔnuwo (Ewe Customs)*. Accra: Sedco Publishing, 1990.
Oquaye, Mike. *Politics in Ghana (1972–1979)*. Accra: Tornado, 1980.
Owusu, Maxwell. *Uses and Abuses of Political Power: A Case Study of Continuity and Change in the Politics of Ghana*. Chicago, IL and London: Chicago University Press, 1970.
'Custom and Coups: A Juridical Interpretation of Civil Order and Disorder in Ghana'. *Journal of Modern African Studies* 24, no. 1 (1986), 69–99.
Pauvert, J.-C. 'L'évolution politique des Ewé'. *Cahiers d'études africaines* 2 (1960), 161–91.
Pedersen, Susan. 'Samoa on the World Stage: Petitions and Peoples before the Mandates Commission of the League of Nations'. *Journal of Imperial and Commonwealth History* 40, no. 2 (2012), 231–61.
Peel, J. D. Y. '*Olaju*: A Yoruba Concept of Development'. *Journal of Development Studies* 14 (1978), 139–65.
Ijeshas and Nigerians: The Incorporation of a Yoruba Kingdom 1890s-1970s. Cambridge: Cambridge University Press, 1983.
'The Cultural Work of Yoruba Ethnogenesis'. In *History and Ethnicity* edited by Elizabeth Tonkin, Maryon McDonald and Malcolm Chapman, 198–215. London and New York, NY: Routledge, 1989.
Religious Encounter and the Making of Yoruba. Bloomington, IN: Indiana University Press, 2000.
Perbi, Akosua. *A History of Indigenous Slavery in Ghana from the 15th to the 19th Century*. Accra: Sub-Saharan Publishers, 2004.
Peterson, Derek. *Creative Writing: Translation, Bookkeeping, and the Work of Imagination in Colonial Kenya*. Portsmouth, NH: Heinemann, 2004.
Ethnic Patriotism and the East African Revival: A History of Dissent, c. 1935–1972. Cambridge: Cambridge University Press, 2012.
Peterson, Derek and Macola, Giacomo, eds. *Recasting the Past: History Writing and Political Work in Modern Africa*. Athens, OH: Ohio University Press, 2009.
'Homespun Historiography and the Academic Profession'. In *Recasting the Past: History Writing and Political Work in Modern Africa*, edited by Derek Peterson and Giacomo Macola, 1–30. Athens, OH: Ohio University Press, 2009.

Plange, N.-K. 'The Colonial State in Northern Ghana: The Political Economy of Pacification', *Review of African Political Economy* 31 (1984), 29–43.

Pobee, J. S. *Kwame Nkrumah and the Church in Ghana 1949–1966*. Accra: Asempa / Christian Council of Ghana, 1988.

Prempeh, Samuel. 'The Basel and Bremen Missions and Their Successors in the Gold Coast and Togoland 1914–1926'. PhD thesis, University of Aberdeen, 1977.

Pugh, Patricia. 'Jones, Arthur Creech (1891–1964)'. In *Oxford Dictionary of National Biography*, edited by H. C. G. Matthew and Brian Harrison. Oxford, 2004. Online edition edited by Lawrence Goldman (2011). Available at www.oxforddnb.com/view/article/34224 [last accessed 27 November 2013].

'Hinden, Rita (1909–1971)'. In *Oxford Dictionary of National Biography*, edited by H. C. G. Matthew and Brian Harrison. Oxford, 2004. Online edition edited by Lawrence Goldman (2011). Available at www.oxforddnb.com/view/article/34224 [last accessed 27 July 2014].

Ramseyer, F. and Kühne, J. *Four Years' Captivity in Ashanti, Related in Accordance with the Diaries of the Missionaries Ramseyer and Kühne, by P. Steiner*. London: S. W. Partridge and Co, 1901 [1975].

Rathbone, Richard. 'Businessmen in Politics: Party Struggle in Ghana, 1949–57'. *Journal of Development Studies* 9 (1973), 391–401.

Nkrumah and the Chiefs: The Politics of Chieftaincy in Ghana 1951–1960. Oxford: James Currey, 2000.

Rathbone, Richard and Casely-Hayford, Augustus. 'Politics, Families and Freemasonry in the Colonial Gold Coast'. In *People and Empires in African History: Essays in Memory of Michael Crowder*, edited by J. D. Y. Peel and A. F. Ade Ajayi, 143–58. London and New York, NY: Longman, 1992.

Read, Margaret. *From Field to Factory: An Introductory Study of the Indian Peasant Turned Factory Hand in India*. London: Student Christian Movement, 1927.

Rivière, Claude. 'Rites du marriage chez les Evhé du Togo'. *Anthropos* 79 (1984), 377–95.

Roberts, Penelope. 'The Village Schoolteacher in Ghana'. In *Changing Social Structure in Ghana: Essays in the Comparative Sociology of a New State and An Old Tradition*, edited by Jack Goody, 245–60. London: International African Institute, 1975.

Rossi, Benedetta, ed. *Reconfiguring Slavery: West African Trajectories*. Liverpool: University of Liverpool Press, 2009.

Ryan, S. 'The Theory and Practice of African One-Partyism: The CPP Re-examined'. *Canadian Journal of African Studies* 4, no. 2 (1970), 145–72.

Sawitzki, Sonja. *Ho/Wegbe: Die Etablierung einer Missionsstation in West-Afrika*. Bremen: Univ-Buchh, 2002.

Schiffer, H. B. 'Local Administration and National Development: Fragmentation and Centralization in Ghana'. *Canadian Journal of African Studies* 4, no. 1 (1970), 57–75.

Schildkrout, Enid, ed. *The Golden Stool: Studies of the Asante Center and Periphery*. New York, NY: American Museum of Natural History, 1987.

Schleh, E. P. A. 'The Post-War Careers of Ex-Servicemen in Ghana and Uganda'. *Journal of Modern African Studies* 6, no. 2 (1968), 203–20.

Schmidt, Elisabeth. *Mobilizing the Masses: Gender, Ethnicity, and Class in the Nationalist Movement in Guinea, 1939–1958*. Portsmouth, NH: Heinemann, 2005.

'Pan-Africanism, People's Power and Decolonization in Ghana and Guinea: The Uneven Legacy of Kwame Nkrumah and Sekou Touré'. In *Africa, Empire and Globalization: Essays in Honor of A. G. Hopkins*, edited by Toyin Falola and Emily Brownell, 525–53. Durham, NC: Carolina Academic Press, 2011.

Schober, Reinold. 'Native Co-operation in Togoland'. *Africa: Journal of the International Africa Institute* 9, no. 4 (1936), 485–94.

Schuerkens, Ulrike. 'The Notion of Development in Great Britain in the Twentieth Century and some Aspects of its Application in Togoland under British Mandate and Trusteeship'. *Sociologus* (1995), 122–35.

Du Togo allemand aux Togo et Ghana indépendants: changement social sous régime coloniale. Paris: L'Harmattan, 2001.

Shillington, Kevin. *Ghana and the Rawlings Factor*. New York, NY: St Martin's Press, 1992.

Skinner, Kate. 'Reading, Writing and Rallies: The Politics of 'Freedom' in Southern British Togoland 1953–1956'. *Journal of African History* 48, no. 1 (2007), 123–47.

'Local Historians and Strangers with Big Eyes: The Politics of Ewe History in Ghana and its Global Diaspora'. *History in Africa* 37 (2010), 125–58.

Smith, Noel. *The Presbyterian Church of Ghana, 1835–1960: A Younger Church in a Changing Society*. Accra: Ghana Universities Press, 1966.

Spieth, Jakob. *The Ewe People: A Study of the Ewe People in German Togo*. Accra: Sub-Saharan Publishers, 2011 [1906], trans. Emmanuel Tsaku, Marcellinus Edorh, Raphael Avornyo and Mary Esther Kropp Dakubu.

Sprigge, R. G. S. 'Eweland's Adangbe: An Inquiry into an Oral Tradition'. *Transactions of the Historical Society of Ghana* 10 (1969), 87–128.

Staniland, Martin. *The Lions of Dagbon: Political Change in Northern Ghana*. Cambridge: Cambridge University Press, 1975.

Stoler, Ann. *Along the Archival Grain: Epistemic Anxieties and Colonial Common Sense*. Princeton, NJ: Princeton University Press, 2009.

Talton, Benjamin. *Politics of Social Change in Ghana: The Konkomba Struggle for Political Equality*. New York, NY: Palgrave Macmillan, 2010.

Terretta, Meredith. 'Cameroonian Nationalists Go Global: From Forest *Maquis* to Pan-African Accra'. *Journal of African History* 51, no. 2 (2010), 189–212.

'"We Had Been Fooled into Thinking that the UN Watches over the Entire World": Human Rights, UN Trust Territories and Africa's Decolonization'. *Human Rights Quarterly* 34, no. 2 (2012), 329–60.

Petitioning for our Rights, Fighting for our Nation: The History of the Democratic Union of Cameroonian Women 1946–1960. Oxford: Langaa RPCIG, 2013.

Nation of Outlaws, State of Violence: Nationalism, Grassfields Tradition, and State-Building in Cameroon. Athens, OH: Ohio University Press, 2013.

Taviefe Evangelika Presbiteria Hame ŋkekenyuie 1903–1978. Accra: Presbyterian Press, 1978.

Tété-Adjalogo, Tetevi Godwin. *Histoire du Togo: La palpitante quête de l'ablodé, vol. 2*. Paris: NM7 Editions, 2000.

Histoire du Togo: le régime et l'assassinat de Sylvanus Olympio, vol. 3. Paris: Editions NM7, 2002.
Thompson, W. Scott. *Ghana's Foreign Policy 1957–66*. Princeton, NJ: Princeton University Press, 1969.
Titmus, Colin and Steele, Tom. *Adult Education for Independence: The Introduction of University Extra-Mural Work into British Tropical Africa*. Leeds: Study of Continuing Education Unit, University of Leeds, 1995.
Togbe Kpegba Tegli II. *Eveawo fe hogbe tsofe ŋutinya*. Publisher and printer unknown, c. 1974.
Toulabour, Comi, ed. *Le Ghana de J. J. Rawlings: Restauration de l'état et renaissance du politique*. Paris: Karthala, 2000.
Tsekpo, G. K. *Lododo Xletigbale 1953*. Accra: West African Graphic Co. Ltd., 1952.
Sasadu: ŋutinyagbale I. Hohoe: Hope Press, 1952.
Togo Nukae Hiawo? Accra: West African Graphic Co., 1953.
Sasadu: takpekpe adelia II. Accra: Mawuli Press, 1954.
Togo Ŋutinya Akpa II. Lomé: Mawuli Press, 1961.
Ustorf, Werner. 'Norddeutsche Mission under Wirklichkeitsbewätigung: Bremen, Afrika under der Slavenfreikauf'. In *Mission im Kontext: Beiträge zur Sozialgeschichte der Norddeutschen Missionsgesellschaft im 19. Jahrhundert* edited by Werner Ustorf, 121–215. Bremen: Im Selbstverlag des Museums, 1989.
Mission im Kontext: Beiträge zur Sozialgeschichte der Norddeutschen Missionsgesellschaft im 19. Jahrhundert. Bremen: Im Selbstverlag des Museums, 1989.
Ustorf, Werner. *Bremen Missionaries in Togo and Ghana 1847–1900*. Legon: Legon Theological Studies Press, 2002 [trans. James Greig].
'Missionary Education in West Africa: A Study in Pedagogical Ambition'. *Journal of Beliefs and Values* 32, no. 2 (2011), 235–46.
Vail, Leroy. *The Creation of Tribalism in Southern Africa*. London: James Currey, 1989.
van Brakel, J. *The First Twenty Five Years of SMA Missionary Presence in the Keta-Ho Diocese (1890–1915)*. Nymegen: CMPA Publications, 1990.
van der Linden, Marcel. 'The Pre-History of *Post-Scarcity Anarchism*: Josef Weber and the Movement for a Democracy of Content (1947–1964)'. *Anarchist Studies* 9 (2001), 127–45.
van Rouveroy, E. A. B. 'Chef coutumier: un métier difficile'. *Politique africaine* 27 (1987), 19–29.
van Walraven, Klaas. 'Decolonization by Referendum: The Anomaly of Niger and the Fall of Sawaba 1958–1959'. *Journal of African History* 50, no. 2 (2009), 269–92.
The Yearning for Relief: A History of the Sawaba Movement in Niger. Leiden: Brill, 2013.
Venkatachalam, Meera. 'Slavery in Memory: A Study of the Religious Cults of the Anlo-Ewe of Southeastern Ghana (c. 1850 to Present)' . PhD thesis, SOAS, London, 2007.
'Between the Devil and the Cross: Religion, Slavery and the Making of the Anlo-Ewe'. *Journal of African History* 53, no. 1 (2012), 45–64.
Watson, Ruth. *'Civil Disorder is the Disease of Ibadan': Chieftaincy and Civic Culture in a Colonial City*. Oxford: James Currey, 2001.

Weissflog, Stephan. 'Vietor und sein Konzept des Leistungsfahigen Afrikaners'. In *Mission im Kontext: Beiträge zur Sozialgeschichte der Norddeutschen Missionsgesellschaft im 19. Jahrhundert*, edited by Werner Ustorf, 293–304. Bremen: Im Selbstverlag des Museums, 1989.

Welch Jr., Claude E. *Dream of Unity: Pan-Africanism and Political Unification in West Africa*. Ithaca, NY: Cornell University Press, 1966.

Welman, C. W. *The Native States of the Gold Coast: History and Constitution, Part I: Peki, [1925] Part II: Ahanta [1930]*. London: Dawson's of Pall Mall, 1969.

Westermann, Dietrich. *Wörterbuch der Ewe-Sprache I. Berlin: D. Reimer, 1905; Wörterbuch der Ewe-Sprache II*. Berlin: D. Reimer, 1906.

Evefiala or Ewe-English Dictionary. Nendeln: Kraus Reprint, 1973 [1928].

Whitehead, Clive. *Colonial Educators: the British Indian and Colonial Education Service 1858–1983*. London and New York: I. B. Tauris, 2003.

'The Historiography of British Imperial Education Policy, Part II: Africa and the Rest of the Colonial Empire'. *History of Education* 34, no. 4 (2005), 315–29.

Wilks, Ivor. *Asante in the Nineteenth Century: The Structure and Evolution of a Political Order*. Cambridge: Cambridge University Press, 1975.

'"Unity and Progress": Asante Politics Revisited'. *Ghana Studies* 1 (1998), 151–79.

'Asante Nationhood and Colonial Administrators, 1896–1935'. In *Ethnicity in Ghana: The Limits of Invention*, edited by C. Lentz and P. Nugent, 68–96. London: Macmillan, 2000.

Yagla, Omaa W. *L'édification de la nation togolaise: naissance d'une conscience nationale dans un pays africain*. Paris: L'Harmattan, 1978.

Les indigènes du Togo à l'assaut du pouvoir colonial 1920–1958: L'histoire politique d'un peuple africain, grandeurs et faiblesses des hommes. Lomé: Les Nouvelles Editions Africaines du Togo, 1992.

Yankah, Kwesi. *Free Speech in Traditional Society: The Cultural Foundations of Communication in Contemporary Ghana*. Accra: Ghana Universities Press, 1998.

Yayoh, Wilson. 'Krepi States in the 18th and 19th Centuries'. *Transactions of the Historical Society of Ghana* 6 (2002), 67–81.

'Local Government in Ewedome, British Trust Territory of Togoland (Ghana) 1920s-1970s'. PhD thesis, SOAS, London, 2010.

'Protests against Amalgamation in Colonial Ewedome, British Mandated Territory, 1920 to 1948'. *Journal of History and Cultures* 2 (2013), 1–16.

'British Policy of Direct Taxation among the Northern Ewe of Ghana' (article in preparation).

Yousif, Abelwahid Aballa. *The Origins and Development of University Adult Education in Ghana and Nigeria, 1946–1966*. Bon-Bad Godesberg: Verlag Neue Gesellschaft, 1974.

Zachernuk, Philip. *Colonial Subjects: An African Intelligentsia and Atlantic Ideas*. Charlottesville, VA: University Press of Virginia, 2000.

Zimmerman, Andrew. *Alabama in Africa: Booker T. Washington, the German Empire, and the Globalization of the New South*. Princeton, NJ: Princeton University Press, 2010.

Index

Books in This Series

1 *City Politics: A Study of Léopoldville, 1962–63*, J. S. La Fontaine
2 *Studies in Rural Capitalism in West Africa*, Polly Hill
3 *Land Policy in Buganda*, Henry W. West
4 *The Nigerian Military: A Sociological Analysis of Authority and Revolt, 1960–67*, Robin Luckham
5 *The Ghanaian Factory Worker: Industrial Man in Africa*, Margaret Peil
6 *Labour in the South African Gold Mines*, Francis Wilson
7 *The Price of Liberty: Personality and Politics in Colonial Nigeria*, Kenneth W. J. Post and George D. Jenkins
8 *Subsistence to Commercial Farming in Present-Day Buganda: An Economic and Anthropological Survey*, Audrey I. Richards, Fort Sturrock, and Jean M. Fortt (eds.)
9 *Dependence and Opportunity: Political Change in Ahafo*, John Dunn and A. F. Robertson
10 *African Railwaymen: Solidarity and Opposition in an East African Labour Force*, R. D. Grillo
11 *Islam and Tribal Art in West Africa*, René A. Bravmann
12 *Modern and Traditional Elites in the Politics of Lagos*, P. D. Cole
13 *Asante in the Nineteenth Century: The Structure and Evolution of a Political Order*, Ivor Wilks
14 *Culture, Tradition and Society in the West African Novel*, Emmanuel Obiechina
15 *Saints and Politicians*, Donald B. Cruise O'Brien
16 *The Lions of Dagbon: Political Change in Northern Ghana*, Martin Staniland
17 *Politics of Decolonization: Kenya Europeans and the Land Issue 1960–1965*, Gary B. Wasserman
18 *Muslim Brotherhoods in Nineteenth-Century Africa*, B. G. Martin
19 *Warfare in the Sokoto Caliphate: Historical and Sociological Perspectives*, Joseph P. Smaldone
20 *Liberia and Sierra Leone: An Essay in Comparative Politics*, Christopher Clapham
21 *Adam Kok's Griquas: A Study in the Development of Stratification in South Africa*, Robert Ross
22 *Class, Power and Ideology in Ghana: The Railwaymen of Sekondi*, Richard Jeffries
23 *West African States: Failure and Promise*, John Dunn (ed.)
24 *Afrikaners of the Kalahari: White Minority in a Black State*, Margo Russell and Martin Russell
25 *A Modern History of Tanganyika*, John Iliffe
26 *A History of African Christianity 1950–1975*, Adrian Hastings
27 *Slaves, Peasants and Capitalists in Southern Angola, 1840–1926*, W. G. Clarence-Smith
28 *The Hidden Hippopotamus: Reappraised in African History: The Early Colonial Experience in Western Zambia*, Gwyn Prins

29 *Families Divided: The Impact of Migrant Labour in Lesotho*, Colin Murray
30 *Slavery, Colonialism and Economic Growth in Dahomey, 1640–1960*, Patrick Manning
31 *Kings, Commoners and Concessionaires: The Evolution and Dissolution of the Nineteenth-Century Swazi State*, Philip Bonner
32 *Oral Poetry and Somali Nationalism: The Case of Sayid Mahammad 'Abdille Hasan*, Said S. Samatar
33 *The Political Economy of Pondoland 1860–1930*, William Beinart
34 *Volkskapitalisme: Class, Capital and Ideology in the Development of Afrikaner Nationalism, 1934–1948*, Dan O'Meara
35 *The Settler Economies: Studies in the Economic History of Kenya and Rhodesia 1900–1963*, Paul Mosley
36 *Transformations in Slavery: A History of Slavery in Africa*, Paul E. Lovejoy
37 *Amilcar Cabral: Revolutionary Leadership and People's War*, Patrick Chabal
38 *Essays on the Political Economy of Rural Africa*, Robert H. Bates
39 *Ijeshas and Nigerians: The Incorporation of a Yoruba Kingdom, 1890s–1970s*, J. D. Y. Peel
40 *Black People and the South African War, 1899–1902*, Peter Warwick
41 *A History of Niger 1850–1960*, Finn Fuglestad
42 *Industrialisation and Trade Union Organization in South Africa, 1924–1955*, Stephen Ellis
43 *The Rising of the Red Shawls: A Revolt in Madagascar 1895–1899*, Stephen Ellis
44 *Slavery in Dutch South Africa*, Nigel Worden
45 *Law, Custom and Social Order: The Colonial Experience in Malawi and Zambia*, Martin Chanock
46 *Salt of the Desert Sun: A History of Salt Production and Trade in the Central Sudan*, Paul E. Lovejoy
47 *Marrying Well: Marriage, Status and Social Change among the Educated Elite in Colonial Lagos*, Kristin Mann
48 *Language and Colonial Power: The Appropriation of Swahili in the Former Belgian Congo, 1880–1938*, Johannes Fabian
49 *The Shell Money of the Slave Trade*, Jan Hogendorn and Marion Johnson
50 *Political Domination in Africa*, Patrick Chabal
51 *The Southern Marches of Imperial Ethiopia: Essays in History and Social Anthropology*, Donald Donham and Wendy James
52 *Islam and Urban Labor in Northern Nigeria: The Making of a Muslim Working Class*, Paul M. Lubeck
53 *Horn and Crescent: Cultural Change and Traditional Islam on the East African Coast, 800–1900*, Randall L. Pouwels
54 *Capital and Labour on the Kimberley Diamond Fields, 1871–1890*, Robert Vicat Turrell
55 *National and Class Conflict in the Horn of Africa*, John Markakis
56 *Democracy and Prebendal Politics in Nigeria: The Rise and Fall of the Second Republic*, Richard A. Joseph
57 *Entrepreneurs and Parasites: The Struggle for Indigenous Capitalism in Zaïre*, Janet MacGaffey
58 *The African Poor: A History*, John Iliffe

59 *Palm Oil and Protest: An Economic History of the Ngwa Region, South-Eastern Nigeria, 1800–1980*, Susan M. Martin
60 *France and Islam in West Africa, 1860–1960*, Christopher Harrison
61 *Transformation and Continuity in Revolutionary Ethiopia*, Christopher Clapham
62 *Prelude to the Mahdiyya: Peasants and Traders in the Shendi Region, 1821–1885*, Anders Bjørkelo
63 *Wa and the Wala: Islam and Polity in Northwestern Ghana*, Ivor Wilks
64 *H. C. Bankole-Bright and Politics in Colonial Sierra Leone, 1919–1958*, Akintola Wyse
65 *Contemporary West African States*, Donald Cruise O'Brien, John Dunn, and Richard Rathbone (eds.)
66 *The Oromo of Ethiopia: A History, 1570–1860*, Mohammed Hassen
67 *Slavery and African Life: Occidental, Oriental, and African Slave Trades*, Patrick Manning
68 *Abraham Esau's War: A Black South African War in the Cape, 1899–1902*, Bill Nasson
69 *The Politics of Harmony: Land Dispute Strategies in Swaziland*, Laurel L. Rose
70 *Zimbabwe's Guerrilla War: Peasant Voices*, Norma J. Kriger
71 *Ethiopia: Power and Protest: Peasant Revolts in the Twentieth Century*, Gebru Tareke
72 *White Supremacy and Black Resistance in Pre-industrial South Africa: The Making of the Colonial Order in the Eastern Cape, 1770–1865*, Clifton C. Crais
73 *The Elusive Granary: Herder, Farmer, and State in Northern Kenya*, Peter D. Little
74 *The Kanyok of Zaire: An Institutional and Ideological History to 1895*, John C. Yoder
75 *Pragmatism in the Age of Jihad: The Precolonial State of Bundu*, Michael A. Gomez
76 *Slow Death for Slavery: The Course of Abolition in Northern Nigeria, 1897–1936*, Paul E. Lovejoy and Jan S. Hogendorn
77 *West African Slavery and Atlantic Commerce: The Senegal River Valley, 1700–1860*, James F. Searing
78 *A South African Kingdom: The Pursuit of Security in Nineteenth-Century Lesotho*, Elizabeth A. Eldredge
79 *State and Society in Pre-colonial Asante*, T. C. McCaskie
80 *Islamic Society and State Power in Senegal: Disciples and Citizens in Fatick*, Leonardo A. Villalón
81 *Ethnic Pride and Racial Prejudice in Victorian Cape Town: Group Identity and Social Practice*, Vivian Bickford Smith
82 *The Eritrean Struggle for Independence: Domination, Resistance Nationalism, 1941–1993*, Ruth Iyob
83 *Corruption and State Politics in Sierra Leone*, William Reno
84 *The Culture of Politics in Modern Kenya*, Angelique Haugerud
85 *Africans: The History of a Continent*, John Iliffe

86 *From Slave Trade to 'Legitimate' Commerce: The Commercial Transition in Nineteenth-Century West Africa*, Robin Law (ed.)
87 *Leisure and Society in Colonial Brazzaville*, Phyllis Martin
88 *Kingship and State: The Buganda Dynasty*, Christopher Wrigley
89 *Decolonization and African Life: The Labour Question in French and British Africa*, Frederick Cooper
90 *Misreading the African Landscape: Society and Ecology in an African Forest–Savannah Mosaic*, James Fairhead and Melissa Leach
91 *Peasant Revolution in Ethiopia: The Tigray People's Liberation Front, 1975–1991*, John Young
92 *Senegambia and the Atlantic Slave Trade*, Boubacar Barry
93 *Commerce and Economic Change in West Africa: The Oil Trade in the Nineteenth Century*, Martin Lynn
94 *Slavery and French Colonial Rule in West Africa: Senegal, Guinea and Mali*, Martin A. Klein
95 *East African Doctors: A History of the Modern Profession*, John Iliffe
96 *Middlemen of the Cameroons Rivers: The Duala and Their Hinterland, c.1600–1960*, Ralph Derrick, Ralph A. Austen, and Jonathan Derrick
97 *Masters and Servants on the Cape Eastern Frontier, 1760–1803*, Susan Newton-King
98 *Status and Respectability in the Cape Colony, 1750–1870: A Tragedy of Manners*, Robert Ross
99 *Slaves, Freedmen and Indentured Laborers in Colonial Mauritius*, Richard B. Allen
100 *Transformations in Slavery: A History of Slavery in Africa, 2nd Edition*, Paul E. Lovejoy
101 *The Peasant Cotton Revolution in West Africa: Côte d'Ivoire, 1880–1995*, Thomas J. Bassett
102 *Re-imagining Rwanda: Conflict, Survival and Disinformation in the Late Twentieth Century*, Johan Pottier
103 *The Politics of Evil: Magic, State Power and the Political Imagination in South Africa*, Clifton Crais
104 *Transforming Mozambique: The Politics of Privatization, 1975–2000*, M. Anne Pitcher
105 *Guerrilla Veterans in Post-war Zimbabwe: Symbolic and Violent Politics, 1980–1987*, Norma J. Kriger
106 *An Economic History of Imperial Madagascar, 1750–1895: The Rise and Fall of an Island Empire*, Gwyn Campbell
107 *Honour in African History*, John Iliffe
108 *Africans: History of a Continent, 2nd Edition*, John Iliffe
109 *Guns, Race, and Power in Colonial South Africa*, William Kelleher Storey
110 *Islam and Social Change in French West Africa: History of an Emancipatory Community*, Sean Hanretta
111 *Defeating Mau Mau, Creating Kenya: Counterinsurgency, Civil War, and Decolonization*, Daniel Branch
112 *Christianity and Genocide in Rwanda*, Timothy Longman
113 *From Africa to Brazil: Culture, Identity, and an African Slave Trade, 1600–1830*, Walter Hawthorne

114 *Africa in the Time of Cholera: A History of Pandemics from 1817 to the Present*, Myron Echenberg
115 *A History of Race in Muslim West Africa, 1600–1960*, Bruce S. Hall
116 *Witchcraft and Colonial Rule in Kenya, 1900–1955*, Katherine Luongo
117 *Transformations in Slavery: A History of Slavery in Africa, 3rd Edition*, Paul E. Lovejoy
118 *The Rise of the Trans-Atlantic Slave Trade in Western Africa, 1300–1589*, Toby Green
119 *Party Politics and Economic Reform in Africa's Democracies*, M. Anne Pitcher
120 *Smugglers and Saints of the Sahara: Regional Connectivity in the Twentieth Century*, Judith Scheele
121 *Slaving and Cross-cultural Trade in the Atlantic World: Angola and Brazil during the Era of the Slave Trade*, Roquinaldo Ferreira
122 *Ethnic Patriotism and the East African Revival*, Derek Peterson
123 *Black Morocco: A History of Slavery and Islam*, Chouki El Hamel
124 *An African Slaving Port and the Atlantic World: Benguela and Its Hinterland*, Mariana Candido
125 *Making Citizens in Africa: Ethnicity, Gender, and National Identity in Ethiopia*, Lahra Smith
126 *Slavery and Emancipation in Islamic East Africa: From Honor to Respectability*, Elisabeth McMahon
127 *A History of African Motherhood: The Case of Uganda, 700–1900*, Rhiannon Stephens
128 *The Borders of Race in Colonial South Africa: The Kat River Settlement, 1829–1856*, Robert Ross
129 *From Empires to NGOs in the West African Sahel: The Road to Nongovernmentality*, Gregory Mann
130 *Dictators and Democracy in African Development: The Political Economy of Good Governance in Nigeria*, A. Carl LeVan
131 *Water, Civilization, and Power in Sudan: The Political Economy of Military-Islamist State Building*, Harry Verhoeven